GAME WITHOUT FRONTIERS

Popular Cultural Studies

Series editors: Justin O'Connor, Steve Redhead and Derek Wynne.

The editors are, respectively, Senior Research Fellow and Co-Directors of the Manchester Institute for Popular Culture where this series is based. The Manchester Institute for Popular Culture, at The Manchester Metropolitan University, England, was set up in order to promote theoretical and empirical research in the area of contemporary popular culture, both within the academy and in conjunction with local, national and international agencies. The Institute is a postgraduate research centre engaged in comparative research projects around aspects of consumption and regulation of popular culture in the city. The Institute also runs a number of postgraduate research programmes, with a particular emphasis on ethnographic work. The series intends to reflect all aspects of the Institute's activities including its relationship with interested academics throughout the world. Current theoretical debates within the field of popular culture will be explored within an empirical context. Much of the research is undertaken by young researchers actively involved in their chosen fields of study, allowing an awareness of the issues and an attentiveness to actual developments often lacking in standard academic writings on the subject. The series will also reflect the working methods of the Institute, emphasising a collective research effort and the regular presentation of work-in-progress to the Institute's research seminars. The series hopes, therefore, both to push forward the debates around the regulation and consumption of popular culture, urban regeneration and postmodern social theory whilst introducing an ethnographic and contextual basis for such debates.

Titles already published

Rave Off: Politics and Deviance in Contemporary Youth Culture
The Passion and the Fashion: Football Fandom in the New Europe
The Lads in Action: Social Process in an Urban Youth Subculture
Hosts and Champions: Soccer Cultures, National Identities and the USA World Cup
Game Without Frontiers: Football, Identity and Modernity
The Margins of the City: Gay Men's Urban Lives

Game Without Frontiers

Football, identity and modernity

edited by

Richard Giulianotti
John Williams

Published by
Arena
Ashgate Publishing Limit
Gower House
Croft Road
Aldershot
Hants GU11 3HR
England

Ashgate Publishing Company
Old Post Road
Brookfield
Vermont 05036
USA

British Library Cataloguing in Publication Data

Game Without Frontiers: Football, identity and modernity - (Popular Cultural Studies)
    I. Giulianotti, Richard II. Williams, John
    III. Series
    306.483

ISBN 1 85742 219 8 (Hardback)
ISBN 1 85742 220 1 (Paperback)

Printed and bound in Great Britain by
Hartnolls Limited, Bodmin, Cornwall

Contents

Preface

The origins of this collection can be traced back to an international conference held in Aberdeen in 1992, attended by leading football and sports academics from four continents. A key interest at the conference was the way in which football clubs at all levels are both determined by, and are the social symbols of, the historical influences of tradition and modernity, and the subsequent forms of individual and group identity to which these processes give rise. In this light, a pluralistic approach to research takes centre stage, a pluralism founded not solely upon a respect for historical and cultural variations but also on an acknowledgement of the valuable insights provided by an inter-disciplinary approach to football cultures. The leitmotif of methodological and cultural variety therefore underpins this collection of essays from leading researchers on football culture and history.

The collection opens with an introductory chapter by the editors on the role of the United States as hosts for the 1994 World Cup Finals, and the questions which this raises about the future financing, presentation and popular appeal of the sport. The remaining fourteen papers are divided into three sections. The first section explores the generalized cultural thematics and historical experiences of tradition and modernity in European football; the second examines social identities within world football, at local, ethnic and national levels; and the concluding section refocuses attention on the social conflicts arising in European football through subcultures of opposition.

The international range of the collection is established immediately. **Pierre Lanfranchi** contributes an insightful and persuasive historical essay on the diverging traditions of British and European football cultures. The three papers which follow provide detailed historical and ethnographic studies of the changes and continuities in three specific football club cultures. **Roman Horak's** analysis highlights the primacy of Vienna in Austrian football's development, and how modernity has signified a challenge to the capital's footballing preeminence. A more ethnographic perspective is offered by **Raymond Boyle** in his detailed and critical questioning of the role of 'tradition' in the exploration of the historical and personal identities of Glasgow Celtic fans. In the article about French football which follows, **Michel Raspaud** shows how the paternalism underlying the successes of the 1970s St Etienne club, has been superseded by Bernard Tapie's high-profile, entrepreneurial approach to business with Marseilles in the late 1980s. The final paper in this section, by **Vic Duke**, is an account of the 'modernizing' pressures for ground redevelopment in British football. Duke examines how the infrastructural changes sought by the 1990 Taylor Report have combined with business interests to threaten both the financial futures of many British clubs, and the cultural senses of 'place' to which their core supporters are deeply attached.

The book's second section explores the symbiotic relationship between football and socially concentric identities, at local, ethnic and national levels. **John Williams** opens with an ethnographic and historical study of local football in England which focuses on the struggles and successes of Highfield Rangers a leading local 'black' club in Leicester.

A comparable case of sorts is provided in **Siegfried Gehrmann's** paper, an historical study of the remarkably successful 'Pole and Prole' German *Bundesliga* club, Schalke 04, which retains a strong local bond with the small city of Gelsenkirchen. However, **Wray Vamplew's** study of contemporary Australian football indicates that ethnic club identities can also have particularly violent consequences. For example, ethnic conflict inside the former Yugoslavia has been replayed at Australian league fixtures between teams founded by Mediterranean immigrants. Elsewhere in the southern hemisphere, as **Eduardo Archetti** demonstrates, the nationally galvanizing possibilities of football have been more successfully exploited. Since the game's arrival in Argentina, an increasing premium has been placed on its national significance, in ways which supplant local, regional, ethnic and class identities. Finally, as **Neil Blain & Hugh**

O'Donnell argue, drawing upon media representations of international football and tennis players, national sporting identities themselves become negatively defined through critical representations of competing others.

The theme of conflicting identities in football is given explicit consideration in the final section. **Patrick Mignon** discusses the complex historical and social genesis of French football hooliganism, in a way which is informed by his own ethnographic work with young Paris Saint-Germain fans. Conversely, an anthropological perspective underpins **Gary Armstrong's** fieldwork study of the rivalry between English football hooligans at Sheffield and Leeds United. Armstrong's paper provides a fresh reading of the locally centred and meaningful conflicts which surround football related disorder. **Richard Giulianotti's** study of Scottish football hooligans at Hibernian demonstrates that their collective identity is also heavily imbued with varying opposition to local subcultures. The final paper is by **Antonio Roversi**, and examines the 'ultras' phenomenon in Italian football. His research into the history of fans' disorder shows the bases for spectator alliances and rivalries, and thus highlights the cultural distinctiveness of European football subcultures.

Acknowledgements
We would like to thank Steve Redhead for helping to get this collection to print and our contributor colleagues abroad for their patience and fortitude. We also owe a debt of thanks to Janet Tiernan for her work in preparing the manuscript.

About the authors

Eduardo P. Archetti is professor in social anthropology at the University of Oslo. His main research interests are in identity rituals of masculinity and social and cultural changes in complex societies, and he has published extensively on football and tango in Argentina. His most recent books are *El mundo social y simbolico del cuy* (1992), and (as editor) *The Anthropology of Written Identities* (1994).

Gary Armstrong is currently a research fellow in the Department of Anthropology, University College, London. His book on Sheffield United fans will be published later this year. Following various research projects and teaching in the area of criminology, he recently began an ethnographic study of an inner-London neighbourhood.

Neil Blain is co-author of *Sport and National Identity in the European Media*, Leicester University Press (1993), and he publishes widely on issues of Scottish and European identity. He teaches media and cultural theory at Glasgow Caledonian University.

Raymond Boyle works at the University of Stirling and is both a member of the Media Research Institute and lecturer in Film and Media Studies. He has researched and published in the area of sport and identity and is co-author of *Sport and National Identity in the European Media*, Leicester University Press (1993). He has a professional and personal interest in the fate of Glasgow Celtic.

Vic Duke is a lecturer and researcher in sociology at Salford University in Manchester. He has a special research interest in

Eastern Europe and has recently been researching football culture in South America, while maintaining a determination to visit all the top League and non-League grounds in Britain before stadium redevelopment takes it's full historical toll. He admits, if pushed, to having a 'special relationship' with Manchester City.

Siegfried Gehrmann, is a social historian with a special interest in football in the Ruhr region of Germany. He is a teacher and researcher at the Universitat Gesamthochschule in Essen, and he has written widely on issues relating to sport and class especially as they involve the history of the Schalke 04 club from Gelsenkirchen.

Richard Giulianotti is a researcher in the Department of Sociology at the University of Aberdeen. He has published several essays on football fan behaviour, hooliganism, drug subcultures and youth culture. In 1992 he organized the international conference, *Soccer, Culture and Identity* in Aberdeen, and is co-editor of the collection *Football, Violence and Social Identity* (1994), Routledge.

Roman Horak is a researcher and writer at the Institute for Kulturstudien in Vienna and he teaches at the University of Vienna. Roman is an expert on Austrian football culture, and he has a special interest in popular culture and football in Vienna. In 1991 he edited, with Wolfgang Reiter, *Die Kanten des Runden Leders* and Roman shares an academic interest in Austrian football culture with a fan's affinity for the currently ailing Rapid Vienna.

Pierre Lanfranchi is a social historian from France who, until recently, was based at the Centre for Research on European Culture at the European University Institute in Florence. He has a special interest in football and football culture in both France and Italy and is likely to extend his comparative work in this area as a result of his recent move to the Department of Humanities at the Leicester De Montfort University.

Patrick Mignon is a writer and researcher who lives in Paris and, who works at the IRIS-Universite Paris IX Dauphine. Patrick has written widely on football, youth culture and popular music in France and recently published an authoritative official report on football hooliganism in France. He is currently preparing a book on rock music entitled, *L'Invention Sociale du Rock.*

Hugh O'Donnell lectures in the Department of Language and Media at Glasgow Caledonian University. He combines a wide-ranging knowledge of European languages with an interest in all aspects of mediation. He is co-author of *Sport and National Identity in the European Media,* Leicester University Press (1993).

Michel Raspaud is Maitre de Conferences at the Universite Joseph Fourier, Grenoble, France. His doctoral thesis explores football culture from an anthropological perspective. He has examined the politics and symbolism of football hooliganism, and the influence of industrial firms in the organizational culture of football clubs. Michel is currently undertaking research into the historical sociology of mountaineering in the Himalayas.

Antonio Roversi is a researcher in sociology in the Department of Political Economy at Modena University, Italy. He is author of several essays about football fans and hooliganism. His book *Calcio, Tifo e Violenza: il teppismo calcistico in Italia* was published in 1992. In 1990 he also edited a book about football hooliganism in Europe.

Wray Vamplew is an internationally renowned sports historian who is perhaps best known for his seminal study of the early years of professional sport in Britain, *Pay up and Play the Game.* Wray recently returned to Britain after a lengthy stay in Australia and is now the Director of the Faculty of Humanities at the Leicester De Montfort University.

John Williams works at the Sir Norman Chester Centre for Football Research at Leicester University. He has co-written three books on football and football fans and, with Stephen Wagg, edited *British Football and Social Change* for Leicester University Press in 1991. He has recently been involved in research on football stadia, in oral history work and research on local football. He approves of another 'Bootle boy', Roy Evans, as the new Liverpool manager.

Introduction:
Stillborn in the USA?

John Williams and Richard Giulianotti

This collection of chapters about football in Europe, South America and Australasia has been put together on the very brink of football's greatest modern adventure. The staging of the 1994 World Cup Finals in the United States, a country with no established professional soccer league and little apparent interest in the professional game, represents an extraordinary triumph for the dollar over culture and marks a key shift in the way in which the world game is administered and financed.

The Brazilian entrepreneur, Joao Havelange, industrial businessman, insurance broker and, since 1974, unopposed President of football's world governing body, FIFA, is the main architect of these changes which mirror a wider global and commercial transformation of the governance of football. Havalange's commercial and marketing instincts contrast sharply with those of his paternalistic British predecessor, Stanley Rous, a referee and schoolteacher, a patron of the game at every level and a man manifestly at home in the FIFA of the 1960s which, "was quaint, it was antiquated, it was just like going back to a Dickensian novel." (Simson and Jennings, 1992, p.38). Havelange rose to power on the basis of his accusations that FIFA favoured Anglo-Saxon countries, and through his tireless lobbying of African and Asian FIFA members for Rous's removal. Needless to say, FIFA's World Youth Cup, inaugurated under Havelange in 1977, has resolutely avoided the old European power bases (Wagg, 1994).

Havelange has also strongly avoided FIFA's traditional advocacy of independence from major commercial sponsors. Coca-Cola are the long term sponsors of the World Youth Cup and a major sponsor of World Cup '94. Adidas, under Horst Dassler, have virtually monopolized kit and equipment sponsorship of World Cup tournaments since the early 1970s. Until his recent death, Dassler was a key Havelange advisor, and a central figure in the latter's extraordinary nomination for the Nobel Peace Prize in 1988 - effectively the drive of FIFA for 'nation state' world status (Simson and Jennings, 1992). Dassler, with Havelange's support, also set up the ISL marketing company in 1982 and, naturally, secured the rights to market all FIFA tournaments from that date.

Werner Fricker, ex-head of the US Soccer Federation (USSF) is the man who helped secure World Cup '94 for the US against poor competition from Brazil and Morocco. Fricker, however, opposed aspects of ISL's involvement in marketing the Finals and was quickly replaced in the USSF by the FIFA sponsored candidate, Californian lawyer, Alan Rothenberg. The latter had been the Commissioner for Soccer and commercial mastermind behind the 'privatised' and profitable 1984 Los Angeles Olympics, and an expressed admirer of the "creative and innovative" philosophy of the now defunct National American Soccer League (NASL), of "push, push, push and score, score, score." (*The Guardian*, 21 February, 1992). Rothenberg's "key appointment in the modernisation process" of the USSF was that of Hank Steinbrecker, as Secretary General, a Brooklyn-born soccer player and coach but, more importantly, a former Quaker Oats director of sports marketing; the marketing force behind the massive recent international profile of the Gaterade sports drink (*World Soccer*, December, 1991). These were the marketing men to sell soccer and its associated products to the US.

Adidas are a USSF 'marketing partner' for World Cup '94 and the only equipment manufacturer on the sponsorship slate. In this potentially huge new market for soccer and its products in which Nike and Reebok are kings and Pepsi a 'troublesome' soft drinks competitor, Adidas and Coke have aimed to make a considerable World Cup killing. With an estimated 50 million Americans somehow "involved" with football, the potential returns are obviously considerable (*The Guardian*, 21 February, 1992). Pepsi and its products will not have been seen near the World Cup stadia, of course, and the ubiquitous Adidas three stripes will have been everywhere on Final day. The stakes here are very high indeed.

Quite apart from the sponsorship business in train - the Finals saw 11 official sponsors paying $15 million and eight 'marketing partners' contributing $7 million - local economies also aimed to make a buck. A recent survey by the Economics Department of the University of California estimated that the Finals would generate some $4 billion worth of spending in the US (*USA Today*, 18 February 1993). In January 1994, Las Vegas managed to turn what was, in effect, a 10 minute World Cup draw into an hour-and-a-half showbiz non-spectacular for US TV; there was also talk early in 1994 of a separate two hour opening ceremony for the Finals staged for a national TV audience. Welcome to the USA.

Lost tales of Belo Horizonti: soccer in the US

Some of the strongest reservations held by soccer commentators and supporters about FIFA's choice of the Americans to host the '94 Finals pivot, of course, on the arguments that the US is demonstrably a 'non-soccer' nation, and that in order to ameliorate this fact, the modern game will be re-defined to cater for a peerlessly rampant and global consumer culture. We will return later to the issue of globalised commercial excess and World Cup '94. On the more general matter of soccer and the US, however, it should be remembered that the Americans are by no means football novices. The USA competed in the first two World Cups and even reached the semi-finals of the inaugural competition, an admittedly weakened tournament in Uruguay in 1930.

In fact, soccer has been played in the United States at least since the 1860s and Oneidas, from Boston, established in 1862, is credited with being the first US soccer club (Waldstein, 1994; see also Guttman, 1993, p.129). The United States Soccer Football Association (USSFA) was granted formal recognition by FIFA in 1914, and the American Soccer League (ASL) was formed in 1921 and ran for eight years with 8-12 competing clubs drawn mainly from working class east coast mill towns. Crowds averaged around 5,000 spectators but Fall River, from Massachusetts regularly attracted 12,000 fans (Waldstein, 1994).

Following the demise of the ASL, ailing finances and growing US political and cultural isolationism helped reduce the number of registered soccer clubs in the US from 200 in 1930 to only eight in 1941. A sensational 1-0 win by the Americans over England in Belo Horizonte, in Brazil, in the 1950 World Cup Finals was dismissed in England as an unlikely triumph engineered by 'foreign mercenaries' (in fact, only four of the American side were not US citizens) and, worse, in the US as an inconsequential blip in an equally inconsequential un-American sporting activity.

The later success of England in the 1966 World Cup helped stimulate a 'new wave' of popular and, especially, commercial interest in soccer in the US which produced, in 1967, the North American Soccer League (NASL). By 1968, the NASL had 17 member clubs in the US and Canada, but in less than a year, as commercial expectations turned into hard economic realities, only five clubs remained. Re-launched with a lower budget base under Lamar Hunt, at its peak in 1978 the NASL housed 24 clubs, with crowds averaging 15,000 spectators. Foreign players, especially from Britain, were widely recruited to improve the quality of 'the product', but it was the arrival of the Brazilian star, Pele, in 1975 which captured national attention and which preceded an influx of aged international stars from abroad. Crowds boomed, with Pele's New York Cosmos averaging close to 50,000 spectators per match in 1978. However, the lack of a development strategy for home grown talent to match Pele's, and the problem of recruiting a second wave of foreign stars to match the profile and quality of the first meant that by the mid-1980s the NASL, and thus professional soccer in the US, was in a deep downward spiral. By 1983 TV coverage of US soccer had gone, one year later only nine NASL clubs remained and by 1985 the league disappeared as it had arrived, quietly and quickly (Waldstein, 1994).

The short term success of professional soccer in the US did, however, leave a longer term legacy. Today, soccer is reputedly the most popular *participant* sport in the US, with 15 million male and female players, but it is one without an apex of 'excellence' on the player pyramid (Scarisbrick-Hauser, 1992). Indoor soccer, in the shape of the Major Indoor Soccer League (MISL), was widely promoted by US sports entrepreneurs in the 1980s as the means of solving the 'culture gap' between an 'entertainment' orientated US sports audience and an alien, difficult to market foreign import. Here was soccer re-invented for a TV McDonalds culture, with sirens, spotlights, organ fanfares, dry ice and non-stop action on a plastic surface with few 'complicated' rules, and a guaranteed audience pay-off with matches averaging eight goals a game (Wangerin, 1992). By 1982, the MISL had grown to 14 teams coast-to-coast, but as TV interest waned and home-spun basketball began to re-assert its central place in the schedules, so too did indoor soccer in the US follow its outdoor equivalent into receivership: the league finally folded in 1992.

Outdoors, the localised soccer focus is on the minor US inter-regional Soccer League (USISL), which attracted four new New York State teams for 1994, with club budgets as low as $50,000 and some local stadia able to house just 2,500 fans. The more broadly based, low profile, low budget, American Professional Soccer League (APSL) embarked on an interlocking schedule between its Western and Eastern (American) Leagues in 1991 but from 22 clubs in 1990 - some averaging crowds in the hundreds - just five clubs remained in 1992, growing again to seven in 1993. 10,000 spectators saw the League's championship game in 1993 between the Colorado Foxes and LA Salsa, but the League's wider prospects look bleak. The APSL's popular Commissioner, Bill Sage, was head-hunted by the USSF in 1993 with the brief of setting up a new professional league following the hosting of World Cup '94. However, true to the values of a 'free market' entrepreneurial sporting culture, in September 1993 an 'unattached' marketing executive, Jim Paglia, revealed his own plans for a new national soccer league in the US, which were to be based, improbably, on the building of 12 new soccer stadia in city suburbs with an estimated total start up costs of some $480 million. The USSF, already resigned to having no national professional league in place before World Cup '94, sought immediate 'negotiations' with Paglia, but their threats that all professional players would have to be registered with the national governing body seem likely to cut little ice in the US law courts where restraint-of-trade lawsuits are common, and successful, legalistic fare (*World Soccer*, November, 1993).

A post-'94 US soccer boom?

Given the history, particularly the recent history, of soccer in the US, it seems likely that cultural and business communities there will be highly selective in their appropriation of soccer post-1994. At least five socio-cultural factors seem immediately relevant here in addition to the shaping *commercial* backcloth to the Finals and the cultural and political isolationism which we have already touched upon and which provides for a national focus in the US on specifically 'American' sports (baseball; gridiron, etc). Firstly, in contrast to soccer's affective properties in other cultures (cf. Dal Lago & De Biasi, 1994 on Italy; Forsyth, 1990 on Scotland; Hopcraft, 1971 on England), American soccer's appeal to participants tends to be defined according to a pragmatic, negative syntax. Unlike baseball, for example, it has not retained a traditionally working class image there; it does not require expensive equipment nor does it involve potentially life-threatening interaction (unlike ice-hockey or American football) hence its appeal to the sons and daughters of the white American middle class; and, contra basketball, it does not de facto exclude those of relatively average build (cf. Murphy et al, 1990, pp.16-17). Indeed, with American females currently soccer World Champions, World Cup '94 may at least boost *women's* involvement in the game, worldwide.

Secondly, American soccer's development in terms of excellence is unlikely to be assisted by the fact that many of its top US players are white, middle-class and committed to further education. Accordingly, soccer does not typically serve as a sporting forum for persistently contesting American social inequalities and prejudices, in the way that basketball does for African-Americans or baseball does for Latin Americans (Albena, 1993).

Thirdly, at collegiate, and current 'professional' levels in the US, soccer is light years from the demographic and financial scale of player sponsorship and coaching enjoyed by virtually all other major sports.

Fourthly, the tendency of the American public and especially American TV to individuate and 'measure' sports performance may flounder with soccer. Eschewing the endlessly pre-planned manoeuvres of gridiron, the batter - pitcher duals of baseball, and the point/rebound/assist frame of basketball, soccer is quintessentially a team game in which players' performances are mutually interdependent to a very high degree. Attempts in Britain, for example, by the popular team selection game, *Fantasy Football*

League, to represent individual player contributions, fail miserably because they are unable to reflect the complexities of the sport or to teach playing and viewing skills honed from a supportive culture. Put simply, just how is it possible to 'measure' the skills involved in setting an offside trap, or those required in 'reading' midfield passing options, or in losing a tight marker near goal?

Finally, and perhaps crucially, with American network television stations having already lodged billions of dollars with the marketing controllers of American football, baseball, basketball, golf, tennis, ice hockey et al., there is unlikely to be a welcoming hand extended by TV to a 'guest' sport which dilutes the secure audience saturation of these domestic 'bankers', no matter what its global significance. The national ABC TV network showed just one game 'live', the final, during World Cup '82; in 1986, NBC showed nine 'live' matches but were rewarded with derisory audiences. For Italia '90, with the USA present as qualifiers, there was no major network interest in the US. A handful of games were shown 'live' in the US on cable TV. For the first time, in 1994, no network in the host country is willing to bear the cost of producing the international signal which provides the basic coverage for foreign TV networks. Instead, the European Broadcasting Union (EBU) will supply technicians, equipment and pictures under contract with FIFA. ABC has agreed to take 11 weekend games 'live' during the 1994 Finals, with the 24 hour cable network ESPN showing the remaining 41 games to a potential reach of 70 million US homes. Bidding to show the Finals on TV in the US has not been fierce. However, nor are the Americans *quite* as disinterested in the tournament as some European commentators might suggest. A poll by SRI early in 1994 suggested that at least 57% of Americans planned to watch *some* World Cup matches on TV (Zahradnik, 1994). Disadvantages such as these within the established American sporting infrastructure highlight the naivety of Havelange's own proposed tinkering with the geometry of soccer per se, in a bid to render the game more palatable to American 'tastes'. Twenty-five minute soccer quarters (to increase TV advertising) and increasing the size of the goals in order to 'improve' scoring ratios, were the more infamous of the mooted changes (Wagg & Goldberg, 1991 p.249). FIFA also allowed its own rules on minimum pitch width to be contravened in order to stage matches at the Giants Stadium in New York State. Rothenberg himself, mindful of the low 'entertainment' value of the matches and of the muted (European?) formal presentations of Italia 90, but obviously not of the strategic nuances of the game itself, was reported to be in favour of outlawing the 'complicated' offside rule for World Cup '94. He, knowingly, told *World Soccer* in December 1991 that:

> Soccer purists certainly don't want to hear Americans criticising this wonderful game. But, I come from a basketball background and that sport exploded after a couple of changes to jazz it up.... FIFA are going to have to act like business people to make it more attractive.

There is nothing new, of course, about the commercial manipulations of aspects of the sport, about attempts to "jazz it up", into an Americanized, consumer friendly commodity. In 1971, the sociologist, Ian Taylor, complained of British football's incipient 'Americanization', with its introduction of pre-match and half-time displays of athletics and dancing girls. Vic Duke (elsewhere in this volume) reports on the response of English football fans to attempts by satellite TV's Sky Sports, more than twenty years later, to present the game as a 'family' package complete with fireworks, the inevitable dancing girls (exactly whose family are we attracting here?) and half-time giant rubberised sumo wrestlers.

In the same year as Ian Taylor's comments were made(1971), in a newly published Penguin edition of Arthur Hopcraft's classic account of *The Football Man*, there were timely warnings for the Americans about the dangers of trying to import a properly *cultural* product via a high profile, top-down sponsorship and marketing campaign: in short, that, "Football is an inner compulsion: it cannot be settled on people like instant coffee. The world must wish the game well in the US; but the only way it can possibly grow is to start in the cradle." (Hopcraft, 1971, p.193).

Today, the incessant end-to-end rhythm of basketball, ice hockey and, even, American football is parodied in some modern soccer in Britain, partly at least, as a result of tinkerings with the laws of the game, such as FIFA's recent half-hearted amendment of the game's back pass rule which is designed to speed up play, increase the number of goals scored and, thus, increase spectator 'entertainment'. It is Nick Hornby who has pointed out, contra Havalange's apparent determination that the game be located and understood simply as part of a malleable and global 'entertainment industry', that football is no mere diversion or 'entertainment' for those who are deeply involved, but rather an alternative universe as stressful and rewarding as, say, work is for some; that, "Complaining about boring football is rather like complaining about the sad ending of King Lear: it misses the point somehow." (Hornby, 1992, p.135). In much British soccer this change in the game's back pass laws has been articulated as a simple re-endorsement of the 'long-ball' game; an exercise in the (further) de-skilling of players in which goalkeepers and defenders routinely punt the ball the length of the field into the opposition corners, hoping that defensive incompetence will prove profitable, but really expecting the ball to be rapidly returned, with interest. FIFA's recent piloting in youth tournaments of the 'kick-in' as a substitute for throw-ins seems to confirm a troubling obsession with greater speed, mobility and physicality in soccer that struggles to mirror the performance of these properties in mature North American sports. It smacks, too, of the constant concern for looking at new ways of 'modifying' the game in order better to deliver the *real* product of a guaranteed TV audience for increasingly influential sponsors, advertisers and channel subscribers.

Missing you already: soccer and television in the US

If we look beyond these technico-rational 'adjustments' to the game by soccer's ruling bodies, there are three main issues of socio-cultural importance arising from the United States tournament. Firstly, in a very general sense, there is an unparalleled and profound climate of ambivalence in Europe about this stubborn, (final?) attempt to complete soccer's global sporting hegemony according to, as yet, uncertain terms. With the tournament being staged in a country which has produced, in Bill Brewster's unkind words, "more world-renowned serial killers than it has footballers"(*When Saturday Comes*, April, 1992) fears remain about the further impact of the *mediazation* and *Coca-Cola-ization* of the world's most popular sport. Sports stadia in the United States, for example, with their TV screen playbacks and electronic exaltations to support, represent vertiginous test sites in which the game's 'postmodern' future is relayed with ultimate clarity to an audience horrified by its own fascination (cf. Williams, 1994a).

Already in Britain and elsewhere, of course, we have the tailoring of soccer for maximized television consumption, through the scheduling and clustering of fixtures for prime-time viewing. The growing role of satellite TV in the consumption and staging of matches seems to be especially analogous to the near determining role of TV in the shaping of US sport (Williams, 1994b). But other features suggest a recent more 'business like' approach to selling soccer, which has similarities to the corporate ideologies about sport and the marketplace which are more common in the US. These include: the massive marketing of club 'leisure wear' and other 'fashion' goods and the endless re-styling and re-packaging of playing kits - now in non-traditional blacks, pinks and greens, complete with names and squad numbers - for a satiated market (Taylor, 1993); the 'Americanisation' of soccer sports goods - the 'Glasgow Rangers' baseball caps, the 'West Ham' 'college' supporter jackets etc; the endless promotion of the game in *social* terms as a 'family' sport, in order, it seems, to chime with the *commercial* ideologies which go with drawing in wealthier fans/consumers (the era of the £30 ticket for some *League* matches in London); the important and necessary new stadium developments which also voraciously promote consumption in choice-filled concourses and, increasingly, unfettered corporate enterprise - one new stand at an English ground, for example, is enthusiastically publicized as 'The Business Stadium'; the collages of brand names and the names of club sponsors which are synonymous with commercial sports (Bourdieu, 1993, p.125). Of course, the TV packaging of 'Americanised' sport aimed at an affluent 'family' audience contains an inner-contradiction. Attempts, for example, to replicate the idyllic suburban living room in giant form in the stadium - for the first time, World Cup matches in the US will be staged in 'weatherless' indoor domes - may lead sports' consumers to settle for the 'real' thing, at home. This kind of vision for sport, does perfectly illustrate the terroristic hyperrealism of our world, a world where a 'real' event occurs in a vacuum, stripped of its context and visual from afar, televisually .... No one will have directly experienced the actual course of such happenings, but everyone will have received an image of them. A pure event, in other words, devoid of any reference in nature, and readily susceptible to replacement by synthetic images (Baudrillard, 1993, pp.79-80).

The distances and time zones involved meant, of course, that even 'live' spectators at World Cup 94 were principally TV viewers of the Finals. Ironically, however, the template for the eerie scenario outlined above is not provided by North America, but, instead by Europe, where club matches are already played 'behind closed-doors' as a punishment for the misdemeanours of over-participatory or violent fans. The absence of England from the Finals means the prospects for soccer hooliganism at World Cup 94 - and, thus, for its 'resolution' by armed police - are much reduced (though kit manufacturers in the US were soon astutely advertising soccer products as the sorts of goods Europeans 'riot' over). Once again for a major international sporting event in the USA, concern about public order problems will probably focus much more on the resentful and preying violence of domestic 'street gangs', which are excluded from this sporting extravaganza, than it will on the tourists/spectators who can afford the prohibitive costs of attending the 'world's greatest sporting event' (Williams, 1986). But it does raise the question of how American police respond to 'carnival' fans, such as those from Ireland and Norway, whose sometimes raucous behaviour can mistakenly suggest imminent hooliganism (cf. Giulianotti, 1991).

Despite the scale of the event, the rhetoric about fan 'involvement' in World Cup '94, and the determination of the US authorities to make tickets widely available, costs and ticket restrictions means a *very* selective audience at top matches. An astonishing 3.6 million tickets were advertised for the Finals, with more than two million of these made available for public sale in the US and 1.3 million on sale abroad. However, ticket prices for top matches were far from cheap, ranging from a hefty $55 to a positively leaden $475. With an average overall tournament ticket price of $58, there is still little here to attract the football supporting, but mainly poor, American-Hispanics. For the Final itself, at the Pasedena Rose Bowl, only "between 5,000 and 10,000 tickets" were planned for general public sale, a situation justified by Alan Rothenberg on the basis that for other major sporting events in the US there are no public ticket sales at all. Inevitably, sponsors and "other commercial affiliates" were down for a sizeable slab of the 80,000 'missing' tickets (*World Soccer*, December, 1993).

The services on offer at American stadia may still put English facilities to shame (see, Zahradnik, 1994), but the detached 'concrete bowl' architecture offered by many American sites for sport - the Foxboro Stadium in Boston, for example, is "a concrete box in a wood ... a soulless chip off a dreary design box" (Davies, 1993), *and* 30 miles out of town - seems to offer little of the historical cultural purchase of 'place' of the kind associated with sport in Europe. Scepticism about the possibility of the USA's 'conversion' to soccer following World Cup '94 is underpinned by the low degree of 'topophilia' associated with mobile and media dominated sports. In explaining the social development and continued public warmth for football in Britain, for example, researchers such as John Bale (1993), John Clarke, (1978), Ian Taylor (1982), and Alan Clarke (1992) have usefully emphasized the role of the traditional 'topophilic' triangle - between the soccer club, the club ground and the affective support of the surrounding community. There is, clearly, something to recommend this approach. However, the empirical research for the thesis is rather scant and its consequent tendency to romanticize the past undoubtedly adds to its appeal. More seriously, its traditionalist inclinations mean that it underplays the full functions of modernity in interpolating soccer's continuing popular and trans-national appeal. Increasingly, for its controllers and 'armchair' fans, for example:

> Sport as a spectacle would appear more clearly as a mass commodity, and the organization of sporting entertainment as one branch among others of show business ...." (Bourdieu, 1993, p.124).

Thus, we can begin to explain the mass, globalised appeal, even to millions of non-attenders, of teams such as Real Madrid, Milan, Juventus, Manchester United and Glasgow Rangers, as being beyond the constraints of national boundaries, local identities and the effects of international social mobility. Nevertheless, there is also an important sense (invention?) of 'place' and 'identity' which infuses the nature of, and the support for, these clubs and which mobilizes their representative communities: the heart of Spain at the Bernabau; La Vecchia Signora of Italy against the suburban Milanese of the San Siro; the imaginative attacking of the Red Devils at Old Trafford; and, the continuing, staunch Unionism of the Light Blues at Ibrox. In the globalised future of televisual sports, the collage of traditional methods and the importance of the cultural rootedness of place and established localisms seems to count for increasingly little in the desperate pursuit of commercial success. Alt (1983, p.100) paints a singularly pessimistic picture of the instrumental pursuit of victory which he argues is central to American sporting culture:

> There being no longer any loyal identification with a local team or a ritualistic sublimation of the game, individuals shop around the sporting franchise marketplace for that team which embodies the necessary winning traits (TV having largely dissolved local team identification). And those teams which are no longer winners or are consistent losers are dropped with disinterest and even disgust.

Indeed, American sporting teams' lack of symbolic fixity is reflected in their own geographical mobility, to locations where better financial incentives predominate e.g. New York Giants to San Francisco, Baltimore Colts to Indianapolis, St. Louis Cardinals to Phoenix, Oakland Raiders to Los Angeles (cf. Sullivan, 1987). Even in these cases, of course, the sports fans do not easily forget, and dislocated teams live on in local memories in the shape of caps and jackets worn out of time. Brooklyn Dodgers' baseball memorabilia is still widely popular in New York, for example, almost thirty years after the club was controversially transplanted to Los Angeles. These sorts of scenarios are not yet apparent in Europe, where capitalist development and the funding of football clubs has traditionally had more strongly localised links and where the corporate financing of sports is still relatively underdeveloped (see Raspaud, this volume). (In the US, of course, sporting concerns, tellingly, are *franchises*, not clubs at all). But again, the question is where, in an era of talks about trans-national media-funded, soccer 'Super Leagues', might this kind of hard-headed corporate marketing, and the sorts of men who control it, lead the international game?

This brings us to our third observation. With a sense of space that is so uniquely mobile and capricious, what are the initial indications for a longer term cementing of American interest in soccer? Perhaps one is to be found in the nature of contemporary patterns of consumption of popular culture. Bauman (1992) and Maffesoli (1988) argue that stability in the era of the social has been superseded by the mutability of sociality:

> The characteristics of the sociality are that the person (persona), plays roles within his professional activities, nurturing the various tribes in which he participates .... Sociality necessitates taking into account everything previously considered frivolous, anecdotal or nonsensical .... the concern for the present (Maffesoli, 1988, pp.147-8; 1990, p.91)

An overwhelming predilection for the present hardly confirms a stable or lasting future. We have, therefore, the prospect of a tactile World Cup, in which American participation has all the investment of a 'fad': a pleasurable leisure experience while it lasts, and perhaps profitable for sponsors and manufacturers, but unlikely to be replicated through a settled and successful national American league to replace the failures of the past.

Feels like going home?

On a more optimistic note, perhaps, we would suggest that there are at least three important areas in which the World Cup may have definite reverberations on the United States. Firstly, the types of fandom and identification which the World Cup germinates indigenously are likely, once again, to throw the ethnic distinctiveness of the USA under the international spotlight. Italians and Irish Americans on the East coast are the most obvious examples of those locals who are liable to reclaim a non-American collective biography at least for the duration of the Finals. Additionally, German, Greek, Dutch, Swedish, Norwegian, and Hispanic fans are set to emerge, anew, from the melting pot which makes up the host nation's populace. 22 million of today's Americans were not born in the US. An international soccer tournament held in the US in 1993 and involving Brazil, England and Germany was televised only on an Hispanic cable channel and to a 90% non-native audience (Davies, 1993).

Most disturbingly of all to the US WASP psyche could be the scale and visibility of familiar non-European ethnic groupings during the tournament, provided in particular by the Mexicans and to a lesser extent the Koreans. The presence of African teams, with their own distinctive styles, will also, no doubt, promote visible and enthusiastic support from black nationalist groups and other black people in the US. The US team itself is also made up of players drawn from a range of ethnic, mainly European, backgrounds and the manager, Bora Milutinovich, is a Serb by birth who has previously managed the Mexico and Costa Rica national teams. All of this provides a symbolic, if not an economic and publicly demographic, challenge to the effective segregation of ethnic groups in many major American cities. Sennett (1977) draws attention to the racial intolerance nurtured within these ecological enclaves (the 'uncivilized communities') in New York. Davis (1992) offers a more contemporary and subsequently more disturbing picture of its manifestation on the West coast, where white, middle-class 'ecologies of fear' have effectively barred Hispanics and African-Americans from large public spaces and buildings in California. In one account he describes this as the 'South Africanisation' of Los Angeles (Davis, 1990), a city in which gang connections with sport are limited to the wearing of team shirts and caps as fashion accessories, and to the negotiation with the authorities of temporary 'truces' to allow visiting sports spectators to go about their business unmolested. Los Angeles, home of Alan Rothenberg, and, significantly, not otherwise noted for its enthusiasm for, or connections with, soccer, will stage three of the four final matches in World Cup '94, including the Final itself.

Secondly, the packaging of the tournament by the American media and tournament organizers poses some interesting linguistic and cognitive questions. Sports commentators and journalists are engaged to provide a textual narrative on sports events which gives the action meaning and historical significance, while enabling the speaker to retain control over interpretation. Which technical codes are to be adopted by American sports journalists within these narratives to avoid them becoming too esoteric to most readers and

15

viewers, or too simplistic to the few who are *au fait* with the sport? Catering for the relatively uninformed looks set to dominate because of concern with circulation and viewing figures; we should expect, therefore, an importation and pastiche of American sporting terms into a soccer context. However, as a counterpoint to the 'artificial' presentation of sports events, Whannel (1992, p.93) points out that there is a high awareness (and distrust) amongst some sports audiences of the processes of mediation involved in television presentation. The underlying interest in seeing the event 'as it really is' rather than in the way it is portrayed, may encourage some American journalists and commentators gradually to educate their publics into the finer aspects of the game.

Finally, there are the likely effects on the one ontological field which, according to Bertholet (1991, p.400), is too often ignored in the sociology of sport, namely the cultural construction of the body. John Hargreaves (1986) and Jennifer Hargreaves (1982, 1993) have separately noted how the body in sport is a crucial site for the reproduction of inequalities, along class, gender and ethnic lines. Shilling (1993, pp.130-1) identifies the material realities of manual labour and limited recreation time as central to the generation by the working class of a pragmatic approach to sport and bodily exercise, emphasising strength and effort against the middle-class pretentiousness for health and fitness. However, with widespread unemployment and the new politics of identity emphasising consumption over production, the class autonomy of popular cultural practices is being broken down in at least two directions. Firstly, as Turner (1991, p.19) indicates, we have the ascendancy of the fit 'lifestyle' body, as signifier of an arrested ageing process. This is achieved through specific bodily regimens, ranging from the varied disciplines of boxercise to the monotony of the step exercise. Perhaps some of the exercise and play disciplines in soccer will be extracted from the sport to impact upon the fitness disciplines of the conspicuous consumers in California, where major games in the World Cup are taking place.

The second impact of this class exercise rapprochement has potentially more serious consequences for soccer. Here, the effort involved in 'getting fit' takes on an operational rationality all of its own. Vinnai (1973) and Brohm (1978) drew attention to this self-perpetuating instrumentalism over a decade ago, as part of a critique of the professional rationale invading soccer and sport generally. Today, in the light of the fitness boom, the alienation of the body through sport is far more diffuse and privatized: "Making the body run soon gives way...to letting the body run...like a somnabulistic and celibate machine." (Baudrillard, 1993, p.47).

However, the poetic grace and flow and the unpredictability of soccer at its best still belies the alienating and repetitive machismo of its North American equivalent, and is likely to survive even the symbolic bruising of its exposure and mediated consumption across the Atlantic. Perhaps a T-shirt worn by an all female high-school soccer team at a match in Pontiac in 1993 is instructive here (*When Saturday Comes*, August, 1993,p.24): it depicted, from left to right, a caveman, an American footballer, a male soccer player and a female soccer player. Underneath these images was the single word, EVOLUTION. Fittingly, the most effective point of publicity for soccer in America is in its appeal to a winning team.

Bibliography

Alt, J. (1983) 'Sport and cultural reification: from ritual to mass sport', *Theory, Culture & Society*, 1(3).

Bale, J. (1991) 'Playing at home: British football and a sense of place', in J. Williams and S. Wagg (eds) *British Football and Social Change: getting into Europe*, LeicesterUniversity Press, Leicester.

Baudrillard, J. (1993) *The Transparency of Evil: essays on extreme phenomena*, Verso, London.

Bauman, Z. (1992) *Intimations of Postmodernity*, Routledge, London.

Berthelot, J. (1991) 'Sociological discourse and the body', in M. Featherstone, M. Hepworth & B.S. Turner (eds) *The Body*, Sage, London.

Bourdieu, P. (1993) *Sociology in Question*, Sage, London.

Brohm, J. (1978) *Sport: a Prison of Measured Time*, Ink Books,

London.

Clarke, J. (1978) 'Football and Working Class Fans: tradition and change', in A. Ingham (ed) *Football Hooliganism: the wider context*, Inter-Action Imprint, London.

Dal Lago, A. & R. De Biasi (1994) 'Italian football fans: culture and organization' in R. Giulianotti, N. Bonney & M. Hepworth (eds) *Football, Violence and Social Identity*, Routledge, London.

Davies, P. (1993) 'Tomorrow, the world', *The Guardian Weekend*, 26 June, pp.6-12.

Davis, M. (1992) 'L.A. was just the beginning. Urban revolt in the United States: a thousand points of light', *Open Magazine*, Pamphlet Series, 20.

Davis, M. (1990) *The City of Quartz*, Verso, London and New York.

Forsyth, R. (1990) *The Only Game* Mainstream/McEwan's Lager, Edinburgh.

Giulianotti, R. (1991) 'Scotland's Tartan Army in Italy: the case for the carnivalesque', *Sociological Review* 39, (3), pp.503-530.

Goldberg, A. & Wagg, S. (1991) 'It's not a knockout: English football and globalisation', in J. Williams & S. Wagg (eds.) op. cit.

Guttman, A. (1993) 'The diffusion of sports and the problems of cultural imperialism', in E. Dunning, J. Maguire & R. Pearton (eds), *The Sports Process: a Comparative and Developmental Approach*, Human Kinetics Publishers, Champaign, Illinois.

Hopcraft, A. (1971) *The Football Man*, Penguin, Harmondsworth.

Hornby, N. (1992) *Fever Pitch: a Fan's Life*, Gollanz, London.

Maffesoli, M. (1988) 'Jeux de Masques: postmodern tribalism',

Design Issues, 4.

Maffesoli, M. (1990) 'Post-modern sociality', *Telos*, 85.

Murphy, P. Williams, J. Dunning, E. (1990) *Football on Trial*, Routledge, London.

Scarisbrick-Hauser, A.M. (1992) 'Is the stadium half-empty or half-full? The story of the success of American soccer'. Paper given at the international conference: Soccer, Culture and Identity, University of Aberdeen, April 1-4.

Sennett, R. (1977) *The Fall of Public Man*, Faber & Faber, London.

Shilling, C. (1993) *The Body and Social Theory*, Sage, London.

Simson, V. and Jennings, A. (1992) *The Lords of the Rings: Power, Money and Drugs in the Modern Olympics*, London: Simon and Schuster, London.

Sullivan, N. (1987) *The Dodgers Move West*, Oxford University Press, New York.
Taylor, I. (1971) 'Soccer consciousness and soccer hooliganism', in S. Cohen (ed), *Images of Deviance*, Penguin, Harmondsworth.

Taylor, I. (1982) 'Class, violence and sport: the case of soccer hooliganism', in in Britain', in H. Cantelon and R. Gruneau (eds.) *Sport, Culture and the Modern State*, University of Toronto Press, Toronto.

Taylor, I. (1993) 'It's a whole new ball game: sports television, the cultural industries and the condition of football in England in 1993', paper presented to the Centre for the Study of Sport and Society, University of Leicester, 18 June 1993.

Turner, B. (1991) 'Recent developments in the theory of the body' in M. Featherstone, M. Hepworth & B. S. Turner (eds) *The Body*, Sage, London.

Vinnai, G. (1973) *Football Mania*, Ocean Books, London.

Wagg, S. (1994) 'The missionary position: football in the societies of England, Ireland, Scotland and Wales,' in S. Wagg (ed) *Football on the Continents*, Leicester University Press, Leicester.

Waldstein, D. (1994) 'An Un-American activity? football in US and Canadian Society'. in Wagg, S. (ed.) op cit.

Whannel, G. (1992) *Fields in Vision*, Routledge, London.

Williams, J. (1986) 'White riots: the English football fan abroad', in Tomlinson, A. and Whannel, G. (eds), *Off the Ball*, Pluto Press, London.

Williams, J. (1994a) 'Sport, postmodernism and global TV,' in Earnshaw, S. (ed). *Postmodern Surroundings*, Rodopi, Amsterdam.

Williams, J. (1994b) 'The local and the global in British football and the rise of BSkyB', *Sociology of Sport Journal*, (forthcoming).

Zahradnik, R. (1994) 'Stars and gripes', in *When Saturday Comes*, March, 1994, pp.22-3.

Tradition and modernity in European football

1 Exporting football: Notes on the development of football in Europe

Pierre Lanfranchi
Translated by Dr J. Roach

Writing in the mid-seventies James Walvin entitled a chapter in his book *The People's Game*, 'England's most durable export'. The game invented on the playing fields of the English public schools in the latter part of the nineteenth century is today an integral part of the leisure activities of the continent as well as of Africa and South America, to such an extent that it is of direct interest to the European Parliament, the Council of Europe and the Commission of the European Union. The European Cup, introduced in 1955, has grown from strength to strength in popularity and the idea of a European Super League is regularly and increasingly put forward. At first sight one might therefore agree with Walvin when he writes:

> From the time when football became entertainment for the masses in England, the game had clear international potential. In the complex process of making football a game of worldwide interest, the English influence remained of paramount importance.[1]

However, recent monographs on clubs and numerous studies of football in Europe have shown the need for a broader perspective of the British influence on European football and the ways in which football has been developed outside Britain. How, from very different cultural and ludic traditions,[2] did a sport which in Britain was associated with a social class, i.e. the working class, the industrial revolution and the massive influx of unskilled workers into the new industrial centres, come to be assimilated within some forty to fifty years in regions so dissimilar as the Ruhr, Lombardy, Catalonia, Provence and the Languedoc in France and in Switzerland, to become in many instances the expression of a local heritage and of a specific community?

To answer this question it seems essential to identify the development of the first practitioners, the hard core around which the clubs were able to organize themselves, as well as looking for possible constraints in the process of the assimilation of an imported ritual, elements able to explain the permeability of local networks. Should one confine oneself to seeing in the playing of football the manifestation of one form of British imperialism? Or, on the contrary, can one define football's expansion in Europe, perhaps even in South America, as the sign of an innovation comparable to electrification or the expansion of railways, the spread of which symbolizes the passage from an archaic to an industrial society?

I want to focus then on the autonomous phase of the sport in the various regions during the inter-war years, following a phenomenon which Eric Hobsbawm has termed, 'the invention of traditions'. This appropriation, which is so evident today, often expresses itself through antagonistic national styles as much as by differences in the idea of what constitutes sport as a spectacle and in the kind of support one finds for teams in Naples, Marseilles, Prague or Manchester.

British models

1. The aristocratic model

They (the English) have a primary commitment to strength, to the full (indeed the fullest possible) development of physical energy. They do not seek to obtain that strength through excessive physical exercises, weakening the body by gymnastic feats of strength. They have, on the contrary,a remarkable understanding of the ordinary conditions of Are you not aware that at the present time we are trying to introduce to our country the English style of physical exercises? We are trying to have them replace our awful regimented gymnastics which is nothing more than another set of instructions, a useless form of instruction wholly lacking in spontaneity. We are stuck in the same old routine! ... There can be no doubt that such games are highly conducive to physical development. Furthermore, they promote composure and self-control since these are essential for victory.(3)

Echoing Pierre de Coubertin, Edmond Demolins, one of the founders of the *Ecole des Roches* saw in English team sports a form of education "aimed, not as in France, at discipline, but at the gradual emancipation and self-revelation of youth".(4) English sports were indeed practised in France just as in Switzerland or Italy, as alternatives to gymnastics and traditional sports.(5) If certain devotees of physical education, such as Paschal Grousset, sought to popularize such local activities as the costumed 'calcio' in Florence, 'la soule' and 'la barette' in France, their attempt bears the mark of an anachronism.(6) In its original form the most famous example, the Florentine calcio, a prestigious display and game for local aristocrats, relegated the citizens to mere spectators. The relaunching of the game at the end of the nineteenth century with rules and a mode of recruitment which cut it off from its origins made it nothing more than a folklore spectacle.(7)

Where a local aristocracy was interested in sport, it quickly chose to promote a game which more fully reflected its new ideals, ideals which sought to reproduce the myth of the English aristocracy which Pierre de Coubertin expresses in his book *Education in England*.(8) Through sport and athleticism aristocratic youth could be inculcated with 'superior' qualities but above all the rising industrial bourgeoisie's ambitions could be tempered. It is clear that playing football contributed to the reproduction of English propensities so admired by the continental aristocracy. This 'anglomania' is evident in the choice of clothes, of names which these elites bestowed on their sons and in the growth of a certain type of society throughout Europe in the latter part of the century: the Jockey Club.(9) A very restricted society, the Jockey Club recruited its members by co-option and in its activities a style of life and the preservation of thoroughbred horses went together. However, the English 'sportsman' exemplified by the Jockey Club is not a practitioner, he is a dedicated follower. He personifies the gentleman and manifests his sporting attributes by his bearing and his presence on the racecourse. As in the difference one or two centuries previously between the popular sports 'la Soule' or 'la Barette' and the aristocratic sports such as real tennis, the distinction resides in the display of physical effort. In real tennis physical contact between the players is replaced by agility and technique. In racing the horse runs, the jockey rides and the sportsman parades and wagers.

In the French provinces, the members of the Jockey-Club were often responsible for the introduction of English sports, such as rugby or football. Such aristocrats saw in football a palliative to the harmful effects of national gymnastics which produced circus animals and canon fodder.(10)

The membership of the committees of the first national football federations at the beginning of this century reveals the interest shown by certain elements of the aristocracy in the growth of the new sport. But such people represent a certain type of aristocracy, a bourgeois aristocracy, the elite of local notables as described by Paul Adam writing in the first years of this century:

> In the capitals, in summer and winter resorts in all those places where major congresses are held, this elite is supreme and grows. Those who form it, doctors, financiers, professors, rentiers, writers, diplomats, dandys, artists, princes and all kinds of dilettantes more or less agree on a hundred or so essential truths... surgeons from Moscow, Glasgow, Montpellier, Chicago have more in common with each other than they do with their half-educated compatriots.(11)

Baron Edouard de Laveleye, who was President of the Belgian Federation from 1895 to 1924, and his successor Count Joseph d'Oultremont typify this sporting aristocracy which held key positions in the various committees but which quickly lost or gave up control of the actual playing of the game as the number of aristocratic players or even referees rapidly diminished.(12) If on the level of discourse the English influence was still evident in the notions of the 'gentlemen' and 'fair play' in sporting values, it appears that on the continent, the main theme for those promoting football, was a combination of an aversion to traditional intellectual values and of football as an allegory of liberalism. As Eric Hobsbawm and Gordon Craig note, this hymn to liberalism calls for a struggle against the predominance of the aristocracy and the church so as to highlight and codify the tastes and interests of an enlightened middle class not attracted by aristocratic extravagances which found an ideal mode of expression in the motorcar.(13)

2. The technical-commercial model

The aversion one notes in 'sporting' aristocrats, finds a strong echo among the advocates of a new practical knowledge, that is, the knowledge of engineers and technicians promoting technical progress.

One cannot fail to note a parallel between the growth of football and that of a caste of highly qualified technicians. From 1850 to 1914 the number of students in English engineering departments multiplied by forty. In Switzerland, the Zurich Higher Technical Institute trebled its intake from 1890 to 1914.(14)   A considerable number of its graduates went abroad thereby exemplifying the rules of a new expansionist capitalism.(15)   They were exporting a technology, a practical knowledge which they disseminated in its entirety and I would suggest that football was one of the elements.

More specifically, if one sees an English influence on those responsible for setting up football clubs on the continent, that influence was not from the England of the Jockey Club and the turn of the century 'gentleman- sportsman'; nor was it from the England of the working class pub, but rather the England of the engineering departments, the England of the industrial revolution.   It is extraordinary to note the number of Swiss, Austrians and Germans who, together with Englishmen, created clubs on the continent.(16)

In Catalonia, Barcelona FC was founded in 1899 by Swiss and German technicians who had learned the game at university. The rival club, Espanol was founded a few years later by engineers who were opposed to Barcelona's cosmopolitan nature. Nevertheless, the two clubs drew their support from the same new urban elites.(17) The history of the Italian club, Genoa, founded in 1893 (or 1894) is even more revealing. It is a fact that the Genoa Cricket and Football Club was initially, exclusively for the British expatriates of Genoa. Equally, it is true that the founding father of the club, Dr Spensley, a British doctor and passport holder, was the first to permit Italians to play for the club, but, as Antonio Ghirelli notes:

In Genoa there was a significant English population made up of businessmen, consular agents, international traders, who were so attached to the city that they never left it.(18)

And it was from a core of young engineers, some English but mostly Swiss and Italians, that the club flourished.   In Bologna, Bari, Naples, Milan and Lyons the original team bore an English name: 'Sporting Club', 'Black Star', 'Football Club' or 'Racing Club', without having any links with England. In France especially, such designations distinguished the clubs from the shooting or gymnastic clubs with more 'plebian' origins which called themselves 'The Gaulois' 'The French', or 'The Patriotic' and whose membership rules were much stricter, excluding foreigners from membership.

One of the most striking characteristics of the first European football teams is undoubtedly their cosmopolitan nature. In all these original clubs, the common factor is not at all their 'Britishness' or that they 'learned' the game from the English elites, as one too often reads in the history of the clubs: it is rather that they are examples of the integration of a modern, urban and transnational society. Walvin, for example, cites the case of Vittorio Pozzo, manager of the Italian national side which won the World Cup in 1934 and 1938, who had learned English in Manchester and Bradford.[19] But Pozzo had previously studied technical subjects at Winterthur, the home town of Hans Gamper. Pozzo no doubt played football there since the Technical Institute at Winterthur had two football teams in 1901. If, in the early years of this century, football in England symbolized 'working class culture', on the continent football was the manifestation of technical progress and, as Christiane Eisenberg has shown, in countries such as Germany up until the 1930s football was a 'white collar' game.[20]

Continental peculiarities

Though there were no national leagues in continental countries before the First World War, there were numerous friendly matches between cities or provinces from different countries. In northern France, the Flanders Lions most usually played against Belgium, Dutch, English or even German teams rather than teams from southern France. In the south, the Marseilles Swiss Football Club (*Stade Helvétique de Marseille*), winner of three French championships in 1909, 1911 and 1913, played each year against Barcelona and almost as regularly against Geneva, and only played three games in Paris in the ten years before the Great War. The players, who were at the same time the club directors, were business partners. The games were opportunities to strengthen links.

The game of the young urban elites

In Naples, the Italian-British Society and a group of Swiss traders were the major financiers of Naples FC, while the Zurich Chamber of Commerce supported the development of football in Marseilles.(21) It is indeed striking to note the extent to which the spread of football parallels the development of the electrical industries and railways. Thus in Germany, the first places where football was played on a regular basis were not the major cities but middle- sized cities with institutes specializing in these technical sectors, for example, Karlsruhe and Darmstadt. If I might suggest an area of further research, it would be a thorough network analysis of these original practitioners, great travellers who at each stop in the course of their professional travels seized the opportunity of creating a football team.(22) In many cases, such as in Nîmes for example, whose managing director was a young local banker, Henry Monnier, football was an expression of modernity.

In this particular case, urban history is a fundamental element for an understanding of the mechanisms of the spread of the game and the playing of the game.(23) The structures of Nîmes, which had grown from a town of 50,000 to 80,000 inhabitants over a few years at the end of the nineteenth century, were favourable for the development of new elites, who were quickly able to consolidate their power.(24) Nîmes became a railway turntable between the Languedoc, Provence, the Mediterranean basin and the Rhone Valley. The growth of Nîmes was to the detriment of the regional capital Montpellier which at the time had no comparable attractions.(25) In the early years of this century Nîmes developed new economic activities, in particular the wine trade and the railway repair workshops of the PLM (Paris-Lyons-Marseilles) Company, together with a rapidly increasing administrative sector,(26) which pulled in a considerable number of people from the Haut-Languedoc region and thus created a new urban population. In 1872, the Inspector for Schools in Nîmes wrote of the use of French in primary school teacher training colleges: "the use of the local dialect, the environment in which the students have grown up, all this makes the teaching of French difficult."(27) Thirty years later, the founders of the Sporting Club of Nîmes were to be the flag bearers of a completed 'Frenchifying' of these new local elites.(28)

In his book on the modernization of rural France, Roger Price stresses the primary role of transport and commerce in the economic growth of Southern French towns such as Nîmes.(29) Thus, should one not challenge the primacy of industrialization in the spread of football on the continent pre-1914? In Germany, as Essenberg and Gehrmann have shown, teams from the Ruhr, for the most part drawn from miners, only began to play a significant role at a national level in the 1930s.(30) In Spain, while it is true that the leading clubs, Barcelona, Irun, Huelva, Bilbao owe their growth to the concentration of new industries in the north, workers were not really associated with the game. In France, few industrial centres were also bastions of football before 1914. One example is the Paris region where there were only a few clubs on the periphery, so much so that in 1910 in in the industrial and working class suburb of Pantin, a football match attracted a mere 200 spectators a small number when compared to those frequenting the town's casino.(31)

Protestantism

The English technico-commercial model on the continent is also not impervious to religious divides which had a significant role in Barcelona and Marseilles as well as in Nîmes. In all three cities the club founders were Protestants and the Protestant community which, more than any other, was united around an active core of members, was a marginal fringe of the population, and as such promoted all forms of activity which brought the community together.(32) Starting from a similar observation, by counting Olympic medal winners Allan Guttmann concludes that modern sports had a more precocious and successful growth in Protestant countries than in southern Catholic countries. His conclusions tend to set this determining link between the Protestant religion and the propagation of ludic activities of English origin on the continent against Marxist and post-Marxist interpretations, particularly in Germany, whereby football would only be propagated in those capitalist countries of which it would be a form of secretion.(33) The basis of his theory could only be developed by transposing Max Weber's ideas to the context of sport with the notion of asceticism as a backcloth. Thomas Arnold, William Webb Ellis and John and Gut Muth (the advocates of gymnastics in Germany), were all Protestants, but a causal relation is still difficult to establish.(34) Perhaps, instead, one should recognize Protestants, right from the seventeenth century, as passionate defenders of the new sciences, so that numerous scientists, such as Pierre Curie, would exemplify the perennial nature of this thirst for progress?(35) Whatever the case may be, the fact is that even in 1912, a match between Barcelona and Auckland Wanderers was refereed by a Swiss Protestant minister(36), while the founding members of the Swiss FC Marseilles were part of that migrant fringe who were recommended to arrive in Marseilles already equipped with "a knowledge of French, also English if possible, short-hand and accounting".(37)

A means of integration

As we have seen, it was a number of young, bourgeois businessmen, entrepreneurs, mobile, highly qualified people, seeking openings and new markets, who encouraged the development of football and created the first organized teams in Europe(38). This large category of people does not exclude the English students and traders who came to continental Europe to improve their language skills or the European students who undertook a period of study in the British public schools (39). In the Languedoc only one team was founded by a homogeneous English group before 1914, that was the Vergèze Cycling Club (*Union Cycliste de Vergèze*). Its founder was the English engineer, Reginald Southwell, who was the manager of the only sizeable business in this town of 2,000 inhabitants, namely, the Source Perrier at Bouillens.(40) He personified a new technical knowledge, as did all those engineers who, from the second half of the nineteenth century had broken free of a long military tradition inherited from the Ancien Regime and were now carrying out major civil engineering projects, such as railways and the telegraph network, all over the world.(41) Their migration to the four corners of Europe during this time provided the opportunity for the transposition of the leisure activities they followed as students in the engineering institutions, activities, that is, which gave them their badge of distinction. There is in this transposition a determination to retain an element of the national culture, a sort of extra-territorial privilege but, as is shown by a study of the introduction of baseball in Japan, this quickly tends to produce a certain ambiguity. When exporting a technology, a practical knowledge,(42) all the elements are transferred. In the case of football in Europe and in South America or baseball for the Americans in Japan,(43) both sports are an integral part of the entrepreneurial culture. In certain regions, a sport which is exclusive to the members of a closed community, accentuates the gap with the sport's origins. Football played by a few persons within a closed community soon becomes no more than a few training sessions and one or two games per year, as was the case with the Sporting Club of Nîmes between 1901 and 1903.

The contacts between teams which developed rapidly in the first decade of this century reflect the movement of people and also commercial mutations; they have a logic which breaks free of the national centralizing cliché. In 1888, following the devastation caused by phylloxera, the port of Sète became the outlet for Spanish wines in France.(44) In 1921, when Sète FC played host to FC Barcelona, the club's newspaper still highlighted the bonds of friendship and the commercial links between the two Mediterranean ports.(45) Until the War, football in Europe seems to have been more a way of meeting than of competing. The English model of leagues was not introduced in any country and the national federations which were created here and there only reflect, in a very imperfect way, the development of football.(46)

Towards a national concept of the game

The French ethnologist, Christian Bromberger, commented in his work on the crowds at football matches that today, teams represented a remarkable crucible for identification.(47) Undoubtedly one can identify the inter-war period as the start of the European public's passion for football. The instances of nationalist sentiments manifested at games between neighbouring states are numerous, so much so that a journalist on a Paris paper could write about a match between France and Switzerland in 1923 that:

> It was fortunate that the referee was English and that he was unaware of the feelings of extreme passion and chauvinism which fill continental footballers.(48)

This departure from the ideal British model of fair play, from the illusory aristocratic model, plunged football into a process of the wider nationalization of the masses. Thus, in 1928, following the victory in Paris of FC Nuremberg against Red Star, the mayor of Nuremberg could say to his team's goalkeeper:

I am delighted that I stayed for the game Mr Suhlfauth! What you and your team have achieved for us and for German sport, ten diplomats could not have achieved!"(49)

Ten years later the Bologna daily *Il Resto del Carlino* reported the victory of the local team against Chelsea in the international tournament of the Paris exhibition, in the following terms:

This victory for Bologna is a brilliant victory for Fascist Italy. Indeed it was recognized as such by all those who hoped for our defeat forgetting that each time an Italian citizen has to fight, in his country or abroad, he always knows how to ensure the victory of the colours of Italy.(50)

From this, should one conclude that competitive football at the highest levels was, in the thirties, a highly promoted shop window of international rivalries? As the manifestation of a team sport - thus, more the representation of a collective will than of an individual talent - a football match has the characteristic of a popular spectacle; but it is also a confrontation (on equal terms and with common values) between two quite distinct groups, thus allowing for the creation of a clear hierarchy on the continent. Unlike previous decades, the confrontation now was all the more significant given that football associations throughout Europe could rely on a greater number of players than any other sport as well as on an ever growing public.

'System' and 'method' against 'WM': the birth of national styles

The improvement of the spectacle had brought about a degree of specialization among the players, the concentration of the best within a recognized elite and the development of a market in players.(51) This evolution was in fact only the reproduction of changes which had occurred in Britain some 50 years previously and which had succeeded in giving football the status of a popular leisure activity. However, there was still a long way to go on the continent before achieving the figures recorded by the British game. In 1913 the average gate for an English First Division game was 23,000, whereas on the continent only a few hundred curious bystanders watched a game.(52) England remained the model for continental footballers, and the French, German and Italian press of the twenties regularly used 'goalkeeper', 'forward', 'off-side', 'draw' or 'away' rather than indigenous terms. The English domination in terms of thoroughness, tactics and sheer technique remained complete.

To this imbalance in strength which prevented continental amateurs from competing against English professionals, one has to add the effects of the 'Versailles mentality' which prohibited matches between the War victors and their former enemies.(53) Indeed, the Germans, Hungarians and Austrians were excluded completely from the 1920 Olympic Games in Anvers. This 'mentality', as Gabriel Colome points out, forced sporting federations to choose sides, so that, for example, when the German-speaking Swiss representatives were in favour of organizing a game against Germany in 1919, the French speaking Swiss were strongly opposed.(54) In the twenties, England withdrew from FIFA and picked only amateurs to play against selected continental teams. However, though the English believed, with good reason, that they were the masters of football, the overall development of the game on the continent was tending to cast doubt on their claim to a fundamental superiority which tended to exclude the possibility of a non-British challenge.

The growth of continental football was far from uniform. The game progressed most in central Europe. But the shackles of the war-time alliances left little scope for confrontations designed to establish a ranking on the continent. While almost all continental countries adopted the British model of championships, a model based on sporting prowess(55), the application of the same system at an international level, was to take the form of a revolt against the all powerful English, expressed in a desire for autonomy and the affirmation of indigenous qualities as much as for a different concept of the game and style of play. Against the political realities, the bitterness and the patriotic pieties inherited from four and a half years of war, was set the appropriateness of the norms of English professionalism, the faith in a sporting ethic. Since the English seemed to want to have nothing to do with the continent, the renewal was to be initiated in central Europe. Unlike the masters, miserly in their continental appearances, the Austrian, Hungarian and Czechoslovakian teams showed themselves ready to confront each other and to assert themselves through football and disregarding prohibitions these teams sought to demonstrate their talents to everyone. In the case of Italy, the strong influence of Hungarian and Austrian football benefited from the diplomatic rapprochements with these two nations begun by Mussolini and Grandi his Foreign Minister.(56) The friendship and co-operation treaty between Italy and Hungary which brought to an end the diplomatic isolation of Budapest was signed in April 1927 a few weeks before the Mitropa Cup, the central European cup, for which Italian teams competed. The central European teams were evolving a very technical style of play quite different to the English 'kick and rush'. The comparison which had been avoided in Britain evolved quickly in Europe and international matches were more and more means by which to establish a hierarchy. The dissemination of Hungarian and Austrian coaches from the mid-twenties onwards with their stress on a subtle, technical game was to establish the reputation of the 'Danube School' as an alternative to the English style of play.(57) As Eduardo Archetti has shown, the innovations of the Austro-Hungarians in the post-war period went far beyond the boundaries of continental Europe and had a determinant influence on Argentinian football.(58)

Football achieved an excellent standard in the major cities of central Europe, Vienna, Budapest, Prague. More than a pastime for boys, football became an export product for these capitals without hinterlands. The endemic economic crises which characterized the nations of central Europe in the twenties, the weakness of the markets and the difficulties which these 'new little nations' encountered on the international scene, further accentuated the importance to them of football. Since they were masters of their craft at a continental level, these teams sought to achieve real gains from the hitherto symbolic gains achieved on the field of play. At the end of the decade professionalism was introduced in the three countries, which made it possible to set up a real market linked to football. Players were not only paid by their clubs but they represented assets and thus a potential source of profits. By transferring them to foreign teams, their clubs could achieve substantial revenues.(59) In a professional sports market based on a large number of players and the low costs of domestic transactions, the sources of revenue were limited to gate receipts and foreign tours. Only very rarely did teams benefit from revenue from advertising or public donations or the sponsorship of a powerful, private patron.(60) Thus, in order to make ends meet, a considerable number of central European teams played in countless tournaments all over Europe, which led Edvard Benes (then the Czech Foreign Minister) to say that his nation had no better ambassadors than the clubs of Slavia Prague and Sparta Prague.(61)

The national football styles may be considered to be a claim made for identity and superiority, through the tactics employed and the technique of the best players, something which can have an effect on the whole community, which brings us back to the comments of Bromberger.

France and Germany, which during these twenty years had no great success, never laid claim to an autonomous style. On the contrary, in France, the thirties were simply a long period of withdrawal from England, whose football had inspired French football in the twenties, and a period in which there was a rise in the number of players recruited from Central Europe.

The militarization of football in Italy and Germany in the thirties sums up the development of football in those twenty years rather less well than the game which brought together central Europe against western Europe in Amsterdam, in July 1937. The western Europe team was made up of players from Belgium, France, Holland, Germany who played an English style while the central European team, which easily dominated the game, featured Italians, Hungarians, Austrians and Czechs, that is, the only countries which had developed their own style of a game originally brought in from elsewhere.

Conclusion

In England football is the sport of the working class. However, throughout this article I have chosen to ignore working class football in Europe. But should football be considered as 'class leisure' in the old continent? For too long the 'continental' analyses of football have neglected a major difference they have with England: on the continent people do not play cricket. The polarities between town and country, amateurs and professionals, the Empire and the UK which these two sports bring out, have no equivalents on the

Continent.(62) Thus, it is to be hoped that future studies of European sport will be less the reproduction of British analyses and based more, instead, on specific research focused on the local growth of an 'English' game.

Notes

1. J. Walvin (1975), *The People's Game*, Allan Lane, London, p.112.

2. I shall limit myself to the most recent texts. In the case of France: J. M. Mehl (1990), *Les jeux au Royaume de France du XIIIe au début du XVe siècle*, Fayard, Paris; and the reference book reprinted in 1986 by Slatkin (Geneva), Jean-Jules Jusserand (1901), *Sports et jeux d'exercice dans l'ancienne France*, Plon, Paris. For Italy: Stefano Pivato (1991), *I terzini della borghesia. Il gioco de pallone nell' Italia dell' Ottocento*, Leonardo, Milan, on the Italian version of real tennis.

3. E. Demolins, (1899) *A Quoi tient la superiorite des Anglo-Saxons?*, Firmin-Didot, Paris.

4. E. Weber (1972), 'Pierre de Coubertin and the introduction of organized sports in France', in *Journal of Contemporary History*, No. 2, p.6. See also: J MacAloon (1981), *This Great Symbol. Pierre de Coubertin and the Original of the Modern Olympic Games*, Chicago University Press; Richard Holt (1981), *Sport and Society in Modern France*, Macmillan, London, and comments by P Bourdieu (1984), *Questions de sociologie*, Ed. de Minuit, Paris, pp.178-181.

5. From the vast literature on gymnastics and sports at the end of the nineteenth century, the following are of particular relevance: J Defrance (1987), *L'excellence Corporelle. La formation des activités physiques et sportives modernes 1770-1914*, P U de Rennes, Rennes, pp.99-121 on the opposition between gymnastics and sports; P. Arnaud (ed.) (1987), *Les athlètes de la République*, Privat, Toulouse; Marcel Spivak (1987), 'Un concept mythologique de la Troisième République: le renforcement du capital humain de la France', in *The International Journal of the History of Sports*, No. 4, pp.155-175.

6. J. J. MacAloon, *op. cit*, pp.109-113 and 158-160.

7. For the history of the Florence Calcio see: L Artusi, S Gabrielli (1986), *Calcio Storico Fiorentino, Ieri e oggi*, Florence; L Artusi

and G Sottani (1990), *Il calcio storico nella Firenze anni 30*, Florence.

8. P. de Coubertin (1901), *L'Education en Angleterre*, Paris, Librairie Universelle.

9. J A Roy (1959), *Histoire du Jockey-Club de Paris*, Riviere, Paris.

10. I have argued this further in, 'Rugby contro calcio. La Genesi delle due pratiche sportive nella Francia meridionale', in *Ricerche Storiche*, XIX, (1989), No. 2, "Sport, Storia, Ideologia", pp.339-351.

11. E. Adam (1902), *Etre Chic, De la morale sportive a la morale des sports*, Paris.

12. V. Bouin (1949), *Het Guldea Jubileumsboek van de KBVB*, Bruxelles.

13. *N. de Saint-Martin*, Jeux nobles, *Aches de la Recherche en Sciences*

14. R. Jaun (1986), *Management und Arbeiterschaft*, Zurich, Chronos, Zurich pp.375-377. R A Buchanan (1986), 'The Diaspora of British Engineering', in *Technology and Society*, pp.501-524.

15. G. A. Craig (1989), *Geld und Geigh*, Beck, Munich, pp.127-155.

16. I have tried to develop this point in two articles: 'Gli esordi di una pratica sportiva. Il calcio nel bacino del Mediterraneo occidentale', in, G Panio and L Giacomardo (ed.), *Università e Sport*, Rome, FIGC, (1989) pp.41-45; 'Calcio e progresso tecnologico', *Lancillotto e Nausica*, (1990), No. 7, 1-3, pp.58-65.

17. J. Garcia Castell (1968), *Historia del Futbol catala*, Ayma, Barcelona; E. Perez de Rozas and A. Reiano, 'Barça, Barça, Barça', *El periodico*, 11 May 1989; G Colone (1992), 'Il Barcelona e la Catalonia', in P. Lanfranchi (ed.), *Il Calcio et suo pubblico*, Napoli, ESI, pp.59-65

18. A. Ghirelli (1990), *Storia del calcio in Italia*, Einaudi, Turin, 1990 (4e), p.21 ff.

19. J. Walvin, *op. cit*, pp.94-95.

20. Ch Eisenberg, 'Le origini del calcio in Germania', in, *Il calcio e suo pubblico*, cit: pp.31-48 id. 'Fussball als Bestandteil der Angestelltenkultur', EUI Colloquium Paper, (1990).

21. G. Panico (1988), 'Dai salotti alle pelouses: le origini del football a Napoli', *Nord e sud*, No. 1, p. 219-245; R. Lopez (1987), 'Les Suisses à Marseille: une immigration de longue durée' *Revue européenne des migrations internationales*.

22. See the biography of Hans Gamper and his visits to Geneva and Lyons in Garcia Castell, *op. cit.*

23. Tony Mason and Charles Korr (1990) have highlighted this point in their work. T. Mason, 'I blu ed i rossi. Storia dei club calcistici dell' Everton e del Liverpool', *Ricerche Storiche*, 20, No. 1, pp.99-120; C. P. Korr (1986), *West Ham United*, Duckworth, London.

24. L. Page Moch (1983), *Paths to the City, Regional Migration in Nineteenth Century France*, Sage, Beverly Hills, pp.85-121.

25. R. Price (1983), *The Modernisation of Rural France. Communications Networks and Agricultural Market Structures in Nineteenth Century France*, Hutchison, London, p. 216. L. Dermigny (1955), *Naissance et croissance d'un port: Sète de 1666 à 1880*, Montpellier, p. 112.

26. L. Page Moch and Louise A Tilly (1985), 'Joining the Urban World: Occupation and Family in Three French Cities', *Comparative Studies in Society and History*, 27, pp.33-56, gives a pertinent illustration in the context of our research by comparing activities in three middle sized cities of the period, Amiens, Nîmes and Roubaix.

27. E. Weber (1983), *Peasant Into Frenchman 1870-1914*, (French

version) Fayard, Paris, p. 455.

28. Henry Chabrol, for example, was born in Nîmes in 1897, his family were Protestants from Lassalle in the Cévennes. A student at the Ecole Normale Supérieure and 'agrégé de lettres'. he was both a teacher and writer. He was also an excellent footballer from 1910-1927, selected to play for the French army team he would undoubtedly have played for the national side but for the war, see his biography: Max Soulier (1969), *Le Football Gardois*, Nîmes, pp.117-119.

29. R. Price, *op. cit.* p. 296.

30. S. Gehrman (1988), *Fussball, Vereine, Politik*, Hobbing, Essen.

31. L. R. Berlanstein (1984), *The Working People of Paris, 1871-1914*, John Hopkins, Baltimore, pp.132-133. On the Red Star, a major team in the twenties, see G. Hanotean, *Le Red Star*, Seghers, Paris, pp.25-40.

32. J. D. Roques (1974), 'Nouveaux aperçus sur l'église protestante de Nîmes dans la seconde moitié du XIX Siècle', in *Bulletin de la Société de l'Histoire du Protestantisme Français*, No. 120, pp.48-96.

    In spite of the divisions between reformers and othodox within the community, the associations flourished throughout the period. The dynamic was driven by local notables, the banker Bruneton, the barrister Donnedieu, or the president of the chamber Pelon.

33. Allen Guttman (1978), *From Ritual to Record, The Nature of Modern Sports*, Columbia University Press, New York, pp.57-89.

34. In France, the Young Christians Union did indeed represent an innovative factor with regard to sports bringing in new sports such as basketball as early as 1893. cf. G Cholvy (1987), *Mouements de jeunesse*, Le Cerf, Paris.

35. cf. T. Zeldin (1980), *France 1848-1945*, Oxford, Vol. 3 'Taste and Corruption'.

36. J. Garcia Castell, *op. cit.*, p. 107.

37. R. Lopez, *op. cit.*, p. 161.

38. J. P. Rioux, 'Sport et association, remarques de précaution', in, P. Arnaud & J. Camy (eds.) *La Naissance du mouvement Sportif associatif en France*, Lyon, PUL, p. 169.

39. L. Allison (1978), 'Association Football and the Urban Ethos', *Stanford Journal of International Studies*, No. 13, pp.203-228, outlines three stages of the process (p.218): (1) English and Scottish bankers, entrepreneurs and engineers settle abroad and begin to play matches against each other; (2) the local aristocrats and elites are brought into the games; (3) finally the local working class is introduced to the game.

40. cf. M. Soulier, *op. cit.*, pp.49-53.

41. On French engineers see A. Thépot (1985), (ed.), *L'ingénieur dans le Société française*, Ed. Ouvrières, Paris. In this work, H. Lasserre (p.239) identifies three phases in the evolution of the profession: the inventor, the inventor-organizer, the organizer.

42. R. A. Buchanan (1985), 'Institutional Proliferation in the British Engineering Profession 1847-1914' *The Economic History Review*, 38, pp.42-60: "Entry to the profession was essentially pratical, via an apprenticeship and adherence to the rules of professional institutions."

43. Donald Roden (1980), 'Baseball and the Quest for National Dignity in Meiji Japan', *American Historical Review*, pp.511-534.

44. L. Dermigny, *op. cit.*, pp.114-115. cf. also the relative growth of the ports of Barcelona and Sète in the second half of the nineteenth century.

45. *Les Dauphins*, No. 30, 2, 1 January 1921:

> Numerous bonds unite us in this thriving city of enterprise, strong in its francophile feelings: bonds of friends and bonds of commerce. Are not Sète and Barcelona in constant daily contact?

> The sons it sends us will thus find in us, players and spectators, the same sympathy, the same warm welcome that we enjoy when we visit their city.

46. cf. J. Bale (1980), 'The Adoption of Football in Europe: An Historical-Geographic Perspective, in *Canadian Journal of History of Sport*, 11, No. 2, pp.56-66.

47. C. Bromberger (1987), 'L'Olympique de Marseille, la Juve et la Torino. Variations ethnologiques sur l'engouement populaire pour les clubs et les matchs de football', *Esprit*, avril, pp.175-195.

48. *Le Miroir des Sports*, 6 May 1923.

49. T. Riegler (1953), *Als Stuhlfauth noch im Tor Stand ... Ein Buch vom deutschen Fussball*, Porta, Munich, p.112.

50. *Il Resto del Carlino*, 8 juin 1937.

51. cf. R. Holt, *Sports and Society in Modern France, op. cit.*; Ch. Eisenberg, *Il calcio..., op. cit.*, A. Wahl (1989), *Les archives du football*, Archives Julliard Gallimard, Paris; E. Weber (1971), 'Gymnastics and Sports in Fin de Siècle France', *American Historical Review*, No. 7, pp.70-98; P Lanfranchi, 'Rugby contro calcio' *op. cit.*

52. W. Vamplew (1983), *Pay Up and Play the Game: Professional Sport in Britain, 1875-1914*, Cambridge University Press, p. 63; Ch. Korr, *West Ham United, op, cit.*, pp.12-14, passim.

53. F. Klippstein (1926), (ed.), *Festschrift zum 30 jaehrigen Bestand der schweizerischen Fusball - und Athletik-Verbandes 1895-1925*, St. Gall, pp.148-159.

54. id. p.153; G. Colome, 'FC Barcelone e l'Europa', paper given at the Football and Europe Conference, Florence, May 1990.

55. This is an elite within which are concentrated the best teams based on their sporting ability. The aggregate of the results obtained on the field throughout the season establishes the champions but the formula also incorporates a system of promotion and relegation which rewards the ability of each team. This principle contrasts with the American one in baseball or basketball where there is a fixed elite. The results only determine which teams play out for the championship. On this point the English export is perfect.

56. On the matter of diplomacy see, J. Rotschildt (1977), *East Central Europe Between the Two Wars*, University of Washington Press, pp.163-177.

57. Bologna which dominated Italian football from 1921 to 1942 had six coaches all from central Europe; see, R. Lemmi-Gigli and G. G. Turrini, *Il mezzosecolo del Bologna*, Poligrafia del Resto del Carlino, Bologne, 1959; P. Lanfranchi (1990), 'Il Bologna che il mondo tremare fa! Una squadra di calcio all' epoca fascista', in *Azzuri 90. Storia del calcio a Bologna*, Roma, La Meridina. Minor teams in the second and third divisions had the same experience. Thus at Udine the twelve coaches between 1920 and 1940 were all Hungarian, R. Meroi, *Storia dell' Udinese calcio*, Campanetti, Udine, 1989, p 323.

58. E. Archetti, *In Search of National Identity. Argentinian Football and Europe*, paper given at the Conference, 'Football and Europe', p.5.

59. See the account given of his transfer by one of these Austrian players, Gusti Jordan, an inside forward who moved from Vienna FAC to the Racing Club de Paris in the Summer of 1933. G. Jordan (1947), *Football européen*, Paris, Triolet, pp.63-67.

60. P. Fridenson (1989), 'Les ouvriers de l'automobile et le sport', *Actes de la Recherche en Sciences Sociales*, 89, septembre; G. Baudouin (1984), *Histoire du F.C. Socaux Montbelliard*, Le

Coteau, Horvath, pp.9-24.

61. L. Serra (1964), *Storia del calcio,* Bologna, Palmaverde, p.58.

62. The books by Richard Holt (1989), *Sport and the British,* Oxford University Press, and Tony Mason (1989), *Sport in Britain,* London, Cambridge University Press, will perhaps enlighten continentals about these fundamental distinctions.

2 Austrification as modernization: Changes in Viennese football culture

Roman Horak

In the spring of 1905, the First Vienna Football Club invited two English League clubs, Everton and Tottenham Hotspur, to Austria to give a demonstration of the strength and power of English football. These clubs played several matches against various Viennese teams and then, as top of the bill, on May 7 they played each other. This particular game attracted a crowd of more than 10,000, which broke all Austrian spectator records at that time. Almost ten years later, on 2 May 1914 24,000 went to see the Austrian team (which was in fact a Viennese team) play Hungary. However, these were relatively small crowds compared to those that could be seen at Austrian international and top league games in the years between World War I and World War II.[1] Football had turned into a sport that moved the masses.

This development is demonstrated best when looking at the numbers of spectators watching the international meetings of the Austrian (i.e. Viennese) team against Hungary (including the games where Vienna explicitly played Budapest).

The number of teams and players in Austria also grew rapidly. In 1914 we find 14,000 registered players in the whole of Austria and in 1921 this number had increased to 37,000 players. Most of these players came from Vienna, where most of the teams, and definitely the most important teams, were based. In 1932, 25 professional teams[2] playing in two leagues, came from the capital. (Schidrowitz 1951, p.255 ff).

Table 2.1: Attendances at international matches between Austria and Hungary

1902-1937

Year	Attendance	Year	Attendance
1902:	500	1919:	25000
1903:	?	1920:	20000
1904:	2000	1921:	45000
1905:	no games	1922:	65000
1906:	no games	1923:	40000
1907:	800	1924:	45000
1908:	4000		45000
1909:	2000	1925:	45000
1910:	6000	1926:	40000
1911:	7000	1927:	45000
1912:	13000	1928:	40000
1913:	18000	1929:	49000
1914:	24000	1930:	40000
	5000	1931:	43000
1915:	?	1932:	60000
	2000	1933:	55000
1916:	15000	1934:	55000
	9000	1935:	40000
1917:	6000	1936:	46000
	12000	1937:	45000
	15000		
1918:	20000		
	15000		

It is not necessary, and it is also confusing, to mention all the names of these clubs, so, instead, I am going to talk in more detail about two clubs which still play an important part in Viennese (and Austrian) soccer. What is more important is that these clubs embody the two main themes of Viennese football culture. It is not difficult to guess that these two clubs are Austria Wien and Rapid Wien. Let us start with the latter.

The *Erste Wiener Arbeiter-Fußballklub*/First Vienna Workers Soccer Club was founded in September 1898 with the intention to "introduce the highly popular sport to the colleagues of the working class who fancy sport". The club had to change its name in January 1899 due to official pressure. The name was changed to Sport-club

Rapid, but the label of 'working class club' remained.

Although the SC Rapid, even at its beginning, was maintained not just by workers, and though a number of clubs were founded at the beginning of the century which would have deserved the label 'workers club' a lot more, it was not by accident that Rapid became to be perceived as the typical Viennese workers' club; the representative of rough playing styles. Also, the culture of the club represented something of a puritanical tendency within Viennese football culture. An article in the *Illustriertes Sportblatt/Illustrated Sportspaper*, from the 8th October 1927, for example, characterized the club as follows:

> They (the players of Rapid) have never disappointed their audience since they never give up and fight right up to the end. Their raw material, the players, are nearly exclusively "home bred", the management is conservative and adventurous business politics are not their cup of tea. The roots of Rapid lie within the population and it never loses contact with its home ground. The 'Green and Whites' are a suburban club in the best sense of the word.

The same source characterized the second club, the Wiener Austria, as the team of "salary football" fuddled by "dense coffeehouse smog". It should not surprise us that the same paper later praises this club concerning its lightfooted and brilliantly, clever way of playing, and celebrates the club as the most typical representative of the Viennese soccer school. This refers to the second branch/tendency within Viennese soccer culture. 'Austria', which was founded in 1911 under the name of *Wiener Amateur-Sportverein/Viennese* Amateur Sportsclub, as a split off of the Vienna Cricket and Football Club, one of the oldest Austrian clubs, very soon developed an aura of the club of the liberal (Jewish) Viennese middle class.

In April 1990, Karl 'Vogerl' Geyer told me that he had joined the 'Amateure' in 1920 when he was 21 not only because of the salary on offer, but also to become part of a - as he put it - "more intelligent social group". This suits the proud self-image of this club, which is revealed best by a contemporary article in the club brochure:

> The 'Violets' represent their own grade, not just in Viennese but in all Austrian football. They had never been what one could call a

'tough' team, probably because the club was always eager to be not just a football club but also a society club. Most of the players were intellectuals, students and merchants. Unintentionally, the head of the team was always a doctor or professor. (*Viennese Amateur Sportsclub*. Brochure for the summer tournament 1919-1920, Vienna O.J. 1920)

Of course, one should not take all of this literally. Nevertheless, a look at the headquarters/office of the club, which were always coffee houses in the city, helps us to understand why the 'Austria'(the name was accepted in 1926 in the third year of professionalism) was always understood as the liberal (Jewish) club of the Viennese middle class.

The geographical spread of soccer in Vienna

Next to the club structure we find a special geographical order of places where football was first played in Austria. In the early years, soccer was played on meadows in the outskirts of Vienna, and only later on do we find the establishment of soccer grounds. (In 1900, Vienna had only three such soccer grounds!). Together with the growing number of teams that were founded especially in the densely populated working class districts, the number of grounds grew.

Due to the rising interest in soccer, more and more grounds were constructed that were exclusively built for soccer. The early twenties saw the completion of a number of important stadia, especially in the Southern and the Western working class areas and the ones in the North of Vienna, across the Danube. This nails down the profound characteristic of Viennese football, concerning its geographical structure. Compared to the inner city locations popular in various cities in Britain, the Viennese stadiums were located at the outskirts of Vienna.

Vienna's inter-war suburbs differed, fundamentally, from the outskirts of most of the other European metropolis'. Being more or less grey areas, where urban and agrarian culture are merging indistinctly, they embody the successive integration of the 'flat country-side' into the urban structure. But *Vorstadt* (suburb) also meant particular spheres of life, and particular outlooks and mentalities: levels of a specific cultural, political and aesthetic feeling, which in many respects reflect the the character of transition so typical of the suburb as a whole. These correlations, between rural consciousness and ways of living, were embedded in swiftly developing processes of industrialization and urbanization.

Since the last third of the 19th century, the industrial exploitation of the suburbs was virtually unlimited. The development scheme of the area followed a very strict pattern, characterized by the mingling of residential buildings and industrial plants. In between, extensive free spaces had developed, which were neither of agricultural nor industrial use. This was a kind of 'no-man's-land', which was also without effective social control. These localities became places of primary socialization, above all for those for whom the stigma of rebellion was somehow 'naturally' attached: the suburban juveniles. Being appropriated for social use, these localities became central places of cultural learning, leisure time activities and reproduction. It comes as no surprise that football became so important here. It was the suburbs where the majority of the spectators and most of the players came from.

Into the 1920s

Up until this point I have tried to describe the special features of the early situation of soccer in Vienna. Analysing them I want now to split my account into three strands of development during the twenties and thirties. These three guiding strands often overlap and sometimes seem very close to each other but sometimes they move very far apart. They are:

1. The strand concerning mass respectable popular culture, including bohemian elements. It is characterized best by the idolization and stardom focused around 'the tank' of the twenties, Josef Uridil, and by the tight connection which existed between literary Viennese coffeehouse culture and the world of soccer. The Ringcafe was not only seen as the birthplace of the "Wonderteam" but also as a central meeting point for people interested in football. (Cf. Horak and Maderthaner 1992)

2. The strand of the highly centralized social democratic working class culture of 'Red Vienna'. This is characterized best by pointing to the regular differences between the small amateur clubs

organized within the frame of social democracy and the 'unpolitical' big clubs. Also, the social democratic sports movement constantly tried to extend the soccer structure with the intention of democratizing the sport by taking over its power and by forcing the breakthrough of the 'real and honest' sport.

3. The strand that runs next to, under and across the official party culture - the 'workers football culture'. This is characterized by loyalty to the club, close connections to the home district, but also the fact that major parts of the Viennese working class population was organized within various cultural organizations of the social democratic party, but were not afraid to watch games of their favourite professional 'bourgeois' clubs although the heads of the party were absolutely against that. From the autumn of 1924, more than a few working class players tried to join these clubs, even as professionals.

Between the Wars, Viennese soccer gained its social and cultural importance through the interactions of the various interpretations of the authorities. The social democrats could not really condone soccer because, in the last instance, they felt that sport prevents the workers from participating in class-conflict(3). The workers found their political voice in the party but they did not want to miss out on soccer. Beyond abstract class solidarity, soccer was able to reflect and take the form of concrete local (suburban) district/street identities. The *feuilleton*, always after new subjects, turned specific players into figures of literature, thus presenting them as immortal. All this formed the basis (and the burden) for the period after the Second World War. The fifties, sixties, seventies and eighties saw not just changes the game itself but also changes in the conditions which provided the backcloth to the game. Old structures and old ways of interpretation changed or disappeared completely.

Post-war football in Vienna

In between the wars football had turned into an important popular cultural phenomenon in Austria, that drew its fans from different social groups. This enthusiasm was so great that discussions in the Austrian Parliament were interrupted because of the radio transmission of a match played by the national team (Gastgeb, 1933) and thousands of Viennese gathered on the Heldenplatz, in the centre of Vienna, to listen to the live coverage of the game Austria vs. England in December 1932.

Austrian soccer in between the wars was formed by the rupture of the different organizational associations. From 1926 onwards, the (bourgeois) *Osterreichische Fußballverband*/Austrian Football Association, which ran the professional league opposed the (socialist) *Verband der Arbeiterfußballvereine Osterreichs* /Association of Austrian Workers clubs (see, Marschik 1991, 1992). But this political split was not taken too seriously by Austrian working class football fans, so that games of the professional league were mostly watched by workers. During the years of Fascism (John, 1992, p.81 f.), but especially at the beginning of the Second Republic, soccer was able to keep its popularity alive. In the years immediately after 1945, it even gained in popularity.

Up until then this 'football euphoria' was more or less a phenomenon that occurred only in the capital Vienna and partly in its surrounding provinces (Lower Austria and northern Burgenland). That the situation was the same at the beginning of the Second Republic can clearly be seen when looking at the interest of the spectators and the number of active players and clubs.

Especially after 1945, there was a new wave of club formation . This was partly because new clubs were founded and partly because old clubs that had been closed down either in 1934 or 1938 were revived. The spirit had changed since before the war and soccer had turned into a 'sport for all' and was no longer based on ideological differentiation (see Friesenbichler, 1985, p.17). The climate of general social consensus and a new 'Austrian awareness in the young Second Republic led to a new structure for soccer. The *Staatsliga* (national league) was founded in order to bring together the best clubs from all over Austria. Until the 1948/49 season, the Viennese football champions were automatically labelled as the Austrian champions, an equation that was unique in Europe. Austrian soccer was clearly identified with Viennese soccer, whose premier rank was accepted without reservation.

The introduction of the *Staatsliga* announced the end of the Viennese predominance, but for the time being the capital remained the centre of Austrian soccer. Under the patronage of the Viennese Football Association, 10 clubs played in the *Staatsliga*; 14 in the

Viennese League; 28 clubs in the two Second Leagues; 56 in the four Third Leagues; and 27 in the lower divisions. In all, 232 clubs were active in 1949/50. Towards the end of the 1940s the number of clubs in the provinces increased rapidly. The official statistics of the Austrian Football Association indicate the number of clubs for 1951(see, Table 2.2).

The decline of Viennese domination

The important change occurred in Austrian football in the middle of the sixties. In 1964/65 the LASK club (a club that came from Linz the capital of Upper Austria) became the first non-Viennese club to win the Austrian League. But this cannot be interpreted in a simple sense as a sign of the end of the Viennese hegemony (Langisch, 1979). At that time, four well known Viennese players and the coach, Karl Schlechta, who had managed several clubs in Vienna, were employed by the LASK club.

The decline of Viennese football dominance became obvious only a few years later. The proportion of Viennese clubs in the first division decreased within a couple of years from 60% to under 30% (1963 to 1967). At the same time, Viennese clubs no longer dominated the top places in the league table. From 1969/70 onwards, only two Viennese clubs were regularly among the top five clubs in the country. Apart from that, we also find that, starting in 1969/70, the title of Austrian Champions was won five times in a row by a club which was not Vienesse.

Table 2.2: Clubs and players in Austria in 1951

Region/Province	Number of Clubs	Number of Players
Vienna	265	26.000
Lower Austria	358	27.600
Burgenland	103	6.000
Styria	137	13.460
Carinthia	54	3.950
Upper Austria	150	12.500

Tyrol	43	3.300
Salzburg	47	4.000
Vorarlberg	27	2.600

Source: OFB, 1951

We can see that the great change which took place in the second half of the sixties, was the changeover from a Viennese football culture to an all Austrian football culture. The relegation of Viennese soccer, and therefore of east-Austrian soccer, was the result of the increase in efficiency of the Styrian and Upper Austrian clubs, but even more strongly of the dramatic increase in performance of clubs in the Western part of Austria, led by Salzburg and Innsbruck.

This process changed the structure of Viennese football dramatically. Out of the 'Great Four' (Austria, Rapid, Wacker, Vienna), only two clubs remain important today - Rapid and 'Austria'. Vienna, the oldest Austrian football club, survives but makes a bare living as a club that regularly gets relegated to the Second Division only to return to the First the following year. Even more sad is the case of Wacker Wien, a club that was the strongest in Vienna at the end of the 1940s but was relegated into the Second Division a couple of times during the 1960s. In 1970, Wacker merged with another traditional Viennese club, Admira, that had moved to Lower Austria some years before, due to financial and sporting reasons. (In this context it is interesting to realize that fans of both Admira and Wacker founded new local clubs that they renamed Wacker and Admira in order to keep the traditional culture of these clubs alive in the districts from which they originally emerged).

We can safely assume that professionalism and the commercialization of soccer, a phenomenon that occurred in the whole of Europe, had a lot to do with these changes, since nowhere did more than two big clubs in one city dominate domestic soccer. It is also obvious that only Rapid and 'Austria' kept pace with the changes in a way that made it possible for them to stay relatively successful. We can draw the conclusion that Viennese football culture included some elements that were incompatible with professionalism. The importance of these various factors will be examined later. One important facet should not be overlooked, however: this is the general decrease in the number of clubs and active players in Vienna during the 1960s, while the number of clubs in the provinces stayed more or less stable (Löschnauer 1983).

In 1951, 265 Viennese clubs existed but this number dropped down to 157 within 20 years (1973). In 1990, only 142 clubs remained. (This figure includes only clubs that are officially registered with the Austrian Football Federation, OFB). But was the demise in Viennese club football also reflected in falls in levels of match attendance in Vienna and elsewhere? We examine this issue next.

Games involving the national team or international club matches do attract a large crowds in Austria, but the Austrian League that runs nearly throughout the whole year remains the basis of soccer for the players as well as for the supporters. (The Austrian Cup has never gained as much popularity as, for example, the FA Cup has in England). The championship, as it is held in Austria since 1911, is still the 'spine' of Austrian football and therefore the appropriate basis upon which to measure the national interest in soccer.

Figure A shows the general spectator trends (average number of spectators at home matches) in Vienna. For this comparison we have chosen four prototypical clubs: 'Austria' and 'Rapid', the two biggest Viennese clubs which best represent the two traditions (coffee-house club and workers club) of football in Vienna. Neither club has ever descended into the Second Division. Together with these two clubs we have chosen two other traditional Viennese clubs that show a very close contact with their districts: 'Vienna' from Döbling (a socially mixed part of Vienna; partly bourgeois, partly working class) and the 'Wiener Sportclub (WSC)' from Hernals (traditionally a working class and lower middle class district).

Starting with the 1962/63 season, the numbers of spectators reflect the official figures of the Austrian Football Association. For the period between 1945/46 and 1962/63 there are no official figures, so we have reconstructed them by using contemporary sources like daily papers and sports magazines. The same goes for the average attendances at matches in the lower leagues.

Firstly, one could describe the interest of 'live' spectators as continually decreasing, at least if we look at the examples we have presented here. Shortly after the Second World War our four chosen clubs attracted a total of 60,000 people every weekend, but in the 1980s we find that the number goes down to approximately 10,000 to 15,000 spectators and varies only slightly. Figure A also shows that this decrease affected Vienna and Sportclub much more than 'Austria' and Rapid.

The early post-war years for Viennese football were, like for the rest of city life, primarily dominated by clearing work and rehabilitation, by hunger and lack of money. At this time football was the only affordable spare time occupation for many people. Although there was a high number of immobile supporters (difficulties in crossing the zone borders, hardly functioning public transport, etc.) there was an enormous influx of spectators during this period, a fact that manifests itself not only when looking at the high average number of spectators (Figure A) but also when having a closer look at individual football 'occasions'. The Vienna 'derby' (Austria vs Rapid), for example, but also other games often attracted more than 50,000 spectators, especially on days when two games per day were played in the same stadium. This usually happened in the Viennese stadium since it was the only one able to house such large numbers of supporters. Rapid's average crowd in season 1947/48 was 27,000 and the 'Austria' club, but also the Vienna and Wacker Wien clubs, held an average of 20,000 visitors per game for quite some years. These sorts of attendances have never been reached before or since.

Figure A also shows how much the post war-years were characterized by this particular soccer enthusiasm, almost regardless of opposition. Later, fans chose the games they where watching by first checking who the opponents happened to be. It is clear that even at that time (late 1940s) that top matches (those including teams like 'Austria', Rapid,Wacker, etc.) did attract bigger crowds. Yet, it also has to be mentioned that even the games of some smaller clubs could sometimes attract more than 30,000 spectators. In many ways, of course, this pattern of spectator attendance also mirrors that in countries such as Britain.

Since the second half of the 1950s, the number of spectators at Austrian football matches decreased rapidly. The economic situation became stabilized which especially changed ways of living in the capital. Increasing salaries, less hours of work, the 'free' Saturdays and the increasing demands for a certain amount of holiday time did not leave the traditional male working class football weekend untouched. Increasing numbers of holidays with the family, such as the trip to Italy, shows that a new geographical mobility had taken over. All this clearly signals changes which had taken place.

The likelihood of one going to a football match began to become more and more dependent on the club's successes. This explains the relatively small decrease of spectator numbers for the bigger clubs

('Austria' and Rapid) as well as the fact that the 'Wiener Sportclub' when it was very successful towards the end of the 1950s, attracted large numbers of spectators which mostly disappeared again when the club did not maintain its success.

Let us have a brief look at another typical Viennese club. Simmering, (named after the district which houses the club) is a typical working class club with a strong regional community spirit concerning the players, but especially the supporters. Simmering was in the top division from 1951/52 till 1965/66 but in the following 15 years it started to alternate between the First and the Second Divisions.

Compared to the decline of the number of spectators that the bigger clubs had to deal with, the number of spectators Simmering attracted (average: 7,000) stayed stable through the fifties (See: Figure B). Because of its inconsistent performance, Simmering was definitely not attractive for supporters that orientated themselves to success. Instead, the fact that the club promoted a strong regional solidarity was decisive for the large numbers of spectators who remained loyal. The fans did not attend Simmering games because they wanted to watch a top Austrian game but, basically, because the participation of their local club really was an event for them (4).

The years between the mid-fifties and the end of the 1960s show a drastic decline in attendances at football matches in Vienna, apart from a short recovery around 1961(5), when the so-called 'Decker Era' (named after Karl Decker, the manager of the national team of that period) was too quickly labelled as the days of the 'Second Wunderteam', once again raising the ghost of Austria as a great soccer power. The changes in leisure time activities in connection with the increase in TV coverage (concerning not only the matches of the national team, but also top League games) turned soccer into one among many options offered by the growing leisure industries. It was subject to completely different socioeconomic conditions and, under the pressure of competition from other spare time activities, football was not very flexible.

The end of the 1960s proved to be an important juncture in the world of Viennese football, a fact that can be clearly demonstrated by what happened to trends in 'live' spectatorship at matches. Whereas the Austrian statistics at this time do not point out relevant changes, the Viennese attendances dropped drastically. Up until the season of 1967/8 the number of fans in Vienna (measured by 'Austria', Rapid,

Wacker and Vienna) was always clearly higher than in the provinces but afterwards we find a sudden conflating of the Viennese and other Austrian figures. We see that this shift is a result of changing patterns of attendance at Viennese football.

The end of an era

The end of the 1960s saw a definite end to the weekly ritual of masses of spectators at the Viennese football grounds; neither the worsening performances nor the lack of conveniences in the stadiums, neither the bad conditions of the public transport system nor the presentation of soccer in the media could, on their own, have caused this rapid change. It is much more likely that the reason was the discernment that the era of the so-called 'Viennese school of soccer'(6) had come to an end. The stronger presence of clubs from the provinces; the internationalizing of soccer (e.g. via the European Cup) including the necessity of professionalizing and of sophisticated management as a precondition of success; but mainly the increased understanding of the importance of financial matters (although the dependence on financial resources already played an important part in the twenties), made a continuation of the specifically semi-amateur Viennese conception of football impossible at the highest levels of the sport.

Since the beginning of the 1970s we have to talk about *Austrian* soccer, no longer, simply, about Viennese soccer. The trends in attendances throughout Austria are approximately the same: crowds stagnated or decreased slightly, with the exception of the years after 1978 when Austria was able to step out into the international limelight (World Cup, European Championships, etc.). Regional particularities are only apparent when success meets with regional factors (f.e.Innsbruck, Austria Salzburg) and sometimes even when regional bonds are carefully directed (e.g. the relocation of Sturm Graz back to its original location, the *Gruabn*.).

The remains of the Viennese football culture, as we found it in the 1960s, are only present in a few areas. Most likely they exist in lower class Viennese clubs where certain traditions (faithfulness to the club, strong connections with the district, the community of the players, the administrators and supporters) from the time between the wars have survived.

If we want to set off the aspects of typical Viennese soccer culture against the general trends in the field of (soccer) sport it is necessary to treat these changes of 'modernization' in all their Austrian varieties. The commercialization of soccer, especially in Austria, is not a development that originally occurred in the Second Republic although it unfolded its effects then. "Soccer cannot live off sponsors, it needs spectators", was one announcement of Dr.Heinz Gerö when he made his inaugural address as president of the Austrian Football Federation in 1970. (Langisch 1979, p.105). This simple statement needs no further explanation. Much more interesting is the timing of the statement. At the end of the 1960s, the time had come, even in Austria, when sponsors of football started to carry out more and more analysis concerning the publicity value of soccer sponsorship to be able to assess the value of their patronage (Schulz 1981; Schagerl 1981).

The development which occurred in the post war period cannot only be explained by the fact that clubs had greater financial support. What seems important is the fact that in the late sixties adverts on the team strip were introduced in addition to adverts on the perimeter boards and adverts in loudspeaker announcements. The removal of the traditional Viennese suburban club, Admira, to Lower Austria, which occurred in 1966 because of financial reasons, also aroused a lot of debate. But the economic dependence of football on sponsors did not become a matter for larger public debate until the beginning of the seventies, when the national media also joined in.

Football and the media in Austria

Whatever has been said about the tendencies towards the commercial reorganization of Austrian soccer can also be applied to the media. Reports of football events in papers and on the radio (e.g. the reports by Willy Schmieger in the 1930s) have always had a great tradition in Austria. Nevertheless, a new step concerning the media was taken in the fifties and sixties, namely the improved quality and range of television transmission. As has already been mentioned, not only international games but also Austrian League games were transmitted live on TV at the weekends[7].

Since the late 1950s we find confrontations between the Austrian Football Federation (OFB) the *Staatsliga* (the union of the top division clubs, dominated by the Viennese) and the Austrian television

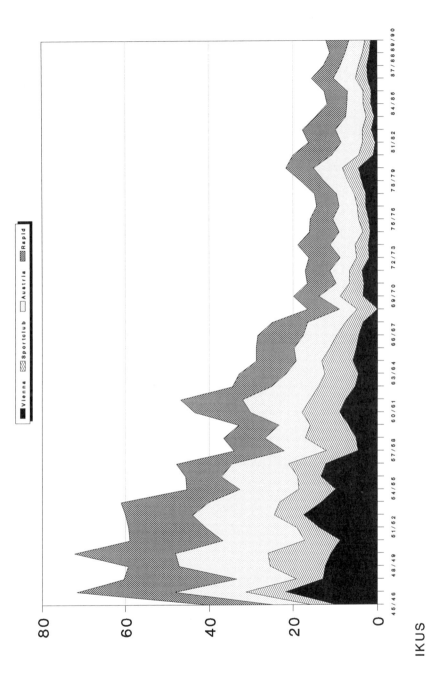

Figure A: Attendances at home matches (1st Division) - average number of spectators

Season/Team	Simmering	Vienna	Sportclub	Innsbruck	Austria	Rapid
45-50		13.570	9.991		16.742	20.516
50-55	7.333	12.664	7.885		18.312	18.059
55-60	7.131	8.411	8.592		11.759	10.632
60-65	3.769	5.244	7.957	9.181	8.849	10.034
65-70	2.322	4.078	5.135	7.515	6.930	8.391
70-75	2.331	2.575	2.776	8.422	4.617	7.001
75-80	1.121	3.151	2.820	5.828	5.389	5.610
80-85	812	1.036	2.404	5.159	5.290	7.333
85-90		1.902	1.903	7.322	4.214	4.760

(Source: ÖFB, till 1960 IKUS)

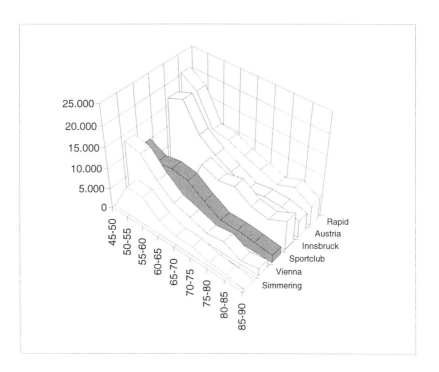

Figure B: Attendances at home matches (1st Division) - average number of spectators within a period of 5 years

62

network concerning the broadcasting of soccer games. In April 1964 the OFB decided that only if at least 60,000 tickets had been sold five days before an international game (played at the Prater Stadium) would a live telecast be allowed(8). A year later it was decided that for some time no international matches at all should be transmitted from the Prater.

The clubs of the *Staatsliga* tried to attract larger crowds by engaging more and more international players. Players, mainly from Yugoslavia, Germany, Hungary but also from Turkey and Brazil, were bought on the international market. This led to a major change in Austrian football. Vienna had been, at least since the end of the thirties, an exporter of successful and good players but now even the smaller clubs of the top division tried to attract more spectators and they became more successful by importing foreigners. In the summer of 1962, the media started to talk about a new invasion of foreigners and to discuss the pros and cons of this situation. Sometimes the style of the coverage did not lack a certain racist undertone, especially when the media used terms like 'Negro players'.

As early as 1961 the manager of the 'Austria', Joschi Walter, brought his plans for reforming and professionalizing the Austrian football into the public domain. The development of the German *Bundesliga*, which was installed during the season of 1963/64, was his model. In 1964 he was provisionally appointed manager of the Austrian team and in May this appointment was confirmed with Bela Guttmann as his assistant. He kept coming up with more ideas for reform but these were only partly taken up by the OFB. They took up the plan to create a national league consisting of not more than 12 clubs under the direct supervision of the OFB; the reduction of the number of foreign players to two; and the recognition of three different types of player - the amateur, contract players and licensed players (the latter were only allowed to play in the top division). The granting of a license for the national league was made dependent on economical criteria which had to be fulfilled by the clubs.

In October 1964 Joschi Walter quit his job because he felt that his ideas for reform were not taken seriously and he felt mistreated and ignored by the *Staatsliga*, the provincial unions and by leading OFB administrators. Quite obviously, he did not see a chance of carrying through his programme (*Welt am Montag*, 12 December, 1964).

In fact, neither the reduction of the number of the First Division clubs, nor the economic recommendations he made were ever carried out. Only the creation of the National League and new regulations concerning the status of the players were put into practise. Walter himself drew back from the so-called reforms; he never forgot to mention in public that "he was not the only one who proposed the rules in this form" (*Express*, 19 July 1965).

Modernization and reform in Austrian football

Since these first attempts, the modernization of Austrian (and therefore also Viennese) football constantly shifts between reform and counter reform. This process emphasizes and speeds up the split between top level and lower level soccer in Vienna. Two clubs with international aspirations ('Austria' and Rapid) oppose other clubs that still embody elements of the old Viennese football culture (ties to the home district, local roots). But even these two big clubs are, due to their history (that is, their semi-professional structure), stuck within this structure. Although they try to break away they do not really succeed. An almost tragic example was provided recently by the Rapid club. The establishment of a Rapid Limited Company (in 1991) which, in fact, now owns the club's players, made the club *de facto* an appendage of the company but it did not at all bring out the hoped for and expected success.

It is not by chance that the most important recent attempt to establish a big Austrian club that could come up to international standards occurred in the provinces. The short history of the FC Tirol club, lasted from 1986 to 1992 and would not have been possible in Vienna. It is unimaginable that Rapid or the 'Austria' club would change not only their club colours but also their name. This happened in Innsbruck without any difficulties. The FC Swarowski Tirol club, sponsored by the international Swarowski company, took over the First Division licence of Wacker Innsbruck, employed Ernst Happel as manager, and was actually quite successful in the Austrian Championship. It attracted its 'supporters', or more accurately the watchers of their home-games, by creating an image of a club standing against the (historically) dominant Viennese football culture. It is not only motives concerning football which play an important part here. It is also the general anti-centralist, more precisely anti-Viennese, attitude of the spectators which is important. But that covers only one side of the matter. Because of the image of professionalism and modernization - built up following the model of Bayern Munich - this new club attracted the representatives of the new middle class of the whole of Austria, even the Viennese, a class that was very much orientated towards success. This is the sort of 'football-interested consumer' who has actually got few ties to the club but chooses his club by checking the results. Soccer for him is just one of many different spare time attractions. From time to time - should it be opportune - he even calls himself a soccer fan and really believes it. I want to end this essay by setting up the following thesis: the half-hearted modernization of Austrian football in the course of international modernizations during the sixties, seventies and eighties is, in fact, an attempted internationalization and a practical provincialization.

'Austrification' here means nothing more than the combination of modern economic strategies of management with an explicit anti-metropolitan attitude. At the same time, it brings with it the deconstruction of the traditional and, itself contradictory, Viennese football culture and the creation of something that could be called the 'general Austrian soccer supporter'.

Notes

1. A four division league, including only Viennese clubs, was installed during the season 1911-12.

2. A professional league, with two divisions, was established in 1924 - again including only clubs from Vienna.

3. Not unlike their British colleagues, Austrian socialists could not really understand the significance of sport in popular culture (cf. Hargreaves 1992).

4. A famous Viennese comedian of the fifties and early sixties, Helmut Qualtinger, coined the phrase: "Simmering versus Kapfenberg - that's brutality". In doing so he actually referred to the working class origins of both clubs.(Kapfenberg was the club of a small industrial city in Styria).

5. Rapid, a club which was always regarded as the one attracting the biggest crowds, had to cope with a decline in spectators from around 18,000 per home match in the first half of the 1950s to 8,000 in the late 1960s.

6. As early as 1964 the daily *Neues Osterreich* complained about the inability of both Viennese players and audiences to cope with the new direction the sport has taken:

    > Our spoiled audiences and our comparatively 'soft' players cannot come to terms with the development of football around the world. Everywhere else the players are tougher, more athletic and more reckless. The appealing actions (the good move) become less, success is the only thing that counts. (*Neues Osterreich*, 8 August 1964).

7. Precise analyses are - unfortunately - impossible since the ORF (Austrian Broadcasting Cooperation) has got no data available for this period.

8. The price of a live transmission was 300,000 AS. On the 8th October 1961 this was carried through for the first time when

Austria played Hungary. How strong the fascination is for TV soccer games was shown by the fact that 90,000 tickets had been sold for the match but 8,000 of these tickets where not used after it was reported that the game could be seen on TV (*Welt am Montag*, 9.10.1961).

Bibliography

Berg, J. (1978) 'Fernsehen, fußball, fernsehfußball,' in *Ästhetik und Kommunikation*, Jg. 9, Heft 33, September .

Eschenbach, R. Horak, C. and Plasonig, G. (eds.) (1990) *Modernes Sportmanagement. Beispiel Fußball: Entwicklung eines integrierten Managementsystems*, Vienna.

Featherstone, M. (1991) *Consumer Culture and Postmodernism*, Sage, London.

Fischer-Kowalski, M. and Bucek, J. (eds.) (1980) *Lebensverhältnisse in Osterreich. Klassen und Schichten im Sozialstaat*, Frankfurt/New York.

Friesenbichler, G. (1985) *Sport frei!. Arbeitersport in Wien 1945 - 1985*, Vienna.

Gastgeb, H. (1933) 'Panem et circenses', in *Der Kampf*, 26.Jg, Nr.1/1933.

Gruber, H. (1991) *Red Vienna. Experiment in Working-Class Culture 1919 - 1934*, New York/Oxford.

Haller, M. (1982) *Klassenbildung und soziale Schichtung in Osterreich*,Frankfurt.

Hargeaves, J (1992) 'Sport and socialism in Britain', in *Sociology of Sport Journal*, Vol.9, no.2.

Holt, R. (1989) *Sport and the British: a Modern History*, Oxford University Press, Oxford.

Horak, R. (1991) 'Football Spectators in Vienna. From the local club supporter to the soccer-interested consumer', Paper presented at the NASSS Conference, 6-9. November 1991, Milwaukee, Wisconsin.

Horak, R. (1992) 'Viennese football culture: some remarks on its history and sociology,' in *Innovation in Social Sciences Research*, Vol

5, no 4.

Horak, R. and Maderthaner, W. (1992) 'Vom Fußballspielen in Wien. Überlegungen zu einem popularkulturellen Phänomen der Zwischenkriegszeit', in: Peter Muhr, Paul Feyerabend, Cornelia Wegeler (eds.): *Philosophie, Psychoanalyse, Emigration. Festschrift für Kurt Rudolf Fischer*, Vienna.

Horak, R. and Marschik, M. (1994): *Vom Erlebnis zur Wahrnehmung. Der Wiener Fußball und seine Zuschauer seit 1945*, Vienna (in print).

John, M. (1992)   'Bürgersport, Massenattraktion und Medienereignis. Zur Kultur- und Sozialgeschichte des Fußballspiels in Osterreich', in *Beiträge zur historischen Sozialkunde*, No.3.

Kastler, K. (1972) *Fußballsport in Ostereich. Von den Anfängen bis in die Gegenwart*, Linz.

Langisch, K. (1964) *Geschichte des österreichischen Fußballsports*, Vienna.

Langisch, K. (1979) *Fünfundsiebzig Jahre ÖFB. Eine Dokumentation des Österreichischen Fußballbundes*, Vienna.

Lindner, R. (ed.) (1983) *Der Satz 'Das Leder ist rund' hat eine gewisse philosophische Tiefe. Sport,Kultur,Zivilisation*, Berlin.

Löschnauer, R. (1983) *Der Fußballsport im Burgenland. Band II: von 1970 bis Juni 1983*. Hrsg. vom Burgenländischen Fußballverband zum 60-jährigen Bestandsjubiläum 1983, Eisenstadt.

Maderthaner, W. (1992) 'Ein Dokument wienerischen Schönheitssinns. Matthias Sindelar und das Wunderteam', in *Beiträge zur historischen Sozialkunde*, No. 3

Mason, T. (1980) *Association Football and English Society*, Harvester Press, Brighton.

Marschik, M. (1991) 'Arbeiterfußball im Austromarxismus', in:

Horak, R. and Reiter, W. (eds.), *Die Kanten des runden Leders. Beiträge zur europäischen Fußballkultur*, Vienna.

Marschik, M. (1992) *Wir Spielen nicht zum Vergnügen Arbeiterfussball in der Ersten Republik*, Vienna (in print).

Mattl, S. (1988), 'Stagnation und gesellschaftliche Krise. Das österreichische Beispiel', in: Maderthaner, W. and Gruber, H. (eds.), *Chance und Illusion/Labor in Retreat. Studien zur Krise der westeuropäischen Gesellschaft in den dreißiger Jahren/ Studies on the Social Crises in Interwar Europe*, Vienna/Zürich.

OFB, (1951) *Fussball in Osterreich*, Offizielles Jahrbuch 1950/51 des Osterreichischen Fussball-Bundes, Vienna.

Schidrowitz, L. (1951) *Geschichte des Fußballsportes in Osterreich*, Vienna-Wels-Frankfurt/M.

Schagerl, F. (1981) 'Der Sportklub als absatzorientiertes sozioökonomisches System', unpublished PhD thesis, Vienna.

Schulz, J. (1981) 'Fußball-Management', unpublished PhD thesis, Vienna.

Schulze-Marmeling, D. (1992) *Der gezähmte Fußball. Zur Geschichte eines subversiven Sports*, Göttingen.

Simmering, O. J. Sport Club (ed.) *80 Jahre 1. Simmeringer Sport-Club*. Jubiläumsbuch, Vienna (no date available).

Taylor, I. (1976) 'Spectator violence around football: the rise and fall of the 'working class weekend', in *Research Papers in Physical Education*, vol. 4, no. 1, August.

Tomlinson, A. (ed.) (1990) *Consumption, Identity and Style*, Routledge, London.

Wegs, J. R. (1989) *Growing up Working Class: Continuity and Change among Viennese Youth 1890 - 1938*, Pennsylvania/London.

Whannel, G. (1992) *Fields in Vision: Television Sport and Cultural Transformation*, Routledge, London.

Williams, J. and Wagg, S. (eds.) (1991) *British Football and Social Change. Getting into Europe*, University of Leicester Press, Leicester, London and New York.

3 'We are Celtic supporters ...': Questions of football and identity in modern Scotland

Raymond Boyle

I just wonder if anyone who has not grown up in the West of Scotland can truly comprehend what has been going on here for the last century, and so discover some level of understanding of just how important the fortunes of the Old Firm are in daily lives. It isn't Brooklyn or the Bronx, New York or even Chinatown. IT'S MUCH MORE SERIOUS. (Alan Davidson, 'Let's get serious Liam', *Evening Times*, 6 Sept. 1991).

"...We've got Cheers, Friday Sportscene and Scotsport Extra Time on the night. This is the night all good punks get to stay in and hurl abuse at Chic Hun." Karen is a punk and a Celtic supporter. A punk by vocation and a Celtic supporter since conception. She's Celtic daft. (Gorden Legge, *In Between Talking About The Football*, Polygon, 1991, p.26).

Introduction

Entry points into the growing debates surrounding the role and position of football in cultural life are numerous, so for the purposes of this chapter I propose to examine some of the more specific issues clustered around two related areas where much of the recent research into aspects of football culture in Britain have centred.[1]

The first is concerned with the role that football plays in the constitution and reconstitution of specific cultural and ethnic identities. To what extent are football clubs important cultural institutions which provide a focus around which specific identities are actively shaped? How is this process being shaped by (or indeed helping to shape) wider cultural agendas that enjoy prominence within local, regional or national spaces?

The second entry point centres on debates surrounding the modernization of football in Britain, and the potential tensions that exist between the drive to modernize, and the need to retain some of the more 'traditional' aspects of football culture.(2) In the case of Rangers and Celtic, we appear at first glance to have a microcosm of some of the wider dilemmas facing football at present. Rangers are portrayed as personifying the modernizing face of football, while across the city Celtic seem to represent a club locked into a more 'traditional' past. Rangers chairman, entrepreneur David Murray, is contrasted with a Celtic board that has been tightly controlled by three families, the Grant's, Kelly's and White's, since the turn of the century. Rangers are associated with business, money and power, while Celtic are portrayed as a club being left behind by the commercial forces that are driving the modern game (Fynn *et al.*, 1989; Moorhouse, 1991).

While not disagreeing with this analysis, I would qualify it by emphasizing the division that can exist between the club as a concrete institution and as an idea which is largely personified or existent through its supporters. In other words, while both are interlinked, I would like to concentrate not necessarily on the public pronouncements of the club, but on the discourses that circulate and enjoy prominence among supporters and which may be supportive of, or oppositional to, those favoured by the club. I will return later to some of the recent commercial developments that have been occurring at Celtic FC, such as the appointment in early 1991 and the subsequent sacking of the club's first Chief Executive, Terry Cassidy.

Some notes on methodology

While this chapter focuses primarily on Celtic FC and in particular its supporters, the debate is broadened out where necessary. At a primary level, this research draws in part from recent work carried out by the National Identity Research Unit based at the Caledonian University in Glasgow.(4) At a more qualitative level, interviews conducted by the author with groups of Celtic supporters both in Scotland and Ireland are used to augment both the empirical data and secondary material. The five interviews with groups of six to eight members took place during the period of May and June 1991. In extracts from transcripts names have been changed.

I should emphasise that in the fieldwork I was interested in the views and opinions of the most committed supporter, i.e. the fan who goes almost every week and follows the club both home and away. As to the class, age, and gender composition of the supporters surveyed and interviewed, the report concludes that:

> The majority of the most committed Celtic supporters are basically young, blue collar workers, from catholic backgrounds (although not necessarily practising) and Labour voters (Boyle, 1991, p.9).

Initially, let us turn to matters historical.

History, identity and football in the west of Scotland

> It's a grand old team to play for,
> It's a grand old team to see,
> And if you know your history,
> It's enough to make your heart go oh, oh, oh,...
> (*The Celtic song*, as sung by Celtic supporters)

> And all you've got is your history.....
> (*The Celtic song*, as sung by Rangers supporters, Celtic v Rangers match 1991).

The historical origins of the 'Old Firm' and the religious and ethnic divisions that have characterized their two sets of supporters have been well documented elsewhere.[5] However, the origins of sectarianism in the west of Scotland and the role played by football in this process have not been an uncontested area of scholarly debate. Gerry Finn (1991a & b) has attacked the orthodox historical interpretation that the setting up of Celtic FC (viewed as an Irish catholic club in the west of Scotland) acted as the catalyst which prompted a reaction from the indigenous Protestant population who rallied behind Rangers.[6] He suggests that anti-Irish racism has been recycled in contemporary histories of the clubs and argues that the setting up in the late 19th century of Irish-Scots football clubs, 'signalled the willingness of the community to participate in Scottish sport'; far from being sectarian, this was the only way that immigrants could be guaranteed participation in the sport. He goes on to argue:

> the setting up of the clubs reveals the complex collective social identity of a community which believed itself to be Scottish but wished to retain a pride in its Irish ancestry: the football clubs reveal the dual identity of the clubs as *Irish-Scots* (Finn, 1991b, pp.370-371).

These historical debates are important, for as we shall see later, few sets of supporters are more acutely aware of their club's history (or particular versions of it) than those of Celtic and Rangers. For example, many of the current discourses circulating among modern day Celtic supporters are inflected through the historical positioning of the club in the cultural life of the west of Scotland. Before proceeding, it is perhaps useful here to say something with regard to the question of identity and how it relates to the work that follows.

Issues of identity

While Finn talks of the dual identity of the Irish-Scots, we can also discuss identity in a manner which emphasizes its multi- faceted nature. Within the realms of social and political science, debates surrounding issues of national and cultural identity have focused on the inter-relationship between politics, economy and culture.[7] Kellas (1991), highlights the importance of what he calls 'psychic income' which he argues, 'refers to those things which satisfy the mental and spiritual needs of human beings' (Kellas, 1991, p.67).

Drawing from the field of social psychology, and work on group identities, concepts such as 'relative deprivation' and 'cultural deprivation' can be useful in opening up debates which link the material conditions of existence with perceptions of group difference which may be articulated through cultural activity: in this case football, with clubs acting as cultural institutions.[8]

Such a role could be assigned to Celtic FC for example, drawing as it does the majority of its support from people with a shared religious (Catholicism) and ethnic (of Irish ancestry) background. As we shall see later, this is not to suggest that that these religious and ethnic traditions are monolithic. They are themselves multi-faceted, and indeed the very act of following Celtic can also be viewed as part of the process which both defines and expresses these areas of identity. As I argue throughout, the internal group identities of minorities are forged in part by external majority group perceptions of, and reactions to, that minority.

Ian Spring (1990), talks about the nostalgia that Glasgow Catholics have for their ancestral homeland, and claims:

> Their homeland, however distant or reconstructed, is part of a national mythology - the Irish club, Ceoltas piping competitions, the shamrock ceilidhs in the James Elliot Centre, Celtic Football Club, St. Patrick's day etc. (Spring, 1990, p.87).

He wonders why the Irish Protestants who also immigrated to Scotland around the same period don't maintain, or appear to exhibit, this same affection. The reason for this can partly be explained by the fact that with their religious and historical background, they were more readily accepted by the dominant community, while the Irish-Catholics were not, and in part responded to this rejection with the setting up of their own cultural support apparatuses. I will return to the debates surrounding Irish/Scottish cultural identity later when attention is turned to the modern Celtic supporter.

Social groups and boundaries

Individual identities are not fixed, but are continually being constituted and reconstituted. When individuals come together in larger social groups this concept of identity as a process helps us to understand how boundary marking is of central importance in group and intergroup relationships. As boundaries are constructed, a process of inclusion and exclusion takes place, ingroups and outgroups are identified.

In the west of Scotland for example, allegiance to Celtic or Rangers illustrate this process of identity demarcation. On stating support for either of the two clubs, people tend to be identified (accurately or inaccurately) with one particular cultural configuration (e.g., catholic or Protestant) which has its roots in the historical socioeconomic development of the west of Scotland. To what extent the perceptions among groups as to the internal content of these configurations are themselves changing, will be examined later when we discuss the interviews among younger and older supporters.

Let us turn our attention to the related and contested area of the role of tradition in football culture, specifically as to how it pertains to debates surrounding Celtic and its supporters. This also provides an entry point into the two areas of debate highlighted at the beginning of this chapter: namely, the role that clubs play in any process of identity formation; and the potential tension that exists between modernizing impulses in the game, and the maintenance of tradition.

Tradition and identity among Celtic supporters

> I couldn't have imagined the intensity of feeling in this city [Glasgow]... The shock of how big the thing [Celtic/Rangers] is, of how everyday it is, is hard to overcome (Then Celtic manager, Liam Brady, *The Guardian*, 14 March 1992).

> ...it would kill me if I didn't go to a game... with Celtic it's not a football club, it's an identity (Celtic supporter, male, 19).

> ...I suppose it stems back to when everybody didn't have much, because they were a minority in Scotland. It gave them a thing to cling onto, and we've still got that (Celtic supporter, male, 18).

Tradition, as Stuart Hall argues:

> ...is a vital element in culture, but it has little to do with the persistence of old forms. It has much more to do with the way elements have been linked together or articulated. These arrangements in a national-popular culture have no fixed or inscribed position, and certainly no meaning that is carried along, so to speak, in the stream of historical tradition, unchanged (Hall, 1981, p. 236).

Thus how particular traditions are articulated and what they constitute can differ widely, depending, in part, on the interests served by the dominance of any one 'version'. What I want to do is examine the meanings attached to this term when it is used by supporters, and in so doing develop our investigation into the role of the club in any process of identity formation.

In the questionnaire work carried out (Boyle, 1991), supporters were asked: "How strongly do you identify with each of these elements of Celtic F.C?" They were then given a list including such things as ground, players and such like and asked if they identified *very strongly*, *quite strongly*, or *not at all strongly*. The item on the list which polled heaviest in the category of *very strongly*, was that of Club History/Tradition (85% Scottish based supporters, 92% Northern Ireland based supporters). The least identification was reserved for the Board (71% Scotland, 84% N. Ireland). It was clear then that the history/tradition associated with the club in the eyes of the supporters, was an important factor in generating a sense of loyalty to the club among fans.[9] For the majority, the initial act of following Celtic was something that was part of a wider socializing process passed on through family influence. The younger supporters (under 25) seemed acutely aware of the role that family and school played on their decision to follow the club.

> Very few people choose a team that's different from their family... you are obviously dominated, especially in the catholic schools (Group 3, Brian, 18).

> I think in particular with Celtic and Rangers it would be that way... I think in Liverpool you might get a father following Liverpool and a son following Everton, in Glasgow it's more polarised (Group 3, Anthony, 19).

When asked to discuss what they thought constituted part of the Celtic tradition elements, they included the attacking style of play; the never say die attitude of the team until the very last minute of the match; and great emphasis was placed on the historical origins of the club and its links with Ireland. The use of Rangers FC as an oppositional force, against which 'our' tradition could be sketched was also important.

> Well politically I think the Celtic tradition has always been a working class tradition. Playing the underdog thing... I don't know about the football but I'm identifying with the crowd much

more. Celtic have always had sort of working class traditions with its supporters, so have Rangers, although not so much. It's [Rangers] always had a rich element, Rangers have always had rich people support them (Group 4, Paul, 25).

However fans were also aware of how tradition could be mobilized for a negative purpose, as well as being something that was important because it gave the Celtic supporter that 'sense of difference'. "The Board misuse that tradition, they use it to try and cover our eyes by saying we shouldn't do this because we don't want to break with tradition" (Group 3, Brian, 18).

Another example was the Board's failure to invest in improving the 'traditional' poor facilities at Celtic Park because, they argued, these were the facilities that the fans preferred. There were also significant, if understandable, differences between the discourses of tradition that existed among the Scottish and Irish based supporters. For example, the latter placed a heightened significance on the importance of particular symbols as part of the Celtic tradition.

In the survey (Boyle, 1991), these Irish based supporters identified more strongly with the football ground (Celtic Park) than the Scottish based supporters (64% compared with 38% identified very strongly). The importance of the Celtic jersey, with its green and white hoops, and the flying of the Irish tricolour flag above Celtic Park were recurring elements when tradition was discussed among Irish based supporters. The role that symbols play in the building and reinforcing of identity has of course a heightened cultural and political significance within Northern Ireland.[10] The importance of these concrete symbols of the Celtic tradition were also given as some of the reasons in explaining why the popularity of following Celtic among young Catholics in Belfast seems to be increasing.[11]

I think it's the jersey, Celtic are unique in the green and white hoops (Group 1, Tom, 40).

You come out of Celtic Park and there is thousands and thousands of people in green and white. There are tricolours everywhere which you never see here, kids can't get over that, that they can get that over in Scotland, but you can't get it here (Group 1, Peter, 45).

To these supporters in particular the Irish connection with the club, and the maintenance of this, is of central importance. They invest a great deal both financially and emotionally in following the club, and it is an important part of their cultural life: another element which helps sustain a sense of a particular identity in the north of Ireland.

A more usual expression of identity occurs when people, living away from their original homeland, maintain links with symbolic events which are used to reinforce a sense of 'who they are'. For instance, Graham Walker (1990, p.146), writing about Rangers, notes how some Scots living abroad use support for Rangers FC and the celebration of both the Burns Supper and St. Andrew's Day as a way of holding 'on to their Scottish cultural identity'. He emphasizes the linking of religious identity to Scottish cultural identity by stating that:

> Rangers, especially in the post war era, were thus part of a celebration of Scottishness which can be underpinned by a strong unionism or loyalism. It can be argued that the Unionism was viewed as essentially an expression of Protestantism, following the traditional Orangeist rhetoric of loyalty to the crown and constitution and the defence of civil and religious liberties (*Ibid.*)

However, what he is talking about here is a very narrowly defined conception of 'Scottishness'. A Scottishness of exclusion as much as inclusion, and one that posed problems for groups such as Catholics, and Irish-Scots. I shall return later specifically to the question of Scottishness and the modern day Celtic supporter later, and also comment on the apparent shifting political allegiance of the Rangers supporter.

Tradition v modernization: a false dichotomy?

> (Football fans) do not simply select a 'product' depending on what the competitive market has to offer... choices are constrained by and dependent on a number of more traditional considerations (Curran and Redmond, 1991, p.28)

Let us now shift the focus of debate surrounding aspects of tradition onto the area of the role (if any) it plays in the modernizing of the game in Britain.(12) By modernizing, I mean the attraction of new money into the club which will allow the club to progress both on and off the pitch. In part, Celtic are responding to economic and political pressures exerted by the Taylor Report (1990), as well as the commercial revolution that has taken place at Rangers FC over the last number of years (13). Moorhouse (1991, p.209) has suggested that Celtic and its supporters:

> cling to a conventional view of what football 'is about' in Scotland, a posture which seems to block any initiative and to stultify any sensible response to the big changes which European developments seem likely to forge.

He presents Rangers as being the shining European lights of Scottish football, and suggests that the pull of Europe may be strong enough to dislodge Rangers from their indigenous base within the Scottish game as they gravitate towards a European Super League.

A number of points are worth making. We have to distinguish between those who run the club, and the supporters of that club; too often these elements are grouped together. I agree that Celtic (the Board), have been slow to halt the relative decline of the club which has been taking place since the early 70s, and indeed the battle for control of the club and the shaping of its future direction, and the Board's proposal for a new £100m Celtic stadium to be ready for 1994 (which remains unresolved as of September 1993) have been very much in the news recently.(14) However, I don't feel that this narrow definition of 'tradition' is shared by Celtic supporters. Neither do I feel for all the Euro rhetoric that comes out of Ibrox, that the club is ready to leave the Scottish scene. Like a lot of big city European clubs, they are guaranteed success in their domestic league; they also thrive on a successful 'Old Firm' rivalry. As to a European Super League that would pull clubs out of domestic leagues, the current set up of the latter stages of the European Champions Cup competition means that a Super League exists in all but name.

Again, I think it's important to emphasize the way that media discourses surrounding football tend to present a more coherent club view than may actually exist among supporters. In the process of modernization, Rangers have cleverly plugged into a 'traditional' folk culture that allows them to connect one version of tradition with commercial acumen. As journalist and writer Kevin McCarra suggests:

> In a way, as well as going forwards they have also gone backwards. They have revived the Bill Struth era of the 1940/50s when they were the dominant force in Scotland and expected to win ... I think they have struck a chord, almost a folk memory with Rangers supporters, by creating this imposing edifice at Ibrox, and these [commercial] developments link well with Rangers' past (Interview with author, 28 January 1992).

This division of 'official' club discourses, amplified by the media (sometimes uncritically), and other discourses articulated in part through an alternative media network such as the fanzine, is important and returned to later in the chapter.

Tradition as commodity

Much debate took place among the interview groups of Celtic fans about the potential clash between the need to attract capital to the club, and its traditional links with Ireland.

> Multi-national companies are not going to put money into Celtic when there are people on the terraces singing 'Oh Ah up the Ra (IRA)', because they can't get involved in that political stuff " (Group 5, Chris, 30).

As in many discussions among the supporters, comparisons were drawn with Rangers:

> Rangers have been a very clever football club in the marketing of its image, simply because they have managed to market themselves as a traditional Scottish club ... They've divorced sectarianism from the club now that they've turned around and signed a catholic. They've divorced sectarianism from the club in the eyes of the media, but the fans haven't changed a bit, and the fans aren't getting hassled for singing 'The Sash' (Group 4, Pat, 24).

Later, when the point was made that some 'traditional' songs might scare off potential sponsors from the club, this was countered with:

People are proud of their team, of their religion, you're talking about the fans not the club, you're talking about how the business is affected by what the fans sing... aye, "We're up to our knees in Fenian blood", what's all that about then, eh? I can't see Scottish and Newcastle [brewers and Rangers sponsors] pointing the finger at the Rangers fans and saying, "Come on guys pack in singing 'The Sash', that happened four centuries ago what are you still singing it for?" (Group 4, John, 26).

Many supporters felt that the traditional elements of Celtic FC (however you wished to define them), could be better exploited for commercial gain, and saw little tension between commercial development and adhering to the symbolic aspects of the club. They felt the club should be marketed on its sense of difference, its uniqueness, rather than as another bland football club (examples here included Tottenham Hotspur and Arsenal). They emphasized the need to harness Celtic's traditions, not to reject them for short term gain.

The introduction in 1991 of the club's first Chief Executive, Terry Cassidy coincided with an increase in the merchandizing of the club. Season 1992-3 saw the launch of the Celtic catalogue with an extensive range of endorsed products. The club are developing and extending the commercial areas in which they are involved, be that corporate hospitality, merchandizing of club products or products endorsed by the club and such like. To what extent Celtic's support (with its large working class element), will provide as lucrative a market for the club as Rangers more affluent supporters have provided for them, remains to be seen.

In addition the sacking of Cassidy and the recent departure (October 1993) of Liam Brady again highlight the club's instability. The recent outcome of the ultimately unsuccessful current struggle (October/November 1993) to gain control of the club by a consortium led by Scots-Canadian businessman Fergus McCann will dictate the future direction and commercial viability of the club.

A commonly expressed and related concern among supporters was that, as the cost of attending matches looks certain to rise with the development of all-seater stadia, there would be a danger of pricing the ordinary working class supporter out of the game. This concern is not unique to Celtic supporters.(15)

Let us now turn our attention to the issue of football and the construction of cultural identity, and focus on Celtic and the modern day Celtic supporter.

Football and identity, Glasgow: west of Scotland?

Gerry Finn (1991a & b) has argued that much of the debate surrounding the cultural role of Celtic in Scottish life has used as its premise an exclusive and narrow definition of 'Scottishness'. He argues that for many Irish-Scots the club was important because it gave them an entry point into Scottish cultural life that was denied elsewhere.(16)

Celtic represented a concrete institution, part of a cultural way of life that they could actively participate in, and be proud of. As Tom Gallagher (1987, pp.352-3) has noted:

> (W)orking class Catholics in particular find it difficult to relate to the symbols of Scottish nationhood. The custodians of Scottish national identity have tended to be bourgeois institutions like the law, the Presbyterian religion and education and these are alien entities to many working class Catholics.

In part they responded by showing loyalty to other institutions such as Celtic FC and the catholic church. This is not to suggest that some clear-cut 'cultural division of labour' takes place. As I've argued, identity formation is a multi-faceted, and indeed at times contradictory process. What is clear is that many facets of what constituted the official cultural apparatus of Scottish culture, excluded particular groups from its rituals.

Today much of what constitutes the identity of the Celtic supporter is passed on via a process of cultural osmosis. There exists within football fan culture a tribal library from which younger fans select and put together aspects of their footballing identity. They learn about the club, its past, its heroes, its villains, its enemies and such like. In the case of Celtic this takes place in the home and in schools, as well as forming part of the fan culture at matches. This is not to suggest that this process is taking place in some sort of hermetically sealed environment, it is subject to internal (e.g. age differences), and external pressures (e.g. political and economic pressures). Also I wish to emphasize that when I say fans *choose*, I am talking about a strictly limited choice. To extend the library analogy further, it is a selectively stocked library, and the range of items in it have been constrained by various socio-cultural forces.

When discussion with fans shifted onto the area of defining one's individual national identity, the multi-faceted element of identity was very much in evidence. The following are typical of responses from supporters in the groups, and are worth quoting at length.

> I'm Scottish, I'm thinking about it in two senses. If I go abroad and meet someone, they'll ask me where I'm from, and I'll say 'Scotland' and I'm Scottish cos that's where I've been born and brought up, but there is always in your mind that most of your characteristics are portrayed through the Irish way of feeling, you've got that (Group 2, Bill, 20).

> The Scottish thing is the fact that you were born here, that's a tangible thing; you can't hide where you were born. But I'm talking about it in terms of what you feel and where you feel you belong, who you've got an identity with. I've got to be Scottish cos I'm integrated, I speak the same and look the same as the Scots (Group 5, Alan, 18).

Many of the supporters expressed their sense of identity through this 'feeling of belonging'. What was interesting was that the linking with 'Irishness', was more pronounced among younger supporters (under 25). Indeed among the older groups there was a feeling that many of the younger supporters were 'more Irish' than Celtic supporters have ever been.

This split is an interesting example of how football and football culture can provide a concrete arena for expressing or articulating various strands of identity. Firstly, 43% of the supporters in the survey (Boyle, 1991) expressed a greater commitment to the Republic of Ireland football team than the Scottish national team. This degree of support can be attributed to a number of factors, including: the recent success of the Republic at international level; the perception of ill treatment of Celtic players playing for Scotland by sections of the Scottish support; and the positive identification of a number of Celtic players with the Republic of Ireland team.

Another factor in this age split in experiencing a sense of Irishness, is the linkage between football and youth culture.[17] Kevin McCarra has commented on how some fans:

> ...see some sort of radical chic in playing up their Irish heritage, this has become a fashion accessory. This political identity, following Ireland during the [1990] World Cup, I find it related to style rather than substance (Interview with author, 28 January 1992).

It also provides an oppositional point of reference to perceptions of Rangers FC and their supporters. As one supporter commented:

> They sell Rangers with all this 'Aye Ready' shite. They've always sold on the Protestant work ethic, Calvinist bit of working hard and tough, and playing hard and tough, and having fans who were hard and tough (Group 2, Dave, 24).

Every perception of difference reinforces that internal sense of group identity, and acts, as Cohen (1985, p.118) argues, as 'a resource and repository of meaning and a referent of their identity.'

Another factor which contributes to this boundary marking, particularly in the case of football supporters, can be success (or lack of it) on the pitch. Celtic's lack of success has been mirrored by a number of successful years for Rangers FC It could also be argued that any discontent among Rangers supporters, regarding the recent direction of the club, has been more difficult to articulate when the team has been continually successful. In football, the regular acquisition of trophies can appear to act as a panacea for many ills.

Before we turn to the discussion of political identity and the Celtic supporter, I want to examine briefly some of the issues surrounding the apparent lack of support for the Scottish national team among Celtic supporters. This in turn fuels suggestions of disloyalty among these supporters to all things Scottish, and reinforces older and deeply embedded beliefs among sections of the population about the role of the Irish-Scot in the socioeconomic development of modern Scotland.

Scotland: the national question

It has been noted elsewhere that international sport provides an attractive arena for the expression of various shades of nationalistic sympathies, as the symbolic representation of 'official' or 'unofficial' nationalisms.(18) The linkage between national identity and international sport often appears clear and unambiguous. Loyalty to national sporting teams finds itself being mobilized in populist rhetoric by some politicians as an indicator of civic loyalty to a country.(19)

Finn has argued that historically Celtic players were discriminated against when the Scottish national team was selected (a discourse that still circulates among Celtic supporters of all age groups). He has argued this was important in the wider social context of Scottish life because, 'sport, relying on open competition, is usually one of the first social arenas in which minority communities can break through to demonstrate their equal competence' (Finn, 1991b, p.375). This perception of discrimination against Celtic from various sources, in particular sections of the media, is still strongly felt among many Celtic supporters today.(20)

Related to the comments above have been recent debates that have centred around the location of Scotland's home internationals. With the re-development of Hampden Park (The National Stadium), Ibrox Park, the home of Rangers, has become the venue for internationals, accompanied by claims from David Murray, the owner of Rangers, that most Scotland supporters are Rangers supporters anyway. By implication, the Celtic supporter is portrayed as less than loyal in his commitment to the national team.

Graham Walker (1990, p.146), in an article discussing the link between Rangers and religious identity in Scotland, states that, 'Celtic supporters were largely indifferent to the national team till the 1970s, they viewed the Scottish football authorities as biased towards Rangers.' The point isn't made that a lot of Celtic supporters felt excluded and alienated when they did go to matches supporting Scotland.

Many older supporters (over 35) claimed that they used to go and watch Scotland, but stopped doing so due to the abuse directed at Celtic players from sections of the Scottish support. The importance of specific fan cultures in the dissemination of ideas and attitudes can be seen by the universal reference made by supporters of all ages to the abuse received by Celtic winger Jimmy Johnstone while playing for his country in the late 1960s and 1970s.

There are guys on the park playing for their country, these supporters are supposed to be there to support their country. There's a guy down there playing every Saturday in green and white hoops and now he's playing in a blue shirt, and they're standing there abusing him (Group 5, Jim, 35).

Look at all the players who got hassled for not playing as well for their country as they did for their club: Kenny Dalglish, Paul McStay, Nicol and Hansen at Liverpool. I can't think of one Rangers player who gets it in the neck (Group 2, Paul, 24).

Why don't I follow Scotland?... A number of reasons, they're dross, they reflect Scottish football; also there are all the other reasons, namely the bigotry on the terraces (Group 3, Brian, 18).

It appears that as the suspicion of prejudice in team selection has receded, the perception, reinforced through commonly circulated personal experiences, of being made unwelcome on the terraces has increased.

While no comprehensive survey of the club allegiances of the Scottish supporter exists, its probable that many of the travelling supporters are not 'Old Firm' fans. To many supporters of smaller clubs in Scotland following their country (particularly abroad), gives them the opportunity to experience the big match football atmosphere, and the excitement of following a football team abroad, that they don't get at a domestic level.[21] Also many Celtic supporters stated that while they may no longer go to Scotland matches, they did follow and support the team through television coverage of matches.

What becomes clear is that any simplistic reading of a national sporting team with some homogeneous support, masks a number of tensions and contradictions that can exist within that culture. Of course this is not unique to Scotland or football, and simply emphasizes the internal diversity of all supposedly *national* cultures.

Political football: political identity and the 'Old Firm'

To reduce the majority of Rangers and Celtic supporters to specific political voting patterns is, of course, to generalize. However what

I'm interested in doing here is to examine broad aspects of political identity as articulated by Celtic supporters. The results of the survey of supporters (Boyle, 1991) seemed to emphasize the strong historical link between Catholics and the Labour Party in the west of Scotland, with 88% of the survey voting for that party. What emerges from the group interviews is the strong perception of the SNP as being a party with links with Orangeism and Protestantism. This perception is particularly strong among the younger (under 25) fans: 'They (SNP) are a Protestant party, catholics aren't welcome' (Group 3, Pat, 17). Another supporter commented how he had heard that there was a stall outside an SNP conference that was selling 'Keep Scotland Protestant' pens. While he felt that this may have been an unofficial stall, he also felt that it must reflect the attitude of some of the people in the conference hall.

> Maybe we're being accused of paranoia which has been flung in our faces. I definitely think the identity of Scotland is to be Protestant and that is what they (the SNP) are trying to achieve ... I couldn't vote for them (Group 5, Graham, 18).

While recent shifts in the SNP support suggest that some Labour voters are switching their allegiance, what emerged among the Scottish based Celtic supporters was a strong linking of the SNP with negative religious connotations. As in other areas of identity formation, the use of groups as external reference points which confirm an internal 'sense of difference' is also evident here when Celtic supporters talk about those of Rangers. Many view the latter as either Tory or SNP voters, and find this assumption reinforced by the symbols displayed by Rangers supporters at matches, such as the Union Jack and the singing of God Save The Queen.

> They sing God Save The Queen, and then they go home to Bridgeton and they've got an outside toilet, haven't got hot water and they're living in slums. They're singing, but they obviously haven't thought this through ... there's no logic in it (Group 2, Tom, 19).

However, if large sections of the Rangers support were not voting Labour, the political map of Scotland would be of a significantly different complexion. The editor of the Rangers fanzine *Follow*

Follow has stated that he feels the majority of supporters are, 'right wing Labour' (Walker, 1990, p.152). If Rangers views itself as the establishment club, and is attracting a greater degree of support from the middle classes, it is highly likely that there are more Conservative and SNP voters among its supporters than exists among the Celtic support.

Graham Walker has noted how he feels an 'ideologically sound' cult has been created around the Celtic supporter (in part mediated through the fanzine *Not The View)*, which may not stand up to closer scrutiny. While this may be true, his own attempt to portray Rangers club officials in a progressive political light also has a hollow ring to it, particularly when he fails to mention some of the extreme right wing groups such as the British National Party that are connected with elements of the Rangers support, however small.

To what extent symbols displayed at matches represent loyalty to the club, and not to any specific political configuration is of course important. While David Murray, owner of Rangers, has recently stated his support for the maintenance of the Union between Scotland and England, a letter to the *Scotland on Sunday* newspaper noted how at a recent Premier League football match, Hearts supporters, when confronted with Union Jack waving Rangers supporters had sung *Flower of Scotland*. The letter writer concluded by stating it was: 'a "time to choose" for Rangers supporters. Is it to be the Union flag or the Saltire?' (*Scotland on Sunday*, 9/2/92). A letter the following week noted,

> If a poll was conducted among Rangers fans on the issue of which flag they would want between the Union Jack and the Saltire, I firmly believe the Saltire would win and contrary to a lot of folk's belief most of the fans are either Labour or SNP supporters (*Scotland on Sunday*, 16/2/92).

Thus, while I believe significant political differences do exist between the majority of supporters of Celtic and Rangers, related to religious and historical factors, there can be no simplistic linkage between symbolic sporting displays of allegiance and collective political orientation. For example, a small group of the Celtic supporters surveyed (who travel regularly to matches) were born and currently live in England. When they were asked which was their national team, they replied that despite following a Scottish club with overt symbolic Irish connections, they viewed it as being England.

Some concluding observations

Any process of group identity formation is shaped by internal and external pressures. In his investigation of Protestant youth culture and sectarianism in Northern Ireland, Desmond Bell notes that:

> ... once one accepts that ethnic identity is a relational affair, i.e. groups establish and sustain their collective sense of themselves as a distinct group by reference to other 'outsider' groups from whom they wish to be distinguished, then our attention must of necessity focus on the socially-constructed and maintained boundary which embodies that sense of discrimination (Bell, 1990, p.49).

To a particular group, Celtic FC are an important badge of identity, a concrete element that helps to sustain and create a sense of difference. Within urban working class culture issues of territory and collective identity are particularly important, and it is no coincidence that both are issues that are central in the culture of football supporters.

This is not to suggest, as is the case in Belfast, that there exists geographical religious-ethnic ghettos which divide various strands of working class life in Glasgow and the west of Scotland. Indeed, one of the crucial points of difference between the Celtic supporters who lived in Belfast and those who lived in Glasgow, both from similar class backgrounds, was the former group's acute awareness of living in a polarized society, and how supporting Celtic took on a heightened political significance because of that: '

> In Scotland most of us found that they (Celtic and Rangers supporters) drink together, they work together ... (Group 1, Vincent, 35);

> Over here [in Ireland] they don't, you live apart, they don't mix and that's just it, Rangers supporters here are much more bitter than those in Scotland (Group 1, Pat, 30).

Football cultures and subcultures can both promote that sense of difference as well as raise a sense of a shared collective identity. In the case of Celtic supporters the club is just one part of a wider cultural network that includes religion, education and politics. However it should also be noted that certain aspects of football culture can also act as repositories of prejudice, sectarianism and racism, however uncomfortable that may be to some involved in the game and its related culture industries.

As we have noted, what comes to constitute a particular tradition is a matter of struggle and contestation over interpretation. In the case of Celtic it is a term that can be politically mobilized to serve and defend particular actions.

As I have shown above it is useful to focus the debate at two levels and locate it within wider debates centred around the modernization of football in Britain. The first relates to the political economy of the football industry. As we move towards the end of the century are the 'traditional' ways of running football clubs viable in the light of the financial pressures being brought to bears on the clubs? Are there alternative models of football club ownership and control? Is the existing structural framework capable of implementing the changes demanded by the Taylor Report of 1990?

At another level, and of course closely linked to the first one, is the role of the supporter in the club. In the case of the Celtic supporter, identification with the club is inexorably bound up with issues of identity and community shot through with religious and cultural overtones. The central question remains the extent to which there has to be a trade off between the first set of problems facing the game, and the latter set of cultural connections that so informs the relationship that exists between football and its 'customers'.

It is perhaps useful here to make some brief observations on the role that public media discourses play in this process of identity formation. Both television and the popular press play an important role in setting the parameters within which issues relating to football get discussed.(22) Recently an alternative channel of communication among supporters has developed through the growth of the fanzine movement.(23) While these publications, by fans for fans, can articulate concerns not treated in the mainstream media, it is important to note the awareness among supporters of existing media discourses, and their ability to plug into these and either reinforce (if positive) or challenge (if negative). This is a social practice that has played an important part in the recent restructuring of the image of the Scottish football supporter that exists south of the border and elsewhere in Europe. Richard Giulianotti noted this during Italia '90:

> In presenting themselves to the world through media-friendly significations, Scots declare images of English hooligans to be accurate indices of national isolationism. They in turn, manipulate this recognition of media power, through the enactment of a bizarre internationalism *ad infinitum* (Giulianotti, 1991, p.510).

Again the oppositional element is important in defining the characteristics of the 'in group', in this case the Scottish supporter. It was a process that was very much in evidence at the 1992 European Football Championships in Sweden, were the Scottish supporters were voted by UEFA 'the best behaved fans of the tournament.' The same is true in the case of the relationship that exists between 'Old Firm' supporters.

Other areas of civil society also play a role in this process of socialization, such as educational and religious institutions. Another area is the media which continually emphasize (and develop?) the uniqueness of the 'Old Firm' rivalry, and in so doing also boost newspaper sales and television viewing figures. Thus the circulating of media discourses relating to Celtic and Rangers are not just important in cultural terms, but also in material terms for the Scottish media.

Media discussion of the sectarianism and racism in Scottish society, noted earlier, is more problematic. For the media the dilemma lies in the fact that while they have no problem discussing the 'unique atmosphere' of Glasgow derbies, they find it more difficult to tackle or examine the sectarian overtones which in turn help to generate that atmosphere. Instead it gets reduced to a 'colourful' characteristic of life in the west of Scotland, which is exemplified through humour. Perhaps too much navel gazing on this aspect of Scottish culture would prompt too many uncomfortable questions, too close to home.

Acknowledgement

A special thanks to all those people who participated in the various interviews used in this work.

Notes

1. See Williams and Wagg (eds.) (1991), and Duke (1991).

2. See Ian Taylor (1991).

3. For example, see Moorhouse (1991), and Fynn, A. *et al.* (1989).

4. What is striking is how little is known about the social composition of modern day football supporters. See Williams (1989), CLR (1984) and Boyle, (1991).

5. In particular see Murray (1984) and also Gallagher (1987).

6. Contrast Finn (1991a & b), and the work of Walker (1990). Also see the heated exchange between Pia (1988a & b), and Walker (1988), over the role that Celtic and their supporters have played in the cultural and political development of modern Scotland.

7. In particular, see Gellner (1983), Schlesinger (1991) and Kellas (1991).

8. For a general introduction see, Abrams & Hogg (1990). For work on Northern   Ireland, see Bell (1990).

9. For a fuller account see Chapter 5, 'Tradition, Loyalty and Commitment', in Boyle (1991).

10. An article in *The Observer* (24/3/91) gave an account of Rangers supporters travelling over to an Old Firm match in Glasgow: "Supporting one of the Glasgow Giants is an act of faith for Northern Irish football supporters". For a detailed account of Protestant working class youth culture in Northern Ireland see, Bell (1990).

11. The media were also viewed to have played a key role. In particular, official and unofficial video tapes of games and especially the club's history had helped to generate a substantial degree of interest among a new younger audience.

12. In particular, see Ian Taylor (1991), as well as Lord Justice Taylor (1990).

13. See the chapter, 'Glasgow Belongs to Me', in Fynn *et al.* (1989).

14. See newspaper articles such as, 'Pitched Battle for the keys of Paradise', *The Scotsman,* 22 February 1992; 'Grounds for complaint on road to Paradise', *Scotland on Sunday*, 19 January 1992; and 'Flattened: Paradise must go as Celts decide to move', *Evening Times*, 12 March 1992. For details of the new stadium see *The Celtic View,* 15 April 1992; and for potential problems with the proposed site see *The Herald*, 27 August 1992.

15. With regard to the fears expressed by Rangers supporters see, Walker (1990).

16. See Gallagher (1987, 1990).

17. For a study of the link between aspects of youth culture and football, see Redhead (1991).

18. In particular, see Allison (1986); and, the chapter 'Sport and National Culture', in Blain *et al.* (1993).

19. For example, take Conservative MP Norman Tebbit's famous 'cricket test', where he questioned the civic loyalty of those people, living in Britain, who actively supported the opposing team when England played cricket. To do so, he suggested, was an indicator of an individual's lack of British (English) patriotism.

20. See Chapter 4, 'Celtic and the media', in Boyle (1991).

21. For a recent account of Scottish supporters travelling abroad, see Giulianotti (1991).

22. For a comparison between the British popular press and its European counterparts (particularly within the arena of sports journalism), see Blain, Boyle and O'Donnell (1993).

23. See Jary, Horne & Bucke (1991).

24. See Rogan Taylor (1991) and 'The silent majority finds its voice', *The Independent on Sunday*, 8/3/92 .In relation to questions of supporter loyalty and the fan as an irrational consumer, see Davies (1990).

Bibliography

Abrams, D. and Hogg, M.A. (eds.) (1990) *Social Identity Theory: Constructive and Critical Advances*, Harvester, London.

Allison, L. (ed.) (1986) *The Politics of Sport*, Manchester University Press, Manchester.

Bell, D. (1990) *Acts of Union: Youth culture and Sectarianism in Northern Ireland*, Macmillan, London.

Blain, N., Boyle, R. and O'Donnell, H. (1993) *Sport and National Identity in the European Media*, Leicester University Press, Leicester.

Blain, N. and Boyle, R. (1994) 'Battling along the boundaries: sports journalism and Scottish identity', in Jarvie, G. and Walker, G. (eds.) *Ninety Minute Patriots? Sport in the Making of the Scottish Nation*, Leicester University Press, Leicester.

Boyle, R. (1991) 'Faithful through and through: A survey of Celtic FC's most committed supporters', National Identity Research Unit, Caledonian University, Glasgow.

Centre for Leisure Research (1984) 'Crowd behaviour at football matches: A study in Scotland', Centre For Leisure Research, Edinburgh.

Cohen, A. (1985) *The Symbolic Construction of Community*, Tavistock Publications, London.

Curran, M. and Redmond L. (1991) 'We'll support you evermore? Football club allegiance: a survey of When Saturday Comes readers', Working Paper, Sir Norman Chester Centre for Football Research, University of Leicester.

Davies, H. (1990), 'Selling Spurs short', in Lansdown, H. and Spillius, A. (eds.) (1990) *Saturday's Boys: The Football Experience*, Willow Books, London.

Duke, V. (1991) 'The sociology of football: a research agenda for the

1990's', *The Sociological Review,* Vol. 39, No.3, August.

Finn, G. (1991a) 'Racism, religion and social prejudice. Irish Catholic clubs, soccer and Scottish identity I: The roots of prejudice', *International Journal of the History of Sport,* Vol. 8 No. 1, May.

Finn, G. (1991b) 'Racism, religion and social prejudice. Irish Catholic clubs, soccer and Scottish identity II - Social identity and conspiracy theories', *International Journal of the History of Sport,* Vol. 8 No. 3, December.

Fynn, A., Guest, L. and Law, P. (1989) *The Secret Life of Football,* London, Queen Anne Press.

Gallagher, T. (1987) *Glasgow: The Uneasy Peace,* Manchester, Manchester University Press.

Gallagher, T. (1990) 'Blue and green in Scotland', *Socialist Scotland,* Summer.

Gellner, E. (1983) *Nations and Nationalism,* Oxford, Blackwell.

Giulianotti, R. (1991) 'Scotland's Tartan Army in Italy: the case for the carnivalesque', *The Sociological Review,* Vol. 39, No. 3, August.

Hall, S. (1981) 'Notes on deconstructing the popular', in Samual, R. (ed.) *People's History and Socialist Theory,* Routledge, London.

Holt. R. (1989) *Sport and the British: a Modern History,* Oxford University Press, Oxford.

Jary, D., Horne, J. and Bucke, T. (1991) 'Football "fanzines" and football culture: a case of successful "cultural contestation"', *The Sociological Review,* Vol. 39, No. 3, August.

Kellas, J.G. (1991) *The Politics of Nationalism and Ethnicity,* Macmillan, London.

Moorhouse, H.F. (1991) 'On The Periphery: Scotland, Scottish Football and the New Europe', in Williams, J. and Wagg, S. (eds.)

op. cit..

Murray, B. (1984) *The Old Firm: Sectarianism, Sport and Society in Scotland,* John Donald, Edinburgh.

Pia, S. (1988a) 'A grand old team: 100 years of Glasgow Celtic', *Cencratus,* Summer.

Pia, S. (1988b) 'Not the view', *Cencratus,* Autumn.

Redhead, S. (1991) *Football With Attitude,* Wordsmith, Manchester.

Schlesinger, P. (1991) *Media, State and Nation: Political Violence and Collective Identities,* Sage, London.

Tajfel, H. (ed.) (1982) *Social Identity and Intergroup Relations,* Cambridge University Press, Cambridge.

Taylor, I. (1991) 'English football in the 1990's: taking Hillsborough seriously?', in Williams, J. and Wagg, S. (eds.) *op. cit..*

Taylor, Lord Justice (1990) *The Hillsborough Stadium Disaster: Final Report,* HMSO, London.

Taylor, R. (1991) 'Walking alone together: football supporters and their relationship with the game', in Williams and Wagg (eds.) *op. cit..*

Walker, G. (1988) 'The Rangers view', *Cencrastus,* Autumn.

Walker, G. (1990) '"There's no team like the Glasgow Rangers": football and religious identity in Scotland', in Walker, G. and Gallagher, T. (eds.) *Sermons and Battle Hymns: Protestant Popular Culture in Modern Scotland,* Edinburgh University Press, Edinburgh.

Williams, J. (1989) *Football and football spectators after Hillsborough: A national survey of members of the Football Supporters Association,* Sir Norman Chester Centre For Football Research, Leicester University.

4 From Saint-Etienne to Marseilles: Tradition and modernity in French soccer and society

Michel Raspaud
Translated by Tony O'Callaghan and Dawn Webster

The world of professional football should be considered in two ways. On the one hand it is an autonomous social domain; that is to say it has its own history, a legal status, and governing rules and institutions, which guarantee its practice and values, in relation to both the individual and social groups. On the other hand, the world of professional football also interacts with society as a whole. And, in this way, it is subject to social influences and either adapts or does not to new societal norms of social function.

As an autonomous social domain, the world of professional football can be considered as a 'field', in Pierre Bourdieu's sense of the word.(1) It is a particular space consisting of positions whose properties can be regarded as theoretically independent of those who fill them. Each field has its own mode of operating (which is linked to its particular history), and is situated within a hierarchy of fields.

In this chapter, we do not attempt to explain the distinctive and significant elements within the field of football itself. We only attempt to pinpoint two forms of sporting success, which are linked to two perceptions of the market and competition, within the very restricted social domain that French professional football occupies.

The two forms and their related perceptions are sequential historically, but they are also contemporary. Their historical changes, or diachronicity, point to distinctions between the traditional and the modern. Yet this does not rule out a synchronic understanding of them. However, taking into account the current shape of football, society and the economy, we will opt for the following definition: tradition refers to the recent past (the 1970s) and modernity to the present (the late 1980s/early 1990s).

The objective of this chapter is to show how two professional clubs embody tradition and modernity in a historical and special social context. In particular, it is argued that assumptions about the social universe can be modified inside one field, such as football, to alter broader social thinking, and perceptions of governing institutions. However, individuals will, within a given historical time, come to personify these changes, becoming emblematic of them, with the underlying social structure predominating.[2]

French football in an international context

In contrast to the great European football nations (for example, England, Germany, Italy, Spain), French professional football's distinctiveness is dichotomous.

Firstly, it has a constitutional status whose purpose is not profit-orientated, thus implying the voluntary nature of its leaders, whereas in England, Scotland, Italy and so on, the clubs are privately owned. Additionally, French sports associations (especially professional football clubs) receive subsidies, sometimes as much as several million francs, from territorial organizations, principally from the regions that the clubs represent. Recently, this financing was denounced by a Dutch Member of the European Parliament, who considered this to be supportive of unfair competition. However, this financing does not guarantee positive results at this level.

Secondly, the trophies won by French footballers can easily be counted on one hand, thanks to the sole successes of different national teams: European Junior champions in 1949 and 1983; European Nations champions in 1984 and Olympic champions in the same year; and European Under-23 champions in 1988. The reader can note the truly French peculiarity of never having won any of the three European club trophies: the European Champions' Cup, the Cup Winners' Cup, and the UEFA Cup.

Repeated failures in continental competition have created, with the passing of time, a real psychological problem, a failure syndrome, for French players, coaches, club presidents and the media.[3] Any good sports season for a French club, especially one which leads to the semi-final or final of the European Cup, is experienced as an epic by players and supporters, and is presented accordingly by the press.(4)

Table 4.1: French clubs in the quarter-finals, semi-finals and finals of the European club competitions

Years Winners	Quarter-Finals	Semi-Finals	Runners-up
1955-56			Reims (1)
1956-57	Nice (1)		
1957-58			
1958-59			Reims (1)
1959-60	Nice (1)		
1960-61			
1961-62			
1962-63	Reims (1)		
1963-64		Lyon (2)	
1964-65	Strasbourg (3)		
1965-66			
1966-67			
1967-68	Lyon (2)		
1968-69			
1969-70			
1970-71			
1971-72			
1972-73			
1973-74			
1974-75		St Etienne (1)	
1975-76			St Etienne (1)
1976-77	St Etienne (1)		
1977-78			Bastia (3)
1978-79			
1979-80	Strasbourg (1) & St Etienne (3)	Nantes (2)	
1980-81	St Etienne (3)	Sochaux (3)	
1981-82			
1982-83	Paris-SG (2)		

1983-84		
1984-85	Bordeaux (1)	
1985-86	Nantes (3)	
1986-87	Bordeaux (2)	
1987-88	Bordeaux (1)	Marseilles (2)
1988-89	Monaco (1)	
1989-90	Auxerre (3)	Marseilles (1)&
	Monaco (2)	
1990-91	Montpellier (2)	Marseilles (1)
1991-92		Monaco (2)
1992-93		Auxerre (3)&
		Paris-SG (3)

Marseilles (1)

(1)   European Cup (since 1955-6) = 38.
(2)   European Cup Winners' Cup (since 1960-1) = 33.
(3)   Fairs Cup (from 1955-6 until 1970-1) = 13; UEFA Cup (since 1971-2) = 22.

In the same way as the transfer of a French footballer abroad is a rarity, every player to be taken on by a big European club (Raymond Kopa by Real Madrid, Michel Platini by Juventus of Turin, Eric Cantona by Leeds United, Jean-Pierre Papin by Milan) is followed attentively by the media which reports emphatically each success or failure.

If we study the European history of French clubs (see Table 4.1), we may note two periods: the first charts the birth of the European cup competitions, from 1955 to 1968, with few positive results despite reaching two finals (Stade de Reims 1956 and 1959); the second period (from 1974-75 to 1991) during which French participation in the quarter-finals was twice that of the preceding period.[5] Three finals were reached: AS Saint-Etienne in 1974, SEC Bastia in 1978, Olympique de Marseille in 1991 (and then AS Monaco in 1992). However, there was still no victory. Between these two periods, six years passed without any participation in a quarter-final match. The second period (1974-75 to 1991) when positive sports results multiplied, was marked by what the media called the 'epic of the Greens', namely L'Association Sportive de Saint-Etienne: semi-finalists in 1975, finalists in 1976, quarter-finalists in 1977. Through this club, French football entered the modern era. However, we also consider *Les Verts* ('the Greens') to be the product of tradition, a paradox which we explain later. Modernity, on the other hand, is represented by the Olympique de Marseille, who followed a trajectory almost identical to that of AS Saint-Etienne: semi-finalists in 1990, then finalists in 1991 in the European Cup. The difference is that O.M. had already participated in a semi-final of the European cup-winners' cup in 1987.

The evolution of professional football in France

Since the 1970s French professional football has developed greatly. We may even say that it has modernized its structures, in the following ways:

- Remodelling the championship into a pyramidic structure linking elite and average players, into divisions 1, 2, 3, 4, and the regional championships. Previously, the professional clubs were radically separated from the amateur clubs. The new system will be modified in 1993-94 by the reorganization of the second division.

- The systematic creation of training centres at professional clubs, the *Fédération Française de Football* having given the lead with the *Institut National du Football* (first set up in Vichy in the 70s, then transferred to Clairefontaine at the end of the 80s).

- The establishment, after 1968, of a 'time contract' i.e. a contract of fixed length. Players are now able to sign for any club once their contract has terminated. Previously, they were tied to their clubs until the age of thirty-five.[6]

Of course, these developments partly explain the improved results of French professional football teams. At the same time, these performances have generated wider social interest, in particular from financially important circles directly associated with professional football, such as television channels, sponsors and company directors. It is also apparent that professional football, whilst being autonomous, also undergoes other influences which affect clubs organizationally. These relate to monetary support for club budgets, and those individuals who keep the club in business.

The transformation of capitalism

Between 1970 and 1990, French society underwent a transformation within its economic organization. We use the term 'transformation' according to its definition by Roger Bastide and Georges Balandier, as 'any change which is defined as a movement from one structure to another, or as a disruption of the "system"'.(7) In other words, the economic structures themselves are rapidly and significantly modified to produce rather different and stable results.

Firstly, France had to confront two oil crises in 1973 and 1975 which led to economic deceleration and large increases in unemployment, from 300,000 in the early 70s to 3 million today. Secondly, the economy which had been based on industrial production, was transformed into a largely tertiary economy, a backward step taken at the turn of the 70s. The new economy is based on service industries with all the sociological consequences implied, in terms of changes in lifestyle and social outlooks. Thirdly, even the forms of capitalism were rapidly altered. The low-paid workers' culture still predominant at the beginning of this period, involving an industrial society and the power of collective forces (exemplified by the unions) is now in full retreat.(8) This outmoded culture had stemmed from the industrial sector, which had evolved over more than a century and which had had a stabilizing influence on civil society.

Transformations are also taking place within capitalism itself, with leading multinationals achieving growth in two complementary ways. Firstly, growth by external means involves regrouping assets and taking control of operating companies; stock market speculation and extended competition between multinationals also exemplify this business method. Secondly, internal growth involves company development and the creation of new production capacities to challenge the market shares of competitors. The first type of growth seems the fastest and most cost effective. To maximize external growth, it is necessary to be able to react quickly and, above all, to have access to required banking support. Thus, company size almost automatically reflects financial power. The company therefore seeks an 'absolute size effect'.(9) This is achieved through the meeting of four factors: the internationalization of markets; the promotion of a brand name; the possession of an international market; and, having financial power.

> The major problem for a company is its competitive position. The totality of comparative advantages (of cost, organization, technology, etc.), when comparable to that of its competitors, including the advantages directly linked to size, enable it to maintain and if possible extend its share of the market. The effect of size also appears *in fine* to be one of the necessary elements in the search for competitiveness.(10)

So there are two forms of logic in this economy, one 'industrial', the other 'financial', which find themselves in competition. The first, which relies on economic rationality spanning a lengthy period of time, works through internal growth and produces innovation and wealth. It is more sound than the second whose quick profitability is built, above all, on simple functional rationality. The 'capitalism of creation' conflicts with a 'capitalism of speculation'.(11)

The market of 'perfect and pure competition' requires several conditions for it to function, in particular 'transparency' (12). It must, therefore, be 'irrigated with widely spread, true information'(13). Alternatively, a lie in its different forms appears to be an important strategic weapon for conquering markets. For example, when Bernard Tapie bought the German company Adidas he said, 'we will not make a "return trip" because we are here to stay for at least ten years - long enough to invest in sport'.(14) Two years later Mr Tapie tried to sell Adidas to the British group Pentland, before selling it to a consortium!

Commenting on a book by Alain Minc, an adviser to the Italian businessman Carlo De Benedetti, Eric Izraelewicz stressed that previously 'immorality was "secret and invisible". Today it spreads in daylight. This is one of the differences between oligarchic capitalism and democratic capitalism, to go back to the original concepts'.(15)

The transformation of professional football

Football has also been the subject of transformations. We have already stressed the role of results as well as changes in the general organizational structures. However, economic factors have been extremely important if not decisive. Without prejudging the issue of bad quality management of professional clubs (which is not peculiar to France, for example Spanish or British clubs, notably Tottenham Hotspur FC), it must be stressed that the economic development of football has been achieved through internal developments enabled by different sources of income. The revenue from spectators has increased but this is less important than television royalties. The latter is due to, firstly, the privatization of state channel TF1 and the creation of new private channels (Canal +, a coded channel which is payable, La Cinq and M6), all of which are very interested in football's appeal to viewers. Secondly, there is the role of sponsorships, either through shirt advertising or various forms of partnership with or through the club.

These two forms of revenue started to take on importance at the end of the sixties but it was not until

> around nineteen-eighty [that] football slowly entered an era of insanity on the financial front. Because the spectacle has become a greatly demanded focus of publicity, considerable amounts are at stake'.(16)

Financial investors are well aware of this development, since 'all things being equal, sponsorship permits a gain in popularity and notoriety quicker than traditional publicity', as one SOFRES study has highlighted.(17)

And so at the same time that the average number of spectators went from 7000 in 1969 to more than 11,000 in the 80s, the revenue raised by French club football multiplied by thirty-two. The increased rate of inflation which followed the oil crisis in 1973 and which was only curbed in the 1980s cannot by itself explain such a phenomenon. Table 4.2 illustrates the breakdown of monetary revenue changes in French professional football clubs over the last twenty years.

Similar to capitalism, professional football has undergone changes, because between the two fields there are very close connections which go far beyond the simple and continuous processes of financing. These organic relations include capitalists who also deal in football, some European examples being Mr Silvio Berlusconi and Milan, Mr John Cordier and the F.C. Malines, Mr Jesus Gil y Gil and Atletico Madrid, the multinational company Philips and PSV Eindhoven, the Bayer company and the Leverkusen and Uerdingen clubs, etc.

Table 4.2: French professional football financial sources (18)
(in millions of francs (MF) and percentage, first division)

Years	The spectator	The Mayor	The sponsor	TV income	Total	Deficit
1970-71	30MF (81%)	7 MF (18%)	0.5MF (1%)	(100%)	37.5MF	
1980-81	125MF (65%)	38MF (20%)	28MF (14%)	2MF (1%)	193MF (100%)	26MF
1990-91	420MF (35%)	240MF (20%)	260MF (22%)	280MF (23%)	1200MF (100%)	800MF

French football, with the media and economic importance it possesses, has become a stake for wider economic powers. And so between 1967 and 1990 the shares held by directors, company directors and other economic figures amongst first division presidents has gone from 45 to 75% (see Table 4.3). The decision makers have taken power in the clubs and have transferred their company management policies to the football association.

Table 4.3: Division 1 Club Presidents, 1967-68

Club	President	Age	Profession
Aix	Garcin	47	?
Ajaccio	Biggi	46	Industrialist

Angers	Doizé	?	Industrialist
Bordeaux	Martin	?	?
Lens Mine	Hus	54	Director of the Lens co-op
Lille	Barbieux	47	Negotiator
Lyon	E. Rocher	?	Doctor
Marseille	M. Leclerc	?	?
Metz	Molinari	34	Industrialist
Monaco	Principale	50	Assistant director of a social benefits office
Nantes	Clairfeuille	?	Sales representative
Nice	Charles	56	Solicitor
Red Star export	Doumeng	?	Director of an import-company
Rennes	Girard	54	Public works officer
Rouen	Paturel	?	Forestry worker
St Etienne	R. Rocher	47	Public works officer, director or Forezienne
RCP-Sedan	Laurant	42	Industrialist
Sochaux	Deur	?	Manager of the Peugeot club
Strasbourg	Muller	?	Surgeon
Valenciennes	Lenclus	?	?

This represents a qualitative change, in the sense that these company directors now retain financial dimensions, on the one hand, and on the other, a field of action which is incomparable to that of twenty years ago. In 1967, Mr Jean Doumeng, president of Red Star FC, was only the managing director of an import-export company of agricultural products essentially dealing with the USSR and East European countries. In 1990, Mr Bernard Tapie, managing director of the holding company Bernard Tapie Finance, controlled the Adidas company, one of the three or four biggest multinational sport products companies and formerly the world leader.

If some of these presidents failed, other investors of great financial and industrial calibre have still tried their luck. And so Mr Jean-Luc Lagardere during the 80s, managing director of Hachette, of Matra and other companies, transformed, with the revival of the Racing Club de Paris, Matra-Racing, in a short period of time.

Table 4.4: Division 1 Club Presidents, 1990-91

Club	President	Age	Profession
Auxerre	Hamel	60	Manager of an industrial garage
Bordeaux	Bez	49	Manager of an accounts auditing company
Brest	Yvinec	56	Company managing director
Caen	Fiolet	37	Managing director of a group of estate agents
Cannes	Mouillot	?	Mayor of Cannes
Lille	Balay	?	?
Lyon	Aulas	40	Managing director of CEGID (computers) and other companies
Marseille	Tapie	47	Managing director of the holding company BTF (Adidas, Donnay, etc)
Metz	Molinari	57	Managing director of SODIMA (Iveco)
Monaco	Campora	53	Doctor of gastroenterology
Montpellier	Nicollin	46	Managing director, Nicollin group
Nancy	Brzezinski	?	Director of a savings bank
Nantes	Bouyer	36	Head of distribution companies
Nice	Innocenti	55	Managing director of a food company
Paris-SG	Borelli	56	Managing director of a publishers
Rennes	Soucaret	?	Managing director of Pfizer-France (pharmaceuticals)

St-Etienne	Laurent	52	Director of a high precision screws company
Sochaux	Thouzery	63	Retired (ex-Peugeot engineer)
Toulon	Asse	56	Shop owner
Toulouse	Delsol	?	Retired (ex-property developer)

Therefore today, the coded channel Canal + (which has many broadcasting and sponsorship agreements with the French football federation and the League) has invested money and personnel in Paris Saint-Germain.

Without a doubt, these men leave their mark on the sports association at which they become president. They organize the club and its operation according to their company model. This aspect is illustrated by two principal examples, AS Saint-Etienne and Olympique de Marseille, the last two French finalists in the European Cup. This analysis includes respectively a study of their presidents, their coaches, the signing of players, their organizations, their politics, and their sporting goals. They demonstrate two different modes of operating, reflecting changes in French capitalism. Each president demonstrates, in his own time (the 70s for St Etienne and the 80s for Marseille) success at the highest level, and embodies the form of financial management which enables it.

Tradition and modernity

More precise definition of the terms used are now required. As far as 'tradition' and 'modernity' are concerned, we do not explicitly refer to the classic sociological definitions, but we shall adapt their content to this particular field. Tradition and modernity must have meanings inside this field which have their own histories and their own referents which are structured by the significations which organize them.

Tradition also refers, inside the domain of French professional football, to a classic form of football represented by its British variety. This classicism is linked, firstly, to the fact that football was born on British territory, and that it has been built, developed and shaped through this heritage, through a culture and organization which is perceived to be eminently efficient. The more significant features of football classicism are:

- The status of clubs as private companies.

- The policy of recruiting young players (apprentices) on the first rung to scaling the football ladder and entry into the first team. This investment is paid back to the club through the team's standard of performance, but also through strengthened association with the fans.

- The presence of an administrative organization and a manager.

- The striking presence of the stadium, its architecture, environment and its special position in the town.

- The 'fighting spirit' of the British game (at least that is how we perceive it in France).

Modernity, on the other hand, refers more explicitly to a way of managing and controlling the club, from a financial and sports point of view. The important thing is not to carry on the 'culture' of British football, but to obtain results as quickly as possible. A few characteristics of the modern club are:

- The large recruitment of top level players.

- A massive change in the strength of players, based on results as well as club finances.

- The important role of money in transfers.

- The financial necessity of selling players whilst they still have a market value.

Clearly, economics determine recruitment and results with precise objectives: winning the championship and the European Cup. The domains of tradition and modernity are equally concerned with economic issues. Most certainly, tradition refers to internal growth, which creates wealth through industrial reasoning; modernity belongs to the domain of external growth, based on share dealing and takeover bids, through financial reasoning. These two opposing, and at the same time, complementary forms are historically located, as examples of success in post-1968 French professional football. These were and remain structurally important, as major reference points in speeches made by club presidents. Moreover, their significance cannot be evaded by the French football authorities as far as the internal political relations of national football are concerned.

L'Association Sportive de Saint-Etienne: the traditional image

The president in 1976, Roger Rocher, arrived at the *Association Sportive de Saint-Etienne* in 1957. He became president in 1961. Born into a family of mining contractors, Rocher and his brothers inherited the company in 1945, seventeen years after its foundation. In 1946, foreseeing the decline of industrial mining, the two brothers created a new company, *La Societe Forezienne de Travaux Publics* ('The Forezienne society of public works'), which amalgamated with *Rocher Pere et Fils* ('Rocher, Father and Sons') in 1951. The two brothers parted ways in 1964, leaving Roger Rocher with control of Forezienne.

The president of AS Saint-Etienne emphasizes in one chapter of his autobiography, significantly entitled *Une vie de bâtisseur* ('A builder's life'), that 'the notion of solid foundations explains, basically, all my work'.[19] This notion is certainly linked to the area of company activity (the construction of works of art) but also with a general outlook on life, in which everyone's place is known: 'Here and there, I have always built with men for men'. In the company 'the human resource of Forezienne guarantees success'; 'the sports director was never any different to a contractor'.

The actions of company leader Roger Rocher are based on a few fundamental principals: *absolute team spirit*, to work under the best conditions;[20] delegation of responsibilities to the lowest possible levels; information on a regular basis, through *L'Echo de la*

Forezienne, the company news-letter; development of social activities at each level; dialogue with management staff; improvement of staff resources through permanent training centres.

We cannot confirm that all these principals were scrupulously respected within the enterprise itself nor that they were applied to the *Association Sportive de Saint-Etienne*. At least three are present, and constitute the major axes of the club organization: team spirit, a principal factor in the success of 'the Greens'; information through a supporters bulletin, thus developing links with the local public (based on the British model); creating a training centre in 1967, which, in 1972, was moved to the new club home, at Geoffroy-Guichard Stadium.

"Basic honesty, love of career, and pride in work well done, have constantly dictated the running of an organization." This reference to *La Forezienne* contains, in fact, all the principal values which make up the *AS Saint-Etienne* game. In fact, following the French dictum, the game consists of applying oneself one hundred fold to the job to be done. It's a question of undermining the opponent, and having an iron will to physically impose, which did not find extravagance and creativity until the unexpected arrival of *l'Ange Vert* ('the Green Angel'), the young and apparently fragile Dominique Rocheteau, with the long curly hair.

L'Olympique de Marseille: the modern image

The president of the *Olympique de Marseille*, Bernard Tapie, arrived at the club in 1986, at the request of the then city mayor, Gaston Defferre.[21] He was therefore not prepared for the position of association president by experience (Roger Rocher had been president of *Olympique de Saint-Etienne* from 1947) even if Tapie had beforehand successfully invested his efforts in professional cycling, constructing a team around the champion Bernard Hinault.

Bernard Tapie deals with the O.M. as he does in business which consists essentially of rebuilding stricken enterprises, that is to say buying companies which are in financial difficulty after carrying out a rapid but meticulous audit of the management and function of the company: first diagnose the ailments, then bring the management back up to a standard level in companies 'which are not managed at all'.(22)   Bernard Tapie took over control of the *Olympique de Marseille* by negotiating directly with the mayors' office, over the head of the then president, Jean Carrieu. He negotiated support for public sector subsidies; the construction of a training centre; renovation of the stadium (the lodges), as well as the closure of certain departments. At the same time, he hired the best trainers (Michel Hidalgo, ex-trainer of the French national team from 1976 to 1984, and Gérard Banide his assistant), and the best players, Alain Giresse, Jean-Pierre Papin, Karl-Heinz Förster, as well as ten or so others. He offered attractive salaries to put together a competitive team from the start, with the ambition of winning the league title, in order to become the first French club to win the European Cup. Each year Tapie renews the team, buying new players and selling those who haven't offered satisfaction. During the summer of 1988, *Olympique de Marseille*'s first results were catastrophic, so Tapie did not hesitate before firing Gerard Banide, to be replaced by the second trainer, Gérard Gili: a good move because *Olympique de Marseille* won the cup and championship in 1989.

It is evident that results prevail over personnel in the mercenary approach to business: 'I am not a company boss, I am a manager. Business is nothing but a commodity we buy and sell'.(23)   And whether it's in a football club or a company, it is the quality of employees which make the difference:

> By changing a single manager, Testut passed from losses of twenty million to a profit of ten million. A company is a Formula One racing car, so highly tuned that the quality of the pilot makes all the difference ....(24)

From tradition to modernity

The traditional aspect of the *Association Sportive de Saint-Etienne* is expressed through the 'constructive' orientation of its president. As he forms his company on solid bases, he builds foundations for the club: the formation centre which produces players who progress to the first team; the social seat adjoining Geoffroy-Guichard Stadium such as his apartment which for a while was his company headquarters.

Tradition is expressed through the will to cultivate, realized by the recruitment of young players nurtured in a protected environment; by the paternal image of the man with the pipe; by the trainer (Robert Herbin), an old club player who had first arrived some twenty years earlier. It is therefore continuity which is favoured and, allied with work, (the club was also the first to build covered training grounds) it has secured the creation of wealth.

Of the players then, all but two (the Yugoslavian Ivan Curkovic and the Argentinian Osvaldo Piazza) played their first professional match wearing *Association Sportive de Saint-Etienne* colours. They were all recruited by the club at the age of sixteen, seventeen or eighteen. And it was also while playing with 'the Greens' that they received their first caps for the national team. Merit is therefore earned within the club, which can be subsequently re-negotiated with another club (see Table 4.5).

Alternatively, the *Olympique de Marseille* does not recruit players unless they have already proven themselves, with star foreigners, such as Ayew Abedi-Pelé, Carlos Mozer, Chris Waddle, Dragan Stojkovic; French players who are already internationals, such as Jean Tigana, Manuel Amoros, Eric Cantona, Bernard Casoni, Bernard Pardo, Basile Boli, etc.; or players who have shown their skills, such as Pascal Olmeta, Laurent Fournier. Value, therefore, already exists and should enable the set objective, to win the European Cup, to be attained. As far as the players are concerned, they must be as productive as possible. There will be no hesitation in 'lending' them to other clubs or transferring them if their yield is not optimal (see Table 4.5). The cases of Abedi-Pelé and Eric Cantona are examples.

Table 4.5: European Cup Final players: *AS St-Etienne*, 1975-76

Players	Matches	Ys	M	Caps	Since	Years
Curkovic*	9	32	2	Yugo	1972	4
Janvion*	9	22	9	2	1972	4
Lopez*	9	23	2	2	1969	7
Piazza*	9	29	1	Arg	1972	4
Bathenay*	9	22	3	1	1971	5
Larqué	9	28	8	13	1965	11

H. Revelli	9	29	11	29	1965	11
P. Revelli	8	24	11	4	1968	8
Rocheteau*	8	21	4	3	1971	5
Farison	8	32	1	1	-	-
Synaeghel	7	25	4	2	1969	7
Santini	6	24	1	-	1969	7
Repellini	5	25	7	4	1868	8
Sarramagna*	3	24	5	4	1969	7
Schaer	2	23	4	-	1973	3
Merchadier	1	24	2	5	1969	7

European Cup Final players: *Olympique de Marseille* 1990-91

Players	Matches	Ys	M	Caps	Since	Years
Olmeta*	9	30	1	-	1990	1
Casoni*	9	29	8	16	1990	1
Waddle*	9	30	5	Eng	1989	2
Papin*	9	27	6	29	1986	5
Mozer*	8	30	8	Brazil	1989	2
Germain	8	31	1	1	1988	4
Abedu-Pele*	8	29	3	72	1989	2
Amoros*	7	29	3	72	1989	2
Vercruysse*	7	29	4	12	1988	3
Di Méco*	7	27	8	6	1989	**11
Boli*	6	24	4	27	1990	1
Fournier*	6	26	8	-	1990	1
Tigana	5	25	11	52	1989	1
Pardo	4	30	5	13	1990	1
Stojkovic*	3	26	2	Yugo	1990	1
Cantona	3	25	-	18	1988	3
Mura	2	28	4	-	1988	8
Lada	1	25	7	-	1990	1

European Cup Final players: *Olympique de Marseille* 1992-93

Players	Matches	Ys	M	Caps	Since	Years
Eydelie	*11	27	2	-	1993	1
Deschamps*	11	24	7	31	1990	3
Abedi-Pelé	11	31	4	Ghana	1987	6

Barthez*	10	31	9	-	1992	1
Desailly*	10	24	6	-	1992	1
Sauzée	10	27	7	34	1988	**4
Angloma*	9	27	9	14	1991	2
Boli*	9	26	4	44	1990	3
Di Méco*	9	29	8	6	1980	**13
Boksic*	8	23	4	Croat	1992	1
Voller*	8	33	1	Germ	1992	1
Durand*	6	31	6	26	1991	2
Casoni	6	31	8	30	1990	3
Thomas*	5	28	7	-	1992	1
Amoros	3	31	3	82	1989	4
Martin-Vasquez	2	27	8	Spain	1992	1
Omam-Biyik	1	27	-	Camrn	1992	1
Dobrovolski	1	25	9	Russia	1992	1
Olmeta	1	32	1	-	1990	3
Marquet	1	19	1	-	-	-

* Players in the European Cup Final.
* * Players who had left the club, then returned.

Abedi-Pelé was noticed when he played for the *Chamois Niortais*, and was taken on by Bernard Tapie. However, after one year, he struggled to blend with the rest of the team, especially with Jean-Pierre Papin, Mr Tapie's 'protege'. So, he was sold to *Lille OSC*. However, his performances there were considered to be remarkable, so Tapie went back on his decision and negotiated bitterly with Abedi-Pelé's new club. Eric Cantona, who now plays for Manchester United (after Leeds United), was recruited from *AJ Auxerre* in 1988 for 22 million francs. As an assertive football personality he did not hesitate to say what he wanted or act as he thought best. He openly insulted the French national team's selector at the time which earned him a suspension from the French team. He threw his O.M. shirt on the pitch during a friendly match because the coach replaced him. Bernard Tapie, who does not like people talking about 'his' players more than himself, immediately negotiated Cantona's loan until the end of the 1988-89 season to the *Girondins de Bordeaux*, and then to *Montpellier-La Paillade* for the season, before he returned to O.M. in 1990-91. However, Raymond Goethals, on seeing that Cantona didn't fit into his playing system, put him into the reserve team. In July 1991 he was transferred to *Nîmes Olympique* before giving up football for a while,(25) until his move to England.

As far as transfers are concerned, other examples could be explored, such as those of Stojkovic, Sauzée, Roche or Leo Rodriguez. Furthermore the Maradona episode, during the summer of 1989, must above all be interpreted as a move to situate *Olympique de Marseille* and its president in the field of international football,(26) rather than as a genuine attempt to sign the Argentinian star.

In this context, the coach cannot remain without immediate results. And, contrary to *AS Saint-Etienne* who predicted, one year in advance, that Robert Herbin would replace Albert Batteux in 1972, O.M. sought out a 'technician' whom they considered capable of making the investments profitable. They found the Frenchman Banide (then coach of *AS Monaco*) in 1986; the German Beckenbauer in 1990 (who had won the World Cup with his national side one month earlier); the Yugoslavian Ivic in 1991 (who had just been sacked at Atletico Madrid); and the Belgian Goethals in 1990 (who had just left the *Girondins de Bordeaux*) and 1991 (he had just left the O.M.).

Strategy for a European Cup victory (1991-1993)

In the last two years, from 1991 to 1993, Bernard Tapie's strategy did not change but, on the contrary, became more marked: seven new players were recruited in 1991 (among them Trevor Steven from Glasgow Rangers), followed by ten new players in 1992, among them five foreigners: the German Völler (ex-Roma), the Croatian Boksic (ex-Hajduk Split), the Russian Dobrovolsky (ex-Servette Geneva), the Spaniard Martin Vasquez (ex-Torino) and the Cameroon star Omam Biyik (ex-Cannes). The last two stayed at Marseille only a few weeks, and were transferred to Real Madrid and Lens respectively. Six players, of the thirteen who played in the Munich final (May 1993), were recruited in June 1992.

The trainer's employment was partly dependent on the results of the team, and good relations with Bernard Tapie. Thus, the Yugoslav Tomislas Ivic (ex-Paris Saint-Germain and Atletico

Madrid) left *Olympique de Marseille* after four months, in October 1991; as did Jean Fernandez in 1992. After each departure, the Belgian Raymond Goethals was called for; in fact, in addition to his good results with the team, he is also the only individual whose age, experience, and track record enable him to withstand Bernard Tapie's moods and criticisms. Indeed, perhaps Bernard Tapie did not perceive Raymond Goethals as a media-friendly competitor to him, in the manner of Hidalgo, Cantona or Beckenbauer.

The stability of reference values

Two conceptions of enterprise are exemplified by these two football clubs, with an interval of fifteen years. With *AS Saint-Etienne* it is a paternalistic idea (embodied by Roger Rocher, owner, president and 'father'), inherited from the era of industrial construction, and the culture of a strong company seeking revenue internally. The production of wealth (football success) is thus achieved through work and continuity.

In the case of *Olympique de Marseille*, we find ourselves in the era of managers and the market, represented by a director of a holding company. Here, value is best obtained in the quickest way, immediate profitability being the first condition of investment. Moreover, the buying and selling of players, the employment and dismissal of coaches, are part of the commercial strategy aimed at maintaining media interest (advertising and sponsorship) and at establishing a combination of factors which should enable maximum productivity (football success).

These two approaches, which in each of the eras studied illustrate sports success, should be understood according to the area from which they are drawn, that of the company. Football people, and club owners, come from civilian society, although the game itself seeks to safeguard the autonomy of its institutions and reference points.[27] However, with the playing success and media appeal of *AS Saint-Etienne*, and the important changes in everyday social life during the 70s and 80s,[28] a certain penetration of football by economics has taken place, slightly modifying this state of affairs.

At the same time, significant changes in European clubs football have occurred: the ban on English clubs in the European competitions following the drama of Heysel,(29) the rise in power of big Italian clubs, the success of clubs organically linked to big industrial companies (Eindhoven and Philips, Leverkusen and Bayer, but also Juventus and Fiat) or the powerful financial networks (Milan and Silvio Berlusconi). The principles employed in conceiving, managing or building wealth are also transferable from one domain of activity (that of the company) to another (that of professional football), moves which can be enhanced by particular events (changing the president of the *Fédération*, and therefore relations of power).(30) Even more so, when those businessmen move from the economy into football.

Notes

1. Pierre Bourdieu (1980), 'Quelques propriétés des champs', *Questions de sociologie*, Editions de Minuit, Paris, pp.113-120.

2. Pierre Bourdieu (1979), *La distinction. Critique sociale du jugement*, Editions de Minuit, Paris.

3. This obsessive fear of confrontation from abroad, within Europe in particular, does not limit itself to football but relates to the whole of social life, especially in the current atmosphere of European political nationalism.

4. Roland Barthes (1977), 'Le Tour de France comme épopée', *Mythologies*, Le Seuil, Paris, 1957, pp.110-121; Jules Gritti *Sport à la une*, Armand-Colin, Paris, 1975; 'A l'écoute du compte rendu sportif', *Les Amis de Sèvres*, No. 4.

5. We included the quarter-finals as a reference point because they have been played during the second half of the season (after the turn of the year). However, in the European (Champions) Cup, they have been transformed by the establishment of two groups of four clubs competing to qualify directly for the final.

6. Alfred Wahl (1986), 'Le footballeur français 1890-1926', *Le Mouvement Social*, no.135, April-June, pp.7-30, Les Editions Ouvrieres, Paris.

7. Georges Balandier (1970), 'Sociologie des mutations', in Georges Balandier (ed.) *Sociologie des mutations*, Anthropos, Paris, pp.13-37.

8. Alain Ehrenberg (1991), *Le culte de la performance*, Calmann-Levy, Paris.

9. Jean-Marie Chevalier (1989), 'Les grandes manoeuvres industrielles', *Le Monde*, 14 November.

10. *Ibid.*

11. Jean-Marie Chevalier (1992), 'Fragilites capitalistes', *Le Monde*, 17 March.

12. A. Beitone, C. Dollo, J.-P. Guidoni & A. Legardez (1991), *Dictionnaire des sciences économiques*, Armand-Colin, Paris.

13. Didier Pourquery (1989), 'Le mensonge, une arme économique', *Le Monde*, 12-13 November.

14. 'Tapie chausse Adidas', *Le Dauphiné libéré*, 8 July 1990.

15. Erik Izraelewicz (1990), 'Un jour l'arrogance de l'argent deviendra insupportable à chacun...', *Le Monde*, 3 February, (about Alain Minc's book *L'argent fou*, Grasset, Paris, 1989).

16. Alfred Wahl (1989), *Les archives du football. Sport et société en France 1880-1980*, Gallimard-Julliard, Paris, p.327.

17. *Le Monde Affaires*, 12 March 1988.

18. Table from Jean-Francois Bourg (1992), 'Sport et argent: le football', *Pouvoirs*, No. 61, pp.91-106, Presses Universitaires de France, Paris.

19. Roger Rocher (1983), *Président pour l'amour d'un club*, Flammarion, Paris, 1983, p.37.

20. Our emphasis.

21. 'Gaston Defferre: l'O.M. a besoin de Tapie', interview by Francois de Montvalon (1986), *France Football*, no. 2075, 14 January, pp. 6-7.

22. Bernard Tapie (1986), *Gagner*, Robert-Laffont, Paris, (re-published by Le Livre de poche).

23. *Ibid.*

24. *Ibid.*

25. This followed Cantona's suspension, after he had insulted a referee, then the members of the French League's disciplinary council, before whom he had been summoned.

26. Where it is possible to speak of such a field.

27. Thus, one of the reasons for Jean-Luc Lagardere's failures and for the decline of the Matra company, apart the team's results, stems from their over-forceful attempt to transform the way professional football functions; the way the players operate (in being considered mere pawns of an industrial company); and also the institutions (*Ligue Nationale de Football*). A muddled but virulent reaction then drove the directors of Matra-Racing towards a dead-end.

28. A. Ehrenberg, *op. cit.*.

29. Even though they had impressively dominated the three competitions for over ten years.

30. Fernand Sastre, president of the *Fédération Française de Football*, a great architect of re-organization and the success of the national sides, left his post in 1984 (at the same as Michel Hidalgo, coach of the French team) to be replaced by Jean Fournet-Fayard who was rather less assertive than his predecessor. The power relations between the FFF and the LNF (which runs professional football) were altered to the latter's benefit at the time when Jean Sadoul (who died in 1991) had presided for several decades.

5 The drive to modernization and the supermarket imperative: Who needs a new football stadium?

Vic Duke

British football grounds are undergoing the most profound period of change since the beginning of the century. More clubs will relocate their ground in the last decade of this century than at any time since the first decade. Other clubs are busily transforming their current home into an all seater stadium. Yet others are entering/will enter into ground sharing agreements with fellow clubs. This chapter will examine the nature of this process of change particularly with respect to English and Welsh clubs. (For information on stadia development in Scotland, see, Black and Lloyd, 1992).

One of the main reasons for the wave of change is quite simply that English grounds (along with Welsh and Scottish) are the oldest in the world. Both association football and rugby football originated in England, and the development of the first professional leagues in both codes followed on from this. Table 5.1 below documents how long the current 92 professional football clubs (Premier League and Football League) have been at their present ground. Over a third of the ground locations date from the last century and more than three quarters (70 out of 92) pre-date the first world war. Only four clubs have relocated to a new stadium in recent times, namely Scunthorpe United 1988, Walsall 1990, Chester City 1992 and Millwall, 1993. A further three clubs have been ground sharing at other clubs, although one of them, Charlton Athletic, has recently returned to its *original* (refurbished) stadium. Ground sharing with rugby league clubs is another recent development. Four of the 92 clubs had rugby league tenants in 1992: Bury, Huddersfield Town, Leeds United and Rochdale hosted Swinton, Huddersfield, Hunslet and Rochdale

Hornets respectively.

Table 5.1: Length of time at present ground location for the 92 Premier League and Football League clubs (as of 1992-93)

When located at present ground	Number of clubs
nineteenth century	34
1900-World War I	36
interwar	13
early post World War II (1946-1955)	3
recent relocation (from 1988)	3
recent ground sharing (from 1986)	3
Total	**92**

Data adapted and updated from Inglis 1987 and Twydell 1991.

That the modernization of British grounds should occur now (rather than earlier or later) is largely due to government reaction to a series of disasters at football stadia involving English football supporters (in Bradford 1985, Brussels 1985 and Sheffield 1989). All of these disasters were associated to some degree with the construction and/or maintenance of stadia. Notwithstanding the obvious need for the modernization of antiquated facilities, the discussion below questions the nature of the modernization that is now taking place and also analyses who determines which change option a club will adopt.

A further influence on the route to modernization chosen by clubs is the financial crisis faced by many of them at the beginning of the 1990s. This crisis is reflected in the demise of two clubs - Aldershot and Maidstone United - in 1992, and the fact that, according to financial analysts, Touche Ross, more than half the clubs in the Premier League and First Division are trading at a loss. The gloomy financial scenario (prior to the recent revised television deals by the Premier League and the Football League - see below) has tempted many clubs to consider selling their ground, usually to a supermarket chain (hence the supermarket imperative in my title), and relocating to a new stadium on a greenfield site. Evidence is presented below of football supporters' views on new stadia and relocation, as well as on the issue of the extent to which modernization necessarily requires relocation.

The drive to modernization

Modernization has become a central element in British thinking in the 1990s, appearing as a key word in blueprints for the Football Association, the Rugby League and even the Labour Party. The Taylor Report on the Hillsborough stadium disaster (HMSO, 1990) placed the modernization of British football stadia on the political agenda. Of the many recommendations contained in the report, the Conservative government singled out a switch to all seater stadia as its main policy response. This directive dovetailed neatly with FIFA's ruling that all qualifying matches for the 1994 World Cup must be played in all seater stadia.

Originally, the British government instructed the Football League that all First and Second Division clubs (now Premier League and First Division, respectively) were to be all seater by August 1994, and Third and Fourth Division clubs (now Second and Third Division, respectively) by August 1999. More recently, in July 1992, the conditions were relaxed for the two lower divisions, whose clubs will now be permitted to retain some standing areas inside the ground. In terms of government policy, attention is concentrated therefore on the progress of clubs in the two higher divisions towards 100% seating.

Tables 5.2 and 5.3 below summarize the level of seating in use at Premier League and first division grounds by the beginning of the 1992-93 season. In the Premier League only two provincial clubs - Ipswich Town and Norwich City - had attained all seater status. However, most Premier League clubs had reduced their standing capacity to less than 50% and almost half of them to a third. First Division clubs appeared more reluctant to comply with only a third of them surpassing 50% seating. Barnsley, Bristol Rovers and Millwall display spectacularly low levels of seating but the latter two were already planning relocation to new stadia. Folk in Barnsley clearly prefer standing.

Opposition to the abolition of the terraces at professional football is not restricted to Barnsley fans.

Table 5.2: Percentage of seating at beginning of 1992-93 season for Premier League clubs

Club	Capacity	Seats	% Seats
Arsenal	31,000	18,100	58.3
Aston Villa	40,312	21,102	52.3
Blackburn Rovers	19,778	7,448	37.6
Chelsea	36,965	20,040	54.2
Coventry City	25,311	17,661	69.7
Crystal Palace	30,312	15,712	51.8
Everton	38,578	36,488	94.6
Ipswich Town	22,500	22,500	100.0
Leeds United	30,997	18,000	58.0
Liverpool	44,931	28,451	63.3
Manchester City	34,074	15,631	45.9
Manchester United	33,981	30,425	89.5
Middlesbrough	26,100	12,609	48.3
Norwich City	20,319	20,319	100.0
Nottingham Forest	26,000	21000	80.8
Oldham Athletic	16,850	11,199	66.5
Queens Park Rangers	23,350	15,450	66.2
Sheffield United	32,793	23,444	71.5
Sheffield Wednesday	41,137	23,370	56.8
Southampton	21,909	8,000	36.5
Tottenham Hotspur	32,786	25,379	77.4
Wimbledon (1)	30,312	15,712	51.8

1. Ground sharing at Crystal Palace
Data obtained from the *News of the World Football Annual 1992-93*

According to surveys conducted on behalf of the Football Supporters Association, the majority of supporters favour retention of some standing areas in grounds (See, Williams, 1989). For many working class regular attenders, a lifetime has been spent standing on the terraces. It is a viewing position they prefer and moreover a communal tradition to be valued and defended.

A home terrace with a high proportion of regulars provides a flexible experience of genuine sociability. It remains possible to spend the first half standing in one spot, talking with one group of friends and/or relatives, and the second half in another location with another group. The fixed seat in an all-seater environment restricts this sociability. Even worse, you may, unknowingly, have bought a season ticket next to the most objectionable loudmouth in the stand. On the terrace you can move away, but in the fixed seat you cannot.

Arguments extolling the greater safety and security of seating are far from convincing. As well as possible incitement to violence of the loudmouth cited above, the ease of mobility required to avoid confrontation or to escape violence is restricted in the seats. It is far easier to retreat to safety on the terraces than in constricted rows of seats. Similarly, the police are able to reach the locus of an incident more quickly on the terraces.

The advent of the Premier League in England, the impending Scottish 'Super League' and the increasing probability of a European League (see Duke 1991a), have led the elite British clubs to seek a new kind of football spectator. Executive boxes and expensive seating are cultivated at the expense of the traditional cheaper terrace supporter. For season 1992-93, for example, the minimum price for an adult seat ticket at Chelsea had risen to £20. Redevelopment of the Platt Lane end at Manchester City includes several state-of-the-art executive boxes. These protect the wealthy from the elements, but also provide a balcony thereby offering the opportunity to sample 'the real atmosphere'.

The elitist pretensions of the Premier League and its lucrative link with BSkyB television herald the presentation of football as a part of the wider entertainment industry.   At the same time, football's heritage as the people's national sport, even *the* worldwide sport, is downgraded. Already Premier League fixtures are played on Sunday afternoons and Monday evenings to suit the television schedule, but at the 'live' supporters' inconvenience.

Table 5.3: Percentage of seating at the beginning of 1992-93 season for Football League First Division clubs

Club	Capacity	Seats	% Seats
Barnsley	26,508	2,164	8.2
Birmingham City	27,957	8,4572	30.3
Brentford	12,071	3,500	29.0
Bristol City (1)	23,636	16,332	69.1
Bristol Rovers	8,730	1,040	11.9

Cambridge United	10,206	3,4161	33.5
Charlton Athletic (2)	22,503	11,396	50.6
Derby County	23,000	15,000	65.2
Grimsby Town	17,526	5,021	28.6
Leicester City	22,100	14,000	63.3
Luton Town	13,410	9,060	67.6
Millwall	22,572	2,650	11.7
Newcastle United	30,348	11,725	38.6
Notts County	19,120	16,500	86.3
Oxford United	11,071	2,777	25.1
Peterborough United	15,414	4,000	26.0
Portsmouth	26,352	6,752	25.6
Southend United	13,518	6,124	45.3
Sunderland	30,164	7,753	25.7
Swindon Town	16,432	7,150	43.5
Tranmere Rovers	17,452	3,490	20.0
Watford	24,000	7,000	29.2
West Ham United	22,503	11,396	50.6
Wolverhampton Wanderers	19,500	14,500	74.4

1. Ground sharing at Bath City
2. Ground sharing at West Ham United
Data obtained from the *News of the World Football Annual 1992-93*

The supporters on the terraces remain unconvinced about the new TV deal. At the launch of Monday evening 'Sky matches' in August 1992 the crowd at Manchester City was bombarded with fireworks as well as with a musical and dancing extravaganza at half time. As the teams re-emerged for the second half the response of the Kippax (standing terrace) to the dancing was a familiar terrace refrain - "What the fucking hell was that?"

In addition to the issue of whose version of modernization is on the agenda, a further dilemma centres on who should pay for the modernization of stadia. The government's one contribution has been to reduce football pools betting duty, in order to release £20 million per annum over 5 years initially, which has been extended recently, by a further 5 years and a further £100 million up until the year 2000. Large though these sums appear to be, estimates from the football authorities suggest that three or four times more capital is required to complete the changes required by the Taylor recommendations.

Because of the limited company status of British football clubs, it is the government's view that the clubs themselves should, mainly, finance the modernization. Unfortunately this view appears to rule out the 'continental solution' to stadium redevelopment of state and local authority involvement in the modernization programme. Many of the leading European clubs are multi-sport clubs financed and governed, to a degree, by their membership. In many cases, the stadium is owned by the local authority and not by the clubs, for instance in France and Italy. Hence, the preponderance of municipal stadia - the '*stade municipal*' or '*stadio comunale*' - which are multi-purpose and not used solely for football.

Some English clubs have established financial bond schemes in order to finance redevelopment of the existing ground. These schemes require supporters to pay substantial sums in advance in return for the entitlement to purchase a seat season ticket for life (or some similar deferred gratification). For most working class (not to mention unemployed) terrace regulars, the cost is prohibitive. Such supporters lose their familiar historical terrace and are unable to afford to sit in its replacement. Again, this form of modernization seems intended to change the composition of the football crowd.

Unsurprisingly, some of the bond schemes have met with supporter resistance. Pressure groups were formed such as the *Independent Arsenal Supporters Association* at Arsenal and the *Hammers Independent Supporters Association* at West Ham United. (For more details on the latter, see 'Irons in the fire', *When Saturday Comes* February 1992). The Arsenal and West Ham schemes do at least have the merit of modernization *in situ*, thereby retaining the traditional home of the club.

The possibility of successful modernization *in situ* is demonstrated by the stadia in Genoa and Milan, which were refurbished for the 1990 World Cup finals in Italy. Both of these are examples of modernization with style (*con brio*), which are uplifting in design yet retain the traditional club home. This combination was achieved with considerable municipal involvement, not only in terms of finance and stadium ownership, but also through imaginative transport policies in Milan, such as a regular bus service from large peripheral car parks.

The supermarket imperative

Relocation to a new stadium is only one of three available options open to English clubs, the others being redevelopment *in situ* and ground sharing. Thus far there have been few completed relocations. The main examples are: Scunthorpe United, Walsall, Chester City and Millwall in the Football League; Wycombe Wanderers, Yeovil Town and Witton Albion in the Conference (effectively Division Four); and Hull Kingston Rovers and Ryedale York in Rugby League. Seven of these nine clubs sold their old ground for supermarket development, the exceptions being Ryedale York and Millwall which sold out to housing development. To this list of clubs selling out to shopping can be added the one case in Scotland of St Johnstone abandoning Muirton Park to the ASDA supermarket chain.

The supermarket imperative (or relocation scenario) results from several interrelated factors. Changes in advanced capitalism have nurtured the growth of consumerism among those in employment and at the same time encouraged substantial profits in the retail sector. In the materialist and consumerist 1980s, voracious competition developed between supermarket chains for suitably large plots of urban land. It seemed at one point that every football ground would become a supermarket.

Many of the English grounds were built initially on the urban fringe. However, their longevity has left many of them located in the inner city now, surrounded by streets which were not designed for mass car ownership. There are, clearly, car access and parking benefits to be had from relocation to a new stadium on the outskirts of the modern city. By the same token, however, the area of land covered by a football stadium is adequate to facilitate the construction of a supermarket plus car parking in the inner city. All that is required, additionally, is a suitable market nearby and, of course, planning permission.

The aforementioned financial crisis afflicting the majority of football clubs also played a part in the supermarket imperative. Many clubs perceived that they could not afford conversion to an all-seater stadium and, moreover, they were heavily in debt already. In these circumstances, some clubs regarded the supermarket imperative and relocation as a resolution to their problems with the added bonus of their emerging with a profit.

Reality has turned out rather differently. For many, the vision of the supermarket imperative as a panacea to their problems has proved to be a chimera. Chester City and Millwall have only recently moved into their new grounds, so it is still too early to pass judgement on the outcome of their move. Of the other seven English football and rugby league clubs cited in the opening paragraph to this section, five have experienced a renewal of financial crisis since moving. According to the relevant fanzines, possibly the only beneficiaries in these cases were certain directors who were able to recover money owed to them after the sale of the old ground. The exceptional success story of relocation seems to be Wycombe Wanderers. They have a much praised new stadium, are financially sound and on the playing field gained promotion to the Football League at the end of the 1992-93 season.

Following the Taylor Report, a Royal Town Planning Institute survey of Football League clubs found that 42 were considering relocation as opposed to 37 who favoured redevelopment *in situ* (Shepley 1990). The supermarket imperative was at its zenith. One year later a similar survey reported a marked shift away from relocation towards redevelopment *in situ* (Shepley and Barratt 1991). The supermarket imperative is on the wane. Why is this?

A factor in the shift away from relocation is a changed perception of the relative financial benefits of the two options, particularly given the examples cited above. The overall financial situation for professional football clubs has also improved in the wake of new revised television contracts for both the Premier League and the Football League. The former have a £304 million deal with BSkyB and the BBC, whilst the latter have received a guaranteed £25 million from ITV, possibly rising to a maximum of £40 million.

Relocation has also become less popular because of increased recognition of the problems in obtaining planning approval for a new football stadium. The Department of Environment's guidelines request that local authorities be 'sympathetic' to new all-seater football grounds, but on the other hand, they are not to be approved within the green belt (Department of Environment 1991). Maidstone United (RIP.) were ground sharing at Dartford in 1992 and failed to obtain planning permission for a new stadium in Maidstone. Perceptions of football grounds as a nuisance (see Bale 1990) further hinder agreement on a suitable site. To end this section on a more optimistic note, perhaps the views of supporters on relocation have been taken into account in some cases? Let us examine the evidence.

Who needs a new football stadium?

The beginnings of an answer to this question may emerge by posing a further question: who benefits and who loses through relocation? On the whole, directors may be said to benefit from a move in that the club can wipe out previous debts and the director himself (they are, invariably, male) can recover money previously loaned to the club. Furthermore, if the new stadium attracts more affluent spectators in the more expensive seats, who will spend more money at the new club merchandizing outlets, then the directors again stand to benefit. The police may also gain from a new purpose-built ground with fewer safety and security problems, and state of the art surveillance equipment. One would expect the players to experience improved changing, training and medical facilities in a new stadium.

From the standpoint of regular club supporters, the inventory of gain and loss is much more mixed. Undoubtedly, all fans benefit from improved modern facilities in terms of cover, catering and toilets, but an improvement in comfort brought by new facilities cannot be *assumed* (as will become clear below). If the prototypical new stadium is located on the periphery of the urban area with good access by road (e.g. Glanford Park, Scunthorpe United's new ground), then supporters who travel to matches by car will benefit, whereas those reliant on public transport will be worse off. Further negative aspects from the point of view of regular supporters are the loss of their traditional club home and the inevitable increased cost of sitting in the new stadium.

Tradition is an important element of what it means to be a football fan in Britain. Rocco Da Biasi, an Italian researcher comparing English and Italian football crowds, has commented on the greater sense of history among English fans (Da Biasi, 1992). John Bale (1991) has stressed the importance of the stadium as a sacred place and as a 'home' to football supporters. Several examples of the intimate relationship between a club supporter and his home ground can be found in the collection of essays, *Saturday Boys* (Lansdown and Spillius 1990). For example, Simon Inglis recounts his early impressions of his own club's home ground: "Villa Park had class. It had history. It had eccentric buildings in odd places. It had iron railings and a bowling green" (Inglis 1990b).

There is a strong sense in British football that a football club *belongs* to the community in which it was raised to professional status. British football fans would not tolerate the movement of a franchise from one city to another, which is a regular occurrence in sport in the USA (British Rugby League does, however, offer some examples of the movement of a club from town to town). Bale (1991) has emphasized the place pride and local patriotism associated with football clubs in England.

Two examples in English football of recent battles, on the one hand to retain a club in its community, and on the other hand to return to its community are Fulham and Charlton Athletic respectively. Fulham fans are fighting to remain at Craven Cottage, their traditional and historic home (with two listed buildings), which is on the bank of the river Thames and therefore a prime site for luxury housing development (the supporters' version of events is recounted in their fanzine, *There's Only One F In Fulham*). Charlton Athletic fans succeeded in persuading their club to return to the Valley, its traditional home, in December 1992 after ground sharing periods at both Crystal Palace and West Ham United. Details of this campaign can be found in *The Voice of the Valley* fanzine and in a book, *Battle For the Valley* (Everitt 1992). Perhaps the most amazing case of community attachment to a football club comes, however, from Scotland. Supporters of East Stirlingshire fought successfully in the courts in 1964 to return the club to Falkirk after the directors had moved the club 30 miles to Clydebank (see Inglis 1985, chapter 10).

The differentness and distinctiveness of individual club grounds is part of the fabric of supportership, especially away supportership. Now that much of this heritage has either gone already or is under threat as a by-product of the modernization drive, a phenomenal interest in the history and memorabilia of football grounds has developed. A new literature has blossomed in recent years on grounds old and new. The most notable authors are Simon Inglis (1983, 1987 and 1990a) and Dave Twydell (1988, 1989 and 1991).

The basic premise of this article is that it is important to consider the supporters' views on the way in which modernization of football stadia is to occur. Hence the remainder of this section will do precisely that by examining the reactions of supporters to the first two 'new wave' grounds, at Scunthorpe United and Walsall. The descriptions cited below have been culled from other clubs' fanzines, magazines written by the fans for the fans. Jary et al (1991) have stressed the importance of fanzines as a cultural form and, in an earlier article, I have called for the greater utilization of fanzines as a data resource on contemporary football (Duke 1991b).

Below are three figures presenting the quotes/comments in other clubs' fanzines on the first two relocated grounds in the Football League. Figure 5.1 summarizes the views on Scunthorpe United's Glanford Park. Figure 5.2 highlights opinions on Walsall's Bescot Stadium. Finally, Figure 5.3 contains an item from one fanzine, which relates the two new grounds together.

Figure 5.1: Scunthorpe United's Glanford Park as seen in other clubs' fanzines

(i) I hate Scunthorpe. I hate their characterless concrete stadium; I hate the fact that Andy Flounders always scores against us; and, above all, I hate standing in their all-seated away end and feeling sorry for myself after another Darlington defeat.

(ii) We were most impressed with the geography of the Glanford Park ground, conveniently at the end of the motorway, and the large car park. The ground seemed functional and well-designed, although we stood all the way through the game - so much for 'all-seaters'. *Mission Impossible* (Darlington) April 1991

Glanford Park ... What can you say about this place? It's very French Second Division. Supposedly, an up-to-date safe ground, but in my opinion not so since they stuffed all those seats into such a small away end. If that's the safe future of football, well, give me Belle Vue any day. Not much to say about the character of the ground, basically because it's hard to find. Would be much better if they hadn't pointlessly filled in the corners, so totally cutting themselves off from the rest of civilization.
Catering: **** (four stars) Good fast food joint.
AWAY SECTION: Covered seats, crap view obscured by fences, roof supports, fans, stewards and police officers. *Raise The Roof* (Doncaster Rovers) No.14 September 1991

We arrived at Scunthorpe at 1.20. Glanford Park is a couple of miles out of town, and is thus fairly well away from civilization. Some of the Gills fans managed to find a bar in a hotel not too far away from the ground but the rest of us hung around outside the stadium for a while, and then, with nothing better to do, went inside. It was my first visit to Glanford Park, now a couple of years old. The kindest comment I can make about the place is that it looks like Walsall's Bescot Stadium. The away end is now all seats, but admission was a reasonable £5.50 (1992). *Brian Moore's Head* (Gillingham) No.26 January 1992

(i) Annual Awards
Best ground visited in Div 4 - Scunthorpe 31%

(ii) And so to a trip to a purpose built fridge, in the middle of nowhere, in search of an away win! I won't say too much about Scunthorpe United's 'purpose built stadium'; just put a roof on it and it would make a perfect superstore! But this is the future, like it or lump it. *Golden Days* (Maidstone United) No.6

Scunthorpe, where the terracing was specially built to enable it to be converted into seating. With the seats on it is virtually impossible to walk past people to reach a seat in the middle of a row. Seats are fairly low down, the view through the fence was poor and it costs you £5. *Deranged Ferret* (Lincoln City) No.8 April 1991.

Best away ground - 2nd Glanford Park. *The Peterborough Effect* (Peterborough United) No.6

Figure 5.2: Walsall's Bescot Stadium as seen in other club's fanzines

So, it's a return to the B&Q stadium (looks like it from outside don't it?). This stadium is so without character that it ideally fits in with the more horrendous aspects of architecture in Walsall and the Birmingham area as a whole. However, it does have its good points; for the carnivores out there it is adjudged to have the tastiest meat pies in the Fourth. *Sound of The Shay* (Halifax Town) August 1991

In the Legoland Labyrinth which forms the Barclays Leagues newest stadium. *Golden Days* (Maidstone United) No.6

Yes you've guessed it! It's just like Scunny's ground except it's painted a different colour and if this is a hi-tech ground why the hell are there still pillars blocking the view? *Raise the Roof* (Doncaster Rovers) No.12 March 1991

A brand new ground similar to Scunthorpe's but without seats or fences at the away end (take heed all others with itchy feet, the railway station is adjacent). *Deranged Ferret* (Lincoln City) No.8 April 1991

Watch with Walsall.
Have you been to the Bescot Stadium yet? Yes? No? Can't Remember? Well if you haven't, you've missed out on the delights of Britain's newest football ground. The stadium, which has been influenced by the early eighties "neo-DIY" store form of architecture, has been described by one critic as "a pillar of quality design - in fact, many pillars". Another raved at the breathtaking views (almost as good as sitting near to an Olympic Gallery entrance at Wembley), especially of posts and other obstructions. But there's no need to go all the way to the West Midlands to experience this kind of beauty. Now you can bring that Bescot feeling to your own ground with Proper Shaped Ball's "Bescot Specs". Simply cut out the glasses below, assemble, and - hey presto! That unique neck-craning atmosphere is authentically reproduced. *Proper Shaped Balls* (Cardiff City) Spring 1992

Figure 5.3: Glanford Park and Bescot Stadium seen together in other club's fanzines

1. *Question:* What do the following teams have in common? Scunthorpe United, Charlton Athletic, Maidstone United, Dorchester Town, Chester City, Weymouth, Walsall
   Answer: They all moved into new grounds over the last five years; all they have to show for it are growing debts and dwindling support.

2. What makes you think that things will be any different if WE move out of OURS? *The Crooked Spireite* (Chesterfield) No.29 August 1991

The fans' views analysed

For the purpose of analysing the comments, the two grounds will be treated as one, because they are architecturally almost identical (though the Bescot Stadium has more pillars obstructing the view). Travelling supporters of other clubs are well aware of this similarity as indicated by comments in three of the fanzines; e.g., it looks like Walsall's Bescot Stadium (fanzine three); its just like Scunny's ground (fanzine nine); and a brand new ground similar to Scunthorpe's (fanzine ten).

Overall, the fans' comments are more negative than positive. A positive feature common to both grounds, albeit for different types of supporter, is ease of access. In the case of Glanford Park, it is nearness to the motorway with a large car park, whilst Bescot Stadium is favoured for its proximity to the railway station. Both grounds are praised for their catering facilities, although the latter claim is open to doubt. To the cogniscenti Rochdale have long provided the tastiest meat pies in the Fourth (now Third) Division!

Other positive points mentioned only once were a functional and well designed ground, reasonable admission price and the lack of fences at the away end. Significantly, Glanford Park won two awards in fanzines in the best away ground visited category, first prize from Maidstone fans and second prize from Peterborough fans. Clearly, the facilities for away fans are good in terms of cover, catering and toilets, and these features are appreciated by fans. However, the all seater nature of the away end at Glanford Park is, generally, not approved of.

The most common criticism of the new stadia concerned the poor view at both grounds which is mentioned by four fanzines. When modern cantilever technology is available, it seems perverse to persist with pillars to hold up the stand roof. Three fanzines commented on the characterless nature of the purpose built constructions. There were also complaints regarding cramped seating conditions and the fact that Glanford Park is in the middle of nowhere with nothing to do. This represents the obverse of praising the car access of the ground mentioned earlier.

Another aspect of the new grounds to come in for repeated negative comment is their architectural style. The grounds are variously described as a purpose built fridge, the B&Q stadium, the Legoland Labyrinth, and the neo-DIY store form of architecture. To this I can add my father's description of Glanford Park as a 'toytown stadium'. Furthermore, an article in the November (1992) edition of the national fanzine *When Saturday Comes* describes the new grounds at Scunthorpe, Walsall and Chester as resembling edge of town industrial units and also part of a rash of hi-tech bike sheds.

Confirmation of the lack of aesthetic considerations in the design of the new stadia is evident from the montage of photos included here. Aerial views of the old and the new Scunthorpe grounds are followed by ground level photos of three sides of the old and the new Walsall grounds. The old grounds are an accidental mixture of structures of different size, height and age, which combine to make each ground a unique home for the supporters. By comparison, both the new stadia appear functional but soulless, with their continuous level roofs providing no distinctive feature upon which to focus. In other words, they both look the same and further clones may well ensue.

Finally, the one item in Figure 3 indicates the fans' awareness that relocation has not resolved the financial problems of several clubs. The fanzines are a useful source of information on what football supporters are thinking and such data is available on Scottish grounds also. For instance, two current Clyde fanzines provide both a guide to the other Scottish Second Division grounds (*The Clyde Underground* no.4) and survey responses to Clyde's forthcoming move to Cumbernauld (*Clyde-O-Scope* no.5).

Conclusion

Substantial change is inevitable at British football grounds, both because of the locations and the age of many British stadia. Modernization is inevitable as a result of the set of disasters which befell English football in the 1980s. However, these changes need not herald wholesale relocation of clubs to new grounds, whilst the old locations become hosts for supermarkets.

The 'supermarket imperative' is on the wane as redevelopment *in situ* gains favour at the expense of relocation. Whatever the method of modernization, there is an urgent need for *creativity* in design and better integration of the stadium into the urban transport system. Thus far, the new relocated English grounds are functional but characterless. Where is the imagination and brio characteristic of the new Italian stadia or the refurbished Italian grounds? It is also pertinent to ask, where is the state and local authority involvement in such developments?

Taking the supporters' views into account should be an essential part of the modernization programme. Greater consultation with supporters was one of the many recommendations in the Taylor Report, which have been treated less seriously than the all-seater stadia suggestion. It is the traditional football supporters, who have experienced the disasters of the 1980s, who should be consulted about stadium change and not, simply, the new executive box spectators. Most regular supporters do favour improved facilities, but they also want the retention of club tradition whenever possible.

Respect for the tradition and history of the British game is crucial if football is to retain its status as the leading mass spectator sport. The campaign to retain some standing capacity, even in the higher divisions is partly the defence of a century of working class communal tradition. In the Premier League the battle has probably been lost already, but achieving total all seater status will not resolve all the problems associated with British football in recent years. Indeed it may well stifle the very lifeblood of the game.

Aerial view of the old showground, Scunthorpe United
Source: David Lee Photography Ltd

Aerial view of Glanford Park, Scunthorpe United
Source: David Lee Photography Ltd

Fellows Park, the old Walsall Stadium
Source: Vic Duke

The new Bescot Stadium, Walsall
Source: Vic Duke

References

Bale, J. (1990) 'In the shadow of the stadium: football grounds as urban nuisances' *Geography* 75, pp.325-334.

Black, J. and Lloyd, G. (1992) 'Football stadia redevelopment and the planning system for Scotland.' Paper given at the *Soccer, Culture and Identity* conference, University of Aberdeen, 2-4 April.

Bale, J. (1991) 'Playing at home: British football and a sense of place' in J Williams and S Wagg (eds.) *British Football and Social Change ,,* Leicester University Press, Leicester.

De Biasi, R. (1992) 'Comparing English and Italian football culture', paper given at the *Soccer, Culture and Identity* conference, op. cit.

Department of Environment (1991) *Planning Policy Guidance: Sport and Recreation* PPG17.

Duke, V. (1991a) 'The politics of football in the new Europe' in J Williams and S Wagg (eds.) *British Football and Social Change,* Leicester University Press, Leicester.

Duke, V. (1991b) 'The sociology of football: a research agenda for the 1990s' *Sociological Review,* 39, pp. 627-645.

Everitt, R. (1992) *Battle for the Valley,* London, (no publisher given).

HMSO (1990) *The Hillsborough Stadium Disaster,* Inquiry by the Rt. Hon Lord Justice Taylor. Final Report. Home Office.

Inglis, S. (1983) *The Football Grounds of England and Wales,* Willow Books, London.

Inglis, S. (1985) *Soccer in the Dock,* Willow Books, London.

Inglis, S. (1987) *The Football Grounds of Great Britain,* Willow Books, London.

Inglis, S. (1990a) *The Football Grounds of Europe,* Willow Books,

London.

Inglis, S. (1990b) 'Remember the Sabbath day to keep it holy' in H Lansdown and A Spillius (eds.) *Saturday Boys,* Willow Books, London.

Jary, D. et al (1991) 'Football fanzines and football culture', *Sociological Review,* 39, pp. 581-597.

Lansdown, H. and Spillius, A. (eds.) (1990) *Saturday Boys,* Willow Books, London.

Shepley, C. (1990) 'Planning and Football League grounds', *The Planner,* 76, September, 15-17.

Shepley, C. and Barratt, A. (1991) 'Football League grounds - update', *The Planner,* 77, May, 8-9.

Twydell, D. (1988) *Rejected FC: Volume 1,* Yore Publications.

Twydell, D. (1989) *Rejected FC: Volume 2* ,Yore Publications.

Twydell, D. (1991) *Grounds for a Change,* Yore Publications.

Williams, J. et al, (1989) 'Football and football spectators after Hillsborough: a national survey of members of the Football Supporters Association', Sir Norman Chester Centre for Football Research, Leicester.

Identities:
Local, ethnic, national

6 'Rangers is a black club': 'Race', identity and local football in England

John Williams

It is something of a truism to say that supporting a professional football club, for men, perhaps especially for working class men, says something about who you are, about where you are from and about how you, and others, see yourself as a man (Williams and Taylor, 1994). Despite exhaustive attempts by clubs better to market themselves and to appeal to the discerning and choosing consumer, and despite obvious signs that successful clubs featured on TV do draw on widespread, latent, support and sell more replica shirts, more books and other memorabilia than smaller clubs (Taylor, 1993), there is evidence that the reasons why fans actively support the clubs they do remain remarkably traditional. They are, largely, to do with notions of place, family ties and local traditions of support (Curran and Redmond, 1991). Thus, beneath the thin veneer of many a distant Liverpool or Manchester United 'fan' often lies a deeper attachment to a, smaller, local club. In this sense, clubs 'choose' their followers rather than the other way around and committed supporters soon discover that football loyalty is "not a moral choice, like bravery or kindness; it was more like a wart or a hump, something you were stuck with" (Hornby, 1992, p35).

So far, so good. But there are also some unresolved questions here. We have looked in detail elsewhere, at the strongly *masculine* traditions which underpin active professional football club support in England and I don't want to dwell on that aspect here (Williams and Woodhouse, 1991). Rather, I would like to argue that looking only at the role of *professional* clubs in England in this respect, and to look only at *fans* of those clubs is to touch on barely the thin surface of the wider football community. What, for example, of the role of non-professional clubs and of local league football in the construction of masculine and neighbourhood identities? What about the wider functions of local clubs, which are run on a voluntary basis for little obvious reward? (See, Thomas, 1994). On these important aspects of football culture there is little available research data. This paper is offered then as a small contribution towards rectifying this situation in the hope of stimulating further work in this area. It turns our attention away from the nationally prominent and well researched field of professional football to look in some detail at *local* football and, more specifically, at the story of one local league football club. Firstly, though, by way of context a few general comments about local football in England.

Weekending: a description of local football in England

Local league football rarely attracts the national limelight. Sports programmes on national TV seldom, if ever, touch on the local game, although LWT, using the ubiquitous 'professional cockney' Danny Baker as host, recently ran a series of TV programmes in the London area about Sunday morning football and, very occasionally, the national weekend broadsheets feature local leagues. The only other time local football issues tend to make the national media is in relation to 'crisis' stories about player behaviour, and particularly about difficulties in recruiting and retaining referees. It was recently reported that 4000 referees were being lost to the non-league and local game each year because of player violence and abuse. Allegedly, some of the worst indiscipline comes comes from the *parents* of young players, as evidenced by the fact that a 13 year old in Liverpool was recently banned for five years after his father, and then the player himself, assaulted a local referee (*Liverpool Football Echo*, 25 August 1990 and 22 January 1994). Player indiscipline in local football remains a key focus for the concern of referees and of the football authorities (FA, 1991, p64; Williams, 1994). Generally, however, as we have pointed out, media coverage of the weekend local football ritual is very much left to the local press and local radio.

The involvement of working class men in local football clubs as supporters, administrators and players is, arguably, their most substantial contribution, in time and monetary terms, to any voluntary local organization. (I am talking here, in the main, about clubs which play matches in local town or county leagues, not about 'non-league' clubs which routinely pay players for playing part-time football. The latter involves travel and possible promotion up the so-called 'League Pyramid' and eventually, perhaps, into the Football League itself). Local football clubs at the lowest level in Britain can be set up with the minimum of organizational expertise, requiring only an appointed secretary, a playing kit and a 'home' pitch hired, perhaps, from a local council. Clubs usually survive on small subscriptions ('subs') paid by players and on income from lotteries and fund raising events. FA estimates suggest that, non-league and local league clubs raised on average about £1000 a year from 'events' in 1990 (FA, 1991, p65). Many local clubs, however, survive on the barest resources and the turnover in clubs at the local level is considerable

Clubs originate mainly out of local neighbourhood, kinship, work or ethnic ties but in Britain many local clubs are also formed out of male networks based around local pubs. However, these days, even clubs playing at Sunday league or local Senior League standard are increasingly attracting formal sponsors and they are paying players for their services, thus fraying some of the strongly localistic friendship ties which have traditionally been significant in starting up and sustaining local clubs. Payment for playing at the local level remains, of course, a constant source of fascination and intrigue and tends to generate its own pervasive myths. Nevertheless, some indication of the rewards now sometimes available comes from a story of recent local success. 'Informed' Leicester sources maintain that players at a local Senior League club were recently "on £200 a man" to win an important tie in the FA Vase. Money clearly talks. The tie was duly won, 5-1.

Organized local football has been played in British towns and cities for more than a century. A number of long established local leagues in Leicestershire can be identified in Table One. However, Table One also shows that playing football at this local level has mushroomed in popularity from the 1960s onwards at the same time as attendances at professional matches during that period continued to fall. Five of the major local leagues in Leicestershire were established after 1967. Adult local teams even in Leicestershire, hardly a football hotbed, number more than 450. In 1991, over 41,500 clubs were affiliated to the national Football Association corresponding to approximately 60,000 teams (FA, 1991, p.64). Allowing for the 'double counting' of the large number of players registered at more than one club, this suggests that substantially more than two million men regularly play the game between September and May. These days, of course, local football leagues thrive both on Saturdays *and* Sundays. Football on Sundays, and especially *boys* football had been the real growth area in the 1970s and 1980s. In 1991, 25% of existing affiliated clubs and 30% of all local teams were made up of boys in the 9-16 age range. A recent estimate suggests that 80% of boys football and 60-80% of all adult local football is now played on Sundays (FA, 1991 p64).

Table 6.1: Main local leagues organized under the auspices of the Leicestershire and Rutland County FA, 1991/92

League	Est.	No. of Clubs
Alliance Football League	1976	53
Charnwood Sunday League	1966	64
Hinckley & District Sunday League	1967	62
Leicestershire Senior League	1903	33
Leicester City Football League	1897	53
Leicester & District Mutual League	1900	31
Leicester & District Association League	1958	30
Leicester Alliance Sunday League	1989	69
North Leicestershire Association League	1931	41
Melton & Rutland District League	1978	15
Total number of clubs		**451**

The *character* of adult Sunday football is also quite different to that played on Saturdays. Saturday football tends to provide a higher standard at more organized venues, involving as it does the increasingly widespread paying of players and the majority of the estimated 1000 local clubs which have their own home grounds. Non-contract Saturday players play for their 'second' clubs on Sundays, and often come into contact with poorer facilities, hostile spectators and the more 'casual' park players who lack the commitment (or ability) for the training and play demanded on Saturdays. For reasons such as these, ambitious referees soon give up refereeing Sunday football. One told *The Guardian* (1 December, 1989), for example, that:

> Saturday teams are usually better organized and want to win games to gain promotion in their particular league. On Sunday, you get more pub players and the better players get frustrated at the ones who think it is better to kick lumps out of people than to play football. The worst abuse comes from the teams who are less able to compete properly.

Although there are signs that the Sunday leagues may have passed their peak of popularity, it is by no means unusual for local players to play twice or even three times over a weekend in organized matches. (Players often play for rival clubs, of course, when illegally registered, or under an assumed name). There is also evidence that difficult economic circumstances and rising pitch fees are cutting back on the number of Sunday league teams. According to Alan Grafton, the secretary of the Gorton Sunday League in Manchester, for example, the £40 needed to field a Sunday team each week:

> may not sound a lot, but it requires organization to get the money in each week and if half your players are unemployed it becomes a struggle. Football mirrors life and times are hard. ('Art of course soccer is alive and kicking', *The Observer*, 22 November, 1992).

Mason and Mason (1980) estimate that the *total* spending on grass roots participation in local football in 1980 was £86 million. FA estimates in 1991 suggest that local club spending on kit, footballs, trophies, medical equipment and foreign tours alone amounted to just under £28 million (FA, 1991, p.65). Moreover, if one adds the soccer *played* at the local level to the amount of professional football now *televised* 'live' in Britain at the weekend, then it becomes clear that involvement in football, either as a spectator, player or administrator (or all three), dominates much of the weekend leisure lives of a large number of young British men. The impact of this pattern of use of leisure time on gender and family relations, particularly in working class communities, remains generally unexplored. (But, see below and Taylor, 1976).

Towards the end of local league seasons, when fixtures have piled up and cup finals are in the offing, top local players may find themselves playing five or more highly competitive matches in a week. (A research trainee of mine, a top non-league player who spent some time at a professional club, recently told me that at age 18 he played 14 competitive matches in 16 days at the end of one crowded season). It is for reasons like these, of course, that professional coaches in England complain that young players play too much competitive football and that the English FA has been trying recently to limit top young players to no more than 60 competitive matches a season. (One of the major recent growth areas in local football has been the establishment of youth and junior 11-a-side leagues for children as young as nine years of age). Our continental neighbours are still likely, however, to see this figure as being remarkably high, especially when taking into account the relentless pace and the physical commitment demanded by the British game (Williams, 1992).

Local football and male identities

Local football is a significant activity, of course, for its general contribution to the fitness and health of young men, though there is no available data on the incidence and seriousness of the injuries which routinely occur in matches of this kind, especially to men who may do no other form of serious exercise. (Also, involvement in a physical and testing team sport such as this does not preclude the ritual of the half-time 'fag', or, indeed, a pre-match drink before afternoon fixtures on Sundays. Heavy lunchtime drinking, also, frequently follows Sunday morning play). Local football is important, too, for the opportunities it provides for administrative and organizational experience, especially for working class men, and for the comradely post-match social activities which occur in pubs, club houses, and at fund raising events, etc. It is also important, of course, for its role in the construction of local male identities.

Recollections of the football events, the trips, the goals or the fearless tackles represent for the men involved accounts of their own specific history; of the loyalty, brotherhood and collective struggle involved in raising and maintaining a team and a club (Westwood, 1990, p.69). It is also a culture which can be forbidding and even startling for those who approach it from a different class and cultural background. This is sometimes alleged by players to be one of the reasons why referees get a hard time in local league matches, especially if they are young and are unable to match up to the rigorous standards of manliness expected and demanded by players. It may also explain why around one in three of a sample of local referees have thought about giving up the game because of increasing harassment by players and spectators (Williams, 1994). A recent letter to a national newspaper complained about local football in the north west that, "The language and congratulations are quite horrendous, the touchline is certainly not the place to take young children or the fairer sex on a Saturday afternoon or a Sunday morning" (Reported in *The Observer*, 22 November, 1992). Similar complaints are made by County FA officials about the language of parents who are following the progress of young sons and daughters (See, *Liverpool Echo*, 22 January 1994).

Top players and managers in local league football, can also achieve considerable kudos among other local men for their exploits on and off the pitch. The heavily masculine discourses of local football celebrate its 'hard cases', but it also has a place for the 'skill merchants' and 'loyal servants'; the men who are the 'backbone' of their clubs. Local club managers, publicly anonymous in their paid work, will often become known within local football networks, for example, for their astuteness, or their discipline; for their powers to motivate; or for their capacity to 'nick' players from other clubs, or to draw in the much sought after generous financial backers.

These days, especially as financial rewards have increased even in the local football sector, players can, and do, move between clubs at an extraordinary pace, sometimes changing teams seven or eight times even in a single season. Coverage of non-league and local football in local newspapers and on local radio stations is also now extensive. Top players - including youngsters of 10 years or less - can become minor local 'celebrities', featuring regularly in the local

159

press, and around whom stories about the professional clubs which are, reputedly, 'interested' in them, may grow. Alternatively, adult players may be better known by the rumours about their own alleged 'unsuitability' for the professional game - typically, because of drink, temperament, violence, etc. - rumours which are shaped, embroidered and transformed via the masculine discourses of the touchline or bar. Knowledge of local male networks and of the interface between local, non-league and professional football is a significant currency inside the male communities which manage, play and support the game at the local level. The 'scouts' of professional clubs have a special, near-mystical status in this culture as they trawl the top local leagues in search of young men who have the elusive and indefinable 'right stuff'.

Football, ethnicity and neighbourhood identities

Local football clubs are also significant focal points for the expression of local neighbourhood or ethnic identities. Most major towns and cities in England house local football clubs which are devoted to reflecting or sustaining the ethnic origins of the club's founders - Serbia FC, Leicester Polska, Nicosia, etc. These are an important, and at the local level, highly visible cultural and symbolic resource for the people who support and run them. Britain's Asian communities also, of course, produce local clubs - Nirvana, Khalsa, and Indiana, amongst others in Leicester, for example - though frustration here at local and national resistances to the progression in the game of top Asian players is often, justifiably, intense. A review of professional club playing staff by BBC 2's *Standing Room Only* in 1992 found only one footballer, a trainee at Burnley, of Asian origin. Rajan Datar also recently argued that local Asian leagues have been set up in Yorkshire and London as a response to the "lack of opportunities to play organized [local] football" for many young Asians (*The Guardian*, 28 June 1989. See, also, Westwood, 1990).

Black players in England have had more success as professionals but not without considerable opposition and struggle. Much has been said and written, of course, about traditions of racist football support in England and the difficulties experienced in this respect by black professional players (Hill, 1989; Cashmore, 1982; Williams et al,

160

1989; Williams, 1990). Estimates suggest that around one quarter of professional players in the Football League and Premier League are black, most of them of African-Caribbean origin, but that less than one per cent of supporters at top clubs share these origins (Williams and Smith, 1994). A small number of clubs seem more successful in attracting black support than others; at Arsenal for example, according to black fans at the club, "There are definitely a lot more black supporters now than five years ago. They've been attracted as the team has gained more black players" ('Soccer's true colours', *The Guardian*, 16 August, 1993. See, also Hornby, 1992, pp.188-191). But in the main, English football grounds seem unattractive and inhospitable locations for black (and Asian) people as spectators. Accounts elsewhere in this volume attest to the fact that racism is a problem around European, as well as British, football stadia. The racism routinely dished out to black *players* in England has arguably diminished in its scale and intensity in recent years though it was still seen as a sufficiently serious problem in 1993 for the Commission for Racial Equality to launch a major campaign at Premier and Football League clubs aimed at *Kicking Racism out of Football.*

The academic literature on 'race' and sport is replete with examples of the racist assumptions and expectations which link blacks with sporting excellence (I am talking here and for the rest of this chapter largely about Britons drawn from African-Caribbean backgrounds. For accounts of British Asian males and sport, see, Fleming, 1993, and Westwood, 1990). These range from presumptions about biological difference, stereotypes fixed on the body, on physicality and 'natural' advantage, and on the presumed lack of organizing skills of black athletes, to narrow and racist preconceptions among, for example, white school teachers about the likely sporting (not intellectual) expertise of black youth (Cashmore, 1982). The last named is often associated, in turn, with allegedly 'realist' perceptions of the opportunities which are available for blacks in the wider labour market.

At the local level, however, 'black' sports clubs, especially those organized and run by black people, are more often seen by their male members and by other members of the black community as a site of *resistance.* As Westwood (1990, p.67) points out:

Black men play football because they love the game, but their entry into the game means they are immediately involved in the cultural politics of 'race'. So much of the politics is missed if local amateur [sic] and semi-professional football is ignored.

Involvement in local football in these terms is, in part, a form of *community* 'politics', or a symbol of resistance to domination if not a ready made agent of structural change. It constitutes, however, a form of resistance, expression and involvement which must always articulate with *local* circumstances. As Gilroy (1987, pp.230-1) argues:

> There are good grounds on which to argue that the language of community has displaced both the language of class and the language of 'race' in the political activity of black Britain. Though blacks identify themselves as an exploited and subordinated group, there are marked and important differences between the political cultures and identities of the various black communities which together make up the social movement. Local factors, reflecting the class, ethnic, and 'racial' composition of any particular area, its political traditions, the local economy and residential structure may all play a decisive part in shaping precisely what it means to be black.

"It's about history": the origins of a local club oral history

The short account which follows is of an oral history of a local 'black' football club in Leicester. It should be seen as an example, at least in part, of "a collective mobilization through football that calls up black masculinities as part of the resistances that black men generate against the racisms of British society and by which they validate each other" (Westwood, 1990, p.71). In fact, despite the popular and academic debates about racism and sport in Britain, there are very few *empirical* studies of the involvement of black Britons in sport. The origins of this local club history really go back to a national two day conference on football held at Leicester University in 1988. The conference attracted speakers from all the major footballing bodies, substantial national media attention and drew an audience of more than 350, including the, then, England team manager, Bobby Robson.

162

Members of a local 'black' football club, Highfield Rangers, also attended (See, Williams, 1989).

Over the next few months meetings were organized with members of the black community in Highfields to set up the *Highfields Community Coaching Project (HCCP)* with funds provided by the *Intermediate Treatment Fund* (now, *Divert*). At some of the early meetings in 1988 up to 18 local organizations were represented, and a summer sports coaching project was established in the area to provide temporary employment and training for local people and activities and coaching for Highfields kids. The concern of *HCCP* was always to use sport as a vehicle for wider forms of development and training. As we have already pointed out, stereotypes about black aptitude for sport are pervasive, often racist and damaging. But local black people in Highfields were also concerned that such was the hostility to sport among white and black educationalists and community tutors in the area that the local community college now offered very few opportunities for competitive sport for their children.

One of the Football Centre's new research trainees was also a good local league footballer and he joined Highfield Rangers as a player, as well as being a member of an Oral History Group we had established inside the club to recommend and arrange interviews and to collect press cuttings and photos from club members about the club's history. There was little difficulty in getting a good 'white' player into Rangers. (There was a place for a small number of Asian players, too, though rivalries with local Asian clubs remained fierce). Though profoundly an African-Caribbean club, Rangers has always housed 'quality' white players, especially those raised in the multi-cultural neighbourhood of Highfields itself, where common cultural interests, educational experiences, and shared notions of 'neighbourhood nationalism' (Cohen, 1988, p.63) worked upon any differences brought by ethnic background (see, also, Jones, 1988). 'Mal', a player still lauded today at Rangers, was the only white player in the early Rangers' teams. Unsurprisingly, this distinction brought with it its own problems:

It's funny, I played for a few years where I never really noticed being the only white player and then, I don't know why, I used to think about it a lot.... At school there was always a good percentage of blacks , but I didn't pay any attention to it at the beginning. I did, though, become well aware of it, but I always had a lot of people telling me, opposition-wise, silly things like,'What are you doing playing for these black bastards?' and all sorts of crap. But it didn't interest me. I don't know if they were trying to wind me up, but I weren't interested.

The researcher's role inside the club was important. It meant we were no longer 'academic' outsiders, whose own masculine or footballing credentials might otherwise be openly questioned. The trainee soon became established in the first team squad and he began to talk informally with older club members about the origins and history of the club. He also began to trace stories in the local sporting press concerning Rangers in order to inform his questions and to build up our data base. We were on our way.

The interviews themselves took place sometimes at the homes of club members, on occasions in the University, but mainly at the club itself. Friday nights were a favourite time to corner interviewees, who could be coaxed out of a dominoes or pool game or away from the bar into one of the small offices in the club house. On some occasions, prospective interviewees failed to show or arrived much later than had been planned. As Gilroy (1987, p.210) points out, this 'black' approach to work time and leisure can be read as a critique of the economy of time and space as, "the period allocated for recovery and reproduction is assertively and provocatively occupied instead by the pursuit of pleasure and leisure." It was not unusual for interviews to take place into the early hours of the morning, and it could take three or four hours hanging around to get an interview sorted out, but usually it was well worth it. The later the interview, frequently the livelier and more evocative the account.

The origins of Highfield Rangers

Anyone with a reasonable knowledge of local football or community organizations in the Leicester area knows the Highfield Rangers Sports and Social Club (now, simply, Highfield Rangers). The club was formed in 1970 by a small group of young men who arrived in England as children in the early 1960s with their families from the

West Indies, to find the streets of this country far from 'paved with gold' as they had been told they would be back in the Caribbean. In the words of founder member, 'Delroy':

> We were told this country was supreme: [that] there weren't tramps; there was no stones on the roads; [that] it was the cleanest place you could ever possibly imagine. It was *nothing* compared to the West Indies!

Our 'check list' of issues for discussion with older African-Caribbean interviewees began with their memories, if any, of the Caribbean and of the arrival of their families in England. Memories of school, and especially about early involvements in sport, brought up predictable accounts of enthusiastic participation and also of young black students being excessively encouraged by teachers in this direction to the detriment of their academic work (Cashmore, 1982). In fact, sport, like almost everything else at school in an English winter was a hard initiation to the new climate and cultures of British life. As Rangers' players later recalled, "It was cold, ice cold. Games lessons was just avoiding football because it was so cold." "I just couldn't play with a football. I couldn't put boots on because I'd never worn boots before."

As teenagers, the young men from the West Indies gathered in the evenings at the Youth Club at their local school, Moat Boys. There they talked, listened to music and played basketball, but they were already developing in the late 1960s a real affinity for a winter sport which had, until their arrival in England, been almost entirely alien to them, football. 'Kick about' matches were soon organized. Often teams would reflect the different island origins of local families - 'Antigua' v 'The Rest'. On other occasions 'the youth' would take their chances against older opponents, as 'Sola' recalls:

> We used to play football on Spinney Hill Park. It used to be the old lads against the young lads and it was a challenge for us to go and kick the hell out of them because we didn't have football boots, only shoes. We played football after school and down the youth club afterwards ... It was as if we were destined to be together, do you understand that? It was Delroy, Maurice, Phonso, Tyson, Neil. We had loads of guys who came together

and it was, like, all of us were good.

A report from the [white] full time youth worker at Moat at the time reveals something of the raw, enthusiastic talents of the new arrivals as well as traces of his own paternalistic and untutored early racism. The Highfields' group, according to this worker:

> contained a number of brilliant footballers but their worst enemies were themselves. They were players of extremes; when on top they were devastating, but if they got off to a bad start they would go completely to pieces. A marked shortness of temper characterized this team .... On most nights the club was open, a football would be taken into the sports hall. Sometimes there would be only one or two kicking the ball but on other occasions as many as twenty five. In such a latter case, the game took second place to an uninhibited 'free-for-all'. Perhaps an organized, more structured, game of football would appeal to the connoisseur, but it would take away much of the enjoyment and all of the spontaneity. The tragedy would be to just see it as a game of football and not a tremendous interplay of emotions and reactions (Parkinson 1969, p.14).

Ambitious for competition and success, and specifically for a focus for local *black* neighbourhood aspirations through football, these teenagers rejected a number of self-proposed names for their new club - Raven; Biafran Underdogs - and settled for Highfield Rangers. The reasons were clear as 'Sola' points out:

> It was personal; Highfields in those days was where the black people and them lived. Highfields was recognized for black people. We wanted to be *Highfield* Rangers; well that's how I felt.

It was these neighbourhood and ethnic brotherhoods and the communion provided by an involvement in a physical and skillful sport which provided the main incentives for setting up Rangers. But, the organization and running of the club was also about wider issues concerning the local politics of 'race', about, "representing the people of Highfields. We were trying to show people. We were painting a picture of what we can do" ('Bucky').

The 'politics' of Rangers have never been obviously those of the 'front line', an approach for which they have sometimes been criticized by members of more 'rootsy' (and less successful) 'black' clubs in the city. Rangers' members and organizers range from men and women in professional and skilled work to the young unemployed, but the rules of the club reflect a determination to maintain 'respectable' and 'professional' standards - the prohibition, for example, on the use of soft drugs in the club house at any time does not sit well with some of club's more 'streetwise' detractors in Highfields. A local, rival Asian club has been much better known in Leicester for combining lower level football successes - and, for Rangers, sometimes chaotic indiscipline - with high profile political activism around the focus of 'front line' black and Asian male identities (See, Westwood, 1991).

These young black men from Highfields entered a new, and largely uncharted, world of sporting responsibilities and obligations; of transport, pitch hire and player registrations. According to 'Phonso', "A couple of the guys, both of them, had an idea to go into a league and approached me with the idea. I didn't know what a league was, but I agreed. We then opened a bank account with £5 on Melbourne Road in mine and Edson's name. I was secretary, though I wasn't sure what this meant or what it was." After playing in youth football for two seasons, in 1972 the club joined Division Eight of the Leicester Mutual (Saturday) League. Highfield Rangers, 'the sharpshooters', were born.

Role models, racism and 'style'

Football role models for young British blacks growing up with televised football in Britain in the 1960s and early 1970s were few and far between. There had been black professional players in England, often recruited from Africa, at least since the 1890s, but they were isolated cases (See, Vasali, 1994). It was the late 1970s before numbers of black footballers started to make it into the top professional grade, and 1978 before Viv Anderson became the first black footballer to play for England. Albert Johanneson, a slight, black South African, played for the successful Leeds United team of the early 1960s, but it was the Bermudan, Clyde Best, an imposing centre-forward at West Ham, who had the physical presence and the public exposure to draw the gaze of many local black players. In Leicester, Best made a considerable impression on young football hopefuls in Highfields, as 'Sola' and 'Joss' recall:

> It was important for me to see Clyde Best, a black man; I was proud to be black. I couldn't wait for West Ham to come down here; to see this big, black man playing as a centre forward. The guy was a legend, a hero. Seeing a black man out there was tremendous. It was a good feeling to see one of you out there and be able to say, "If he can do it, I can do it."
> My greatest hero was, obviously, Pele. Another was Clyde Best. I had this picture...of West Ham. I never supported them, but I always liked them because they had a big squad photo and I'd never seen so many black faces in a team... I never knew there were black players at these clubs. I always had a secret admiration for West Ham because they had all these black players there.

A number of the Rangers' players, themselves, had trials for League clubs and had experienced overt racism from coaches and managers ("I guess they weren't ready for us then", 'Wully'). 'Sola' a confident and aggressive goalkeeper, wrote to a number of smaller League clubs for trials and he made a point of stating clearly in his letters that he was black. He wanted no club to invite him down only *then* to be dismayed when discovering his ethnic origin ("I wanted a fair go"). 'Bertie' spent some time at a West Midlands pro. club, though he soon tired of demands that, "Nigger do this, nigger do that." 'Sam', a real pioneer, played ten years visiting the 'redneck' towns in the Southern League without ever lining up against another black player. Another local player's well known League manager openly called him 'nigger' in team meetings in order, as he 'explained' it, to 'toughen up' his 17 year old black player for the treatment he would inevitably meet elsewhere. Finally, 'Jefferson' found the clash of cultures inside a professional club difficult to adjust to and admitted the need for more self criticism in his own case; wearing *headphones* to coaching sessions was unlikely to endear him to any coach, let alone to the retentive and racist contingent *in situ* in

168

English League clubs in the late 1970s.

Of established, white, European players George Best's skillful individualistic dribbling play had its supporters among the young Rangers' players, but it was Brazil, and particularly the expansive *style* of the Brazilian play, compared, especially, to the 'dull', methodical 'English' style, which really captured the imagination of the young British African Caribbeans. Brazil, in 1970, confounded north European obsessions with the footballing work ethic to produce a side which combined technique, attacking power and flair; "a Platonic ideal that nobody, not even the Brazilians, would ever be able to find again" (Hornby, 1992, p.38). The sheer quality of the Brazilian play also made a nonsense, or an irrelevance, of the alleged 'failings' of black players. As 'Skids' put it:

> The 1970 World Cup, the best World Cup ever seen, sort of inspired me. The talk at them times was, "Yeah, the black man has got skill but he can't work." But to me that ain't the point; that ain't the way I know football and a lot of people realise it now. A man who can go there and score a few goals is better than a donkey or somebody working up and down. The way the Brazilians played was so basic and simple but when it was needed, when it looked like it wasn't going anywhere they would just do a bit of magic, just awareness, and, to me, that was the simplest football.

It is important, of course, not to essentialize the racial differences which are made explicit in this account. It is obviously important to Rangers' players that many of the greatest Brazilian players are black. But, Rangers' players are not Brazilian, they are black *and* British and their identities are forged within concrete and particular conjunctures of history, place, culture and class. This is an obvious but important point to reiterate, because the moment the signifier 'black' is torn from its historical, cultural and political embedding and lodged in a biologically constituted racial category, we valorize, by inversion, the very ground of the racism we are trying to deconstruct (Hall, 1992, pp.29-30).

Nevertheless, the cultural underpinning of some of the authentic differences in national football playing styles were also obvious in the earliest traditions of, and mythologies about, playing for

Highfield Rangers. As in other black British expressive cultural forms, Rangers approach to the game has a spontaneity, a performance orientation and a commitment to improvisation as key and celebrated features (Gilroy, 1987, p.199). Matches had to be won, of course, especially when, as we shall see later, racism was so much to the fore among the club's opponents. But it was never enough *just* to win; matches also had to be won *Rangers'* way. 'Jefferson' and 'Denis' explain:

> Something is expected when you play for Rangers. A lot of teams are not worried about the style or finesse in a game but ... I think they are the main features we've got; style and finesse. If you can do that and win, then it's a bonus. I'd sooner play in a game that we've done everything that we enjoy doing, everybody has expressed themselves on the pitch, and lost. I'd enjoy that more than to play like robots and win. It's enjoyment. You enjoy it if something comes off, especially when the crowds are there and you're getting encouragement.
> It is important to play with some flair. If we go out and beat a team 10-0, structured, then we don't want it. If our supporters, and even me as one of the founder members, if we win the game and we do it fast, we do it fluently, we see a lot of skill on the ball, a lot of people falling over by us, beating them, coming out of a tight situation - we prefer that and winning 1-0 or drawing, as opposed to winning 10-0 and it's just mundane. I don't know why, it's just nice. It's nice to see, nice to be part of it, it's just the flair that we have got.

Such accounts, positively provided by black people themselves, are double edged, of course. Racist discourses about black athletes are replete with accounts about black 'flair' coupled with an alleged lack of 'bottle' or organizational skills; that black people have 'the bodies' but not 'the brains' for football (Small, 1992). As Westwood (1990, p59) points out:

> To consider black masculinities as part of the cultures of resistance to racism is not to suggest they are not in themselves contradictory. These areas, the streets and football, are important to consider because it is precisely in these areas that

current stereotypes about black men have been generated and have become part of the commonsense racism of today.

As can be seen from the examples above, however, the involvement of *spectators* also defines an important and positive element of the approach to playing for Rangers. Matches are often recalled, for example, because of the *size* of the crowd, or the response of Rangers' followers and also, crucially, because of the 'historic' moments they are taken to constitute when black spectators (and players) have succeeded in breaching the spatial and institutional enclaves of the local white football establishment - Highfield fans in numbers, for example, at a major and previously 'closed' venue in local county football. (A strong memory is of a large Rangers' contingent present for a famous Senior Cup victory at a local Beazer Homes League ground, bringing cries from the Rangers' supporters that, "The 'ghetto' has taken over the county").

Local football is also a social space where symbolic victories can be achieved as a means of alleviating wider community tensions or of responding to perceived community injustices. Holmes Park, home of the Leicestershire County FA, hosted a 'famous' (Junior Cup) final in 1988 which had particular resonances for many Rangers' supporters and players, as 'Gerry' points out:

We had a District League cup final against the [Leicestershire] Constabulary at Holmes Park...I remember coming out there, it was against the police, and Holmes Park just seemed to be full up with black faces. The game started off and everybody got barracked, both sides, except Natty who for some reason he was the only one. We won the game 2-1, I think, in extra time but by rights we should have lost about 4-1. I'll always remember that, 'cos we started in daylight on a summer evening and finished late under the floodlights ... That was a tremendous game and I was absolutely knackered! I've never played a game so hard 'cos it was constant the whole two hours. It was also the first final I played in with Paul, my brother, and there were three sets of brothers in the same team; myself and Paul, Jerome and Carley and Maurice and Gary. Some people just used the chance to give the police some abuse. The whole team wanted to win so much. That was my most satisfying game.

At Rangers, individual acts of outrageous skill or daring - a mazy dribble from a defensive dead end; a 'nutmeg' at the expense of strategic advantage; an extravagant overhead kick; a 'wicked' shot - are volubly celebrated, and recalled, on the touchline - and often in the manager's 'dug out' - almost as reverentially as any famous victory. These are widely interpreted as signs of the club's unique traditions, origins and status; they are what stand Rangers in opposition to, "a normal English game; two sides playing ping-pong with each other" (Sola). Gilroy (1987, p.214) has argued that black musical performers:

> aim to overcome rather than exploit the structures which separate them from their audiences. The relationship between the performer and the crowd is transformed in dialogic rituals so that spectators acquire the active role of participants in collective processes which are sometimes cathartic and which may symbolize or even create a community.

In the same way at Rangers, expressive football playing styles stand as a marker for the more closely symbiotic relationship between player and spectator at the club. Fans frequently encroach and spill onto the pitch. 'Watching' matches is an *active* and social pastime. Supporters - Rangers' members - *expect* to be entertained, expect to see games won with a flourish, a fact which is understood, accepted and enjoyed on the pitch. Younger Rangers' players are more 'realistic' about the demands of playing at higher levels; about the greater need to organize and to plan when faced with well marshalled, if sometimes technically limited, opponents. For older club members, however, the new generation of black British Rangers' players are, necessarily, negotiating their identities between two cultures, a fact which, it is argued, is reflected in recent changes in club styles of play. What's lamented here seems to be the perceived loss of 'freedom' of the earlier approaches to playing the game, as founder member 'Bucky' explains:

> People from the Caribbean bring special qualities - pace, skill, and they like ... if there is a big crowd watching, to do a few flicks and all that. You can do the flicks and you may be going ten yards back your way, but the crowd like to see something like that. And, if the

crowd like that, then you're alright. The crowd like to see a bit of skill, a bit of the unexpected. They bring a bit of that, not so much now, because most of the kids now are born in England and brought up the English style of way. We like to play like Cameroon; they get the ball and just go, they are not bothered about text-books, and that. That's how we like to play in the early days. I think *then* that is how we played. It's a bit sad now because although we are doing well I still like to see a bit of individual play. They are a dying breed, though, even in the professional game.

Black club, white leagues

From its beginnings as a lowly 'parks' team, Rangers has since gone on to become a thriving African-Caribbean voluntary organization and senior local football club. Rangers has its own grounds, facilities and club house which were 'negotiated' from the local authority following the black street 'uprisings' in the Highfields area in 1981. (Rangers were finally allocated an old rubbish tip, troublingly, three miles out of Highfields and currently being excavated after reported dangers of leakages of pockets of methane gas). The club runs regular social events, three adult, male football teams, a junior (under 14s) team and a new (1992) women's football team. In the summer, the Rangers' cricketers take over.

The club also now hosts a unique £250,000 training project aimed at promoting, with local businesses, white collar training and work opportunities for black and Asian people in the retail and banking sectors. While many other 'black' projects in the city have stuttered or closed, Rangers has survived and grown, gaining in stability and strength. Most of the young men who started the club in 1970 remain involved today as Management Committee members. This longevity of commitment is unusual in voluntary organizations, though less so in sport, and probably points up the enduring attraction of football to working men and the continuing significance of the club as a stable and popular social and cultural resource, especially for black men in the city.

Any meaningful account of the Rangers' past must, of course, chart the often contradictory and gendered role of sport in African-

Caribbean cultures in Britain. But, it must also signal the resourcefulness and resilience of a community faced with the twin barriers of social closure and racism. The club's account of its own past is, inevitably, littered with tales of obstruction, discrimination and exclusion. From the start, especially in the more isolated county locations, Rangers' players faced overt provocation and racist abuse on and off the pitch. On some occasions the only appropriate response to this seemed to be physical retaliation or collective self defence; on others, racism seemed to inspire the team to heightened playing efforts, and frequently to a footballing demolition of their abusive opponents.

Faced with the new factor of a black local league club, many referees seemed to be incapable - or unwilling - to control racism. Inevitably, match officials came to be seen less as neutral arbiters and more as just another hurdle; part of the opposition. Looking back now, Rangers' early years are recalled as an adventurous and near constant struggle against adversity. As 'Bucky' put it, "It was quite an experience, because I don't think we had played in 'the wars' before." 'Maurice' and 'Wully' recall below incidents drawn from many examples of early encounters:

> We seemed to get racial abuse all the time, it's funny because we found it more when we went out to these country teams. I remember one particular incident when there was a little boy, a white family, and we ran out onto this pitch and this little boy's remark was, "Mum, they *haven't* got tails!" And the two of us who heard it just looked round at the mother because you couldn't look at the boy. Others, like, say an incident of a tackle, the first thing was it wasn't a bad tackle but straight away, "God, you black this or black that." Some of the players started to react to that. It was hard to keep quiet about it but we loved playing football so much, we took it as a sport and that's it. We didn't expect to get all this abuse.
>
> Some of the referees we had in the early days enticed the trouble by going and changing in the opposition's dressing room, not in ours, probably 'cos we are black and they were white. So, at once, you knew that once you were on that pitch you had to prove something special, because the referee was on their side. At half-time the ref would have tea or a bit or orange with them, not with

174

us. I can't ever remember a referee stopping at half-time with us. We did once have a black referee, an African. He weren't no good either. I didn't really want a black ref, 'cos if we won the opposition would complain. It wasn't a colour thing for us, but the opposition *made* it a colour thing.

Despite the routine and corrosive problems of racism, Rangers quickly moved up the ranks of junior local football, winning the Leicester Mutual League title a record six times in seven seasons, the Leicester Junior Cup twice (1987, 1988) and the prestigious national *Caribbean Times* Cup in 1987. Arguably, by this time Rangers were the strongest 'black' local league club in Britain and they were unquestionably the best junior club in Leicestershire ('The Untouchables' according to the local football press). Highfield applied to join the Leicestershire Senior League, a natural move for a club with this sort of record. In fact, the club was made to apply to the Senior League three times in ten years; on each occasion their application was turned down. This sort of 'ethnic closure' is, clearly not confined to the local league level of football or to Britain (See, Gehrmann, this volume).

Forced eventually, to move *out* of the county in order to play senior football, Rangers were accepted into the more competitive and prestigious Central Midlands League at first time of asking (1988), a move which also meant travel to play matches around Derbyshire, Nottinghamshire, Lincolnshire and even South Yorkshire, an expense the club could hardly afford. It also sometimes meant new opponents in inhospitable villages with all the usual problems of overt racism. Rangers' treatment at the hands of the football establishment in their home county was bitterly felt inside the club and it seemed to confirm Rangers' status as unwanted 'outsiders' in local senior football circles. 'Sola' comments, with remarkable restraint in the circumstances, on the effects of the local barriers to promotion:

We don't really feel we are part of county football because certainly in my opinion it's like we are the county's Achilles heel. They know we are good, they know we are good enough, but they deny us the status and the avenues to cement that status. If we are going to become recognized at senior football we have to go

175

the long way round; we have to spend ridiculous sums of money on travel to ensure games at the right standard. It's like we are being cut off from the main road and having to go the back route and I feel very strongly about this. I'm disgusted at the way there is this covert attitude towards the club now; at one time it was very open but now it's covert and you can't challenge it 'cos there will always be a 'justifiable' attitude for it happening.

Money, money, money

In 1992, a decade after the club's first application for senior status in their home county, Rangers were eventually admitted into a depleted Leicestershire Senior League. Highfield are currently chasing their first Senior League title (they lie second, January 1994) and seem finally to have achieved a degree of acceptance into their rightful place in senior football circles in the county. Finance remains a problem, however; many of Rangers' main opponents are able, and choose, to pay their players and a number of top Rangers' players have been lured away to other local clubs and further afield (Dion Dublin, for example, eventually all the way to Manchester United). Rangers don't pay players. The feeling inside the club is that ambitious and talented players can't be 'blamed' for seeking rewards elsewhere, but also that the traditions and the 'meaning' of the club should be, and usually are, sufficient to hold players at least from joining local rivals. In many cases of course, and despite the financial offers elsewhere, it is still important for young local black players to *play* for Rangers. As 'Gary' points out:

> I've never thought about leaving Rangers, 'cos ... this is a black club, and all that, and I just don't think I'd fit in with any other club. I'd only leave if I was going to another club where I knew the majority of the other players. I'm committed to Highfield Rangers....It's like a family and to go away and play for another club especially if you have to play against Rangers ... I don't think, personally, I need paying to play for Rangers, a lot of youngsters though seem more money orientated. I just want to play and get Rangers up there.

For 'Morris' and other long standing club members, unsurprisingly, it is important that players come to the club for reasons other than the sort of cash rewards which are widely on offer elsewhere. (Fans of professional clubs often express the same sentiments; that players should play because, like the fans, they *love* the club). Cash contracts threaten some of the traditional functions and patterns of recruitment of local clubs, but the feeling persists at Rangers that the wider 'community' functions of the club will continue to attract local black talent and the sorts of players more generally who insist on 'playing for the shirt' and not for the cash.

There is no doubting in the accounts of Rangers' members their view of the wider importance of the club to the local black community in Leicester. This is perhaps especially so since the club has involved itself in supporting football for women and youth and in promoting training and employment opportunities for members of the Highfields community. That is not to say support inside the club for the women's game is universal; far from it. It is still, also, very much the Highfields *men* who spend two, three, four or more nights a week 'down Rangers' and who often find their relationships with partners and girlfriends fatally compromised by the 'demands' of the club. ("I was playing football Saturday, Sunday, Tuesday, Wednesday, Thursday, Friday, Saturday. I came home on Sunday and all the doors were locked. And she said, 'You don't live here any more; you spend all your time at football!'" 'Sola').

The club is highly valued, of course, for its local standing and for the opportunities and experiences it continues to provide for the people who have built the club and for younger members of the black community who are coming through to take on an administrative role in the running of Rangers. In 'Phonso's' words, "I'm proud of the club, but there are other issues in the community; we're a community organization not just football teams. Take football for what it is, education, careers, advice should really be flowing from the club. There is enough experience in the club and it is not right to ignore issues that surround you just to play football".

Endpiece

Rangers' ambitions are high, some might argue unrealistically so.

The current talk at the club is about floodlights and a little grandstand but it doesn't take much to get older members waxing even about Football League status for the club, "before I die", or about the examples now set by black people in the professional game. There is media talk, and more, in 1994, for example, that Manchester United's Paul Ince will cement his place as the first black captain of the national team. Of special interest here, too, is that at the time of writing (January 1994) three black ex-professionals - Keith Alexander at Lincoln City; Viv Anderson at Barnsley; and Tony Cunningham at Doncaster Rovers - are managing League clubs.

No one is fooled at Rangers, of course, that these overdue and modest successes signal the end of the institutionalized racism in sport which has rendered black athletes, both here and in the US, largely, "seen but not heard" (Lapchick and Rodriguez, 1990; Maguire, 1991). Remarks by Garth Crooks, the Chair of the strangely anonymous Institute of Professional Sport, that, "Sport is a foundation of social integration", and that black involvement in sport, "has allowed people to feel more comfortable with the society we live in because sport shows a truer face of multi-racial Britain", also seem forcefully idealistic and overblown. ('Can blacks win the power race?', The Observer, 6 June 1993). These recent developments in the professional game are, nevertheless, especially hopeful signs which give pleasure at a local football club where the management and administration functions have sometimes been given an understandably stronger emphasis because of the view among its members that it is especially, "important in this day and age that black people are seen to run and organize things" ('Sam').

Acknowledgements

I would like to thank Rangers' players, past and present, especially Laurence Redmond, for their involvement in this research, but also Stephen Small and Sallie Westwood for their helpful comments on an earlier draft of this paper.

Highfield Rangers circa 1970: the 'sharpshooters' are born
Source: Highfield Rangers

Black and white unite: key Rangers' stalwarts of the early 1980s
Source: Highfield Rangers

The untouchables: Rangers pick up another trophy
Source: Highfield Rangers

A Rangers' legend: the late Nigel 'Natty' Burke, FA Vase v Stourport, 0-0, 1990
Source: Leicester Mercury

Bibliography

Cashmore, E. (1982) *Black Sportsmen*, Routledge, London.

Cohen, P. (1988) 'The perversions of inheritance: studies in the making of multi-racist Britain', in Cohen, P. and Bains, H. (eds.) *Multi-Racist Britain*, Macmillan, London.

Curran, M. and Redmond, L. (1991) 'We'll support you evermore?', Sir Norman Chester Centre for Football Research, University of Leicester.

Fleming, S. (1992) 'Sport and South Asian Male Youth', PhD Thesis, Brighton University.

Football Association (1991) *Blueprint for Football*, Football Association, London.

Gilroy, P. (1987),*There Ain't No Black in the Union Jack*, Hutchinson, London.

Hall, S. (1992) 'What is this 'black' in black popular culture?', in Dent, G. (ed) *Black Popular Culture*, Bay Press, Seattle.

Hill, D. (1989) *Out of his Skin*, Faber, London.

Hornby, N. (1992) *Fever Pitch: a Fan's Life*, Gollanz, London.

Jones, S. (1988) *Black Culture,White Youth*, Macmillan, London.

Lapchick, R. and Rodriquez, A. (1990) 'Professional sports: the 1990 racial report card'. *Centre for the Study of Sport in Society Digest* 2, (2).

Maguire, J. (1988) 'Race and position in English soccer', *Sociology of Sport Journal* 5, pp257-69.

Murray, B. (1984),*The Old Firm: Sectarianism, Sport and Society in Scotland*, John Donald, Edinburgh.

Parkinson, N. (1969) 'The Highfields Project 1967/69. A report by a full-time youth worker for Highfields'. City of Leicester Education Department, Leicester.

Small, S. (1992) 'Racialised ideologies, class relations and the state in England.' Paper given at the Critical Theory Conference, University of Nottingham, 6-8 July.

Taylor, I. (1976) 'Spectator violence around soccer: the decline of the working class weekend', *Research Papers in Physical Education*, 4.1.

Taylor, I. (1993) 'A whole new ball game', Paper presented to the Centre for Study of Sport and Society, University of Leicester, 18 June.

Sugden, J. and Bairner, A. (1993) *Sport, Sectarianism and Society in a Divided Ireland*, Leicester University Press, Leicester.

Thomas, J. (1994) 'Non-League football: A survey of clubs in the Diadora League', Leicester, Sir Norman Chester Centre for Football Research.

Vasali, P. (1994),*The History of Black Footballers in Britain*, (forthcoming).

Ward, A., Taylor, R. with Williams, J. (1993) *Three Sides of The Mersey: An Oral History of Everton, Liverpool and Tranmere Rovers*, Robson Books, London.

Westwood, S. (1990) 'Racism, black masculinity and the politics of space', in Hearn, J. and Morgan, D. (eds.) *Men, Masculinities and Social Theory*, Unwin Hyman, London.

Westwood, S. (1991) 'Red Star Over Leicester', in Werbner, P. and Anwar, M. (eds.)*Black and Ethnic Leadership in Britain*, Routledge, London.

Williams, J. (1989) *Football into the 1990s*, Leicester, Sir Norman Chester Centre for Football Research.

Williams, J. (1990) 'Lick my boots: racism in English football', Leicester, Sir Norman Chester Centre for Football Research.

Williams, J. (1992) 'Ordinary heroes?: England international football players in the 1990's' *Innovation* 5 (4).

Williams, J. (1994) 'Foul Play?: a survey of football referees in the Midlands', Leicester, Sir Norman Chester Centre for Football Research.

Williams, J. and Smith, M. (1994) 'The Carling Premiership surveys', Leicester, Sir Norman Chester Centre for Football Research

Williams, J. and Taylor, R. (1994) 'Boys keep swinging: football and masculinity' in Newburn, T. and Stanko, E. (eds.) *Just Boys Doing Business*, London, Routledge (forthcoming).'

Williams, J. and Woodhouse, J. (1991) 'Can play, will play: women and football in Britain', in Williams, J. and Wagg, S. *British Football and Social Change*, Leicester University Press, Leicester.

Williams, J., Dunning, E. and Murphy, P. (1989) *Hooligans Abroad*, Routledge, London.

7 Football and identity in the Ruhr: The case of Schalke 04

Siegfried Gehrmann

At any given time a soccer team's influence on its hometown and on the local economy depends largely on its success on the field. Now, while it is obvious that a team high in the top division generates public interest and draws fans into the stadium, its standing in the community is not simply a matter of winning and losing. The social and economic impact of a club can also be conditioned by its history. In what follows I would like to deal with this aspect of a German professional club. In particular, I will sketch the history of a soccer club from Gelsenkirchen, an industrial city of 350,000 inhabitants which is located roughly between Dortmund and Düsseldorf, that is, in the middle of the Ruhr region, the largest industrial centre in Germany. Let me begin, though, by providing some background information on the Ruhr region itself.

The Ruhr region - structure and development

The Ruhr region is one of the world's biggest industrial agglomerations, and to many visitors it looks like one huge city. However, this region cannot be regarded as a metropolis in the strict sense of the term. It has no centre and no unified administration. Even today, the region is divided up by ancient territorial and traditional boundaries. Important decisions affecting the planning of land uses, communications and industrial and other economic developments, are made outside the region. Basically, the Ruhr region is a high ranking but extremely decentralized urban area. It is an urban association, a city of cities, or an urban realm. This body's loose organization and limited powers contrast strikingly with its constituency - eleven cities with a total population of around 3.6 million spread over 1680 square kilometres, and four districts (Kreise) with some 1.8 million inhabitants covering just under 2,800 square kilometres. The whole agglomeration thus contains nearly 5.5 million residents.(1)

Although mining and metalworking were established early in the Ruhr region, the real economic take-off phase did not occur until the 1840s and 1850s. Outcropping coal had been mined on the slopes of the Ruhr valley to the parallel line of the Hellweg, an ancient trade route running from the Rhine to Middle Germany via Essen, Dortmund and Soest. From now on, the heavy industries became the leading sector of German industrialization.(2)

The characteristics of this early industrial concentration were dictated solely by the profit orientated locational decisions of individual owners, and subsequently of public companies, partly financed by foreign capital. There were no large towns at first; until the middle of the nineteenth century the old-established Hellweg towns remained small, decayed communities, centres of handicrafts and semi-rural pursuits with virtually no central-place functions.(3)

Clearly, the region's existing population could not provide the labour force which this rapid industrial growth required. From the 1840s to the end of the 1860s, a first wave of migration brought 50,000 people into the Ruhr. It was, as yet, short-distance migration from nearby agricultural districts and former areas of domestic industry, where poverty now threatened. From early on, the employers started to provide housing for at least some of their workers, but such 'planning' as this involved did not extend further than the needs of the industrial concerns. Workers' colonies were built as close as possible to the works, since residence in such settlements linked the workers more closely to the enterprise, aided discipline, and discouraged rapid labour turnover. Furthermore, the colonies helped to integrate new arrivals from agricultural areas into an industrial style of life and work.(4)

At first, the indigenous elites in the old Hellweg towns took a sceptical view of this industrial revolution. In the end, however, they integrated with the new, industrial, middle and upper classes. In the town councils, they exercised a growing influence on the continuing physical expansion of industry, to such an extent that some of their actions verged on planning. These efforts were, however, confined to the individual towns. They did not relate to the industrial region as a whole, which was still gradually pushing northwards. Indeed, in the third zone, the Emscher strip (Emscher is a small river which flows parallel to the Ruhr river) matters were completely different. So sparsely settled was this area at first that for a long time the industrialists found no established structures, or interests, other than their own, to worry about. There was no upper class there, and apart from a few prosperous townfolk, and rural craftsmen, there was almost no middle class either. In any case, during the last thirty years of the century these indigenous interests were drowned in a mighty wave of immigration from the east, and notably from East Prussia.

During the period of high industrialization, some 800,000 migrants came into the Ruhr region from the east. They settled predominantly in the newly developing northern part of the coalfield, which meant the northern districts of the Hellweg zone, but even more the Emscher zone and, from the turn of the century, a fourth zone - the Vestische zone - where mining had since been opened up. There were a few model 'colonies' in which the mine owners provided their workers with a small house, a garden and a stable. Most of the new arrivals, however, ended up in hideous, poorly equipped, and overcrowded housing, which was thrown up in the shortest possible time with complete disregard for the pre-existing environment. Whereas, by the end of the century, some kind of urban infrastructure was beginning to emerge in the Hellweg towns, in the newer zones it was completely absent, so that there existed, in extreme cases, settlements of up to 100,000 inhabitants with the legal status of a village. By now, the Ruhr region was regarded throughout Germany as a 'coalscuttle', an area of grime, noise and lowering skies. This image was based principally on the jagged landscape of winding towers, spoilheaps, colliery buildings, crisscrossing transport lines and straggling housing areas which typified the Emscher zone.[5]

It should be clear by now that at the end of the nineteenth century the Ruhr region lacked a unitary structure and did not even possess a single, dominating urban core. At best, the Hellweg strip might be regarded as a core area, but certainly no more than this. The situation was further complicated by the fact that between the cities of Essen and Bochum there ran, from north to south, the historic boundary between the Rhineland and Westphalia. When the whole region was handed over to Prussia at the Congress of Vienna, the boundary remained in existence, to the extent that the western part of the future Ruhr region was included in the Düsseldorf county (Regierunsbezirk) of the newly-created province of the Rhineland, whereas the eastern part was incorporated into the province of Westphalia. To add to the confusion, the eastern areas were further divided between two Westphalian counties. The Gelsenkirchen-Recklinghausen area became part of the county of Münster, while the remainder, a larger area, was made part of the county of Arnsberg.(6) These administrative boundaries remain very significant today. In the second half of the nineteenth century, all three county presidents kept a jealous eye on the soaring economic significance of the Ruhr region, with a view to protecting their established interests and influence.(7)   However, their rivalry was paralleled by competition between the eastern and western Hellweg towns.

Particularly prominent were Essen, which saw itself as 'the heart of the coalfield', and Dortmund, which clung to its proud tradition as a one time free imperial city. Moreover, it was not without importance that the Protestant and Catholic churches of the Ruhr were organized from centres outside the region, their institutions conforming to the traditional boundaries. Particularly significant, however, was the fact that important economic decisions affecting the Ruhr region were not made locally but in more distant cities. Düsseldorf was the main one, but Cologne and Berlin also had their say, because interested banks, and the head offices of numerous public companies active in the Ruhr, were located there.(8)

In spite of some relevant plans and efforts, up to the present the Ruhr region hasn't gained from the formation of a specifically political organization and of a politically compact unit, which is seen for this region - especially before the background of a united Europe - as a question of vital importance.(9) There has been no emergence of a sufficiently strong regional patriotism as a necessary condition for the rise of a politically effective local organization. But in spite of all these difficulties one can identify some trends and developments in the Ruhr region which, on a longer-term basis, are producing a very strong socio-psychological attachment to the area. In this respect the organized soccer of the top level seems to be of exceptional relevance.

Soccer and fans in the Ruhr

In the Ruhr region organized soccer started at the end of the last century.[10] The first soccer clubs were of bourgeois origins. This social profile changed after the First World War. In the twenties, in rising number, clubs which originated from working class areas gained in importance. The most successful clubs here are Gelsenkirchen-Schalke 04 Football Club (Schalke is a suburb of the industrial town of Gelsenkirchen) and Borussia 09 Dortmund.[11] Schalke 04 won the German championship for the first time in 1934, Borussia Dortmund in 1956. These dates were the starting points of a long chain of great successes for these clubs up to the present day. The enormous popularity Schalke 04 and Borussia Dortmund have gained, not only in their home towns but in the whole Ruhr region, resulted without doubt from their brilliant performances. But this isn't the only motive for the enthusiasm of the Ruhr people. To understand more clearly the popularity of clubs like these one must take into consideration the special nature of the social environment in which they grew up.[12] Let us look in some detail at the history and background of Schalke 04.

Schalke 04

Gelsenkirchen-Schalke 04 FC was founded as 'Westfalia Schalke' on May 4, 1904, in Schalke, a suburb of Gelsenkirchen. It was a neighbourhood team composed of youths aged fourteen to sixteen.[13] Most of the team lived in the Hauergasse Lane in Schalke or in the immediate vicinity, near the Consolidation 1/6 colliery and the Kuppersbusch oven factory. The club colours were red and yellow at first to be replaced after the First World War by white and blue, the traditional club colours today.

In the early days of its existence Westfalia Schalke did not belong to a sports association and thus was a 'wild' club, which might play only against other 'wild' clubs. Clubs belonging to the associations were generally forbidden, under threat of severe punishment, to play against non-member clubs. Westfalia Schalke tried twice in vain to enter the *Westdeutsche Spielverband,* or the West German Sport Association (WSV), the largest organization supporting football in West Germany and a sub-association of the *Deutschen Fussballfund,* the German Football Association (DFB). It was finally successful in 1915. After the First World War, Westfalia Schalke amalgamated with the much older 'Schalke 1877 Gymnastic Club' and became the new 'Schalke 1877 Gymnastic and Sports Club'. At the beginning of the 1920s the *Deutsche Turnerschaft* or 'German Gymnastic Association' to which the '1877' belonged, insisted on gymnastics and sports being 'separated completely', and on club members not belonging, simultaneously, to other sports associations. This led to the football section leaving the '1877' again in the middle of the 1923/4 season. It was re-formed in January 1924 as an independent club, not under the old name, Westfalia Schalke, but as Schalke 04 Football Club. In this way the original foundation year of 1904 was incorporated into the club name. Many members of the club lived in the area of Gelsenkirchen, so in 1928, the board resolved to lengthen the name to Gelsenkirchen-Schalke 04 FC, the name which the club still bears today.(14)

In the early days of its existence, Westfalia Schalke was run by Gerhard Klopp and Heinrich Kullmann. Klopp, born in 1890 and a native of Schalke, worked as a fitter in the Consolidation Colliery. Kullmann, born in 1889, was also a native of Schalke and a fitter by trade. Westfalia Schalke was not recognised as a formal club by the municipal authorities because it was run by these lowly young men. Formal recognition was an important requirement for admission into the West German Football Association, to which the club aspired. Eventually, a foreman, Heinrich Hilger, was elected club President in 1909. Hilgert had probably never been an active player for Westfalia, but he took an active interest in the Schalke youth games in the club's early days. During the war, a bank clerk, Robert Schuermann, ran the club and after he was called up for war duty, his wife, Christine, the daughter of a Schalke public house landlord, took over. The temporary amalgamation of the club with the Schalke 1877 Gymnastic Club brought Westfalia Schalke into contact with a man who was to be of great importance for its development, the then president of the 1877 club, Fritz Unkel.

Fritz Unkel had originally been a coal dealer, but he then worked as a goods manager in the Consolidation Colliery, and was from an old-established Gelsenkirchen family: his father had been one of the first works-managers of Consolidation. When the football section left the Schalke 1877 Gymnastic and Sports Club in 1924 and established itself as an independent club, Fritz Unkel stayed with the football players, although he had always been an enthusiastic athlete. He became the first president of the newly-founded Schalke 04 FC and he retained this function, with only short interruptions, until 1939. Then, at the age of 74, he was appointed honorary president. According to the accounts of those who experienced his leadership of the club, Fritz Unkel must, more or less, have been what is typically called the 'soul' of the club; a leading and integrating figure around whom the whole life of the club was orientated. It was mainly thanks to his initiative as goods manager in the Consolidation Colliery that the company supported the club in such a generous fashion. The most obvious example of this support was the construction of the Gluckauf Stadium, completed in 1928. The land for this ground, one of the largest football stadiums in West Germany with a capacity of about 40,000 spectators, was ceded to Schalke by 'Consol', as the colliery was popularly known in Gelsenkirchen, for a trifling rent on a 99 year lease.(15)

The structure and background of Schalke 04

When Westfalia Schalke was founded in 1904 the club had only 16 members. The number increased to 80 or 90 members within 10 years. After the First World War, membership increased considerably. By 1930, Schalke 04 FC had about 1,100 members, including those in the boxing, light athletic and handball sections, which, however, were much smaller than the football section. I shall now attempt to describe more exactly the club's social structure, which these figures conceal. Some preliminary remarks in this connection are appropriate. Firstly, the complete Schalke 04 FC archives, including the personnel register which had been kept in the Thiemeyer club house on Schalke Square, were destroyed in an Allied bombing raid in the Autumn of 1994. Nevertheless, it was possible to discover the occupational background of a proportion of the club membership by means of an evaluation of club records, newspapers, address-books and the files of Gelsenkirchen registration and registry office archives, supplemented by information from former club members.(16)

In this fashion, 254 people can be identified who had been members of Schalke 04 FC for a period in the decades 1904-13, 1914-23 and 1924-34. From 1904-13 a total of 44 people are recorded; of these, 22 were miners, 15 factory workers or craftsmen, five salaried or higher employees, two self-employed. For 1914-23 a total of 88 people are recorded; of these 40 were miners, 33 factory workers or craftsmen, 11 salaried or higher employees and four self-employed. For 1924-34, 122 members were traced; of these, 34 were miners, 57 were factory workers or craftsmen, 22 salaried or higher employees and nine self-employed. According to this investigation, the Schalke members were predominantly manual workers: miners, factory workers and craftsmen, although there is a tendency towards falling numbers of these at times. We must allow for the fact in this connection that the people identified as salaried or higher employees or the self-employed themselves originated from working-class families, with only a few exceptions. Thus, there was, for example, a number of club members, particularly pit foremen, who worked as salaried employees, but whose fathers and brothers were working men. The high proportion of miners among the workers is also noticeable. It was 59 per cent in 1904-13, 55 per cent in 1914-23 and fell to 37 per cent in the third decade. Since a number of pit salaried employees, especially pit foremen, are included in the section 'salaried or higher employees', the total number of Schalke members who were working in the pits was actually far above these figures.

To the fact that Schalke 04 was, in its formative years, a 'workers club' was added the peculiarity that most of the members, or their parents, originated from the southern part of East Prussia and thus from German-Polish border territory. As 'working men' they were numbered among the 'lower class' and as a result of this fact alone were at the bottom of the social prestige scale. But, in addition, they belonged to a national group which had little social esteem in Germany, as 'Polacken', this being the accepted abusive expression for Germans with Polish-sounding names. (In the mid-1920s there were players such as Szepan, Kuzorra, Sobotka, Czerwinski, Jaczek, Krischik, Przybylski and Gottschewski in Schalke 04's first team). In this respect club members felt doubly oppressed by the middle-classes i.e. in both social and national terms.[17] This forms the background to a development which was extremely important for the history of Schalke 04.

As has already been mentioned, Westfalia Schalke joined the West German Football Association (DFB) in 1915. The latter association had been founded in 1898 in Düsseldorf as the 'Rheinischer Players' Club' by clubs whose members, as far as can now be ascertained, originated predominantly from the middle class. When the working class clubs joined the DFB the dominance of middle-class clubs was at first hardly touched. This changed after the First World War. In the western Ruhr region, for example, the Duisburg Football Club 1908, situated in the Duisburg working-class district Hochfield, caused more and more of a stir on account of its outstanding achievements. In the Gelsenkirchen region it was particularly the football section of Schalke 1877 Gymnastic and Sports Club which attracted attention because of its excellent performances.(18)

Class conflict and the DFB

Since 1919, the West German Football Association has had a classification system grading from bottom to top, as follows:C Class, B Class, A Class, County League, District Class. A system of automatic promotion and relegation originally linked the leagues. In 1923 this ruling was interrupted. The new system which was then introduced scheduled a two-year interruption of promotion and relegation. The aim of this 'new way', as the DFB called it, was to counteract the hectic atmosphere in the football world, caused by the principle of achievement and recognizable in the increasingly violent and bitter way the teams fought while playing. This step, justified officially by the DFB as a measure to raise general sporting morale, was regarded in a different fashion by the Schalke camp. The ban on promotion decreed by the DFB was here felt to be an attempt on the part of the middle-class DFB to debar the working-class clubs, especially Schalke, which appeared from 1919 to be ascending the league ladder unchecked (they had climbed from the B Class via the A Class into the Emscher League between 1919 and 1921), one league from entering the elite division of German football - the District Class. Whether this interpretation was justified can be left undecided, since in any case there is no way of proving it. At any rate no-one in the Schalke camp had the slightest doubt about the matter: the middle-class clubs were behind the promotion stop, a measure chiefly directed at the Gelsenkirchen 'Pole and Prole Club'.

"They didn't want to have us in their top division"(19); "the middle-class clubs, Black-White Essen, and so on, wanted only to play against the likes of themselves"(20). Today, these are the views of two former Schalke players, assessing the situation of that time. They and their comrades reacted to the challenge in their own way. Conscious of being victims of envy and ill-will and of forfeiting their well-earned sporting success for reasons of class and national origin, they did not resign but instead mobilized new energies. They closed ranks together in the club more tightly than ever. If the slogan 'conspiratorial community' was ever justified when applied to Schalke club life, then it was especially at that time. Training was intensified and systematized: this was when the foundation for the later famous 'Schalke Top' was laid, a system of playing which united beauty and success in a fashion hitherto unknown; and when, in 1925, the promotion ban had to be abandoned because of decreasing spectator interest in matches, it was to signal the starting-point of a meteoric rise by the Schalkers. The club won seven German championships between 1934 and 1958 and made the name of Schalke 04 synonymous with the highest football ability. The enthusiasm in Gelsenkirchen and the whole Ruhr region aroused by the successful Schalkers was overwhelming. Some impression of this enthusiasm can be gained from a report by the newspaper, *Vestische Neueste Nachrichten*, when Schalke 04 beat Nuremberg FC on 24 June 1934 in the Berlin Poststadium in the final game of the German football championships. In this report, headlined 'A Chaos of Joy', a journalist comments on Schalke's return:

> The return of the eleven miners, who had carried the day at the German Football Championship in their thrilling final contest, in a victory which was well-earned and uncertain until the very last second, was an unprecedented triumphal procession. Fanatical enthusiasm for sport and football mounted in an unimaginable fashion. People lined the streets waiting hours in advance for their football heroes. Traffic had to be diverted. As the express bearing the miners' team drew on to the platform, rapturous sports fever swept all regulations aside. Lord Mayor Bohmert just managed to shake one hand briefly at the train window and then Szepan, Kuzorra and the championship trophy, the

'Victoria', were carried high over the rejoicing heads on to the Gelsenkirchen station yard. An unprecedented number of police had, with difficulty, kept order up to that moment, but when the people saw their sporting idols appear at the station entrance there was no holding them .... Order and discipline were simply swept aside: everything sank in an overwhelming wave of overflowing joy in sport which washed everything away .... and the Schalke miners marched like conquering heroes through the huge avenue of hundreds and thousands of followers to the Schalke market place, where a great civic victory celebration took place.(21)

The club's great days are long gone but by no means forgotten. Its popularity especially among the lower social classes has not suffered. This explains even today its enormous significance for its home town, especially with respect to its general prestige and economic activities. I would like now to turn to this subject.

Schalke 04 FC and Gelsenkirchen today

As already implied, Gelsenkirchen was, traditionally, a city of coal, iron and steel. Its reputation as a densely packed industrial city has lent the area a negative image, similar to that suffered generally by the Ruhr Valley, commonly referred to in Germany as the Ruhr Pot, symbolic of foundries and heavy industry. The traditional image accepted all over the country was that of a ravaged industrial landscape with acute environmental pollution, a paucity of education and cultural facilities and a poor quality of life.

Today, Gelsenkirchen is a city undergoing a process of radical and difficult change. The focal points of industry have shifted considerably; the dominance of coal and steel has given way to diversification involving, as major elements, mechanical engineering, environmental technology, new materials, production technology and energy engineering. Gelsenkirchen industry is no longer geared solely to the coal and steel sectors; the coal and steel complex is currently responsible for only 16 per cent of the area's gross domestic product and employs around 33 per cent of all industrial workers in the city. In the secondary sector, the majority of

195

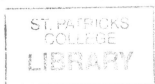

the employees no longer work in raw materials, but in investment goods. But to think of this process as being complete is presumptuous. Above average unemployment rates; the relatively low growth dynamic in the higher quality production orientated services such as marketing and industrial consultancy; the below average growth rates for those unemployed in the service sector; and above-average losses of jobs in production industries and an increasing lack of skilled personnel - all testify to the fact that the structural changes are far from comprehensive.(22)

In this economically difficult situation it is immensely important for Gelsenkirchen to improve its image and that the city's name be associated with a sport that for many people invokes action, excitement, and energy and that such values be spread far and wide. Gelsenkirchen-Schalke 04 FC achieves both of these objectives. Using the name of the city, it still exercises its power over many people. Two examples will demonstrate this point. *Die Bildzeitung* is an inter-regional tabloid newspaper with the largest circulation (5.4 million) of any daily newspaper in Germany. In the 1989/90 football season, which lasted from the beginning of July until the end of March (that is, approximately 277 days), this newspaper published, according to Schalke's own count, 335 stories on Gelsenkirchen-Schalke. In the same period parts of games involving Gelsenkirchen-Schalke were seen on television by 330 million viewers according to the various networks' own statistics. The average length of coverage was eight minutes.(23)

In addition to its public relations value for the city, the club's economic role deserves special attention. Here, a few examples will also prove useful. Despite its relative decline, the club still draws large audiences for home matches. Its average attendance (1992) of 40,000 fans is second only to BV Borussia 09 Dortmund. Approximately half of the Schalke fans do not live in Gelsenkirchen, and some travel as far as sixty miles to attend home games. The yearly income from ticket sales is about 12 million DM (approximately £4 million), of which the city of Gelsenkirchen receives seven per cent, or approximately 840,000 DM, in taxes.(24)

Schalke's stadium grounds include parking facilities, owned by the city of Gelsenkirchen, for 22,000 vehicles. As the stadium lies on the outskirts of the city and can easily be reached by motorways and divided highways, many fans drive to the games, which means that the parking lots generate sizeable revenue. The city thus derives an additional annual income of around 300,000 DM.(25)

The club's most important sponsor is the local branch of a company that makes aluminium wheels for cars. The owner of the company, Rüdiger Hoffken, is also the treasurer of the club and, automatically, a member of its board of directors. He has cleverly succeeded in using the club to advertise his company's trade name RH ALURAD, an anagram composed of his initials plus a German abbreviation for aluminium wheels. This trade name appears on the jerseys of the players, the stadium scoreboard, tickets, team posters, and club souvenirs such as shirts, caps, scarves and jogging suits. The great significance of this advertising for the company can be inferred from the results of marketing research. In January, before the company's advertising campaign with the club was launched, only eight per cent of the population in the Ruhr Valley recognised the company's name. At the end of the year this figure had risen to 60%.(26)

Let us conclude this article by trying to contextualize Schalke 04's more recent economic position by looking at football in the Rhur more generally.

The economics of professional football in the Ruhr

All professional soccer clubs of the Ruhr region raised their budgets for the season 1992/93. At the top were Borussia Dortmund with 17.5 million DM, followed by Schalke 04 with 15.0 million, VfL Bochum with 10.0 million, SG Wattenscheid 09 with 7.0 million and MSV Duisburg with 7.8 million. Most expenses are produced by the salaries of the players who earn about 30,000 to 40,000 DM a month. But there are some exceptions. Stephan Reuter at Borussia Dortmund, for instance, who transferred from Juventus, earned about 120,000 DM a month. To cover their high expenses the clubs use three sources of income: admission tickets, television and sponsoring.

(a) Gate money

All five clubs have big stadiums. The largest is the Parkstadion of Schalke 04 in the northern part of Gelsenkirchen. It has a capacity of

71,000 spectators and will be replaced in 1995 by a new stadium costing about 400 million DM, which can be completely enclosed through installation of a rectractable roof. The stadiums of the other clubs have a capacity of 42,000 spectators (VfL Bochum), 42,000 (Borussia Dortmund), 32,000 (MSV Duisburg) and 20,000 (SG Wattenscheid).

As far as the numbers of spectators are concerned, Schalke 04 and Borussia Dortmund rank in the first place. In 1991/92, Borussia Dortmund had an average of about 44,000 spectators at every home game. Schalke 04 had an average of about 47,000. Each spectator paid an average of about 15 DM to watch matches. Thus, at the end of the season both clubs had gate money of more than 11 million DM. The clubs of Duisburg, Bochum and Wattenscheid received only a third to a half of these sums in gate receipts.

(b) Television money

Television money takes second place in the order of money sources. In Germany in the past ten years the prices for the right to broadcast soccer games on television have risen twentyfold. This rapid increase in cost has been caused by the fact that in Germany, until quite recently, there was a public monopoly on broadcasting and therefore there was no competition in the marketing of the rights to transmission. But now some private television stations have been established and so in recent years the situation has fundamentally changed. In addition to that, one must take into consideration the fact that in Germany there has been a continual reduction of working hours; leisure time has grown in importance and a rapidly rising number of people now watch TV. For the period 1992 to 1997, the German Football Association has sold the rights to transmission to a private television station (SAT 1) for 700 million DM. That means that each club of the First Division gets 4.1 million DM a season. For clubs like VfL Bochum and Wattenscheid 09, these sums are of great importance, because their gate money is relatively low.

(c) Sponsorship

In Germany, apart from tennis, golf and motor sport, football is a kind of sport for which sponsorship is of the greatest importance.[31]

There are three forms of sponsorship. These are the sponsoring of athletes, teams and sporting events. Though in Germany there are some football players who are sponsored, the typical form of sponsorship is that of whole teams. In this context it is remarkable that as a growing trend football clubs and firms sign contracts on a long term basis, of two and more years, in order to secure stable financial advantages.

In 1991, Shalke 04 received 2.3 million DM from their main sponsor, a Bavarian dairy (Alois Müller); Borussia Dortmund received 1.5 million DM from the German assurance organization Continentale and the American clothing firm Nike; MSV Duisburg took 400,000 DM from the German builders and contractors Gotzen Baumarkte; SG Wattenscheid 09 received 500,000 DM from Steilmann, the largest European clothing firm and VfL Bochum 600,000 DM from the German marketing company Trigema.

Teams and players

Until quite recently in Germany professional soccer clubs were allowed to recruit four foreign players. Since July 1 1992, because of the arrangement UEFA reached with the European Community, clubs are now allowed to play only three foreign players. In addition to that ruling clubs can sign an unlimited number of players provided that they come from a country of the European Community. Four of the five professional clubs in the Ruhr region usually play three foreign players.

It seems remarkable, however, that the pools of professional players at all five clubs consist largely of German players. Foreign players constitute about 14% of team squads and foreign players from the European Community only 4%. How far this situation will change remains to be seen. It is noteworthy, however, that representatives of the boards of all five clubs suggested to the author that in the near future they are not going to change their policies in this respect; i.e. there are no local plans to sign considerably more foreign players from the European Community.

Conclusion

If one would want to draw a conclusion from the latter part of this discussion, perhaps one would point to the fact that in view of European unification, with its tendency towards levelling national differences, regional solidarity can be of greatest importance as a manifestation of the protection of cultural differences. It is clear that in the Ruhr region, professional soccer is very relevant as a means to found and stabilize local identity. It might be interesting to apply such an approach via a European perspective. This could be carried through by comparing systematically some European regions of a similar industrial structure as the Ruhr region concerning the local function of professional soccer. So, it would be interesting to research the cities of Milan and Turin in Italy, Barcelona in Spain, St Etienne in France and, for example, Manchester, Sheffield and Liverpool in northern England. It goes without saying that such a comparative study could only be realized, if social scientists of different countries work together to give such work a properly co-ordinated European dimension.

Schalke's players advertise their greatest sponsor
Source: Schalke Kreisel, official club publication of Gelsenkirchen-
Schalke 04, July 1990

Schalke's players advertise their greatest sponsor
Source: Schalke Kreisel, official club publication of Gelsenkirchen-
Schalke 04, 1990/91

Notes

1. The figures relate to 1979 and are taken from the brochure, 'Wechsel auf die Zukunft', published by the Kommunalverband Ruhrgebiet. April 1980.

2. For a good overview of Ruhr history, see Walter Foerst (1967) (ed.) *Rheinisch-westfalische* Rückblende, Koln/Berlin.

3. Hulmuth Croon, op. cit., pp.188-189.

4. For further discussion of the Ruhr housing problem, see Franz J. Bruggemeier and Lutz Niethammer (1978) 'Schlafganger, Schnapskasinos und schwerindustrielle Kolonie. Aspekte der Arbeiterwohnungsfrage im Rurhgebiet vor dem Ersten Weltkrieg', in: Jurgen Reulecke and Wolfhard Weber (eds.) *Frabrik, Familie, Feierabend: Beitrage zur Sozialgeschichte des Alltags im Industriezeitalter*, Wuppertal, pp.135-175.

5. See, Wilhelm Brepohl (1957) *Indusatrievolk im Wandel von der agraren zur industriellen Daseinsform, dargestellt am Ruhrgebiet*, Tubingen, p.20.

6. For the history of local boundaries in the Ruhr region, see Paul Wiel (1970) *Wirtschaftsgeshichte des Ruhrgebiets: Tatsachen und Zahlen*, Essen, esp. pp.2 ff.

7. Ibid.

8. Ibid.

9. See Jurgen Reulecke (1987) 'The Ruhr: centralization versus decentralization in a region of cities', in Anthony Sutcliffe, *Metropolis 1890-1940*, London, pp.387 ff.

10. On this point see: Siefried Gehrmann (1988) *Fussball - Vereine - Politik, Zur Sportgeschichte des Reviers 1900-1940*, Essen, pp.83ff.

11. Cf. Siegfried Gehrmann, 'Football in an industrial region: the example of Schalke 04 Football Club', in *The International Journal of the History of Sport,* Vol. 6. Dec. 1989, No. 3, pp.335-355, and Siegfried Gehrmann (1988) 'Von der Stassenmannschaft und der Junglingssodalitat zum Spitzenclub - "Schalke" und "Borussia"', in: Bernd Faulenbach/Gunther Hogl (eds) *Eine Partei in ihrer Region. Zur Geschichte der SPD im Westlichen Westfalen,* Essen, pp.51-56.

12. Cf. Siefgried Gehrmann, Fritz Szepan und Ernst Kuzorra - zwei 'Fussballidole des ruhrgebiets', in, *Sozial-und Zeitgeschichte des Sports,* 2. Jg., H.3/1988, pp.57-71.

13. Cf. Siegfried Gehrmann (1978) 'Fussball in einer Industrieregion. Das Beispiel FC Schalke 04', in: Jürgen Reulecke Wolfhard Weber (eds.) *Fabrik - Familie - Feierabend. Beitrage zur Sozialgeschichte des Alltags im Industriezeitalter,* Wuppertal, p.382.

14. Siegfried Gehrmann (1988) *Fussball - Vereine - Politik. Zur Sportgeschichte des Reviers 1900-1940,* Essen, pp.90-6.

15. Ibid.

16. Siegfried Gehrmann, *Fussball in einer Industrieregion,* pp.385-6.

17. Cf Heinrich August Winkler (1985) *Arbeiter und Arbeiterbewegung in der Weimarer Republik 1924 bis 1930. Vol. 2: Der Schein der Normalitat 1924-1930,* Bonn/Berlin, p.170; Hendrik de Man (1926) *Zur Psychologie des Sozialismus,* Jena, pp.161-5; Dr Eberhard Franke (1936) *Das Ruhrgebiet und Ostpreussen. Geschichte, Umfang und Bedeutung der Ostpreusseneinwanderung,* Essen, pp.104-8; Siegfried Gehrmann, Fritz Szepan und Ernst Kuzorra - zwei (1988) *Fussballidole des Ruhrgebiets, in: Sozial* - und *Zeitgeschichte des Sports* 2, 3, pp.6204.

18. Siefried Gehrmann, *Fussball in einer Industrieregion*, p.394.

19. Hans-Joachim Teske, 'FC Gelsenkirchen-Schalke 04', paper written at home for 1st State Examination for Teachers of Secondary School I, 1977, pp.81 ff.

20 See note 7.

21. Vestische Neueste Nachrichten, June 26, 1934

22. Kommunalverband Ruhrgebiet/Initiativekreis Ruhrgebiet (1992) (eds.) *The Ruhr. The Driving Force of Germany*, Essen, pp.26-9.

23. *Schalke-Archives*, Gelsenkirchen, Parkstadion

24. *Op. cit.*

25. *Op. cit.*

26. *Op. cit.*

8 'Wogball': Ethnicity and violence in Australian soccer

Wray Vamplew

There is a perceived violence problem in Australian soccer. To some extent this is a product of the media, particularly the Australian press, who have focused on crowd disturbances seeing them as newsworthy in the light of the European experience. Nevertheless, a recent survey of persons actually involved in soccer suggested that it was the most violent of any football code in Australia and that crowd behaviour at soccer matches was rated as the worst of any sport.[1] This paper aims to provide background for on-going academic assessments of the situation by bringing together three major and interrelated themes of Australia history - migration, sport and violence.[2]

Migration and sport in Australia

Immigration has been the major factor influencing Australia's population growth since the invasion of 1788 into a land containing perhaps half-a-million aborigines to the sixteen million or so inhabitants of today.[3] Australia was actually founded as a British penal settlement and between the arrival of the First Fleet in New South Wales to the cessation of transportation in 1868 some 140,000 British convicts found themselves involuntary migrants to the antipodes. Accompanying these early transportees were British administrative and military personnel, themselves often conscripted, though frequently temporary, migrants. From the 1830s, however, immigration increasingly was of free settlers, again predominantly

British in origin. Of the total populace of 1,152,000 in 1861, 723,000 was foreign born and 630,000 of these came from the British Isles. Migrants from Britain have continued to dominate the inflow of population: in 1981, 1,170,000 of the 3,102,000 foreign born residents in Australia were British. However, other nations have dispatched significant numbers including 283,000 from Italy, 153,000 from what was Yugoslavia, and 150,000 from Greece, many of whose relatives first came in the massive post World War Two migration, designed to supply Australia's desperate need for labour. In very recent years Asian migrants have been greatest in number, partly because of the abandonment in the 1970s of the White Australia policy, but also due to the volume of refugees and the ensuing family reunions.

Many migrants retained an emotional attachment to their native land and sport, brought along as accompanying cultural baggage, provided a link with home in an alien environment. In seeking to participate in their traditional sports the British were no different from later migrants such as the Germans, who came to Australia following the European political and religious troubles of the late 1840s, and brought with them skittles, crossbows, target rifle-shooting, and gymnastics. However, the British were more numerous and hence it was their activities which dominated the Australian sporting calendar.

Inevitably, soccer was one of the sports transported from Britain to Australia.[4] Reputedly the first game was held in August 1880 on Parramatta Common between the local King's School and the Wanderers. The recognizably British nomenclature of the latter team was also reflected in the organizing bodies throughout the Australian colonies with the Southern British Football Association in New South Wales, the Anglo-Australian Football Association in Victoria and the British Football Associations appropriately prefixed by the colonial title in Queensland, South Australia and Tasmania. Each new wave of migration before the second World War, dominated as they were by Britons, brought a new influx of soccer enthusiasts. Nevertheless, despite being played in each state, the game never became the major football code in any of them, always ranking behind Australian rules in Victoria, South Australia and Western Australia and rugby league in New South Wales and Queensland.[5]

Whether caused by a favourable climate, boundless land, the high proportion of males in its early population or some other factor, there is no doubt that sport flourished in Australia. Indeed it is often alleged that Australians have been besotted by sport: possessed by an obsession which lasts from the cradle to the grave, from the wearing of nappies in their team's colours to the scattering of their ashes at a favourite sporting venue. Comments of visitors to these shores have reinforced a national self-image in which sport features in the words of one critic, as *the ultimate Australian super-religion.*(6) Although there is an element of hyperbole in the claims advanced for Australia's sporting involvement, it remains true that playing and watching sport is a central feature in the lives of many Australians.(7)

Since sport was part and parcel of the Australian way-of-life, it was an obvious avenue by which migrants could become acculturated.(8) Yet sporting migrants from Europe who came to these shores after 1945 opted for a game with which they were familiar rather than an overtly Australian one. Rugby league and Australian rules were unknown to the vast majority: to them football meant soccer. Unlike the workplace, the soccer field offered them an opportunity to demonstrate their skills without fluency in English. It gave them a sense of community, a link with their homeland, and a base for the socialization of their Australian-born offspring. Soccer clubs emerged out of the ethnic social clubs which developed from the geographical concentration of particular groups of migrants. Throughout Australia teams were founded with ethnic names and such clubs began to dominate the game, particularly after 1957 when the leading ones broke away from existing organizations to set up their own, culminating in the formal establishment of the Australian Soccer Federation in 1961 which took over administrative control of the sport in Australia.(9) So much did soccer become identified with ethnic groups that, despite a long and continuing British involvement, it became disparagingly referred to as *wogball*, a term now enshrined as an Australian colloquialism in the *Macquarie Dictionary*.(10) In recent years the image of soccer as a foreign game has been reinforced by the electronic media: Australian matches are featured virtually exclusively on the Special Broadcasting Service which caters for ethnic groups in Australia.

Australian sport has a violent history. Field sports, perhaps more than any other sporting activity including boxing, were unchallenged in their level of premeditated violence. Game laws in Australia were less restrictive than in Britain and many of the early settlers took advantage of them to combine pleasure with food provision. Others, particularly the upper echelons, who donned hunting garb to chase wild dogs, emus and kangaroos or who chose to shoot rather than ride, rationalized their killing as pest control, albeit an entertaining form. Other brutal - to the modern mind - animal sports included cock fighting, coursing (with live hares) and trap pigeon shooting, all part of the British migrant's sporting luggage. Humans too faced sporting violence. The prize-ring epitomized what was tolerated in the name of sport. Rounds ended only when one pugilist was knocked or thrown to the ground; he was then given thirty seconds to toe a line scratched across the centre of the ring; not till one combatant failed 'to come up to scratch' was the match over. With knuckles protected only by long soaking in brine, damage to a fighter's hands were common; far worse, however, were the horrific injuries inflicted on an opponent, particularly as early match agreements often allowed kicking, gouging, throttling and biting. This was part of an age in which the education system socialized boys into men. In these schools of hard knocks pupils were taught that courage was to be admired, pain to be endured and brutality, in the guise of manliness, to be tolerated.

This was a product of a violent society. Modern Australia was founded by invasion and, like many frontier societies, dealt violently with the indigenous population. Aborigines were massacred and poisoned as the settlers sought to take over their land: even more fell victim to European disease and alcohol.(11) Life for the invaders was also harsh. Transportation, in existence till 1868, was no pleasure trip and convict servitude, with its ever present threat of flogging, no holiday.(12) Even free settlers found life difficult as they struggled first to survive and then to establish themselves in this vast and often unforgiving continent. Blood, sweat and tears made Australia and in the process brutalized many of the inhabitants. Given that sport, as part of Australia's culture, would be subject to the same influences as other aspects of life, it is not surprising that historically Australian sport was often violent.

Many, including the author, would claim that times have changed. However, although it is easy to establish that Australia's past was a violent one, it is more difficult to show that the nation has become less violent. Nevertheless, lower crime rates, legal recognition of

Aborigines as full Australians, hardening attitudes towards domestic violence and child abuse, and a growing tolerance towards homosexuals and ethnic minorities all indicate that Australian society has become more civilized.(13)

As attitudes towards societal violence have changed so too they have towards violence in sport. Boxing remains as legitimized violence in which the ultimate aim is to render one's opponent unconscious. Nevertheless it has become more civilized in that bareknuckles gave way to leather mitts and later padded gloves; new rules outlawed certain blows, limited the number of rounds to be fought; and, to protect the smaller fighters, introduced weight divisions. Boxing would certainly not now be recommended for school children as a form of character building. Indeed *Aussie Sports* and games with modified rules in which height, weight, and even gender are of no advantage, are emphasizing skill development and the fun of sport rather than the competition. Animal sports too have changed under the weight of public opinion. Legislation has outlawed the worst of the abuses and, although some illegal sports activities still exist clandestinely, generally greyhounds now chase mechanical hares and clay pigeons have replaced live birds as shotgun targets. Even the slaughter of birds and animals in the wild has become increasingly restricted and subject to license.

Accentuating the change in society's attitude towards sporting violence has been the role of the electronic media. Previously spectators had to go to the ground to witness the mayhem, but now modern technology, often glorifying violence in order to sell its product, has brought the thuggery into the home with instant replay and sports new grabs reinforcing the perception of increased violence.(14) In doing so it has sparked a backlash by provoking a growing number of people - often with no direct interest in sport - to become concerned at the level of violence being portrayed. For the first time many Australians have become aware of - and viewed with distaste - the violence stalking the nation's playing fields.

Sports violence in Australia

Given that attitudes towards violence in sport have changed should anything be read into the fact that 60% of the survey respondents from soccer felt that player violence in their sport was excessive? There is in fact no hard evidence that on-field violence is any worse than it used to be. The traditional British style, which provided the basis of the Australian game before the second World War, was physically hard even when legitimate and certainly the players from the mining areas of New South Wales were renowned for their fierce tackling.(15) Basically, to cite the observations of Leo Baumgartner, an Austrian import to the local soccer scene in the 1950s, what developed in Australia was a game based on *hit and rush tactics* with *robust tackling* - in effect a tougher version of the British strength, stamina and speed approach.(16) This style of play led to friction in matches against ethnic teams in the 1950s and 1960s. The latter's continental finesse, which emphasized skill rather than muscle, contrasted with the physical hardness of their opponents and when grit and determination faced artistic expression it was not surprising that on occasions trouble erupted.

The low position of the European migrants on the Australian socioeconomic scale and their lack of power in politics and at work must have resulted in massive frustration, both individually and collectively. Soccer gave them a chance to compete against Australians on equal terms and anything which threatened discrimination against them on the field would be regarded as intolerable. No doubt the situation was also aggravated at times by referees who favoured the Australian blood and guts approach and by anti-migrant taunts from Australian players and spectators.(17) Violence could also break out when ethnic teams played each other. The traditional homeland loyalties which underlay the ethnic clubs also included traditional hatreds, so often issues other than soccer were at stake when, for example, Croat faced Serb. In such circumstances cynical tackles and off-the-ball incidents could be seen as political rather than professional fouls. It should be noted that, although most games passed without serious incident, one authority maintains that "European immigrants were ... the common denominator in the majority of cases of violence within soccer." (18)

All this said, it remains true that soccer today is seen by its devotees as being more violent than their counterparts in other sports rate their own games.(19) Before jumping to the conclusion that ethnicity - as the obvious difference between soccer and other sports - is to blame, it must be pointed out that elite level ethnic teams no longer recruit so exclusively from restricted groups: as the rewards for winning have increased so ability rather than ethnic affiliation has become the key variable in team selection. The major site of soccer violence in Australia is not in fact at the elite level but much lower down the player scale. Here, judging from the replies to the survey, ethnic tensions play a role. Yet it must not be forgotten that other factors could be at work, including the poor quality of referees in the lower grades, a matter complained of by 72% of respondents.

Space does not permit an analysis of the many theories of aggressive and violent play, but currently I am pursuing the line that people in groups can behave differently from when they are separate individuals.[20] This can have relevance to player violence in team sports if we introduce the concept of the team as a *gang* with standing up for your mates a requirement of membership. Of course, this will not explain the actions of particular individuals; nor is it applicable only to teams of the same ethnic background. However, it may have relevance when ethnic (including Scots and English) sides play each other or when ethnic slurs are levelled during a game.

The major attack on brutality within soccer has concentrated on the punishment of offenders, though it is worth noting the rehabilitation of the guilty has not been of prime concern. No doubt this approach will continue, although personally the author believes the punishment of clubs by the loss of premiership points would do more to rid the sport of its hatchetmen. In any event it is likely that the law will increasingly intervene and take matters out of the hands of the clubs and even the tribunals.

Perhaps the best long-term solution lies in education. Sports violence is learned behaviour and certainly the Australian male has been socialized into a belief that violence on the sports field is acceptable in our society. Only recently have attempts been made to counter this, first by the teaching of codes of conduct in schools and, second, by the development of games (including soccer) with modified rules to offset the physical advantages which some children have and with improved sportspersonship as an anticipated spin-off.[21] Unfortunately funding limitations on this *Aussie Sports* programme have prevented the development of non English language versions which ultimately may have adverse consequences regarding the behaviour of ethnic players.

Soccer violence and ethnicity

There is little crowd violence in Australian sport but much of what occurs appears to be concentrated around its soccer grounds. One-day cricket has had its disturbances, the annual Bathhurst motorcycle races too saw significant crowd disorder, but it is soccer which is considered to be the site of most trouble. This view is shared by those within the sport. More than a third of the soccer-based respondents to the violence survey believed that spectator misbehaviour at soccer matches was excessive.[22]

Soccer also topped the list for most specific types of spectator disorder: vandalism occurred often according to 14.0% of respondents, throwing missiles (21.6%), pitch invasions (26.0%), racial or ethnic abuse (49.0%), and foul language (80.8%). The most common offence was abuse of officials which was observed by 82.7% of respondents, beaten only by the 83.9% for rugby league crowds. Significantly, however, soccer ranked only sixth at 22.0% for common observation of drunkenness which would suggest that other stimulants besides alcohol triggered disorder at matches. To many, both within and outside the sport, the answer is the obvious ethnic rivalry which permeates soccer in Australia.

To some extent sports nationalism can be viewed as a potential unifying social force within Australia, particularly as historically sport has been a major avenue through which Australia has projected itself as a nation. Today, in the international arena, sport is Australia's only way of competing with - and on occasions even defeating - the political superpowers. Almost every Australian can recall the nationalistic fervour which greeted *Australia II*'s victory in the America's Cup or can note the delight in some quarters when Australia beats the Poms at anything. Yet it has not been established that European migrants, including British ones, have identified with Australia's international sporting success. Personal observation suggests that, at least in soccer, visiting overseas club sides have often had more support than the Socceroos or state sides.[23] The sporting nationalism exhibited by many ethnic groups, particularly those from continental Europe, has been that of their homeland and at times this has led to violence at soccer matches. When, for example, in the 1960s Croatia played Yugal, whose support came mainly from Serbs and Slavs, past political struggles were symbolized and re-enacted.(24) This has continued. Only a month before this conference police were brought in by helicopter to quell a crowd riot at a Melbourne soccer ground where a game was being played between Preston Makedonia and Heidelberg Alexander: the issue which provoked the trouble was a dispute thousands of kilometres away in Europe over whether or not Greece had patent rights to the Macedonian name.(25) The ethnic mix of Australian cities means that the historical and contemporary political problems of Europe are condensed into a relatively small area. This downside to multi-culturalism in Australia is not unique to soccer. An academic study of public disorder in contemporary Australia found that of 288 politically motivated disturbances 32 which involved the participating of ethnic groups were related to events outside Australia.(26)

The responses to the violence survey show that Australian soccer fans do not appreciate having their employment of sport spoiled by spectator misbehaviour. Indeed they supported severer punishments for such offenders than did respondents to the survey in general. Table 1 shows that over ninety per cent would have such offenders expelled from the ground and almost as many favoured some longer-term ban on their presence. Over three-quarters would have them arrested and fined and a majority supported imprisonment as a punishment, though presumably not for isolated incidents of foul language or verbal abuse of officials. Clearly they would have supported the New South Wales government which recently introduced tough anti-hooligan legislation which was backed up by a media advertising campaign.

There is, however, no evidence that harsh punishment acts as a deterrent to crowd disorder. Certainly it is unlikely to prevent heat-of-the-moment, knee-jerk reactions to on-field events. Whether it would lessen premeditated violence, especially that which was politically motivated, is a matter of conjecture. Although the violent player can be relatively easily distinguished, the troublemaker in the crowd is less readily identified. Until the likelihood of being caught becomes a probability rather than a possibility, the deterrent effect of any punishment must be weakened. It can also be speculated that for some of those involved the risk of being caught could be part of the excitement. Nevertheless, it must be conceded that some punishments by their nature would keep the convicted offender away from the game and would also convince the law-abiding spectator that the authorities were trying to do something about the disorder, a psychological marketing ploy not to be underestimated.

Table 8.1: Support for measures to deal with disorderly spectators
(% of respondents)

	Soccer	All Sports
Tolerate	4.2	7.0
Expel	90.7	92.6
Arrest	77.8	61.3
Fine	83.0	69.1
Imprison	51.9	28.5
Ban	88.7	71.1

The recent reaction of soccer authorities, the New South Wales Government and some sports journalists has been to call for a 'de-ethnicization' of the game and, in particular, the dropping of ethnic club names in favour of those reflecting the area in which the club has its ground or headquarters.(27) Even as this paper was in its first draft the Australian Soccer Federation announced that they were *encouraging* the Coca Cola [National] Soccer League teams to phase out ethnic names.(28) Traditionally European migrant groups have been opposed to such a district system of sports teams which has, however, been favoured by most Australian sports administrators. This structure emerged in the late nineteenth century as a concession to the vast distances between major inhabited areas in Australia. In 1891 over 34 per cent of New South Wales' population lived in Sydney and 42 per cent of Victoria's in Melbourne, but the two cities were almost nine hundred kilometres apart, which, considering the state of transportation, was too great for any regularly organized competition: weekly matches were feasible only at the metropolitan level. What emerged were teams based on suburbs, often organized around the electorates of the time. So Australian rules supporters in Melbourne barracked for Collingwood, Carlton, and other distinctively geographically located clubs; and, similarly, rugby league fans in Sydney cheered for Balmain, South Sydney and the like. Such a structure did not appeal to the 'New Australians' who preferred to organize clubs labelled Budapest, Hellas, Macedonia and other nomenclature which signalled the ethnic preference of the members.(29)

Nevertheless some teams have changed their names voluntarily. In Victoria the Dutch side, Wilhelmina, became Ringwood City in an attempt to secure wider support, though it has been argued that the club had a weak ethnic tradition. Another Victorian side J.U.S.T. (Yugoslav United Soccer Team) became Footscray J.U.S.T. in the early 1970s after receiving a $100,000 loan from the local council towards improved ground facilities.(30) At times during the past two decades other clubs too have succumbed to pressure from league officials to at least add a district tag to their official name. Yet this has been for economic reasons, either to secure sponsorship by less overtly restricting the identifiable market or in an effort to attract new spectators to soccer. Crowd behaviour appears to have had no part to play.

There are major problems associated with the attempt to de-ethnicize soccer. First, and certainly foremost, is the resistance by the clubs themselves or more especially by their fans: crowds at Hindmarsh Stadium do not cheer for the West Adelaide Hellas Sharks but for *Hellas*. It is notable that a ban on making ground announcements in languages other than English appears to have fallen by the wayside.(31) Second, such reverse multi-culturalism runs counter to current Australian political philosophy and legislation which encourages diversity of cultural experiences rather than assimilation into a mainstream one. Ultimately such measures by the soccer authorities may be declared illegal. Third, unless the districts themselves are sufficiently varied in ethnic composition the change in terminology may be meaningless. Fourth, if soccer is genuinely de-ethnicized then, to quote Sam Papasavas, at the time chairman of South Melbourne Hellas Gunners and now Australian Soccer Federation Commissioner, "by eradicating the ethnicity of the sport you are eradicating the people who have been following soccer for the past thirty years."(32) Yet, if it is not done, soccer as a major spectator sport may be doomed. Many ethnic-based clubs are on an inclined plane to oblivion simply because their traditional source of support is dwindling as a consequence of a lessening in European migration to Australia. It is quite possible that the crowd problem in Australian soccer simply might disappear along with the spectators.(33)

Acknowledgements

I am grateful for comments and assistance from Robyn Day, Roy Jones, John McTier, Phillip Moore, Bill Murray and Janice Vamplew.

Notes

1. W. Vamplew (1991), *Sports Violence in Australia: Its Extent and Control*, Australian Sports Commission, Canberra. The survey was not directed at any particular sport, but questioned a total of 906 players, coaches, administrators, officials media representatives and spectators across some eighty sports. Forty-seven fully completed surveys referred to soccer. Although a small sample, it is noteworthy that 59.6 per cent of the respondents felt that on-field violence in their sport was excessive as compared to 32.8 per cent for all sports.

2. Soccer, let alone its violence problem, has not received much academic attention in Australia. Bill Murray (La Trobe) and Philip Mosely (Canberra) are writing *A Social History of Soccer in Australia* with a spin-off contribution to B Stoddart & W Vamplew, *Sport in Australia : A Social History* (Cambridge University Press, forthcoming). Mosely also wrote the entry on soccer for the forthcoming *Oxford Companion to Australian Sport* edited by W Vamplew, K Moore, J O'Hara, R Cashman and I Jobling on behalf of the Australian Society for Sports History.

3. This paragraph is based on data in C. Price, 'Immigration and Ethnic Origin' in W. Vamplew (1987) (ed.), *Australian Historical Statistics*, Fairfax, Syme & Weldon, Sydney, pp.2-22.

4. For a brief history of soccer in Australia see P. Mosely, 'Soccer' in Vamplew et al, *The Oxford Companion to Australian Sport*.

5. Although not an exclusive explanation, one reason is that both Australian rules and rugby union (from which rugby league emerged in 1908) established themselves before soccer.

6. K. Dunstan (1973) *Sports*, Sun Books, Melbourne, p.1.

7. For a critical overview of the sporting passion allegations see R. Cashman (1987) 'The Australian Sporting Obsession', *Sporting Traditions*, 4.1, pp. 47-55.

8.	This is a little studied issue in Australian history. One chapter in R. Unikoski (1978) *Communal Endeavours: Migrant Organisations in Melbourne*, ANU Press, Canberra, looks at sporting organizations. Brian Stoddart has come comment in his 'Ethnic Influences' contribution to the forthcoming *Oxford Companion to Australian Sport*. A few Aborigines, far less than in rugby league or Australian rules, have played soccer at an elite level. See, C. Tatz (1987) *Aborigines in Sport*, ASSH Studies in Sport History No. 3, Australian Society for Sport History, Adelaide.

9.	For details on the formation of early ethnic clubs see Mosely's thesis, 297-306. The schism came about because of alleged discrimination by the ruling bodies which did not select ethnic players for representative teams and refused to promote ethnic-based teams beyond the lower grades. S. Grant (1974) *Jack Pollard's Soccer Records*, Jack Pollard, Sydney.

10.	S. Kamasz, 'It's time to Australianise the round-ball code', *Weekend Australian* 11-12 February 1989. English born Johnny Warren, ex-Australian soccer captain and now media commentator, also recalls that when he began to play soccer was considered a **'wog'** game. L. Writer (1990) *Winning: Face to Race With Australian Sporting Legends* Ironbark, Chatswood, New South Wales, p.15.

11.	H. Reynolds (1991) 'Violence in Australian History' in D. Chappell, P. Grabosky & H. Strang, *Australian Violence: Contemporary Perspectives* (Australian Institute of Criminology, Canberra.

12.	R. Hughes (1987) *The Fatal Shore*, Collins Harvill, London. A revisionist attempt to provide a counterweight to the unremitting horror stories of Hughes still shows that over three-quarters of all convicts were flogged at least once and is forced to conclude that there was an "ever present fear of physical punishment" [S. Nicholas (1988) *Convict Workers* Cambridge University Press, Cambridge, pp.181-182].

13. R. Broome (1987) 'Aborigines' in G. Aplin, S. G. Foster & M. McKernan, *Australians: A Historical Dictionary*, Fairfax, Syme & Weldon, Sydney, pp.6-7. S. K. Mukherjee, A. Scandia, D. Dagger & W. Matthews (1989) *Source Book of Australian Criminal and Social Statistics 1804-1988*, Australian Institute of Criminology, Canberra; and S. K. Mukherjee, J. R. Walker & E. N. Jacobsen (1986) *Crime and Punishment in the Colonies: A Statistical Profile*, History Project Inc., Sydney.

14. Depending upon the specific category (in ascending order radio sports programmes, radio commentaries, newspapers, television news, television commentaries and television sports programmes) around two-thirds to three-quarters of **all** respondents to the survey believed that the media glorified or condoned violence in sport.

15. Mosely, thesis, pp.244-245.

16. L. Baumgartner (1968) *The Little Professor of Soccer* Marketing Productions, Sydney, p.104.

17. Mosely, thesis, pp.316-317.

18. Mosely, thesis, p.308.

19. The figures for major male sports were soccer (60.0%), Australian rules (52.8%), rugby league (51.7%), rugby union (46.2%), hockey (45.5%), basketball (43.8%), baseball (40.0%), cricket (26.9%), tennis (22.2%).

20. For a survey see M. D. Smith (1983) *Violence in Sport* Butterworths, Toronto.

21. J. Clough & R. Traill (1989) *Report of Australian Sports Commission Study of Modified Sports*, Australian Sports Commission, Canberra.

22. Figures for other major sports were, in descending order, rugby league (19.4%), Australian rules (18.6%), basketball (16.7%),

baseball (13.3%), netball (10.0%), cricket (8.2%), rugby union (8.0%), tennis (5.6%) and softball (5.0%). For a historical view see R. Lynch (1991) 'Disorder on the Sidelines of Australian Sport', *Sporting Traditions* 8.1 pp.50-75.

23. For a specific case when Australia played Hajduk Split see J. Wells, 'Socceroos' Reception a National Disgrace - But Which Nation?', *Weekend Australian*, 9-10 June 1990.

24. B. James, 'We are Playing Soccer - Not Politics', *Sports Magazine*, 16,.1 June 1963, pp.36-7.

25. *Australian* 17 March 1992.

26. R. J. Holton & P. Fletcher (1988) *Public Disorder in Contemporary Australia*, Report to Criminology Research Council, Canberra, p.43.

27. R. Gatt, 'Ethnic Names Alien to the Game', *Australian*, 6 November 1991.

28. *Australian*, 13 December 1991. This appears to be a marketing attempt to broaden the spectrum of spectators rather than specifically a crowd control mechanism. It should also be noted that not all national league teams are ethnic based though those that are remain dominant both numerically and politically.

29. For the history of the district system in New South Wales soccer see Mosely, thesis, pp.77-78, p.108.

31. R. Gatt, 'Ethnic Feuds Give the Game Its Bad Name', *Australian*, 3 January 1990.

32. Allan, op. cit.

33. In correspondence, Bill Murray rejects this conclusion and argues that Australian soccer is healthy, pointing to the performance of the two youth teams, the Olympic team (almost all of them locally born) and the Australians playing in Europe.

There is, of course, the possibility that new clubs, representative of new migrant groups, will emerge: Perth already has the Chindits, the Assegais and Chile (R. Jones & P. Moore, '"He Only Has Eyes for Poms": Soccer, Ethnicity and Locality in Metropolitan Perth', Paper presented at Australian Sociological Association Conference, Perth 1991, 13).

9 Masculinity and football: The formation of national identity in Argentina

Eduardo P. Archetti

In this chapter I will present some ideas about one masculine team sport, football, in the context of the modernization of Argentina (1900-1930) and how this sport is involved in the formation of national identity. It has been consistently argued that the nation is an 'imagined political community' in the sense that its members share a sovereign boundary and have a strong feeling of communion. The nation is then conceived as a kind of 'horizontal comradeship', that sets aside social differences based on inequality and exploitation.(1) Logically and practically, it is important in nationalist ideologies to imagine a fraternity that is flat and horizontal. Hence, the ideology of nationalism must be integrated in social practices that can create, over time, the image of 'people' having 'something' in common. The 'people' are perceived to be greater than any concrete community and always as fundamentally homogeneous, only superficially divided by status, class, or locality. Therefore, it is crucial to identify social practices which appear to reflect ideas of nationalism and to investigate the 'content' of these practices with respect to the actors involved and the meaning of the values conveyed.

Benedict Anderson's account of the growth and consolidation of nationalism can be seen as a history of active male nationalists (soldiers, generals, bureaucrats, writers, poets, journalists, politicians) trying to realize the destiny of fraternal communion. It seems that Anderson's imagined community only imagines men. In his perspective, nationality seems to have an aura of fatality, of moral obligation and disinterested solidarity. However, he argues that the revolutionary aspect of the idea of 'a nation' is that it is based on the possession of 'a common language', not blood, and, therefore, anyone 'could be "invited into" the imagined community', anyone, in principle, could become naturalized.(2)

I agree with Anderson's analytical perspective, which sees 'nationalism' as a new and fundamentally equalizing ideology. However, there must also be some common ground inherent to nationalist ideologies, in addition to that of language. There must be a history, in the sense of tradition, of events, symbols and ceremonies that are seen as the realization and representation of a bonded, undifferentiated collectivity. A segment of the population - organized nationalist elites, or individual nationalist militants - must generate ideas and implement actions that, over time, will stand for an entire nation. A nation's origin includes both 'foundation myths' and concrete heroes. However, national consciousness must be elaborated and reproduced through different practices in 'normal times'. Education seems to be a preferential arena for national indoctrination (the most advanced form of 'printed capitalism'). However, nationalism is generated in many different social settings and, I believe, located in less institutional contexts. In this direction, modern sport in the age of international competitions has created a particularly privileged arena for the analysis of a 'gendered' rhetoric of nationalism.

Football, without any doubt, is the 'national' sport of Argentina. Other sports are also popular but have a rather clear class bias, for example rugby, or are eminently individualistic in practice, for example tennis. Football is a practice and a passion that cuts across class, ethnic status or regional origin. Through football Argentina became an important actor in the modern world history of sport. However, football was and still is a typical and exclusively masculine sport in Argentina. Thus, a powerful expression of national capabilities and potentialities is overtly gendered, as are the most typical emblems of the modern culture of nationalism: the cenotaphs and tombs of Unknown Soldiers.(3) Argentinian football has constituted a symbolic and practical male arena for national pride and disappointment, happiness and sorrow. The nationalist discourses on sport, in addition to the discovery or the foundation of a 'national style of playing', can then be seen as an influential mechanism through which male cultural power is established.

It has been pointed out that the ideology of nationalism compels one to think in terms of 'nature', of 'natural ties' and, therefore, of deep moral bonds to the nation. Hence, nationalism must be conceived as a cognitive and social arena marked by obligations and not by selfish considerations. Thus, one dominant theme is self-sacrifice, best realized in the contexts of war and martyrdom. Consequently, it is expected that national feelings and identity must be expressed in contexts of competition. Nationalists are always willing to prove that their world is distinct and unique.(4) The ideology of nationalism is the celebration of differences and, if possible, of success and victory. Given this context, the ritual and spectacle of football enable a 'peaceful', masculine, fraternal participation in a public arena opposed to both the domestic and working environments. Football belongs to the realm of leisure in which participants can release creative powers, individual and communal, that allow a play with images, fantasies and social relationships.(5) I think that in the exploration of national images and national identity it is highly relevant to pursue the 'arena of freedom and creativity' represented by the social use of leisure.(6)

The historical context of modern Argentina: immigration and national dilemmas

Modern Argentina is, in a way, the product of massive rural colonization, which began in 1853, after almost thirty years of civil war, and which reached its climax at the end of the century.(7) Initially, the migrants were Swiss, German, Danish, French, English, Spanish, and Italian, with the latter becoming increasingly prominent. In 1869, shortly after the colonization movement started, the first federal census recorded a national population of 1,836,490; in 1895, towards the end of the first wave of colonization, the second census recorded a national population of 3,954,911, an increase of approximately 115 per cent in 26 years. In that period, the imbalance of immigration over emigration was approximately 840,000. This development was very similar to the homestead movement in the United States.

After 1895, the tide of immigration continued to flow into Argentina at even higher levels than before, but rural colonization slowed down. New immigrants were integrated as landless labourers and tenants in the countryside, or remained in the cities, principally in Buenos Aires. The immigrant tide was low in the decade 1891-1900, at only 319,882. However, it rose to its greatest level ever between 1901 and 1910: 1,764,103, against 643,881 emigrants, an imbalance of 1,120,222. From 1857 until 1916, a total of 4,758,729 immigrants entered Argentina with a net immigration of 2,575,021. As a consequence of changing opportunities, Buenos Aires grew rapidly from 187,000 inhabitants in 1869 to 1,576,000 in 1914. By 1930 Buenos Aires had almost 3 million inhabitants, one third being of European origin.[8]

The massive wave of immigration confronted the native political elites with the problems and dilemmas of building up a 'new' nation.[9] They tried to establish a positive answer to immigration, either by pointing out that the development of the country required a labour force and, above all, a skilled one; or by arguing that the new immigrants and their culture could help transform the 'primitive' Spanish cultural influence, which had been based on an aristocratic and hierarchical model of society. Many ideological supporters of immigration believed that the Europeans would bring new values of equality and work, necessary for creating a prosperous, industrial and democratic society. However, by the end of the 19th century nationalists began to perceive immigrants as the main source of cultural contamination, importing 'socialist, class-based ideas', and organizing political parties and trade unions based on the ideology of class struggle. The nationalists argued that these ideologies did not recognize the existence of fundamental equalities of opportunity, which in turn constituted the basis of the Argentinian economic expansion. The community of common interests was at risk.

Thus, in the first decade of the twentieth century, it was discovered that many immigrants suffered from nostalgia: they not only retained their nationalities, but also tried to develop their own school systems. These attitudes were seen as a barrier to consolidating national unity, occurring in a context of changing political rights, which had been provoked by the approval in 1912 of universal male suffrage. Many politicians saw the dangers of a society divided between natives, with political rights, and foreigners, without political rights, which could give rise to a divorce between State and Nation. They saw that the foreigners could easily identify themselves with the State, the legal guarantor of 'private interests', but not with the Nation. In this sense, they felt that the maximization of 'private interests' could supplant the strengthening of 'national identity', and thus the development of an authentic 'community of interests'.

This historical context is crucial to an understanding of the politics and ideology of 'national restoration' which were advanced by the Radical Party, the dominant political party in the first decades of this century. The Radical Party's ideology was strongly impregnated by a moralist perspective, in which national goals supersede sectorial interests. The party perceived itself as the very essence of the Nation, at a time dominated by 'materialist ideologies' that legitimized success without a critical and moral examination of the means employed.(10) The party argued that the main problem was not simply the presence of so many foreigners, but the lack of an accepted ideology putting the emphasis on sacrifice, the postponement of selfish interests and, consequently, on the achievement of national supra-individual goals. It is important to bear in mind that this ideology was fostered in the context of the First World War, when national cohesion was seen as a priority for facing its bloody consequences. The Radical Party, which came to power in 1916 and remained until the military *coup d'etat* in 1930, represents first and foremost the ideology of national cohesion and national consciousness. It is therefore in confrontation with other parties, especially the Socialist, which represent more 'sectorial' ideologies. The impact of football as a national ritual must be seen in relation to, and in the context of, the growing concern for consolidating a genuine and strong national identity.

Football as a source of 'national virtues' and 'national consciousness'

It has been pointed out that sports and games were two of the most important agencies of cultural transmission from Britain to her colonial Empire and to the world.(11) Team sports, especially cricket, rugby and football, were perceived as efficient means for inculcating teamwork values, such as: the importance of accepting leadership; the development of perseverance; courage and virility in the face of adversity; the will to win while respecting the rules of the game; and, perhaps above all, the sense of solidarity and loyalty towards fellow players. The ideology of 'fair-play' and 'gentlemen's competition' permitted a view of sport as an egalitarian and 'apolitical' arena which could transcend social divisions in the colonial order or national societies. Moreover, the team sports which eventually became 'national sports' were played in public by men, being intentionally defined as public cultural performances. The sports activities of women were largely private in character, confined to the spaces of schools, colleges and private clubs.

The spread of soccer in Argentina was due to Britain's power and her active presence in commerce, industrial production and financial investment.(12) By the end of the 19th century, Argentina was integrated in the world economy as a meat and cereal producer. British political influence was decisive and British capital controlled the key sectors of Argentina's external economy (transport, banking and meat factories). Thus, in the case of Argentina, the rapid expansion of the game and its internationalization were also related to the importance of Britain in the last half of the 19th century. By 1890 there were 45,000 British nationals living in Buenos Aires and small cities close to the capital. The Buenos Aires Football Club, a division of the Buenos Aires Cricket Club, was founded in 1867. In the same year, the first recorded match was played between two teams of the same club: the 'Reds', with captain Thomas Hogg, and the 'Whites' with William Held. Many clubs were founded after 1880 and the majority of them sprang from English schools. In the period 1890-1900 the Lomas Athletic Club gained five titles. All the players had been students at the Lomas de Zamora School, a prestigious British boarding school. Alumni, the great Argentinian club at the beginning of this century, was originally the Buenos Aires High School (a British school). After 1900 it was decided that the clubs should substitute their English names, for Spanish ones. However, the first football association kept its English name: the Argentine Football Association. The Association also maintained English as the official language of meetings until 1906. In 1912 the Association was divided, and for the first time, Spanish was partially used. The two factions were called the *Federación Argentina de Football* and *Asociación Argentina de Football*. Not until 1934 was 'football' replaced by the Spanish 'futbol', when the new and definitive association was created: *Asociación de Futbol Argentino*.(13)

Not only was the game a British import but so were its standards and quality of play. In the first decade of the 20th century, football grew under the influence of the great teams that came to play in Buenos Aires and Rosario, the largest Argentinian cities, with a relatively well developed system of club competition. Southampton arrived in 1904 and won all their matches. In 1905, Nottingham Forest played several matches and returned to England undefeated. The first Argentinian victory in 1906 was against a team mixed with British nationals based in South Africa. The game was celebrated in Buenos Aires as a glorious event, and consolidated the image of its winners, Alumni, as a great team. Before the First World War, Everton and Tottenham visited Argentina with great success. In 1923 Chelsea played several matches and won them all. In the wake of these matches, the myth of the invincibility of British soccer was created, which over time was intelligently manipulated by the British themselves, and not only in relation to the Argentinians.(14) Argentinians had to wait almost a century before defeating England in a tournament in Rio de Janeiro in 1964.

From 1895 onwards, football spread all over the country. By 1910 there were clubs and provincial leagues as far North as Santiago del Estero. However, Buenos Aires, Rosario and La Plata remained the main centres of the new game. The rapid growth of Buenos Aires, through the arrival of one million European immigrants in the first decade of this century, conditioned the future composition of the 'national' League. Buenos Aires and small industrial cities close to the capital, like Avellaneda, Quilmes, Banfield and Lanús gradually came to dominate organized football. At the club level, Alumni dominated for the first decade, with a team of players drawn from the boarding schools. All the players' names were English. The expansion of football and the massive creation of clubs in almost every district of Buenos Aires and the surrounding cities made possible what many saw as the 'nationalization' of football. The League victory of Racing Club in 1913 and its dominance until 1920 was perceived as having generated a 'national tradition' in which players with English names disappeared.(15) Soccer shifted from the English schools to the new industrial quarters, where Argentinians, immigrants and immigrants' sons founded the new clubs which dominated the League until 1930. Bayer writes emphatically that 'the "creole" (national) football was born, like the tango, in the poor quarters of Buenos Aires'.(16) The period 1900-30 is, without any doubt, the golden age in the expansion of soccer in Argentina, still reflected by the fact that, in 1985, two thirds of the professional clubs playing in the different divisions of the national League had been founded in this period.(17)

This 'new' tradition was initially supported by the traditional elites and political parties. Both the Conservative and the Radical parties had active members in the different clubs founded in this period. Many of the clubs became 'massive' institutions, with thousands upon thousands of members. Politics and voting developed also as an integral part of the social life of the main clubs in Buenos Aires. Hence, control over the Executive Boards of the most important clubs was regarded as very important by some political leaders. Moreover, the socialists and anarchists had seen soccer as an alienating activity, but this negative reaction was changing and some new clubs were initially supported by active and militant left wingers.(18) Thus, football rapidly became a 'national' sport, an arena in which a public spectacle given by male players definitely established a unique framework for the management of male identity and cultural power. It is a game for and about men. Thus, exclusive masculine participation made possible a gender based definition of boundaries: women were defined and perceived as spectators, as a passive element in a game played by men.(19) Football, then, created a space for male self-definition, and a historical time for producing and 'representing' events, games and players tied to the imagining of 'Argentine qualities'.

In this process, international competition provided a suitable setting for male performances, but also for the encounter of nations. Teams represent nations. In a world that had defined as ideal the model of the political organization of the national state, national teams were perceived as competing nations. The model of the nation, as I have pointed out above, needs a 'community', 'a sense of belonging', in other words a 'national consciousness'. My main argument is that, in the absence of war, sport provides a crucial arena where teams, heroes and victories are produced and reproduced.(20) The history of competition between nations is reflected in the world history of sport, one of the most attractive global cultural scenes for victory and defeat, for heroic exploits and dramatic failures. Sport in general, and in the specific case of football in Argentina, generates male discourses and performances in which 'national characteristics' that are male become the focus of attention and symbolic construction. Let us explore these assumptions more closely.

It is possible to imagine that the 'original' style of Argentinian soccer was British, a very physical way of playing where the game was, obviously, dominated by physical strength, resistance and continuity - known as the 'kick-and-run' style. However, it is important to keep in mind that this style was very effective in obtaining positive results. Concomitantly, Argentina was visited by different European teams, with the 1922 visit of the Hungarian Ferencvaros especially remembered. The Hungarian players were popular for their technical skills and dribbling ability; no kick-and-run methods are recalled. The Hungarians provided the Argentinian players with a kind of mirror in which they could see themselves reflected. It is important to point out that, at the same time, in Europe a 'typical Austro-Hungarian style' was widely recognized and admired. Argentinians believed that their own style of playing was very similar to the football played by Central Europeans teams. In contrast to physical strength and perseverance, ball control and 'fantasy' were emphasized.(21)

For Argentinian national football, the 'foundation myth', (i.e. the emergence of a style all of its own) is located in the 1920s, and is associated with the following aspects: the cult of 'dribbling'; the appearance of 'pairs' in a team (insider winger); and the crystallization of a style defined as elegant, skillful, cheeky and lively. It is interesting to note that the development of trick skills is traceable to 'founding players': the 'bicycle kick' with Pedro Calomino; the 'marianella' with Juan Evaristo; and the 'flying header' with Pablo Bartolucci. Through their ability and technical skills these players were defined as 'models' to be emulated. However, to be established as something unique, a style must be contrasted with other styles. In this respect, the 'founding myth' emanated from the famous tour of Europe in 1925 of Boca Juniors, a first division team from Buenos Aires and one of the greatest teams in the history of Argentinian football. On this tour they won fifteen games and lost only three. Boca's way of playing, the elegant and easy movements of the players, the absolute control of the ball, skill in dribbling; their move to a sort of circus-like, spectacular and artistic mode astonished the Europeans. In addition, Argentinians demonstrated that it was possible to play and to win with less continuity and physical strength than many European teams. In contrast to kick-and-run football, this style was associated with two qualities: playing at different speeds and maximizing control of the ball, even if it was necessary to play it back. What the game lost in intensity and continuity, it gained in precision. The Argentinians gained a positive image in Europe, a genuine admiration based on the way they were able to play the game. The construction by a relevant other of this image of Argentinian football was recognized as an important element in the process of creating a self-identity.(22)

We must bear in mind that in this process a 'national style' was invented as 'tradition': 'fantasy', 'creative imagination' and 'aristocratic elegance' were opposed to 'work', 'discipline and hardness' and 'physical effort'. It is possible to see that in this context football, a rather new social practice related to leisure time and consequently less obligatory than school or work, was 'invented' as being highly relevant to a 'national male style'. In this sense, 'national characteristics' in football tend to be quite specific, in contrast to the vagueness of many values reflected in making and binding together 'imagined communities', such as nations and countries. With great lucidity, Hobsbawm points out that the occasions when people become conscious of 'nationality' or 'citizenship' remain, in many cases, associated with symbols and rituals that are novel and invented.(23) Sport offers this performative context when teams representing 'nations' compete in well-arranged ceremonies, adorned with national flags and initiated with the music of national anthems.

Argentina consolidated her dominant position in South American football when, after defeating Uruguay in the final, she gained the South American Championship in 1921. In this decade not only the South American but also the international competitions were marked by the intense confrontations between Argentinians and Uruguayans. Argentina did not send a football team to the Olympic Games of 1924 in Paris: Uruguay won. After the victory, and once back in Montevideo, Uruguay were challenged by Argentina in a match that for many was considered to be the 'moral Olympic final': Argentina won. Again in 1927, Argentina won the South American Cup, defeating Uruguay well in the final. Finally, at the 1928

Olympic Games in Amsterdam, Argentina and Uruguay both arrived undefeated at the final: Uruguay won. The disappointment and sorrow of the Argentinian supporters after the defeat were replaced by the hope of winning the first football World Cup, to be played in Montevideo, Uruguay, in 1930. Once again Argentina and Uruguay met in the final, and once again Uruguay won. Brera, an Italian sport journalist and historian, describes the match in the following way:

> Argentina play football with a lot of imagination and elegance, but technical superiority cannot compensate for the abandonment of tactics. Between the two 'rioplatense' national teams, the ants are the Uruguayans, the cicadas are the Argentinians (author's translation).(24)

This interpretation was shared by many of Brera's contemporaries. Against the background of these two important international defeats, the myth of the generosity of Argentinians players and their style came to be created and rationalized. This belief perfectly matched the 'national characteristics' of players that were devoted to play with great imagination, elegance and aristocratic flavour. Uruguayans, on the contrary, were interpreted as rude, almost enraged players. The myth of the 'Charrua (Uruguayan Indian) grip' was born, as opposed to 'Argentinian (non-Indian) aristocratic elegance'. This was undoubtedly the way in which Argentinian defeated males preferred to be considered and to imagine themselves. However, the reaction of the supporters was different: the entire national team, but especially the centre-half Monti, were accused of lacking virility. Sixty years later, one Argentinian who played in that final recognized that the Uruguayans were extremely violent, but also admitted that the majority of his team-mates behaved on the field with cowardice.(25)

Conclusion

I have argued that in constructing national identity, traditions of belonging to the same community must be created. This is done through different ways, but a collective memory with shared symbols that emphasized particular events and ceremonies as the initial moments of a tradition must be present. These events and ceremonies appear to be public in nature. Symbolic and practical work is carried out in arenas opposed to the home, the private and the internal. In the constitution and modernization of nation states, the collective rituals of sport facilitate not only a privileged male participation but also, through competition, a confluence between a given male activity and national representation. In this respect, I have tried to demonstrate that in the first three decades of this century, Argentinian football functioned as an efficient 'rite of institution', according to Bourdieu's use of the term: the creation of a separate arena in which the main difference is the one established between the accepted participants and those who will never participate, i.e. the women.(26) In addition, for a 'team' to represent the nation and some of her best qualities, it is necessary to have a process of identification in which, at the end, 'the team is me'. One source of this complex process is what Ricoeur calls 'the semantics of wishes': dreams, myths and rituals which may act as a disguise for the deepest wishes of people.(27)

Football, in the last instance, permits a legitimized definition of a bodily practice as eminently masculine, which does not need to be accepted by the entire male population. Over time, it produces an overlap of practical and symbolic constructions of national characteristics, national values, and national pride and sorrow. The 'national' will thus come to be perceived as 'naturally' masculine. This exclusion implies that women will not acquire the capacities that are a *sine qua non* condition for playing the games. A masculine, fraternal participation recreates, over time, images, perceptions, events, teams and heroes, which allow the playing and replaying, again and again, of the games that can nourish the nation with fulfilled dreams. From this, it follows that women can identify themselves with the 'team as a nation'. They can recognize in men the 'national virtues', so long as they accept the logic of this symbolism, and acknowledge the importance of the active presence of sons, husbands and brothers.

Football as a cultural bond had considerable force in Argentinian society when immigration was so dominant. Argentinians were not born Argentinians; their nationality needed to be invented. A contemporary observer of this process wrote:

On the football fields the national unity, created by the primary school and conscription, was completed and even improved, because differences in terms of age and education disappeared ... Football became in practice a school of democracy (author's translation).(28)

Nationality was, then, a question of 'becoming' rather than 'being'; and it was a 'problem' for Argentinian political and cultural elites at the beginning of the century.(29) Masculine qualities became an important frame of reference for thinking the 'national'. I have shown that the emphasis was put on fantasy, creativity, elegance and aristocratic flavour, and less on leadership, perseverance, determination, courage and virility. This created a masculine world full of ambivalence and mixed feelings. Argentinian soccer was, paradoxically, a symbolic construction which generated a 'discussion' on national values, but also about the limits of a masculine moral world where courage and virility were not at an excess. In each great failure cowardice was identified, but each success was the result of technical superiority and ability.(30)

Acknowledgement

I would like to thank the members of the panel to whom the original paper was presented and my colleague Marit Melhuus for their comments and critical suggestions on the first draft.

Notes

1. Benedict Anderson (1983) *Imagined Communities: Reflections on the Origin and Spread of Nationalism*, Verso, London, pp.15-6.

2. Anderson, *op. cit.*, p.133.

3. Anderson (*op. cit.*, p.17) writes:

    > no more arresting emblems of the modern culture of nationalism exist than cenotaphs and tombs of Unknown Soldiers. The public ceremonial reverence accorded these monuments precisely because they are either deliberately empty or no one knows who lies inside them, has no true precedents in earlier times.

4. See Bruce Kapferer (1988) *Legends of People, Myths of the State: Violence, Intolerance and Political Culture in Sri Lanka and Australia*, Smithsonian Institution Press, Washington; and Bruce Kapferer (1989) 'Nationalist Ideology and a Comparative Anthropology', *Ethnos*, 3-4, pp.162-99. In his comparative analysis of the Australian egalitarian nationalism and the Sinhalese Buddhist hierarchical nationalism, the emphasis is put on the violent aspects of nationalist ideologies and practices. He writes:

    > my argument, certain aspects of which are anticipated by Dumont, is that hierarchy and egalitarianism, separately or in combination, are potentially destructive and dehumanizing. This potential is realized in nationalism itself, which takes particular direction through hierarchical or egalitarian ideology (Kapferer, 1989, p.9).

5. If nation is destiny, as many nationalists could argue, then, in principle, there is no choice. However, national emotions and images can be expressed via different arenas in which choice and uncertain outcomes are dominant characteristics. In this sense, our preference for a given sport is conditioned by taste,

sensibility or simply lack of better opportunities. Sports may represent a space of freedom, not only because we can exercise choice but also because the outcome is uncertain. Victor Turner (1977) in 'Variations on a Theme of Liminality', in Sally F. Moore and Barbara G. Myerhoff, (eds.), *Secular Ritual*, Van Gorcum, Assen/Amsterdam, emphasized the importance of taking seriously leisure as a key dimension in the analysis of modern societies.

6. I strongly believe that 'marginal' themes and unconventional fields are a good entry to the complex, difficult and 'diffuse' topic of relating 'national consciousness' to cultural symbols. For an analysis of the historical process of building up a national consciousness through the production of cookbooks in modern India, see Arjun Appadurai (1988) 'How to Make a National Cuisine: Cookbooks in Contemporary India', *Comparative Studies in Society and History*, 30, pp. 3-24. John Borneman (1988) 'Race, Ethnicity, Species, Breed: Totemism and Horse-Breed Classification in America', *Comparative Studies in Society and History*, 30, pp. 25-51, convincingly shows how the classification of horses in America is linked to the reciprocal influences of cultural symbols, social practices, and the formation of national identity.

7. The historical perspective chosen in the analysis of the formation of national identity is not accidental. I assume that national or ethnic identity is tied to heterogeneous social practices (war, political parties ideologies, the nature of the State, cook books, or sport) and produced in discontinuous times and spaces. This approach is very well presented by G. Carter Bentley (1987) 'Ethnicity and Practice', *Comparative Studies in Society and History*, 29, pp.24-55. Thus, the temporal and the spatial dimensions are very important in revealing the relevance of 'national' symbols and images. The victory of Argentina in the World Cup of 1978 had been 'expected' since the 1920s and was experienced as the historical realization of a long-awaited 'destiny'; it was not lived as an 'accident' but as a 'historical necessity'.

8. For the data on the process of migration I have relied on Oscar Cornblit (1969) *'Inmigrantes y empresarios en la politica Argentina'* in Torcuato S. Di Tella and Tulio Halperin Donghi, (eds.), *Los fragmentos del poder*, Editorial Jorge Alvarez, Buenos Aires; Aldo Ferrer (1963) *La economia argentina*, Fondo de Cultura Económica, Buenos Aires, pp.106-8; and David Rock (1977) *El radicalismo argentino: 1890-1930*, Amorrortu Editores, Buenos Aires, pp.22-29.

9. Tulio Halperin Donghi (1987) in *El espejo de la historia. Problemas argentinos y perspectivas latinoamericanas*, Editorial Sudamericana, Buenos Aires, pp.188-238, provides a brilliant analysis of the relationship in Argentina between immigration policies and ideologies from 1810 to 1914. I follow in this section many of his arguments and insights. For a discussion on types of nationalisms and nationalists see Maria Ines Barbero and Fernando Devoto (1983) *Los nacionalistas*, Centro Editor de America latina, Buenos Aires.

10. In the 1915 Manifesto of the Radical Party, it is stated that:

    the Radical Party is the Nation herself ... The work that we will generously achieve will be for all Argentinians, that coexist inside the national life, and is aimed to imprint fundamental and glorious paths in the process and in the future of our Motherland (author's translation, quoted in David Rock, *op. cit.*, p.65).

11. See, among others, Ronald Hyam (1976) *Britain's Imperial Century, 1815-1914: A Study of Empire and Expansion*, Harper and Row, New York; J. A. Mangan (1986) *The Games Ethic and Imperialism*, Viking, London; Pierre Bourdieu (1984) *Questions de sociologie*, Minuit, Paris, pp.173-95; and Brian Stoddart (1988) 'Sport, Cultural Imperialism, and Colonial Response in the British Empire', *Comparative Studies in Society and History*, 30, pp.649-73.

12. See Tony Mason (1989) 'Football', in Tony Mason (ed.), *Sport in Britain*, Cambridge University Press, Cambridge.

13. For Argentinian soccer history I have relied on Ernesto Escobar Bavio (1923) *Historia del futbol en el Rio de la Plata*, Sports, Buenos Aires; Eduardo Olivera (1932) *Origines de los deportes britanicos en el Rio de la Plata*, n/e, Buenos Aires; Pablo Ramirez (1977) *Historia del futbol profesional*, Perfil, Buenos Aires; Horacio De Marinis (1981) 'La pasión futbolística' in *Serie la Vida de nuestro pueblo*, 33, Centro Editor de América Latina, Buenos Aires; Ariel Scher and Hector Palomino (1988) *Futbol: pasión de multitudes y de elites*, CISEA, Buenos Aires; and, Osvaldo Bayer (1990) *Futbol argentino*, Editorial Sudamericana, Buenos Aires.

14. Mason, *op. cit.*, pp.177-8.

15. Bayer, *op. cit.*, pp.21-2.

16. *Ibid.*, p.21.

17. Scher & Palomino, *op. cit.*, p.31.

18. Bayer, *op. cit.*, pp.23-5.

19. See Pierre Bourdieu (1990) 'La domination masculine', *Actes de la Recherche en Sciences Sociales*, 84, pp.4-31, especially p.26. Umberto Eco (1984) *Viagem na irrealidade cotidiana*, Editora Nova Fronteira, Rio de Janeiro, p.231, observes that in the case of soccer and masculinity it is necessary to transcend the game itself and to focus analysis upon the discourses on and about soccer. Men, he argues, talk and discuss soccer as a kind of play, a pedagogical play, where the issue at stake is to learn how to keep positions and boundaries of power.

20. See Eric J. Hobsbawm (1990) *Nations and Nationalism since 1870: Programme, Myth and Reality*, Cambridge University Press, Cambridge, p.143.

21. Juan Carlos Lorenzo and Jorge Castelli (1977) *El futbol en un mundo de cambios*, Editorial Freeland, Buenos Aires, p.37.

22. Kapferer, *op. cit.*, 1988, p.215 distinguishes Sinhalese and Australian nationalism through the way identity is perceived: while Sinhalese identity is 'in itself' the Australian identity is 'for itself'. In other words, Australian identity is established in relations of competition, conflict, contrast, and opposition. The Australian nation is a collectivized individual identity that, in a sense, can only sustain such identity, and unity in identity, by contrast ... It defines itself in relation to what is not Australian and discovers opposition and conflict founded in the presence of collective national identities that are different.

23. Eric J. Hobsbawm (1983) 'Introduction', in E.J.Hobsbawm and Terence Ranger, (eds.), *The Invention of Tradition*, Cambridge University Press, Cambridge, p.12.

24. Gianni Brera (1978) *Storia critica del calcio Italiano*, Tascabilli Bompiani, Milano, p.98.

25. It is interesting to observe that the title of Bayer's chapter in *Futbol Argentino*, dealing with this period of Argentinian soccer history, is simply 'Charruas y blandengues', where 'charrua' signifies courageous Uruguayans and 'blandengues' signifies Argentinians as softies. I do not have space to elaborate, but I believe that this is quite central to understanding some dilemmas of masculine identity in Argentina.

26. See Pierre Bourdieu (1982) *Ce que parler veut dire*, Fayard, Paris, pp.121-34 and Bourdieu (1990) *op. cit.*

27. Paul Ricouer (1970) *Freud and Philosophy: An essay on Interpretation*, Yale University Press, New Haven.

28. Augusto Mario Delfino (1971) 'Lo bueno del futbol' in Roberto Jorge Santoro, (ed.), *La literatura de la pelota*, Editorial Papeles de Buenos Aires, Buenos Aires, pp.50-1.

29. See Robert Paine (1989) 'Israel: Jewish Identity and Competition over "Tradition"', in E. Tonkin, M. McDonald and M. Chapman, (eds.), *History and Ethnicity*, Routledge, London. He

argues that in looking into questions of national identity in societies that are the product of immigration, and, hence, the meeting of different ethnic groups and contrasting philosophical and religious interpretations, issues of ontology are unavoidable. They arise when dealing normal informants as well as with intellectuals.

30. This remark about the presence of ambiguity and uncertainty, of a tension between 'peaceful elegant superiority' and 'violent victory' is very interesting for the question of Argentinian males - but only if we accept as valid, David Gilmore's (1990) description of Circum-Mediterranean images of manhood in *Manhood in the Making. Cultural Concepts of Masculinity*, Yale University Press, New Haven. I will not deny the presence of competitive and sexually aggressive aspects in the performance of soccer, where the modal relations of father-son, and 'real man' and homosexual are profusely used. See in this respect Eduardo P. Archetti (1992) 'Argentinian Football: A Ritual of Violence?', *The International Journal of the History of Sport*, Vol. 9, 2, pp.209-35; and Marcelo Suarez Orozco (1982) 'A Study of Argentine Soccer: The Dynamics of the Fans and their Folklore', *Journal of Psychoanalitic Anthropology*, 5, pp.7-27.

10 The stars and the flags: Individuality, collective identities and the national dimension in Italia '90 and Wimbledon '91 and '92

Neil Blain and Hugh O'Donnell

The symbolic functioning of sport and sports mediation, within the ideological and political constitution of the national dimension, is inevitably related to many large topics in the social sciences. These include questions of sign/object relationships; of hegemony and the state; of structures of media output, institutions and audiences; of identity and collective identity; and of media imperialism. We begin by briefly outlining some of the most important theoretical questions and positions.(1)

The national dimension

In what follows, we use a variety of phrases related to that aspect of collective identity which is constituted as 'national'. The category which contains ideas such as the nation-state, nationality, and national identity, we call the 'national dimension'. Additionally we try to distinguish aspects such as 'nationality', 'national identity', 'national character', 'national feeling' and 'national difference' with whatever precision we can, in the hope that this will, for example, differentiate processes of auto- and hetero-typification, and help distinguish specific areas of discursive practice; for example, the construction of 'national character' for cultures (often treated as 'races') such as Italy or Germany, or transnational groupings such as 'Latins' or 'Celts'. At all times we assume that this group of ideas is quite distinct from the notion of political mobilisation implied by the group of concepts related to the term 'nationalism'. Where we do point to 'nationalistic'' discourses we make that clear.

Mediation or invention?

Though in this chapter we use concepts like 'representation' and 'mediation', whose deployment generally signals some faith in an objective world beyond discourse, we are also conscious that the vocabulary of the postmodern - 'construction', 'invention' - requires some space in such an analysis also. This is not an attempt to have it both ways, but a recognition that there is yet much to be resolved in the series of arguments between those who continue to make truth claims and those whose position has become 'relativist' and 'textualist' to the extent of claiming to regard questions of what might lie beyond 'rhetoric' as naive.

A position in this debate is, however, obviously very important in the discussion of the constitution of the national dimension in the mass media. We are of the view that what is significant in our study is its examination of the relationship between media constructions of the sporting and political worlds (seen by us as connected), and the real-world relations of dominance which are represented or concealed therein. Our use of terms like 'invention' therefore refers to our perception that media discourses are best approached as fabrications whose relation to their correlatives in the political world is problematic.(2)

Institutional and political frameworks

The relationship between media output, media institutions, states, and political cultures is extremely complex, and we do not have space here to pursue the question in any detail. Nor could we attempt, in any circumstances, such an analysis for every nation whose media we refer to.

But it is necessary before proceeding further to be more explicit about what sort of relationships are in operation when press and broadcasting organizations construct their own and other cultures in national terms. While unable here to address questions of 'the state' and of 'political culture' generally, or, in any more than a glancing way, to investigate the nature of the media institutions whose output we examine, it is nonetheless important to signal that nothing in the relationship of these four domains can be taken for granted.

As we have noted elsewhere,(3) it is therefore desirable to keep in mind probable differences occurring in a variety of relationships between specific cultures, societies, state apparatuses, media institutions and discursive practices. This question is worth exploring in more detail.

1. We know that football is (with various qualifications) predominantly a working class sport, while tennis is predominantly middle class. Yet there is working class interest in tennis and middle class interest in football. When we examine coverage of these sports in the mass media we find, to locate our examples in the UK, that the tabloid press re-invents tennis in such a way as to address what it sees as its readership: tennis coverage may often, as we see below, use the brutal language in which this section of the press chooses to construct the world generally, and especially for its working class and underclass readership. Likewise, quality papers with significant socioeconomic group A, B and C1 readerships require to reach a discursive compromise between, on the one hand, the conventions of journalistic style appropriate for newspapers like *The Herald* or *The Independent*, and, on the other, the symbolic functioning of football in class and gender formations.

2. But if we look beyond the UK, we find not only that the tabloid press as understood in the UK is missing from most European countries (Germany's *Bild* notwithstanding), but that its equivalent readership is also missing, since the breadth and rigidity of British class distinctions is very much a sui generis phenomenon. In particular, the existence of very large culturally and politically disenfranchised working classes or underclasses simply is not replicated in the EC formation: nor elsewhere in the west of Europe. Therefore, to understand the language of *The Sun*, we require to understand the socio-historical conditions of possibility for *The Sun*, and also their national specificity.

3. And just as we need to compare outward from Britain to Europe, we need to compare outward from sport to politics. We require to do this both at macro-levels and in relation to the particulars of discourse. If *The Sun* and its British rivals adopt an especially unacculturated and frequently degraded form of language in

sports coverage, we need to remain aware (a) that it does so in most if not all other areas of its coverage, despite the special licence which sport seems to offer and (b) that this is a political fact and not just a linguistic or journalistic one. It is no coincidence that British tabloid newspapers are strongly conservative in terms of their support for existing relations of dominance. The maintenance of a large unacculturated and potentially reactionary element in British society has clear political purposes. The language of the popular press, with its mockery of radical politics and its sneers at cultivation and culture is above all a political phenomenon, affecting areas such as gender and race as much as class.

At the surface level, rather than the structural, then of course we find an interpenetration of sport and politics in a number of distinct categories: a constantly productive metaphorical relationship between the domains means that sport uses political symbolism, politics uses sporting symbolism, the media use sport politically, cities and countries use sport politically, even races (as in the case of white supremacists) use sport politically.(4)

In this chapter we assume from the outset both homological and real-world ideological and political relationships between the discourse of sports journalism and the discourse of politics. We cannot pause to justify these assumptions here, but evidence is intended to emerge from our examples.

Identity

Then there are the connected questions of collective identities and media constructions of the national dimension. In the final part of his *Media, State and Nation*, Philip Schlesinger (1991) argues the need for an actionist perspective in which identity is seen "as a continually constituted and reconstructed category" (p.173) whose collective dimension is enabled by a process of sustained agency within both "a determinate set of social relations" and definite spatio-temporal conditions, specific conjunctures of which characterize collective identity at the national level.

We take it for granted in this chapter that the national dimension of collective identity is, firstly, centrally important in human experience (historically, in Europe, from the establishment of a fully modern consciousness onward) and, secondly, rendered visible in particularly revealing ways by the sorts of international sports event which we are examining here.(5) We are interested, therefore, both in sports discourse in itself, and also as a component of political discourse; and hence as a constituent of political identity. While we cannot take space in this chapter for an explicit discussion of the national dimension in collective identity, we return to outline some important associated issues in our conclusion.

Football, tennis and the national dimension

In examining media coverage of Italia '90 and Wimbledon '91 and '92 from the point of view of discourses of national identity,(6) a number of differences become immediately apparent.

Firstly, the number of nationalities in relation to whom such discourses emerge is very much smaller in the case of Wimbledon. Of course, a number of nationalities represented in Italy (the Scots, the Irish, the Cameroonians) were not represented at Wimbledon. On the other hand, of those nationalities represented at both events, some attracted discourses of national identity at one of them, but not the other.

For example, the Italians were one of the most striking sources of discourses of the national during Italia '90, based essentially on the notion of 'volcanic passion', but they were entirely inconspicuous at Wimbledon '91, despite the fact that thirteen Italian players started the tournament. Another example is that of the Argentinians, consistently portrayed in Italy (as indeed were all the South Americans) as temperamental and reckless to the point of irresponsibility. No such discourses were to be found in the coverage of Wimbledon, and this despite the fact that Gabriela Sabatini was one of the 1991 women's finalists and attracted concentrated media attention.

The reverse situation is best exemplified by the Swedes. Their team attracted few discourses of national character or identity in Italy, whereas Stefan Edberg at Wimbledon was a major recipient of accounts of Nordic 'coolness' and 'cleanness' (we should note here the susceptibility of Swedes to this dual national/Nordic - or

Scandinavian - identity).

Secondly, both the extent and scope of the discourses of the national dimension differed enormously at the beginning of the respective tournaments. A study of coverage of the early matches of the World Cup showed an abundance of such discourses relating to a wide range of nationalities. During Wimbledon, on the contrary, although such discourses did emerge with great vigour towards the end of the tournament, they were singularly lacking during the early stages of play. We offer a number of explanations for these discrepancies.

Individuals v teams

An obvious difference is that, while football is a team game, tennis is, in every sense, a game played by individuals. In relation to this we might note the following.

Firstly, traditional rituals of national representation are entirely absent from Wimbledon. There are, for example, no national colours (everyone - even Andre Agassi - being subjected to Wimbledon's 'predominantly white' rule), no flags and no national anthems. By way of contrast, the question of national anthems had been an important sub-theme of World Cup reporting, with well publicized interventions by, among others, Luciano Pavarotti and Diego Maradona.

Secondly, this situation is further complicated by the fact that there is genuine confusion in the European media concerning the actual nationality of some of the leading players. For example, during the 1991 tournament there were numerous examples of Martina Navratilova being described as Czech, and of Ivan Lendl being described as American, when it was in fact precisely the reverse which was the case. In the 1992 Wimbledon tournament similar confusions would arise over Monica Seles. She herself avoids references to her nationality. In 1992 she came under direct attack from the Croatian player Goran Ivanisevic in relation to the civil war in Yugoslavia. The German newspaper *Die Welt* (6 July 1992) quotes Ivanisevic as saying:

> Monica is now almost an American, perhaps she doesn't want to recognize her country any more. In any case, if I win I will dedicate the title to my people. Monica doesn't even know which

flag she's starting under. I hope she loses the final.

Similar confusions arise in relation to other less well-known players. 'Statelessness' has been a recurring description of tennis players. There was never such confusion over nationality in reporting of the World Cup. (It is not that such ambiguities were entirely absent. A number of journalists in different countries made the point that several of the players in the Irish team were not born in Ireland - in a radio advert, *The Sun* even suggested that the only thing truly Irish about the team was Jack Charlton's dog - and for political purposes the British press made much of the 'British Isles' unifying potential of the Irish team.)

Trying to fly the flag, anyway

While Wimbledon is not a nation-based tournament in the strict sense of the term, it is nonetheless an obviously international event, and it is also, by any standards, one of the world's major sporting media events. The 1990 final had been watched by 350 million people in 71 countries, while in 1991 some 5.5 million people watched the women's final and 8.5 million the men's final in Germany alone. By 1992, the total viewing figures had increased to 500 million people in 105 countries.

On such a world stage, the emergence of specifically nationalist interpretations of even the most individualistic of sports (not only tennis) appears to be irresistible. As part of the media attempt to present Wimbledon in such a light, discourses of national representation frequently emerge. These include numerous references to national flags, which are conspicuous by their absence at Wimbledon, as well as references to national anthems, which are of course not to be heard before the start of play. Indeed, Italian journalists went so far as to describe the Italian players (following the nickname of the Italian football team) as the *azzurri*.

And in fact, when there is more than one player from any given country involved, there is a very real sense in which the journalists from that country attempt to create the idea of a team. This notion is normally relatively unsuccessful, since it is frequently players from the same country who knock each other out of the tournament - there were no less than twenty-eight such games in the 1991 tournament -

but it is nonetheless a very stubborn idea. And these efforts towards constructing 'teams' prepare the ground for the later stages. As the tournament proceeds, and both the visibility of surviving players and media interest in them rise correspondingly, discourses of national identity emerge as powerfully as for any other sport.

Stars in teams and stars as individuals

Despite attempts to fly the flag in tennis, the sport is to a great extent a carrier of myths and ideologies about individualism. It is true, of course, that football is also marketed to a varying degree through the use of individuals as stars. The English star Paul Gascoigne was used extensively by the UK's Channel Four television in the latter half of 1992 to market its broadcasting of Italian football, but this was only one of innumerable concurrent such deployments of stars in football marketing as a whole and individual teams in particular.

As in the Hollywood star system, there is not necessarily a rational explanation for the success of sports stars - they are decisively products neither of production or consumption, but appear to succeed as a result of negotiation between producers and consumers. Just as movie stars require more than acting talent to achieve stardom, mere sporting ability is not enough for sporting stardom either. To be a very great player, a Hoddle, a Gullit, a Maradona, a George Best, undoubtedly helps, but, as in cinema, *persona* is likewise important. Sports stars like Ian Botham and Paul Gascoigne may have about them a timeliness, an ability to incarnate something required by the historical moment, in this instance a quality of Englishness which is centrally of its period.

Of course, as in movie stardom, stars should not be seen merely in marketing terms. Richard Dyer's work on movie stars at the end of the 1970s brought together a range of possible economic, sociological and psychological approaches to the phenomenon, many of which are applicable to sport.[7] The phenomenon of the star also provides modes of 'identification' and otherwise conceptualized forms of imaginary relationship between spectator and star; and, by extension, an imaginary connection with forms of cultural and social activity associated with stars. Furthermore, stars operate ideologically. For example, the strong, independent male star (a Clint Eastwood or Arnold Schwarzenegger persona) appears to offer an individual and often reactionary solution to what is often a social and collective problem (there are intriguing parallels in sport). It may be, therefore, that the combination of strong individual performances in a game such as tennis, when coupled with significant national identities - particularly German identity, which is one of our main focuses below - result in a particularly potent signifying combination. (Though, in truth, no amount of militarist accounts of German sporting prowess, which we note below, will turn Michael Stich into Chuck Norris.)

Most television producers - on BBC, NBC, Sky, for example - carried a Wimbledon section of tennis programming which offered what Sky termed the 'Player Profile'. (Interestingly, the 1991 Sky Sport profiles periodically demonstrated less *élan* here than their BBC counterparts, though NBC's personality segments, as one might expect, were televisually the most extravagant.) Applying star theory from the cinema, one would expect to find in tennis, an interest, from television's point of view, in players as a form of outlay, a form of capital and a major marketing component of the coverage. Players can cost money in various ways: their cost is implied in the purchase price of rights to broadcast, or incurred by their employment (for example, Jimmy Connors on NBC) as commentators or summarizers. Yet stars can be seen (variously inflected in the differing cases of commercial companies on the one hand and the BBC on the other) as forms of capital, as guarantors of ratings success ultimately translatable into further financial gains, or other kinds of gains equal to financial gains. Their central role in marketing tennis and keeping viewers is probably considerably greater still than in football.

Tennis (and other sports) stars may also be televisually constructed and decoded according typologies similar to those previously explored in sociological work applied to cinema.[8] McEnroe, like the one-time delinquent Nastase, is a Bad Guy, Agassi, a Rebel (the Rock'n Roll Kid), Sabatini is a Dark Latin Beauty: in this instance (like the Ice-Borg), a strong flavour of national (here actually transnational) flavouring enters the definition of the Type. Most commonly in Wimbledon 1991, as we see below, this happens in tennis when the players are German.

This discourse of stardom is widely found in the press also. When Agassi lifted the title in 1992, the dominant discourse in the British press was one of cheeky, glitzy, brash Americanness, with a strong emphasis on gambling, reflecting his origins in Las Vegas: 'The lights always shine in Las Vegas and Agassi has grown up in their glow', writes the *Sunday Express* (5 July 192). "He gulps Coke for breakfast, searches the world's finest gourmet centres for a McDonald's burger and has three sugars in his coffee", continues the *Daily Mirror* (6 July 1992), adding:

> he came from the deserts of Las Vegas to strike like a rattlesnake and win the game's premier prize... The dice finally fell right for Agassi ... he trains on a liquid diet of Coke, Coke, and more Coke, in between wolfing down burgers and fries at all hours of the day and night.

Such constructions are not confined to the tabloids. *The Times* joins in with the following description:

> the street urchin with the flowing locks became king of the turf, the rebel found a cause and the bastion of tradition gained a champion coined in the mint of Las Vegas: ear-ring, squirrel's tail hair, baggy shorts, bicycle pants and all.

During the fourth set, when Agassi looked as if the game might be slipping from him, it adds: "For the first time Agassi had the glazed look and the weary step of a penniless gambler on the Vegas strip". (Or, we might reflect, it could be Paul Newman in *The Hustler*.) Commenting on the peculiarities of grass-court play, it continues:

> It suits the Las Vegan in him: the odds maker ... Grass-court tennis is like cutting cards for a tenner every time ... Every stroke of the racquet is a high stakes business.

We might note of this approach to what seems above all to be *individuality* that it is nonetheless approached as a mythic *American* individuality - there is a strong national element not only animating but enabling this account.

But it is possible to find stars in team games, too. During Italia '90,

Maradona, among one or two others, is accorded this sort of treatment. The Spanish daily *El País* (9 July 1990) describes him as "a chubby, swarthy Paul Newman", while the Austrian *Kronen Zeitung* (24 June 1990) describes the Argentinian team as "Diego Maradona and ten extras".

The cult of the star is in Maradona's case only one step towards the cult of the idol. At times Maradona becomes almost incorporeal. The Soviet weekly *Sovetskaja Kult'ura* (30 June 1990) describes the key moment of the Argentina-Brazil game as follows:

> What did Maradona do? Something unbelievable. He passed through a wall of six feet which were kicking him, six hands which were pulling him back, six shoulders as powerful as battering rams.

He acquires superhuman powers. *France-Soir* (5 July 1990) informs us that "he was able to inspire in his team mates an almost supernatural will to win". He finally turns into a God. The Austrian daily *Kurier* (24 June 1990) describes him as a 'god of football', while France's sports daily *L'Equipe* (25 June 1990) calls him an 'all-powerful god'. The article in *France-Soir* mentioned above is titled 'Diego is still god', and in another issue (19 June 1990) it observes that "in Naples they revere one God, Maradona". On the day of the final the Swedish daily *Dagens Nyheter* (8 July 1990) comments that "the need for football gods is inexhaustible, and Maradona will always play that role, whatever this evening's result".

The same person can, of course, be presented as the personification both of evil and of good depending on who is writing. Following Italy's defeat by Argentina the Italian daily *La Stampa* (4 July 1990) carried the headline "Defeated by the diabolical Maradona", while its sister newspaper *Tuttosport* of the same day said simply "Maradona is the devil".

Such descriptions can be found throughout the European press. And although Maradona may perhaps represent the highest point of this process, he is not the only beneficiary. "The myth is definitive!" announces the Spanish daily *El País* of Schillaci, whom *Kurier* (4 July 1990) describes as a 'folk hero', and *Sovetskaja Kult'ura* (30 June 1990) as a 'hero of the nation'. *France-Soir* (26 June 1990) describes the German player Klinsmann as a 'mythic hero': the same thing happens to the German player Matthäus.

But whereas stardom in football is one economic and signifying component among a number, in tennis it is considerably more important, a constituent which requires a greater frequency of distribution in the operation of the sport. Football is arguably conceivable without stars, but tennis is not. Tennis is physically organized in such a way as to enable a televisual approach to participants with something in common with the cinematic construction of stars. Cinematic stardom was to a great extent consequent, historically, upon the spread of the close-up, a close visual interest on the individual. Tennis, with its structured pauses between serves, its periodic breaks, enables a particularly personal form of interest on the part of the camera, something not attainable to nearly the same extent with fast-moving team games.[9]

English fans v German teams

Only two identities achieved significant levels of presence in both Italia '90 and Wimbledon '91 in terms of the national dimension. These were the English and the Germans. But there were two entirely different kinds of interest here. (We might note in passing that some nationalities, presumably because of - very broadly speaking - their historical salience, offer to those who comment upon them a much richer repertoire of myth than others whose political visibility has been lower.)

The English and the Germans have been historically important enough to merit not only a high visibility but, so to speak, a richer mythic texture. The Germans are not only militaristic in myth (despite their provocative non-involvement in the Gulf war which had preceded some of the later press coverage we analyse) but also of course, hard working and, naturally, efficient, though these traits may display some thematic links. There is, in aspects of both the British and the continental European coverage of Italia '90 and Wimbledon '91 some continuity in the operation of myths of Germanness. This is because the chief vehicle of discourses of Germanness was on both occasions the players, presumably because of a certain relative decorum on the part of German fans.

But the fact that England fans were the main focus during Italia '90, whereas the event of Wimbledon itself became the source of discursive generation during Wimbledon '91 means that we find a striking sort of mythic pluralism at work when overviewing the two events. In fact there is virtually no discursive continuity at all. There are instead at least two different accounts of Britishness developed and we return in the conclusion to the question of how compatible they are.

The English

Italia '90

Discourses of Englishness during Italia '90 related overwhelmingly to the behaviour of the English fans. These discourses were not, however, static, and showed a clear development as the tournament proceeded, though this development was not uniform in all the countries studied.

Prior to or in the early stages of the World Cup, a number of negative and at times extremely alarmist articles concerning the English fans appeared in many sections of the European press. For example the Spanish weekly *Cambio 16* (4 June 1990) carried an eight-page article on the subject, with photographs from Hillsborough and Heysel, bloodstained fans and beleaguered bobbies, and a caption announcing that "the objective is to humiliate the greatest number of people possible". Elsewhere in Europe, in Germany, France and the Soviet Union, articles could be found depicting the arriving English fans as marauding barbarians coming to put not just Italy, but in some sense all of Europe to the sword. The English football hooligan was coming to pillage the holy sites of Italian civilisation, and with it the cultural values of Europe as a whole.

However, we may note that, with two significant exceptions, such discourses did not survive long in European World Cup coverage, and that the European press is in the main generous about English football fans. Thus in Germany the *Hannoversche Allgemeine Zeitung* (27 June 1990) quotes the Italian *La Repubblica* saying that the "English are victims rather than causes of tensions". The Spanish sporting daily *As* (1 July 1990), says that "that section of the English support made up of hooligans was violent and noisy - fortunately they are a minority and in no way represent the fan from the islands". In France, *Le Nouvel Observateur* (5 July 1990) observes that the Cameroonians:

> provided the British fans with an opportunity to show that they are also human - imagine, the hooligans from Manchester and Liverpool stood to applaud the lap of honour of Milla and his gang!

The Italian *Gazzetta dello Sport* (6 July 1990), speaking admiringly of the sporting virtues of the English players, talks about those 'fans' who are so different from the players: "if there is a group who do not deserve the hooligans, it is precisely the English players".

The two significant exceptions to this generous attitude are the Spanish press and the Soviet press. We do not have to look far for an explanation of this Spanish attitude. The myth of the English football rowdy has its meaning constantly redefined by that other English invader, the drunken holidaymaker who arrives in great numbers on Spanish shores every summer. The Soviet case is more complex, and responded to ideological imperatives of the time which we have analysed fully elsewhere, but which limitations of space do not allow us to detail here.[10]

Wimbledon '91

Discourses of Englishness relating to Wimbledon '91, based essentially on the site of Wimbledon itself and those who frequent it, turn essentially on the notion of a country which is anachronistic, hide-bound by tradition, and in the final analysis class ridden and inegalitarian in the extreme. Since in fact, despite the persuasiveness of this account, we do not really believe that European journalists see Britain in quite the way they write about it, we return in our conclusions to the idea that this form of writing has some ulterior, enabling function.

These versions were encouraged greatly by the fact that, as a result of the backlog due to heavy rain during the first week of play, games were played for the first time ever on Middle Sunday, and what are presented as 'ordinary, real fans' gained unaccustomed entry to the ground. There is a relationship here with the Italia '90 coverage: Wimbledon in Britain is ruled by aristocrats but the real people who get into Wimbledon on Middle Sunday are (at least) cousins of Britain's horrible but real football fans.

The scale of these accounts is simply too enormous for us to do more than merely scratch their surface here, but what follows is very representative. For example, the notion of disturbance, of challenge to an antiquated class society, is emphasized in some Continental reports by the use of the English term 'shocking' (i.e. this word appears in English in these foreign-language reports). Thus *Le Figaro* (29 June 1991) writes:

> Shocking! For the first time in the history of the Wimbledon tournament matches will take place on Sunday on the courts of the All England Club. This time, meteorology was stronger than tradition.

The Austrian *Neue Kronen-Zeitung* (1 July 1991), making a reference to football fan behaviour on Middle Sunday, adds:

> No sign of the usually supercooled atmosphere, the joy of finally being in these 'august surroundings' was celebrated with the Mexican wave. In Wimbledon!
> However, some respectable gentlemen found this 'Shocking!'

According to the Italian magazine *Matchball* (12 July 1991), these "young and enthusiastic spectators bring football stadium songs" to tennis. In fact, they turn the aristocratic world of Wimbledon 'upside down':

> The world is upside down. From the centre court come unaccustomed yells. As they await the beginning of the matches, the crowds do the 'ola', known here as the 'Mexican wave'. It goes on for twenty-five minutes. It's never been seen before at Wimbledon. Will we ever see it again? (*L'Equipe*, 2 July 1991)

The notion of the importing of football fans is put forward by numerous newspapers, many suggesting an implicit victory of the working class over the aristocracy. Thus the Spanish sports daily *El*

Mundo Deportivo (1 July 1991) writes:

> (It was) a different audience. Young, healthy people with innovative habits, who did not hesitate to start doing 'Mexican waves' on a Centre Court which yesterday did not seem so mythical, so venerable.

Kurier (3 July 1991) mentions the party atmosphere which prevailed:

> ...some people turn up their nose when matches are played on Sunday. Not to mention this wave, 'la Ola' or whatever it's called, which comes from football and has even made its way to Wimbledon. It felt a bit like a public festival.

The longest and possibly most highly developed article on this theme was to be found in *Gazzetta dello Sport* (2 July 1991). Entitled 'The revenge of the ordinary spectators', it requires very little comment.

> The first Sunday of play in Wimbledon made room for the people: they took over the terraces of the Centre Court and the entry of the masses gave a genuine flavour to an aristocratic and stuffy tournament.
> However, the abolition of privilege, even if only for a single day, had a revolutionary effect.
> The people took over the terraces of the Centre Court in a joyful tumult reminiscent of the storming of the Bastille ... and the entry of the masses, although authorized, brought a unique flavour, of real supporters, to a tournament which too often hides behind polite applause a profound lack of interest in tennis.

The Germans

Apart from the English, the nationality which attracted the most sustained discourses constructing national character both during Italia 90 and during Wimbledon 91 was the Germans. In stark contrast to the discourses of Englishness mentioned above, the discourses of Germanness were essentially the same in both cases. They were of a militaristic, aggressive, highly disciplined nation which either blasted or steamrollered its opponents out of existence. A few examples from coverage of both tournaments will serve to illustrate this point.

Italia '90

The Italian *Gazzetta dello Sport* (25 June 1990), for example, describes the game between Germany and Holland as "the metaphor of the war", and Austria's *Kronen Zeitung* (24 June 1990) entitles its report on the same game, 'The Thirty Years War'. The headline in *The Sun* of 4 July also equates football with war: "We beat them in 45 ... Now the battle of 90". The Spanish sports paper *As Color* (8 July 1990) describes Matthaus as "the resurgence of the German Luftwaffe", his legs are like 'machine guns', and he combines "Wagnerian musicalinity with his usual steamroller style". The Soviet newspaper *Izvestia*, (26 June 1990) speaks of Klinsmann as "the man who literally blasted the Dutch defence". The Spanish daily *El País* (9 July 1990) describes the Germans as "moving with the heaviness of a tank" and as "always looking to measure up to armies like their own". The German press itself recognises that its team is internationally knows as a 'Teutonic panzer' (*Spiegel*, 11 June 1990).

Wimbledon '91

In the case of Wimbledon these discourses are if anything even more highly developed. They accumulate primarily around the figure of Michael Stich. Thus we find references to his 'explosive game' (the Spanish daily *el Periódico*, 8 July 1991); to his 'deadly forehand cross' (*Dagens Nyheter*, 8 July 1991); his 'fatal' serve (*La Libre Belgique*, 6 July 1991); his 'brutal serve' (*ABC*, 8 July 1991); his 'explosive serves' (*Gazzetta dello Sport*, 7 July 1991); his 'bomb-serves' (*Corriere della Sera*, 5 July 1991); his 'serve missiles' (*Dagens Nyheter*, 5 July 1991); his 'violent' serves (*L'Equipe*, 6 July) which 'bombard' his opponent (*El País*, 1 July 1991), which 'pound' or 'destroy' him (the Spanish regional daily *La Voz de Galicia*, 6 July/8 July 1991), with Becker "being pummelled by the bullet-like serves of Stich" (*The Glasgow Herald*, 8 July 1991).

These military metaphors also extend to Steffi Graf. Thus she is referred to as 'the battleship Graf' (*Gazzetta dello Sport*, 6 July

1991). She is 'hyper-aggressive' (*Le monde du tennis*, 1 August 1991) and has a 'deadly forehand return' (*Dagens Nyheter*, 7 July 1991) which is a 'killer blow' (*Bild*, 6 July 1991).

The Spanish daily *ABC* (8 July 1991) opened its report on the final between Becker and Stich with the following metaphor: "A duel of high precision bombers took place in the Centre Court at Wimbledon". But, nowhere were these discourses more notable than in the British press. Even 'quality' newspapers such as *Scotland on Sunday* took part (7 July 1991):

> For most, it will be as difficult to watch the first all-German Wimbledon men's final ... without flinching as it is to heed Basil Fawlty's advice: Don't Mention The War.
> Oh well, here goes. Before Becker won the first of his three titles in 1985, Germany's greatest impact on Wimbledon occurred in October 1941 when the Luftwaffe dropped 16 bombs on the All England Club, ripping a huge hole in the roof of the Centre Court stand. There, least said soonest mended.
> Happily, other sons of the Fatherland have treated the manicured lawns of SW19 with warm affection.

The most highly developed version of such discourses belong, however, to the British tabloids. For example, *The Star* of 8 July 1991 carried an article entitled 'Stich as a parrot'. It is surrounded on all sides by the following exclamations: 'All mein says Hun-known hero'; 'Hun-believable'; 'Stich it up your Junker'; 'Triple champ Boris throws in ze towel'; 'Deutschlark'; 'Michael's the new power Kraut'; 'Wunderbar'.

A number of these themes also appear in *The Sun* of the same day. Its back-page article is entitled 'FANTA-STICH. He tears Becker to blitz', and it tells of Stich's 'devastating straight-set blitz of fellow German Boris Becker'. It continues later "Fanta-Stich! He blasted down an amazing 15 aces to brush aside the No. 2 seed". Beside it is a photograph almost identical to that of the *Star* with the caption, 'It's a Stich-up'.

Two photographs on the inside back pages carry the captions 'Herr-raising! Hun-believable!' The article, referring to an earlier 'victory for the Fatherland', tells of how Stich "skewered Becker with a forehand return" at match point, and assures its readers that when

Becker embraced Stich, "Junior Jackboot put the boot in ... Stich stuck it up him".

Conclusion

The main conclusions which can be drawn from this comparative study are as follows.

Firstly, discourses of nationality emerge more easily in relation to teams than in relation to individuals, but they are constructed around individuals also. Our view is that images of society and culture, rooted in a belief in the centrality of the national dimension, are so pervasive that they will work in emphatic opposition to 'individualist' accounts. Where appropriate, journalists work hard to create and maintain the notion of a team, anyway, since this makes the notion of typicality easier to sustain: for example the three German finalists at Wimbledon in 1991 were presented as a kind of mini German team. However, as we have seen, the symbolic value of an event itself can surpass that of teams and individuals.

Secondly, when European journalists were dealing with what might pass as the actuality of English fan behaviour in Italy, they were relatively generous to the fans: yet when dealing more or less self-consciously with a mythic Wimbledon, that is talking about it in a decidedly non-realist fashion, their hostility toward English culture often appears strong. In the space we have available we cannot give this fact the attention it probably deserves, since it requires the opening up of a new set of arguments which we will address in work still in progress. But (a) it would seem that the hostility is toward the domain of English/British politics and not in any real sense aimed at the domain of sport. And (b) as we observe below, the tone of whimsy in the Wimbledon reports should be treated carefully.

Thirdly, as we have noted, the English were the outsiders at Italia '90 and the hosts at Wimbledon. But they remain the outsiders in the second event also. There is no doubt of the fact that England is constructed as 'outside' by European journalists (it is distanced in certain parallel ways by American coverage also). So it seems that the discourse of exclusion typical of the Italia '90 coverage belongs to a category much larger than football. In other words the idea that English football fans might be letting the side down is, even if true, probably not important as an event on its own. The 'otherness' of the fans is part of a larger construction of otherness. England is 'outside' even at Wimbledon, in fact particularly at Wimbledon for at Italia '90 the fans could be read as exceptional.

Fourthly, to return to the mythicizing element in European coverage of Wimbledon, what is interesting is how the mythic England relates to what may be argued to be true of the actual England. The England of the 'dainty aristocracy' at Wimbledon (*El Mundo Deportivo*, 8 July 1991) is a metaphor from the French revolution, of course; but it is in another way quite near the mark, insofar as it can be argued that hegemonic relations in the UK do indeed belong in part to pre-modern social structures. Again, the reasons for these constructions taking the form that they do lie beyond the scope of this chapter, but we are dealing neither with naivete (nor just marketing): we are looking at a disguise which masks both accuracy and probably real hostility. To what extent this is actually greater, toward UK political culture, as time goes by, is hard to say though between 1990 and 1992 this seems to be the case. It may be part riposte.

Fifthly, as to the question of whether or not the two accounts of Britain are compatible, there may be some sense in which the people who turned up on Middle Sunday are the football fans. But, of course that would be too neat and in fact there is not in reality that degree of discursive fit. Nevertheless it is, so to speak, through the doors at Middle Sunday that the football fans would come, if they were allowed in.

Generally tennis fans are not seen to be representative of national character and nor in fact are they normally as visible as Middle Sunday made them. Football fans are of course in these respects different. But it should be noted that in predominantly middle class societies like Germany, football fans may aspire to the relative invisibility of tennis fans. This may serve as an index of the degree of modernity and (hence) civility in a society.

Sixthly, visibility of football fans is not restricted to England, as we know, and there might be much to say about why some country's fans take on a symbolic role and some do not. (It is not restricted to *countries*, either, because there is a Latin fan who is transnational.) But it may be that both in terms of auto- and hetero-typification, the prominence of the English fan is not by any means wholly a consequence of social reality, i.e. of actual hooliganism. The myth of the English fan may, in fact, be a boundary-marking function, perhaps related to a need to deal with 'otherness': both on the part of the English psyche and its bewildered continental counterparts. This would not be to suggest that the difference between English fan behaviour and that of other fans is, ultimately, a function of discourse; such a suggestion would be unduly Lyotardian.

Despite evidence of English fan misbehaviour having been talked up during the last World Cup there is little doubt that there are real-world differences in European fan behaviour and that English football fan behaviour is relatively antisocial. Yet its interpretation may nonetheless at home and abroad fulfil this differentiating function.

Finally, our seventh finding is that Germany and Germanness appear to be a central obsession within British media culture and at least as much within sports culture as elsewhere. At the time of writing late in 1992, British-German relations are in poor shape and a cursory glance at the television schedules in the UK reveals many programmes obsessed with World War Two and many others with imagined German monetary perfidy associated with the demise of the British economy. There is little doubt that a separate category requires to be constructed for British media re-inventions of German character. The ahistorical nature of such constructions we assume to be obvious. But their obsessive and pathological nature suggests (a) some unique role for Germanness in defining Britain's own national dimension to the British - or, at least, to the English - and (b) troubled times ahead in the nineteen nineties in what (in politico-economic terms) is bound to be an ever less equal relationship between the two countries; one hardly likely to civilize the attitudes and tone of the British media.

Notes

1. For an extensive discussion of theoretical problems in this area, see Blain, Boyle, O'Donnell (1993), especially Chapter 1 and General Conclusion.

2. The most useful discussion of the earlier, 'modern', debates about issues of 'reflection' and 'mediation' is probably in Raymond Williams (1977), especially part II, 'Cultural Theory'. At another, recent, extreme from Williams's continuing faith in a domain of objects beyond that of signs was Baudrillard (1991), a fairly extreme example of the textualist view of history. See, inter alia, Jean-Francois Lyotard (1988) and Mark Poster (1988). Scepticism and anxiety about postmodernist positions in the political sphere can be found in Dick Hebdige (1988) and Christopher Norris (1990), and more polemically in Christopher Norris (1992).

3. Blain, Boyle, O'Donnell (1993), Chapter 1.

4. See also Whannel (1983; 1992).

5. For contrasting views on the operation of the national dimension in contemporary life, see Hobsbawm (1990) and Nairn (1990).

6. This paper is based on two pieces of research. In the first of these, we studied approximately 3000 newspaper articles on the 1990 World Cup in the following ten countries: Austria, England, France, Germany, Ireland, Italy, Scotland, the then Soviet Union, Spain and Sweden. In the second we studied coverage of the 1991 Wimbledon tournament in the same ten countries, on this occasion adding Belgium (the French-speaking press), Catalonia, Portugal and the United States.

7. R. Dyer (1979).

8. See O. Klapp's (1962) work on social type, cited in Dyer (1979).

9. Goldlust (1987) discusses questions of shot distance and duration in US and Australian coverage of various sports as broadcast on

Australia's Channel Nine (Chapter 4, pp.102-107).

10. See Blain, Boyle, O'Donnell, (1993), Chapter 5.

Bibliography

Baudrillard, J. (1991) 'La guerre du Golfe n'a pas eu lieu', *Libération*, 29 March.

Blain N., Boyle R., O'Donnell, H. (1993) *Sport and National Identity in the European Media*, Leicester University Press, Leicester.

Dyer R. (1979) *Stars*, BFI, London.

Goldlust J. (1987) *Playing for Keeps: sport, the media and society*, Longman, Cheshire, Melbourne.

Hebdige, D. (1988) *Hiding in the Light*, Comedia, London.

Hobsbawm E. J. (1990) *Nations and Nationalism since 1780*, Cambridge University Press, Cambridge.

Klapp, O. E. (1962) *Heroes, Villains and Fools*, Prentice-Hall, Englewood Cliffs.

Lyotard, J. F. (1988) *The Differend: Phrases in Dispute*, Manchester University Press, Manchester.

Nairn, T. (1990) *The Modern Janus - the new age of nations*, Radius, London.

Norris, C. (1990) *What's Wrong with Postmodernism*, Harvester Wheatsheaf, Hemel Hempstead.

Norris, C. (1992) *Uncritical Theory: Postmodernism, Intellectuals and the Gulf War*, Lawrence and Wishart, London.

Poster, M. (1988) *Jean Baudrillard: selected writings*, Polity, Cambridge

Schlesinger, P. (1991) *Media, State and Nation: political violence and collective identities*, Sage, London.

Whannel, G. (1983) *Blowing the Whistle: the politics of sport*, Pluto Press, London.

Whannel, G. (1992) *Fields in Vision: Television Sport and Cultural Transformation*, Routledge, London.

Williams, R. (1977) *Marxism and Literature*, Oxford University Press, Oxford.

Subcultures of opposition

11 New supporter cultures and identity in France: The case of Paris Saint-Germain

Patrick Mignon

Football is, incontestably, the most popular sport in France, and has been for a very long time, but there have always been fewer spectators, and it has aroused less passion, than in other major European countries. No city in France is able to support two teams, and the ends occupied by the 'ultras' seem empty compared to the kops, the curves or the sides elsewhere. This situation arguably reflects the place of the working class in French society in the process of urbanization and in the organization of political life. But, how can one understand the renaissance of passion for football in France which has been articulated over the past twelve years by a marked increase in the number of 'live' spectators and by the development of new forms of supporterism? The sporting successes of French teams - a fundamental condition for the rise in interest of spectators and TV fans - is the result of a meeting between the world of football, *stricto sensu*, clubs and official bodies, and the political, financial and media worlds which seek to mobilize communities, voters, and audiences. This work of 'football promotion', which is also an effort at promoting cities, regions or firms, is opposed by the 'ultra' supporters, who put into play their own interventions, at the same time reinventing the tradition of supporterism.

In this process, the identities put into play - masculine, local, national and social - are modernized, even radicalized, as a function of the condition of the moment. For traditional reasons, which remain a powerful springboard, the love of football in France is enhanced by new processes which are sustained by the crisis of the French model of integration and the definition of identities. These new stakes must take account of the development of hooliganism, French style.

The sport of the people, but which people?

The system of sports

On television, a European Cup game involving a French club can capture 20% of the total TV audience. The figure is higher for a match involving the French national team. Thus, although France had already been eliminated, the World Cup match between France and Scotland in 1990 attracted 45% of the television audience for that day. Football in France sustains important monthly magazines (*France Football, Onze*) a part of the daily press (*l'Equipe*) and occupies an important place in the general press news, especially in the local press. One might also mention here the sale of sports equipment, the popularity of the Panini figurines (models of footballers) and the total number of registered players, which was 1,752,638 in 1988-1989.

Another way of assessing the importance of football in France is to look at the increase in the sums of money invested in it since the beginning of the 1980's (Bourg, 1992). The spending by the clubs, which reached 37.5 million Francs in 1970, totalled 1,200 million in 1991. Club receipts, for the 1990-1991 season were made up of 23% from the rights to televised transmission; 20% from local authorities; 22% from sponsors; and only 35% from spectators. Spectators account for 42% of receipts in Germany, 55% in Spain and Great Britain, and 65% in Italy. The spectator receipts in the budgets of French clubs made up 81% of total income in 1970 but only 50% in 1985-86. This trend towards revenue raising from sources other than gate receipts is a development found throughout Europe. However, it shows that going to the stadium is not the dominant form of relating to the game in France.

The first official statistics on football crowds in France date from 1952. In that year, the average number of spectators per First Division game was 11,140. Despite the statements of the football authorities, the current average is barely higher. It remains three times less than in England, Spain or Italy. For the Second Division, the average crowd over the last fifteen years has been about 2,500 spectators.

The recent growth of football audiences has largely been dependent on the successes of clubs such as Marseille, with an average of about 30,000 spectators per game, and, more generally, those of large cities such as Paris, Lyon, Nantes, Bordeaux. Some football bastions, such as Saint-Etienne and Lens, are also able to count on crowds which are as large when the club is in the Second Division as they are when they are in the First.

A social history of French football

Reliable data are lacking on the social evolution of the football crowd in France. Nonetheless, based on some research on the clubs (Bromberger, 1987) and general data derived from a survey on the Cultural Practices of the French (Ministry of Culture, 1990), it is possible to point out some general traits.

According to the first sources, football crowds reflected the general public: alongside the students and adolescents in high school who often represent 20% to 25% of it, employees and workers supplied the core (between 50 and 60%), the rest being comprised of middle or upper class members. On the other hand, the statistics of *Les Nouvelles Pratiques Culturelles des Français* give more importance to members of the middle classes (middle and upper level managers, merchants, artisans) in attendance at sporting events. In fact, with the exception of the upper classes, all of society is found in the stadium. Unsurprisingly, the working class dominates when the club is located in a working class region, while in Paris it is the office workers and middle level managers who reign. As Bromberger has argued (1987; 1988; 1992), football in France offers a plurality of levels of identification (personality of the players, styles of playing, etc.), which permit each social group to find its reasons for going to the stadium.

Why, when compared to Britain, has there not been in France the appropriation of football by the working class, and why has there been this lesser passion for the game at least until the 1980s? My hypotheses have a bearing on the processes of urbanization, industrialization and the place of the working class in France and on the French model of citizenship.

Football in France is especially the affair of small cities (Marseille, 1990). Auxerre, Sochaux, Saint-Etienne are popular today; Reims were a major force in the 1950s, Alès or Sète during the period between the two wars. The clubs of the large cities, such as Paris or Marseille, only predominated during limited periods, and often knew the pain of the lower divisions, the abandoning of professionalism or even pure and simple disappearance. This was the experience of clubs in Lille, Toulouse, Bordeaux and Paris. Likewise, there are rarely two high level clubs in the same city, while there are seven to eight large London clubs and two large clubs in Madrid, Rome and Milan. Prior to the Second World War, there were, indeed, several clubs in the agglomeration of Lille-Roubaix-Tourcoing, but they did not survive the 1950s. In Paris, there was the Red Star, the Stade Français and the Racing clubs and, more recently, Paris Saint-Germain and Matra-Racing, but the latter has disappeared due to poor results and lack of public support.

Football developed at the beginning of the century in a society which was largely rural and Jacobin. Until the 1950s, the majority of the French lived in small administrative or industrial cities or large rural villages, rather than in the large agglomerations where the major industries were located. Moreover, due to the slowness of the rural exodus during the first part of the 20th century, the French working class remained very heterogeneous for a very long time (Noiriel, 1986). Few workers were sons of workers. Those who were lived alongside the children of farmers who sometimes continued to work the farm or who kept close contact with the rural world. There were thus marked cultural differences among the working classes drawn from the same area, from the points of view of political values, sociability and leisure. Those who continued to have links with the land were less inclined to become integrated in urban leisure pursuits such as football. And, when the local working class community was more homogeneous, it often found in rugby the best means for expressing its values of strength and solidarity. This was the case in the industrial valleys of the Alps and the Jura (Chambéry, Saint Claude, Rumilly), and the Burgundian iron and steel industry (Le Creusot, Montchanin), or for the miners from the South (Carmaux) (Pociello, 1983).

In the big cities such as Lyon or Paris, large concentrations of the working class simply did not exist. People worked in small workshops and were dispersed throughout the urban area, mixed in with other social classes. Paris is not a working class city; it simply has neighborhoods which are more working class than others, such as the East of Paris. Most of the workers live in the suburbs, mixed in with other social groups. As is the case throughout Europe, football in France contributed to a reinforcement of the social bonds among people having no other social or cultural definitions than belonging to a given urban territory and social class. This construction of collective identities took place within the context of relatively restrained communities which, in addition, had not entirely cut their ties with traditional rural society. As this working class was becoming larger and more homogeneous between 1950 and 1974, it would turn to other forms of leisure, which, subsequently, were to lose their importance (Noiriel, 1986; Mendras, 1988).

Professionalism in football was established in France in 1932, but it was not unusual up until the 1960's for talented players to remain amateurs, adding to their salary the benefits of a possible promotion within the enterprise of the local club's patron and the bonuses which he paid (Wahl, 1989). The 'soft' modernization, French style, may take account of the lesser importance of professionalism within the working class. In a context defined by a relative economic stability, professionalism was not a live issue. The salaries proposed by the clubs were not high enough for a qualified worker to abandon his work, or for a semi-rural worker to drop work on the farm. For many, school, the hope of becoming a civil servant, of taking over the family business, or of entering into the steel works like one's father, constituted realistic dreams of social climbing. Only the immigrants - the Polish, Spanish, Italians, then those from the Maghreb - felt that football was the best means of escaping from work in the mines (Beaud, Noiriel, 1990). As a general rule, money from playing football appeared as a sort of extra, and, in this case, rugby and especially cycling with all their intermediate statuses between amateurs and professionals, were sports as attractive as football, perhaps more so in a society in which changing social status was seen as much as a matter of individual as of collective strategy.

During the years when the Communist Party was becoming established in the working class in France, its successive political strategies acted against the 'autonomization' of football as a working class leisure activity. There was, of course, a working

277

culture which was being formed in the 'red' suburbs around Paris and in the valleys of the Lorraine steel and iron works (Verret, 1988; Schwartz, 1990). For the militants and the avant-garde, however, working class culture was not true culture. In France, working class organizations were built up against the idea of an autonomous working class or popular culture. The socialist or communist organizations fought for access to the universal, as they struggled to take over political power. These ideas were well accepted by the elite among the skilled workers. For them, emancipation meant resisting conventional leisure pursuits which brought alienation with them. This did not mean that one could not love football privately, but this love was not a value. In France, until the 1960s, culture was 'great culture', something always linked to the idea of a unified social and national body. The national football team or the Tour de France were things of valour, because they evoked this unity (Vigarello, 1993).

The economic and social transformations in France after 1945 upset this landscape (Mendras, 1982; 1988). The cities were growing rapidly and the rural exodus transformed the peasants into employees and workers. However, this movement was also one of diversificiation in styles of life and leisure, more organizd by generational divisions and by consumption-led individualism. The numerical increase in the working class did not go hand in hand with a reinforcement of the awareness of belonging. The strong communities which combined union and political affiliations remained there where they were, but greater education and a more comfortable daily life weakened the traditional forms of solidarity. The political parties and the unions were transformed into service structures more than into militant organizations (Touraine *et al*, 1984).

In this context, football was still of interest, but less exciting for those who wished to explore modern life. For the young, the cinema, going out, the new forms of music, shopping, television, do-it-yourself work or the purchase of a car, or sometimes an apartment, had more attractions. During the 1960s and 1970s, for a large number of adults, football was nostalgia for the Stade de Reims, or for the World Cup in Sweden in 1958. The same was true elsewhere in Europe, but only in societies in which football had not been established in the large cities. How, then, can the renaissance of

French football be explained?

The new meaning of football in France (1)

Popularity and success

There are obvious reasons for the renewed interest in football in France during the last decade. Rheims, between 1950 and 1962, and the France team in Sweden in 1958, made enthusiasts of the crowds. However, following the collapse of French football, of clubs and of the national team, the public quit the stadiums. The poor quality of football and of its emotional power ceded to other forms of leisure. Later, the stabilization of the attendances, then their growth, was linked to the successes of the various French teams. Firstly, there were those of Saint-Etienne in the European Cup; then the successes of the French national team in Argentina in 1978, and subsequently in Spain and Mexico; and, finally, the achievements of clubs such as Bordeaux and Marseille. Due to these successes, there was an incentive to remain in front of one's television to watch football, and even to return to the stadium. This improvement in performances was also linked to the modernization of football clubs under the aegis of the Federation and the League, and to the arrival of sponsors, investors and local government who were all interested in the success of the French teams in European or international competitions.

Football, the media and the spirit of enterprise

For a long time in France, football was an affair of local notables (industrialists, merchants) who saw in it a means of acquiring a local and national reputation. The legal status of the professional clubs was that of non-profit making associations and reflected this state of professionalism in which the management of a club was an act of good will. This is still mainly the case, but a new wave of club directors has recently appeared who take a more active role in the club, defining a new economy of football. This commitment is based on the notion that football is a universal sport and, at the same time, a universal market. In this new perspective, French football is of interest when it begins to be prominent abroad and can promote French products (Bourg, 1992; Nys, 1990; see Raspaud, this volume).

In addition, just as Taylorism has come to an end and companies are looking for new methods of management, the vocabulary of sports, and especially those of collective sports, will serve as an instrument in the mobilization of the companies' staff around themes of competition and organization in a context of the free market. Individuals must be strong and count on themselves in order to become someone in society and within the company. Thus, football is used by companies as a means of creating staff solidarity around their projects. However, it is also an external means of communication used to promote the fame of brands or of new entrepreneurs. With the end of the 'glorious thirty', those thirty years of unsurpassed economic growth and prosperity, French companies are looking toward new markets and are seeking strong positions against the competition. Sport provides them with the values to do so (Ehrenberg, 1991).

Thus, new, rich investors are appearing: Jean Luc Lagardère at Matra-Hachette; Bernard Tapie Holding at the Marseille Olympic; Canal Plus at Paris Saint-Germain. The structures of the most important clubs are changing; they are becoming public companies with a sports objective. Thus, the Marseille Olympique (OM) was, until recently, part of a holding company in which one found the club, television sports interests, the Adidas company and an agency for the marketing of sports events. Canal Plus, the cable television channel, is the principal stock holder in Paris Saint-Germain SA, part owner of the Parc des Princes, and is now launching a multisport club in the image of Real Madrid by buying basketball, volleyball and handball clubs.

With the end of the state monopoly over television and the creation of three, then six channels, football has become a commodity in the competition among media channels. In 1974, there was barely 10 hours of football per year on the French channels; in 1990, football was the major sport televised, with 425 hours yearly, and it provided one of the largest television audiences. The competition among channels for the recording of large football events has produced a lot of money for clubs' coffers. This input of money has changed the recruitment of new players and promoted more spectacular staging, as well as increased excitement for the spectators. Even if the money coming from television and sponsors is more than that coming from the spectators, it nonetheless remains necessary to attract the latter, since a full stadium has more value for a dynamic entrepreneur than an empty stadium, which has no passion and energy. Thus, Canal Plus and Paris Saint-Germain invited, in their advertising campaign for the 1992-1993 season, the Parisians and suburbanites to "be parochial" and to come "to celebrate Mass every Saturday evening at the Parc des Princes"

"Be parochial": local governments

Sometimes these entrepreneurial strategies are also accompanied by political strategies. Thus, Bernard Tapie had both a financial and a political strategy. Being president of the O.M. meant having greater chances of becoming deputy in the Bouches du Rhône, Mayor of Marseille or a government Minister. However, more generally speaking, at the level of cities or regions political projects prevail. For example, in Paris, the election of the Mayor by universal suffrage (1975) was the departure point for attempts to have a great football team reborn in the capital. In fact, these bonds between football and politics are of very long standing since, as of the 1920's, the football clubs have sought from the mayoral offices the funds necessary for the construction of stadiums and equipment (Wahl, 1989). However, the first far-reaching policy of this kind was that of Gaston Deferre in Marseille in 1965.

What may one expect from a football club? "Be parochial" is a good slogan for local politicians when they think that the representation of French society as a unified body might be transferred to local societies, especially to new regional metropolises. The football team can serve as a support for the image of a municipality, working for the common good, and the stadium for that of the mobilization of the inhabitants around the city, its team and its mayor.

It is thus a question of knowing how to 'sell' a city: have an important team, good economic health, modern, high technology companies, a university, eventually a rock scene, etc. This means being a real city. Football, and other sports, are factors in the strategies used to attract investors, because since the decentralization laws, cities have been competing with each other in this sense. One may cultivate images: wisdom and work ethics (Le

Havre, Sochaux, Lens); know-how (Auxerre); or the grandeur of large projects such as Marseille or Paris. Football has thus become one of the vectors of communication strategies for the most powerful cities or regions.

The new image of football not only projects a new institutional and economic context, but also popular support. The new company spirit, the Tapie model, the renaissance of regional capitals, and the ambitions which accompany it, define new conditions for the encounter between the public, the football authorities, the sponsors, the investors and the mayors. However, this encounter takes place in a society which is no longer seen as on a path leading to citizenship, comfort and modernism; which symbolized the movement which led the people from the country to the large city. Rather, it is seen as a focal concern which seems more and more difficult to attain, and from which one risks being excluded. Therein are the social conditions for a rediscovery of a sense of identity and territory, and, therefore, new reasons for being committed to football.

The new meanings of football in France (2)

Who are the French 'ultras'?

The social background of the 'ultra' supporters or hooligans is quite difficult to establish. The social surveys, via interview and participant observation, do not allow the establishment of pertinent quantitative data. However, the data gathered at the time of observations, and those kept by the police at the time of questioning, allow for the construction of an image of the kop of Paris Saint-Germain and its hooligans which is a little different from that found in Britain. Our analysis is based on 73 persons questioned during the seasons 1988-89 to 1991-92, whose age, sex and background are known. Among these 73, the profession of 30 of them is known.

Some data are not surprising: the hooligans are young people (70 out of 73). The three young girls present in this sample show a feminine presence which was greater in the Parisian kop than in British stadiums. The majority, 62, were between 16 and 22 years of age, with a few, older fans aged 25 and over. The leaders of the associations and those who present themselves as spokesmen or 'connoisseurs' of the kop belong to this older age range.

Their geographical origins correspond to the area of recruitment of the general spectators at the Parc des Princes. What do the data on employment say? Two of the sample were unemployed; there were four students and three 'high schoolers'; military people, one committed and two called up; two apprentices; eight office workers, and eight workers. Among the 'leaders' and interviewees, this same diversity was found : one foreman at the SNCF (French National Railroad); two orderlies; a police officer; a military person; a data processing employee; an unemployed person; a messenger; two 'high schoolers' and two students. That is, although the hooligans are not mainly unemployed people or socially detached individuals, they belong to the working class with an equal balance between skilled and unskilled jobs. Also, the founders of the Boulogne kop, notably the skinheads, come from the upper classes (families of lawyers or top level managers). What was interesting in the case of the Boulogne kop and among the hooligans was the meeting between two social groups, the young workers and employees and the young bourgeois, in 'rupture with their milieu' and seeking to unite with the people. However, between 1985 and 1991, the meetings no longer took place with a view to the revolutionary transformation of society, as it had done in the years after 1968.

The French hooligans and the urban crisis

France is, today, an essentially urban society and during the past fifteen years most geographical mobility has taken place within urban areas. In France, there are no ghettos, as in America, or *favellas* such as those in Brazil, but there is indeed a movement toward a society shared between groups which are well integrated and others which are threatened by the modernization of the economy and by urban renewal. The results of this are that some live in neighborhoods which accumulate a maximum of handicaps. This does not mean that all the hooligans or all the 'ultra' supporters come from these neighborhoods, but simply that this risk of 'dualization' feeds a feeling of dereliction and a fear of social decline. The young supporters who come from the suburbs, do not come from neighborhoods characterized by a social and cultural homogeneity, but rather from areas where there is social fragmentation (Dubet, Lapeyronnie, 1992).

The increase in immigration during the 1970s, which resulted in permanent settlement in France, added its specific weight to this situation (Jazouli, 1992). During the years of economic growth, immigration was perceived as a minor problem. However, today the immigrants are projected as part of this crisis of disintegration of social relationships. With racism on the rise, the difference in life styles between ethnic groups reinforces the tendency which leads individuals to value their private space, which must be defended against the outside world (Wievorka, 1992). Thus, all public housing areas and all the neighborhoods are divided into 'good' and 'bad' sectors filled with immigrants, the unemployed, large sized families and single women.

In the suburbs, the main problems are focused on the young and the question of failure in school and delinquency. In the suburbs the large number of young people from the immigrant population is seen as an obstacle to success in schools. However, the school is also the place where the young Maghrebians and the young Africans learn to mix with other young French children, to share the same values of equality and individualism, and to arrive at the conclusion that they have not much to expect from school. Failure in school, unemployment, and life in the marginalized neighborhoods is the source of this experience of the absence of perspectives, 'la galère' (Dubet, 1986). One of the aspects of this 'galère' is the development of delinquency; of petty thievery, drug trafficking, vandalism, and racketeering in the schools. This delinquency is not exclusively due to young immigrants; in effect, the gangs or groups are often a mixture of all nationalities and ethnic origins. It is simply that the acts committed by the young Maghrebians or Africans are more easily stigmatized.

However, there is also a tendency for gangs to form based on ethnic identity, to the degree that some estates are peopled in the majority by one or another group, and that the local gang defends its territory against the police or the other gangs (Roy, 1991; Giudicelli, 1991). This phenomenon appears to be particularly marked among the young Africans, under the generic name of 'zoulous', because they are often less integrated into French culture than the young Maghrebians. Instead, they have, with their identification with

Black Power and the North-American gangs, references which allow them to build symbolic frontiers (Kokoreff, 1990).

In the suburbs, the groups or gangs who claim the right to be different, that is, to be 'white French', are not the inhabitants of a single unity but rather groups of individuals looking for a territory or who invent a territory to defend. Thus, the skinheads, who are the most spectacular manifestation of the playing up of fears of the loss of status, are not only young people coming from declining neighborhoods but also those from more bourgeois areas. It is here that football is seen as something of a 'solution': alongside traditional forms of supporterism for pleasure and local pride, supporterism develops among individuals who feel the most threatened and it allows them to define themselves against other communities, by claiming oneself to be one within the kop. This seems particularly true in Paris, where the Boulogne kop, at the Parc des Princes, assembles young white supporters coming from the entire Parisian region and expressing the values of the 'petit white'.

Pop culture and the 'rediscovery' of football

In order to understand the renewed interest in football during the 1980s, it is also necessary to explore cultural history. Some sociologists (Mendras, 1988) see 1965 as the year which marked the break between traditional France and modern France. It was the year of the opening of the first supermarket; the inauguration of the University of Nanterre, the symbol of the university for the masses; the expansion of the paperback book; the beginning of a decrease in the birth rate and the increase in the number of salaried women, etc. It was thus, symbolically speaking, the birth of the cultural, hedonistic and individualistic revolution. At the same time, the large socializing institutions (the Church, the school, political parties, the army, etc) entered into a crisis. Football was also in decline. A new field of expression of social relationships was opening up : it was known as 'pop culture'.

For several years, pop culture identified mainly with new forms of music; the promotion of fashion and new hedonistic and individualistic values were opposed, in France, to football as is progress to tradition, or the discovery of new areas of pleasure to the remnants of past leisures. The 'baby boomers' and their parents were those who discovered modernism through consumerism. For parents it was television, the car, and household appliances; for the children it was Anglo-Saxon pop culture, or its French version. Modernism also meant access to school, no longer only to primary school but also to high school and the university, and more generally, to the *experience* of being young (Galland, 1991). In this context, football had no more symbolic value. It evoked childhood and traditional life styles. For the young people involved in higher education or who wished to benefit from modern life, it could even be shameful to be interested in it. Football was thus not a significant practice: rock culture, or the culture of night clubs, cinemas, restaurants, were more pertinent. For those involved in the counter-culture or on the political left, there were more 'constructive' reasons for resisting football: if rock was Woodstock, football was the opium of the people and it stood for chauvinism and macho values.

Today, this 'progressive' scenario has been played out. Everyone is now into pop culture, even the skinheads. The change in attitude toward football occurred during the 1970s. On the one hand, there was the appearance of 'intelligent' football players such as Rocheteau, with his long hair, his taste for rock and his 'anarchistic' stances. In addition, there was the 'official' end of the left and the counter-culture around 1975; the hopes for cultural or political revolution collapsed with the 'discovery' of 'real socialism', the failure of the counter-cultural experiences and the need to 'return' to society to find work or to produce children. For some, the re-ordering occurred propitiously; others experienced a declining mobility. For everyone it was a time to reorganize social and cultural identities. Rock and football provided the symbolic elements for this re-adaptation to the new society.

In rock, one discovered forms such as pub rock, then punk; one became aware of the heterogeneity of what was called 'rock', with all the various subcultures and the punk rebellion against the counter culture. Listening to what is happening in Britain, one construes a romantic and populist vision of urban sociability where pleasure is linked to 'authenticity', music, the competition among subcultures, and the 'ends' in football stadiums with their songs and fights. For those who are militant, the new rock and football are the cultural means of remaining close to the 'people'; of returning to their roots by remobilizing the memories of old rock and football, without betraying the political ideal.

The new supporterism in France

The spectators are thus returning to the stadiums, but with them there is a new kind of supporter, the 'ultras'. Those called 'hooligans' essentially comprise young white males. The regular expression of the new supporterism in France in fact begins in the 1980s. The first hooligan incidents, outside of those provoked by English visitors, occurred during the 1978-79 season and the true foundation of the 'kop' of Boulogne in Paris dates from the 1983-84 season. However, the national expansion of the 'ultra' phenomenon followed the Heysel disaster. The principal associations of supporters were created in Paris, Marseille and Bordeaux during the 1985-86 season, and the only attempt to constitute a national federation of 'kops' and 'ultras' dates from 1987. It was in these years that acts of vandalism in the stadiums and in the cities first occurred and the fights and ambushes, or the use of fascist symbols or racist slogans, became a new routine.

Today, there are 'kops' and 'ultra' groups everywhere in France. In general, the 'kops' are found in clubs located north of the Loire River and the 'ultra' groups are found in the south. This division refers to two styles of supporterism, the English style, and the Italian style. In fact, the tendency toward 'Italianization' has been affirmed everywhere in France, but the labels remain. As a general rule, these 'kops' are composed of a nucleus of faithful fans, between 20 and 50 persons, who give enormous importance to the results of games. Otherwise, these 'kops' are a reflection of the wider audience in the stadium. In Paris, the 'kop' is of course more important; here there is a nucleus of 500 supporters. However, during recent seasons, there have been on average, 2000 to 3000 people in the 'kop' in Paris and, of course, many more for the visits of Marseille Olympique. It is Marseille which appears to have the most powerful groups of 'ultras', with a nucleus estimated at 2000 individuals. However, it is necessary to clarify that in these cities there are two 'kops' or rather two areas in which the most passionate supporters assemble.

In general, there is more atmosphere and excitement in the 'kops' than anywhere else. There are, however, two exceptions. For example, in Lens, the most popular and the most passionate area is found in the stands and not in the 'ends'. There, young people and adults are united, dressed in Red and Gold (the colours of the club), wearing miners' helmets or carrying a lamp, symbols of the former prosperity of the region. Moreover, this stand willingly welcomes the supporters of other teams, sharing beer and French fries with them during half-time. This scenario is repeated between friendly clubs, those who come from working class cities such as Le Havre or Saint Etienne, and it is much less marked when the supporters from Paris or Lille visit.

The final general characteristic is that the 'kops' are frequented by extreme-right groups. In Paris, the creation of the Boulogne kop was largely due to the activities of skinheads from the extreme right and the division between the 'Boulogne' stand and the 'Auteuil' stand is that which separates the supporters who express populist and racist sentiments and those for whom football is essentially the support of the local team and the pleasure of organizing this support.

Boulogne's kop

PSG has, together with Marseille, one of the largest crowds in France, and its 'kop' has the worst reputation. It is the site on which the symbols of the extreme right are most visible: "Blue, White, Red, France for the French"; one sings the 'Marseillaise', linking arms; one wears Celtic crosses, etc. After the game around the stadium and in the metro, some fans chase after Arabs and Blacks. Then there is the routine of smashed seats or vandalized cars. Why and how does this concentration occur? What holds this group together? Can one distinguish between the ritualistic 'war' of the terraces and political influences? On what does this dynamic feed?

Paris Saint Germain (PSG) was created in 1973, nearly ten years after the descent of the Racing Club of Paris into the Second Division in 1964. Between 20% and 30% of current PSG fans come from Paris. Office workers represent 34%, the middle classes 13%, and working class people 8%; 41% are under 24 years of age, and 64% are under 35 years of age. One may also note that the PSG crowd is also made up of Portuguese and Spanish immigrants, of Africans, Antillese and

Jews from North Africa. Fans also come from 'show biz' or the media world, since they like to be seen in a place which has recently become fashionable. Despite the lack of reliable data, it can be said that, with the exception of women and Maghrebians who are under-represented, the Parc des Princes football crowd projects a profile of a multi-ethnic region in which tertiary jobs dominate.

The origin of the 'kop' at PSG goes back to the end of the 1970s when the club began to offer cheap seats to attract young spectators. Very quickly, Boulogne was to provide a welcome for all the Parisian subcultures. The importance of England in the new French pop culture has already been mentioned. The years 1978-1981 were those of the popularization of punk and the skinheads. The latter found in the stands of the Parc des Princes a means of ensuring themselves the street credibility necessary to attract and repel. They left their mark on the stadium area, more so than did the punks, since the latter, especially their leaders, were more orientated toward the extreme left and not very interested in football. Thus, at the Parc, the most marginal punks, those most attracted to populism and who acted as intermediaries for the skinhead subculture, came together.

Skinhead culture

At the outset, skinhead culture was divided between two groups. The first was multi-ethnic and more concerned with the street, with rivalry among gangs in les Halles or 'squats' than with football. Its sympathizers saw as a reference point the English *two-tone* movement, and young Maghrebians or young Antillese were among them. The second tendency was explicitly orientated to the political right. It had leaders who were of more bourgeois origins, and were often students. Traditionally, the youth of the middle class is in the avant-garde in the introduction of the counter-culture or Anglo-Saxon pop culture because they are the ones who read, who travel and who can more easily buy the goods which go with this culture. However, there is also among them a fascination for the extreme right, especially among law students. It was this trend which contributed to the foundation of the Boulogne 'kop'. Its members occupied the previously empty stands at the beginning of the 1980's. They can be seen as the first pop reaction: that is, inscribed in the universe of mass culture, in the victory of the left in 1981, but simultaneously as one aspect of the reconstruction of the extreme right in France during this period.

The 'skin' leaders in the 'kop' are, in effect, in affiliation with organizations such as the MNR (National Revolutionary Movement), and some are members of the JNR, the youth organization of this movement, or La Troisième Voie (the Third Line), of the Oeuvre Française or the Front National, for whom they carry out orders and put up posters. They are present on the rock scene with Oï bands such as Tolbiac Toads, Evilskins or Brutal Combat. They have a music label based in Brest, *Rebelle Européen*, which edits and distributes labels of other skin movements in Europe and which organizes 'Rock against Communism' concerts. Their attendance in the stands is an example, therefore, of the ideological work of the new right in France. It is based on the idea that football is an expression of the roots of the white community or nation, and a rebellion against the 'conformism of the left', 'cosmopolitan capitalism', or 'mixed races'.

The activity of the skinheads in the 'kop' was particularly marked during the years between 1983-85, and then in 1989-90, with the creation of the fanzines *Blood and Beer* and *Pour le prix d'une bière* ('For the price of a beer'), celebrating the foundation and the activity of the 'Pitbull Kop', the avant-garde of the Boulogne 'kop', of a kop which is "100% nationalistic". The *Choc du Mois* ('Shock of the Month'), the monthly publication of the Front National, thus presented this 'kop' as a high point in the struggle against the 'left-controlled' police. However, the skinheads were also largely helped by the media looking for an entirely new popular demon and good television ratings. The Boulogne kop was 'baptized' by a documentary prepared by Canal Plus just after Heysel showing the Parisian skinheads proclaiming to be at one with their English colleagues and apparently celebrating the death of the Italian supporters. This recognition and exposure by the media largely aided the kop 'strategy' of attracting young men to a new macho, anti-conformist movement.

During the 1991-1992 season, the presence of the skinheads was reduced because of arrests, ageing or the entry of leaders into political or politico-commercial careers. However, the presence of the extreme right is maintained by the *Commandos Suicide*, then by the *Army Korps* which is in charge of launching nationalistic and racist slogans or of organizing the chasing of 'beurs' (Maghrebians born in France) and blacks. They are no longer skinheads, but call themselves 'casuals', and among them are the veterans of the 'anti-mixed race' hunt, old habitués of meetings of the extreme right or poster campaigns for the latter.

The skinheads do not direct the Boulogne 'kop', but they symbolize the development of nationalistic and populist feelings among some fractions of French youth and the attraction of rhetorics of violence and male toughness. Their designation as 'folk devils', and the loss of legitimacy and credibility of the ideas of the left in the face of the economic and social crisis, have made Boulogne the place for all challenges.

Although in the spring of 1992 support was strong among the young people, but also among the older spectators in the 'kop', for the success of J. M. Le Pen in the French elections, a number of the members in the 'kop' had voted for Mitterand in 1981 and some of them were very reticent about the marked presence, in the 'kop', of the extreme right. Another example of the divisions here is that of racism. The 'kop' makes the monkey noises when an opposing black player has the ball, but the African players in the PSG club are also among the 'kop's' favourite players. The characteristics of the persons arrested at PSG games also reveal the social heterogeneity of the 'kop'. Although all are young, aged between 18 and 22 years of age, there is also a mixture of self-proclaimed unemployed people and true 'marginal' people; of employees and unskilled workers from the distant suburbs, and of students and militants coming from affluent neighborhoods. The fact is that, today, defiance of legitimacy and the social order means defiance of the left, the values of the left, and, more generally, all universal values symbolized by the left. In the context of a social and urban crisis, identity is a central problem, because of its references to the community and the struggle of the poor against the more privileged, with all the ambiguities inherent in these themes. In this sense, the football team, with its mix of foreigners and French players, stars and beginners, can appear to be a privileged focus for the posing of the often hidden question of how to live with foreigners (Gauchet, 1990). Today, it is the extreme right which has taken the initiative in these interrogations.

One can see that there is a clear line of demarcation between ideology, challenge and populism in the associations of supporters. Besides the skinheads, the Boulogne 'kop' is organized around three principal groups, all founded in 1985: the *Boulogne Boys*, the largest of them; the *Gavroches,*; and the *Firebirds*, which are rather less important. All these associations claim to have relationships with other clubs and other supporters such as those at Inter Milan, Fiorentina, Anderlecht or Bruges. These are all clubs suspected of being 'on the right' and their fans also express their affection for clubs such as Chelsea, West Ham or Leeds, considered to be the bastions of English racism. Each of the Boulogne groups occupies its own place in the stands and has its own style: the *Boys*, with their hats, are very organized and display an Italian style of supporterism with banners, drums and megaphones. The *Gavroches* and *Firebirds* were in the English style, at the beginning, but the *Gavroches* then became more 'Italian'. The *Gavroches* are also more orientated toward team support. They organize travelling, admire the players and participate in fan displays set up in their honour. However, they also include in their ranks some *'imbeciles'*, who are not really violent but who like to do act wildly by breaking a window, pillaging a shop, making vulgar jokes, and responding to provocation from the opposing supporters. They indeed want to be seen as *'gavroches'* or little Parisian *'titis'*.

The *Firebirds* are older and define their association as a select club of people who like the good life. They have ceased to organize travelling to away games because that created too many problems. The game for them is "50% football and 50% madness". They organize after-game dinners and they travel when it is without risk and when they can also do some tourism; they like, for example, to go to Monaco. However, they are also among the most reflective of the supporters and they are clearly orientated politically toward the extreme right. A few years ago they edited a fanzine which was clearly in the business of racist and antisemitic provocation. They are not explicitly violent, but they take part in confrontations against the police, since it is a 'socialist police' and the Boulogne 'kop' is the territory of those who feel marginalized because of their ideas or the reconversion of the PS (Socialist Party) to the values of free enterprise:

> It was like that from the beginning. In the kop, you find all the 'zonards' [the surbanites], all those who have no job, all those who give you shit, all those who are fed up with living in the Casbah. Here we are among our own.

For the *Firebirds*, the important thing is the idea of the fan club as an expression of a community which is in opposition to other communities. They are little interested in the players, whom they see only as professionals, a means of giving pleasure to the community. They have no sympathy for the African players, in contrast to the *Gavroches* : if they are good, all the better, but they simply do their job. They wish to be seen in the modern 'English' style of support, without any props, except, perhaps, scarves and a few songs: supporterism must be the expression of an innate sense of football and the belonging to a community. The problem is that this football culture does not really exist in France, since this sense of community which it would be likely to express, or the ideological unity in the kop, do not exist. This may be the reason for the victory of the Italian model over the English model in French supporting styles.

The Italian style, with its organization and sense of 'theatre', compensated for the absence of a spontaneous football culture and offered opportunities for the development of a supporter-led spirit of enterprise; the organization of travel, the sale of badges and stickers, the design and manufacture of scarves, the sale of videos, the production of a fanzine, negotiations with the club, etc. The associations of supporters, mainly those of the *Boys*, were both politically radical *and* the providers of fan services; they expressed as much a sense of the collective as they did individualistic entrepreneurial values.

The 'kop' as a weekly compromise

As well as the skinheads or the other extremists from the right, the 'kop' also supports slogans, music and noise, which define the atmosphere of the kop and attracts people. The 'kop' is based on the opposition between supporters and spectators, between friends and enemies, but the slogans can be interpreted according to different logics. The songs tell of loyalty and the pride of being a Parisian. As everywhere, supporterism is a question of authentic commitment and the will to actively intervene in the destiny of the club, set against the passivity of the 'normal' spectators. However, since the other portions of the stadium house black or Jewish fans, one may also see oneself as among 'good French people', as opposed to foreigners. Likewise, one can accuse the club directors of being Jewish, cosmopolitan, rich - it all depends.

Supporters from other clubs, of course, are simply 'from the provinces', 'peasants', 'losers', but also 'wogs' when they come from Marseille or Matra Racing. For some members of the 'kop', their location in Boulogne derives from the fact that Auteuil was 'invaded' by foreigners. For others, it is because it is necessary to 'baptize' the enemies. If Marseille and Matra are the worst enemies, it is because one is a cosmopolitan city and the other was accused of seeking support from Maghrebians, and also because both are symbols, with their directors, Tapie and Lagardère, of the triumph of the spirit of enterprise, of social decline and the triumph of the managerial spirit over the sports' spirit. However, it is also because football is only a matter of victory, and how to obtain it.

The 'kop' is an urban territory to be defended, as the Place Saint Michel or les Halles were during the 1970s and 1980s. It is the sociability of a community in which one can be someone among the other supporters and in the face of the other supporters, the police and the media. However, this is a temporary community, since there are broad social and cultural differences; between the 'vicious fighter' and the one who 'goes after wogs', and those who are, simply, anti-police such as the young people from the suburbs. There is a difference between the student on the extreme right who wants to 'play tough' and the young workers; there is a difference between the militantism of the extreme right and the spirit of enterprise, as well as between 'full-time' hooligans and 'part-time' hooligans.

Bibliography

I give below references to French authors or books on France only, although I am greatly indebted to British and Italian authors for my research on football supporters.

Beaud, S. and Noiriel, G. (1990) 'L'immigration dans le football', *XXème Siècle*, avril-juin 1990.

Bourdieu, P. (1993) *La misère du monde*, Seuil, Paris.

Bourg, J. F. (1992) 'Sport et argent: le football', *Pouvoirs*, 61.

Bromberger, C. (1988) 'La moquerie; dires et pratiques', *Le Monde Alpin et Rhodanien*, juillet- décembre.

Bromberger, C. (1992) 'Le football met à nu les antagonismes majeurs de nos sociétés',*Le Monde Diplomatique*, juin.

Bromberger, C., Hayot, A., Mariottini, J.M. (1987) 'Allez l'OM ! Forza Juve ! La passion du football à Marseille et à Turin', *Terrain* n°8, avril.

Broussard, P. (1990) *Génération Supporter*, Robert Laffont, Paris.

Dubet, F. (1986) *La galère, jeunes en survie*, Fayard, Paris.

Dubet, F., Lapeyronnie, D. (1992) *Quartiers d'exil*, Seuil, Paris.

Ehrenberg, A. (1985) 'Les hooligans ou la passion d'être égal', *Esprit*, juillet.

Ehrenberg, A. (1991)*Le culte de la performance*, Calmann-Lévy, Paris.

Friedenson, P(1989) 'Les ouvriers de l'automobile et le sport', *Actes de la Recherche en Sciences Sociales*, 79.

Galland, O. (1991)*Sociologie de la Jeunesse*, Armand Colin, Paris.

Gauchet, M. (1990) 'Les mauvaises surprises d'une oubliée: la lutte de classes', *Le Débat*, mai-août.

Giudicelli, A. (1991) *La Caillera*, Jacques Bertoin, Paris.

Jazouli, A. (1991) *Les Années Banlieue*, Seuil, Paris.

Kokoreff, M. (1991) 'Tags et Zoulous. Une nouvelle violence urbaine', *Esprit*, février.

Marseille, J. (1990) 'Une histoire économique du football en France est-elle possible ?', *XX ème Siècle*, avril-juin.

Mendras, H. (1980)*La Sagesse et le Désordre, France 1980*, Gallimard, Paris.

Mendras, H. (1988)*La Seconde Révolution Française (1965-1984)*, Gallimard, Paris.

Noiriel, G. (1986) *Les Ouvriers dans la Société Française*, Seuil, Paris.

Nouvelles Pratiques Culturelles des Français (Les) (1990) Département des Etudes et de la Prospective/Ministère de la Culture, Documentation Française, Paris.

Nys, J. F. (1990) 'L'Economie du football en France', *Le Football et l'Europe*, European University Institute, Florence.

Pociello, C. (1983) *Le Rugby ou la Guerre des Styles*, AM Métaillé, Paris.

Raufer, X. (1991) 'Front national: sur les motifs d'une ascension', *Le Débat*, janv-avril.

Roy, O. (1991) 'Ethnicité, bandes et communautarisme', *Esprit*, février.

Schwartz, O. (1990) *Le Monde Privé des Ouvriers*, PUF, Paris.

Touraine, A., Dubet, F., Wievorka, M. (1984) *Le Mouvement Ouvrier*, Fayard, Paris.

Touraine, A. (1992) 'Face à l'exclusion', *Citoyenneté et urbanité* , Esprit éditions, Paris.

Verret, M. (1988) *La Culture Ouvrière*, ACL, Paris.

Vigarello, G. (1993) 'Le Tour de France', in Nora, Pierre (ed.), *Les Lieux de la Mémoire* , Gallimard, Paris.

Wahl, A. (1989)*Les archives du football*, Gallimard, Paris.

Wievorka, M. (1992)*La France raciste*, Seuil, Paris.

12 False Leeds: The construction of hooligan confrontations

Gary Armstrong

This chapter focuses on a group of young, male, Sheffield United supporters known as 'the Blades', a name which is also the club's nickname and otherwise used to describe all fans associated with the club. For convenience, however, the term will be used to denote 'The hooligan element' (a difficult concept to apply meaningfully, as we shall see); other supporters will be referred to as United fans. The demarcation is more clearly made when considered from the Blades' perspective. The Blades are young men aged 16-35, who regard themselves as the vanguard supporters of the Sheffield United. They have an unrivalled enthusiasm for United and an antipathy for city opponents, Sheffield Wednesday, and their hooligan equivalents, 'the Owls', who also borrow from their club nickname. This antagonism extends back to the mid-1960s. The Owls and the Blades refer to one another contemptuously as 'the Pigs', while both refer to hooligan formations from outside Sheffield as 'Their Boys'.

Blades involve themselves in rituals of confrontation against these varied rivals, and via this wish for two things: on a national level to be considered a good 'firm' in the hierarchy of hooligan oppositions, spread by a gossip network of interested participants. They also want to be recognized as Sheffield's 'number one' in various ways: stylistically, through control of space and the hooligan ethical code (cf. Giulianotti, this volume). The Owls' dispute this. Whilst match day is one context for Blades and Owls to contest this issue, more frequent clashes occur on weekend nights in the city centre pubs. United claim one street as theirs, the Owls claim another. The competitive collective pursuit of status within the hooligan hierarchy, thus concerns the Blades at both the inter- and intra-city levels; the manifestations which the opposition takes vary with the occasion. With 'Their Boys' the issue is usually conducted when the teams play, and is thus resolved on match day. When the issue is with the Owls, the event is more complicated; there is no particular reason why one man should support one team or another (see Armstrong, forthcoming). That said, once an identity is chosen, it remains for life. The Blades have, since the early 1980s, always rated themselves above (i.e. 'harder') than the Owls, who were harder in the 1970s. Whilst they know nationally which fans are 'nowt' or 'fuck all', others have a challengeable status; thus the Blades are willing to contest the matter with such equivalents from other towns and cities.

Hierarchy, honour and shame

Obviously, an observer will ask why do some men use football rivalries as an avenue of status pursuit? Such a pursuit is not irrational. In a hierarchical society ranking will be prevalent in all forms of social life. Those at the top look down on those below who, in some instances, may aspire to emulate their achievements. 'Football hooligans' are no different; gathering in groups they enact what Victor Turner (1974) would term 'social dramas', the main one being to challenge similar groups. Such events are 'competitions'; borrowing this term from anthropologist Bailey's (1969) study of political disputes, I think the definition he uses is applicable to football hooliganism. For Bailey, adversarial behaviour occurs via rules which could be divided into those that are proclaimed ('normative themes'), which set broad limits to possible action, allowing the players a choice; and, rules that are tacit ('pragmatic rules') which deal with the effectiveness of action, and are wide-ranging in possibilities, from accepted ways of winning without actually cheating, to ways of cheating without being found out. This is not, however, to argue that hooliganism has clearly defined and universally observed 'rules of disorder' (cf. Marsh et al, 1978). Matters are more complex.

Two other issues of principal importance enter proceedings. These have been examined in detail by anthropologists elsewhere; one is the concept of Honour (cf. Campbell, 1964; Pitt-Rivers, 1966; Peristiany, 1966), the other the notion of Performance (cf. Geertz,

1972; Goffman, 1959; Maffesoli, 1988). Honour has been defined in various ways, many of which are applicable to the hooligan phenomenon. As Friedrichs (1977, p.284) argues, "it is both an individual and group attribute which has to be claimed and maintained, and is therefore a power mechanism used to initiate and resolve conflicts." The ultimate vindication of honour, as Pitt-Rivers argues, lies in the use of physical violence. Honour is lost, and shame follows, if a man is found incapable of replying to a challenge (Bourdieu, 1970). Significantly, a notable aspect of challenge and response in terms of honour is that a man ought to respond only to the challenge of an equal (Bourdieu, 1977). The Blades fight only equals; their violence is not random.

My argument with regard to performance is that hooliganism is an experiment in which young men test their responses under certain conditions. In this contrived theatre of hostility, they seek oppositions to provide performances, wherein various selves gain credit or are discredited (cf. Goffman, 1959). In the context of this chapter, the definitions offered by the anthropologist Pitt-Rivers (1966) are more pertinent. He states that the competitive acquisition of social status and reputation are confirmed to individuals through various audiences. Thus, it is a precarious status prone to change, constantly requiring to be re-won.

If we draw together honour, shame and performance in the context of football hooliganism, a paradoxical scenario ensues. Honour and shame are produced simultaneously to various audiences, judging with different criteria, via 'the court of reputation' (cf. Wikan, 1984; Brandes, 1987). Whilst fellow hooligans can be either honoured or shamed by their counterparts, the wider audience (i.e. the public) find the various groups' very pursuit of honour shameful. Yet, the more the audience think them shameful, potentially the more the Blades can obtain honour in the smaller 'court of reputation', the hooligan gossip network. At the same time, there are hooligan acts which the Blades consider shameful, such as indiscriminate vandalism and random assault on those, who by their appearance are clearly not part of the script. Thus, media and public perceptions of hooligan notoriety do not always accord with that within the hooligan culture.

To be more specific, this analysis focuses on matches between Leeds Utd and Sheffield Utd between 1978 and 1992. The aim is to illustrate the following: the negligible levels of 'hooligan

301

organization'; the extent of and levels of violence and racism between and within hooligan gatherings; how football hooligans pursue reputation on both the intra- and inter-city stages; the relationship of hooliganism to media hype and distortions; the effect of policing public order tactics in combating the hooligan; and the subsequent judicial legislation and sentencing of the miscreants. Hooliganism has to move with the times; as police, in their role as umpires, seek to shorten the pitch, the hooligan actors seek to widen it. As such, they construct new ways of manifesting superiority. These are not always obvious to an unknowing audience.

From taking Kops to posing: the changing face of hooliganism

Hooligan competitions are dependent on the construction of 'enemies'. Some enemies are more disliked than others. After city rivals Wednesday, Leeds are the team Blades and United fans most 'hate'. Explaining why is difficult; it could be a symptom of a city-wide issue, over which merits the title of Yorkshire's premier city. Yet, few Sheffielders have reason to visit Leeds and vice versa. In fact, the only reason for large numbers from Sheffield to travel the 35 miles along the M1 is to follow football. Leeds, despite being the only major club in England without a recognized 'derby' match, do not see Sheffield as their particular rivals. In a sense they have bigger fish to fry, preferring to reserve their greatest enmity for Manchester United and Chelsea. The latter is a product of rivalry beginning at the 1971 F.A. Cup Final, the former a product of battles on and off the pitch since the late 1960s.

The issue is not particularly one of football status. Sheffield knows it is the place that 'gave football to the world' and its two clubs, both over one hundred years old, have nearly always been amongst the top twenty in the League. By contrast, Leeds are relative newcomers, based in a city considered to be a 'rugby town' by Sheffielders, and, having joined the League in the 1920s, Leeds have spent much of their time in the relative obscurity of the Second Division. Leeds' glory days from the mid-1960s to the mid-1970s under the stewardship of Don Revie produced the 'Leeds Machine'. This phenomenal side attracted world-wide interest; Leeds supporters clubs were founded throughout Britain and indeed the world. The club was loved by thousands and hated by just as many for its successes and 'calculating' play. The support for Leeds rose from an average of under 20,000 fans in the early 1960s to 40,000 in the 1970s. As their status rose various acts of hooliganism followed. By the mid-1970s, and with their team in decline, the Leeds fans took over the notoriety that their team once had - a reputation stretching from Paris in 1975 (cf. Watson, 1982) to Bournemouth in 1990 (cf. Giulianotti, 1994a; Haynes, 1993). The rivalry with Leeds has intensified from the Sheffield United fans' point of view since the late 1960s to the present day, when Leeds acquired and sustained the financial power to buy Sheffield's favourite players (Mick Jones, Alex Sabella, Tony Currie, Keith Edwards, Brian Deane). Since that time, Sheffield has lived in its neighbour's shadow.

Football hooliganism, as we now know it, began in Sheffield, as it did elsewhere in England, in the mid 1960s. This is when groups of youths gathered with the expressed intention of opposing similar visitors via chants and, ultimately, fights. With Leeds in the First Division and English football hooliganism in its infancy, Sheffield United's home matches against Leeds saw 8,000 away fans arriving, amongst them hundreds of the Leeds 'hooligan element', who would stand on, and therefore 'take', the Shoreham End terrace of Sheffield United's Bramall Lane ground. This was a late 1960s and 1970s procedure, and provided the original manifestation of football hooliganism in England (see Marsh, 1978; Ward, 1989). It was also the unequivocal way for hooligans to demonstrate their 'hardness' and 'reputation'. The visitors had a duty to enter the home 'End' terracing, (usually behind one of the goals) where the home 'lads' would duly form a 'mob' to expel them. For Sheffield United, the local mobs were known in the early 1970s as the 'Shoreham Boot Boys', then in the late 1970s as the 'Shoreham Republican Army' (SRA). The victors were the ones who could repel the invasion or resist the expected attack and remain on the terrace. The police would form a 'thin blue line' between the combatants who would, throughout the match, shout threats, occasionally throw missiles and sporadically scuffle. Non-combatants could occasionally get jostled or knocked over.

This pursuit was mainly confined to young men aged fifteen to early twenties, and was based on getting 'mobbed' up. It combined rowdy behaviour with the symbols of club support, usually the scarf.

The Leeds 'Boot Boys' throughout the 1970s were numerically stronger than the Blades and, after arriving sometimes ninety minutes before kick-off, would 'take' the Kop and remain there, repulsing the Blades' attacks. In this fashion, Leeds could claim to have 'taken the Shoreham' three times.

The Blades, however, did not reciprocate. Visiting Leeds was, at the time, 'risky'; few travelled for fear of 'gettin' hammered'. These were the days when the movement of visiting fans was not as coordinated as it became from the late 1970s onwards. Vehicles arrived without escorts and those on trains walked to the match without police 'supervision'. In later years, when visiting any ground was considered 'safe', more fans went to away games, including hooligans. This is important to their performances because it illustrates that football hooligans rely on a police presence. The participants know that their confrontations will be ended in seconds and that they can enact their performances behind the safety of a police escort. Ironically, this suggests that the intensification of police tactics for dealing with public order at football matches also intensified the public presence and performances of the hooligans (Ward, 1989). More importantly, it demonstrates what Foucault (1977) regards as the wide prevalence or 'capillary' nature of social power in a surveillance- orientated society. This is reflected in the creative ability of football hooligans which has been ignored by much English research on the subject (cf. Taylor, 1982a & b; Dunning et al., 1988). That said, in order to avoid over-restrictive procedures, from the late 1970s hooligans abandoned organized travel on supporters' club coaches and 'football specials'. They made their own travel arrangements. This needed a coach organizer or knowledge of train timetables. Furthermore, with football grounds increasingly fenced and segregated, the shows of power formerly available on the 'Ends' had been replaced by rivals walking about city centres. The home lads had to meet up in pubs before the match to form a 'welcoming committee'. The goalposts had been moved, the pitch widened and the police, as referees, had to be more mobile in pursuit of foul play.

However, being in different Divisions for seven seasons (1978/9 to 1984/85), the Blades had no opportunity to challenge Leeds. Through their escapades in the lower divisions, and the emergence of hundreds of lads in their late teens who were all United fans, the Blades developed a confidence in the 1980s that they were a hooligan force to be reckoned with. What was needed was a chance to confirm, against one of the big names, what the Blades already knew. Such an occasion arose in 1984 with United newly promoted to Division Two.

During the 1980s, Leeds fans' image had been particularly tarnished by both racist chants and publicized association of its fans with right-wing political parties and violence. Leeds fans were involved in serious disorder in Birmingham in 1985 (during which one fan died); and, Bradford, Chelsea, West Brom and Oxford in 1986. To counter fan disorder, the English FA tried to ban Leeds fans from away fixtures in various ways. Eventually, in 1990, following events around a match in Bournemouth, Leeds were threatened with expulsion from the Football League itself. The club responded to this moral panic by introducing a 'hotline' via which anonymous callers can pass on information about fellow fans which is then passed on to the police. Furthermore, any fan found guilty of 'racist' comments faces a ban from the ground and all local council-owned facilities, following a joint declaration between club and local politicians (see Leeds TUC & AFA, 1987).

The Blades generally ridiculed the semiotics of racism, which they considered neither funny nor clever (and certainly not something they aspired to). Whilst to most liberal academic observers the Blades would not be considered 'politically correct', they could be construed as neither fundamentally 'racist' nor 'anti-racist'. That said, their antipathy towards Leeds' fans public displays of racism (Seig Heils, chants, badges, etc.) was based upon pragmatic rather than normative cultural values.

Leeds' 'racism' was one of several issues through which the Blades defined themselves against their local rivals, and sustained the Blades' collective perception of their moral superiority. Furthermore, in contrast to those who would typologize hooligans into a social and moral 'race' (cf. Dunning et al., 1988; Williams, 1986), some Blades were analytical enough, albeit at an amateur sociological level, to categorize Leeds fans' behaviour and habitus according to socioeconomic conditions. They believed these Leeds fans to be from a homogeneous, white, male, socially deprived, local milieu, which attracted peers at a national level. This depiction of the citizens of Leeds and its environs resonates with the equally dismissive opinion of the city advanced by Sheffield men, not necessarily football supporters. More importantly, the Blades were particularly critical of Leeds fans' reputation, as constructed by the media and football authorities, for 'hooligan' behaviour of a kind which the Blades simply did not 'rate'. Vandalism, seat-smashing and fence-pulling en masse did not equate with the Blades' measurement of 'hardness' and therefore with a legitimate fan reputation.

Blades versus Leeds: 1984-1992

1984: 'That surprised 'em'

At this time (mid-1980s), the police were neither fully aware of hooligan procedures nor capable of preventing coach loads of 'football lads' travelling to rival city centres. Reflecting the acephalous and very loosely ordered structure of the Blades (cf. Armstrong & Harris, 1991), two days before the eagerly anticipated match in Leeds in 1984, no Blade knew for certain how many coaches would depart nor where they would stop en route for a drink. The only thing known was the meeting point for all aspiring combatants.

By 9.30 am on Saturday, two hundred Blades had 'turned out' at the rendezvous. Four coaches arrived resulting in a scramble around the entrance. One, run by Benny and Toad and already half-full with locals, took twenty over capacity. Others run by Max, Wasp and Taffy, arriving half full, left over full. This still left fifty Blades without transport; Nev and Welsh simply hired a coach from a nearby garage. By 10.15 am everyone who had turned out (by now over three hundred) was on their way to Leeds. That was the extent of the 'organizing' of the event.

The town of Wakefield was the pre-match stop. Nobody knew who made the decision, but all thought it sensible as the town is close to Leeds. After an hour's drinking many Blades grew restless; a debate ensued, most opining "we should go now." Others warned that police lookouts on the motorway would 'capture' the vehicles, and escort them to the ground, thereby ruining the day. However, Benny, one of the older Blades, argued that as the Blades had the free run of this town's pubs, why travel when drink was available? However, the 'move now' lobby was strongest, particularly amongst young

Blades. Organizers of three coaches then announced that they were leaving; this reflected the majority view, and all four coaches departed ten minutes later. This 'internal conflict' is significant in two ways. Firstly, it demonstrates again the pragmatic nature of leadership which is always related to the consensus view. It also shows that the elders had little or no control over the younger element, in contrast to media and police depictions of football hooligan formations (cf. Armstrong & Hobbs, 1994; Giulianotti, 1994b).

Having driven without police attention into Leeds city centre, two hundred Blades on three coaches alighted and after a short walk found the Leeds 'lads' pouring out of a pub and thus chased them. Police arrived, arrested one Blade and marched the rest to the ground under escort. En route, Leeds regrouped; the police, few in numbers, could not contain the skirmishing, as Blades fans 'ran' Leeds. Police reinforcements arrived, arrested two more Blades and resumed the walk. The Blades entered the ground at 2.15 pm, having, in their opinion, "done t' business."

Meanwhile, another Blades coach was outside a pub in a Leeds suburb. It contained a dozen of the 'old lads', around twenty-five 'young lads', and another twenty undistinguishable Blades; it also reflected some deep divisions within the Blades on what were the day's priorities. Whilst the elders were content to drink, the youngsters were disgusted that they had not yet arrived in the Leeds city centre. The old lads blamed the driver, saying he had refused to drive them there. In the younger elements' opinion, the old 'beer bellies' had desired drink more than a fight and had invited him to stop. This coach arrived at the visitors' car park, under police escort, at 2.45 p.m; occupants could only verbally insult Leeds fans as they walked past their turnstile queues. Missing the pre-match fighting had a deep effect on the young Blades aboard. The following season they vowed never to travel with the older crowd again and organized their own transport. They were to become the vanguard of the Blades for the next few seasons.

Inside the ground, the Leeds 'lads', five hundred strong, were seated in the South stand. They exchanged chants with elements of the four thousand Sheffield fans standing and seated in the west side of the ground. Racist chants by Leeds fans were directed towards black United players and black Blades. Consequently, two black

Blades sat on their mates' shoulders mimicking the Seig Heil salutes of the home fans. Blades shouted 'fat bastard' at noticeably portly rivals, and sang the put down of "what's it like to run at home?" The game ended in a 1-1 draw. Police had matters under control after the game, and by 6.45 pm the Blades were in Sheffield's pub discussing how they had accomplished what they considered no prestigious London crew to have achieved: 'done' Leeds at home.

Stand United: Leeds at Bramall Lane- March 1985

The March 1985 fixture produced the largest and most serious acts of hooliganism around a football match in the city in the 1980s. Had the police not turned out in large numbers (two hundred and eighty) there could have been major disorder. The Blades knew that Leeds would be looking for revenge. They were anticipating, in particular, the so called 'Leeds Service Crew', created and sustained by the media since 1983 (see Haynes, 1993; Walker, 1983). They were supposedly notorious for avoiding officialdom and restrictions by service trains (as opposed to football specials), as well as for the wearing of expensive casual, crewneck jumpers (so as not to look remotely like football thugs were supposed to look). The Blades presumed, however, that for this fixture the Leeds mob would not travel by service train: they would know police would be waiting at the station to 'capture' them. Instead, they 'should' arrive in coaches via the 'Back-Wacks' i.e. minor roads to the north of Sheffield, thus avoiding police patrolling the M1 motorway. By using vans and cars in a convoy, Leeds 'lads' could park together, and 'have a walk' around Sheffield city centre.

Over the previous year the media had exposed how hooligan crews were publishing leaflets about planning violence (Armstrong and Harris, 1991). For this match, for the first time ever, Blades produced leaflets similar to those that they had read about. The first, circulating a month before the game in pubs near the ground before a home match, was produced by Yifter, and known as 'Stand United'. It was a mock leaflet, not intending to convey information; the rendezvous, and its purpose, were already known to all. An attempt to raise the name of the Blades in imitation of what they had read had been made, but 'Stand United' did not carry. One Blade proposed sending the leaflet to the tabloids, another suggested Leeds

United FC itself. Others suggested gluing it to toilet walls in Leeds pubs known to be frequented by 'Their Boys'. Anything, in fact, so long as the artefact got publicity and thus notoriety.

Two of these proposals were acted upon. The leaflet was sent to a national tabloid and locally to the *Sheffield Star*, the city's evening daily. Furthermore, two Blades, whose jobs required travelling via Leeds, pasted leaflets on pub toilet walls which they had heard were frequented by Leeds 'lads'. Another leaflet circulated a week later was produced by Barry. This suggested that both the day's meeting place and time had changed. With it came an exhortation for the Blades to remain together after their day's game, in an attempt to confront Derby 'lads' changing trains on their way to Hull. Derby did not appear, and the suggested name, 'Blades Firm Force' (BFF) was not adopted either.

Despite what some would interpret as 'planned' or 'organized' violence and the fact that around four hundred Blades were on 'patrol' on the morning of the match, not much happened. The Blades gathered in pouring rain from 10.00 am onwards. The pub stated in the leaflets saw the landlord and two PCs at the door; no Blade entered. By 1.00 pm all were packed into two pubs on the High Street. Most left at midday to check a rumour that Leeds had left the train station, unescorted. Walking quietly and quickly through shoppers, the four hundred were turned back by uniformed police having been spotted by two plain-clothed officers. Some subsequently walked to London Road, fearing that Leeds might have arrived in vehicles via back routes. Others returned to the city centre, where they found 40 Owls but no Leeds. The Owls had met in a city centre pub and had told the Blades they would be out on the streets that day. They intended to confront Leeds; however, the arguments of the Leicester Centre based on 'ordered segmentation' (cf. Suttles, 1968) does not work in Sheffield. The Blades did not want the Owls present for two reasons: if Leeds got run, the Owls would claim it was due to their presence; furthermore, Leeds could, in gossip later, blame their defeat on two mobs and not one. When the Blades found the Owls in a city centre pub, the factions stood at opposite ends of the bar. The latter left when a top Blade 'offered out' (i.e. challenged to fight) a leading Owl. The situation was tense, but for now the Blades considered there to be a greater enemy afoot, and so continued their search for Leeds.

309

All coaches and vans were escorted directly to the match. The one pre-match incident occurred at 2.50 pm when one hundred Blades walking to the ground passed hundreds of visitors at their turnstiles. A brief scuffle was ended by dozens of police both mounted and on foot. The majority of the 8,000 Leeds fans were in the Bramall Lane End. A few hundred were in the South Stand, enacting the silent hostilities of stares, smiles and gestures with both sides' restraint prompted by the nearby police. Vociferous rivalry was occurring over a longer distance between Leeds fans on the Bramall Lane End, the three hundred Blades in the John Street terrace and the thousands who sang on the Kop. The former exchange escalated after 45 minutes when, 1-0 down, Leeds fans began throwing seats from the stand onto the pitch as colleagues below in the terracing began doing what they were renowned for - pulling at the perimeter fence. Twenty PCs replied by striking their hands with truncheons. The Blades on the terrace, to signify their willingness to face rivals with impunity, similarly pulled on their fencing and threw a few seats from the stand, a significant event illustrating that if necessary, some would damage their own ground to get at rivals. When all the pulling and swaying had died down after about five minutes, there was one casualty, a policeman struck by a piece of debris thrown by the Blades; he walked away assisted by a colleague.

Half-time brought entertainment provided by rival fans in close proximity. Under pressure of numbers, a police-created 'no-man's land' on the Lane End, was breached by surging Leeds fans, who pushed police aside. In response, the Blades surged against the terrace wall and fencing. Neither faction was anywhere near assaulting the other; between them were three fences, an open piece of terrace and twenty police. But both sides had made their appropriate show. Amidst all this a senior police officer, over the public address system, called for calm, asking Leeds fans to think of the good name of their club. They *were*, of course, but he could not understand this. In response, thousands of visitors jeered him, one climbed onto a wall and, to mass cheers, kicked off the speaker.

The Blades, one hundred and fifty strong in the South Stand, had a less eventful but equally significant first half. They concentrated their attention on both the two hundred Leeds fans, and the forty Owls who had also arrived to observe the day's proceedings. The Blades' response to the latter's chant of "We love you Wednesday", was to clamber towards them, shutting them up as police intervened. A nautical distress flare was fired by a young Blade towards both Owls and Leeds fans, hitting the stand roof and falling harmlessly; the culprit was arrested minutes later. When play resumed both sets of fans settled down to watch an entertaining match which United won 2-1. The second half was uneventful on the terraces except at the end one Leeds supporter forced an advertising hoarding from the wall of the South Stand which fell onto the pitch to cheers from the visitors.

Outside, for some inexplicable operational reason and in contrast to normal procedure, police were allowing both sets of fans out at the same time. In the various back streets around Bramall Lane, scuffles began. Police on foot and mounted hurriedly separated the combatants whilst the escorting of the largest groups to the coach park and railway station began.

The biggest confrontation took place fifteen minutes later. One hundred Leeds lads, having avoided police, met one hundred Blades on a dual carriageway five hundred yards from the ground. Scuffling lasted a minute before police arrived. About ten of each side managed to get a punch in and there were no injuries; the three distress flares fired by the Blades hit no one. A few skirmished en route to the railway station and later outside it, but it was all chasing with no physical contact, with police always nearby. By 6.30 pm, with all visitors departed, the Blades who 'stopped out' were in various city centre pubs discussing how the police had won the day, and whether Leeds could claim a victory in the after match fracas.

The day, in fact, was more to be memorable for what the Blades did to the Owls. Forty Blades entered a city centre pub at 6.15 pm to find twenty Owls inside. After half an hour of an uneasy impasse, two Sheffield Blades, Fats and Mark, challenged them with the watching approval of the rest. Tom, a village Blade, then threw the pub telephone at them. In the ensuing melee, glasses, bottles, stools and punches were thrown. Two minutes later, the Blades departed leaving the Owls under a barricade of tables and furniture. There were four casualties, two from each side, requiring stitches to head wounds. Dozens of glasses and two windows were broken. By the time police arrived, the protagonists had gone. Matters continued later when ten Owls, having heard about, in their view, the despicable bullying, stood around whilst two of their number thumped two Blades in The Blue Bell in retaliation, one suffering a broken nose. Later, the Blades, on learning of this episode, argued in pubs with Owls whom they recognized about who were the worst bullies, and promised vengeance when 'mobbed up'. This issue had repercussions for months.

All aboard: Leeds away - September 1985

Because of the above disorder, Leeds United made the next fixture against Sheffield United an 11 am kick-off and all ticket, on police advice. No pubs would be open beforehand, and therefore no pre-match stop was necessary for visiting fans. Once again a leaflet circulated amongst the Blades, suggesting travel by a local service train, scheduled to arrive in Leeds at 9.30 am. Everyone knew police would be 'capturing' coaches after last time; trains, however, allowed only one exit point, and thus little chance of avoiding police if they were waiting. It was a gamble the Blades decided to take.

However, diverse travel arrangements fragmented the Blades. Around one hundred and thirty travelled by train, others went in coaches, mini-vans and cars. Thus, 'organization' was non-existent; it was each to his own as to how the individual Blade travelled. The police did not have much idea about how to deal with matters at Sheffield station. Having allowed the Blades to board the train they then demanded that they alight. The Blades complied only to board an Inter-City train to Leeds which conveniently arrived on the next platform. Police then demanded that the Blades alight, which they all did again, only to reboard the local service! Police ordered them off this train for a second time, but were overruled by senior officers who demanded that all remain on board.

Awaiting the Blades' arrival in Leeds were plain-clothes police from Sheffield standing with forty uniformed local police, six mounted police and ten vehicles, one of them being the 'Hoolivan' (see Armstrong and Hobbs, 1994) which photographed the Blades for the next half an hour. A following of 3,000 saw United draw 1-1 in a match producing no trouble amongst the 20,000 crowd and with no racist chants from the Leeds lads in the South Stand. At the end a Blade fired a distress flare at them which landed harmlessly wide of the target. The escort back to the station was without incident even though one hundred Leeds lads 'shadowed' the Blades' movements.

Waiting in vain: Leeds home - March 1986

This Tuesday evening fixture was again declared all ticket. In conjunction with the fact that this was also an inconsequential end of season game between two mediocre sides, this helped to account for an attendance of only 9,300, which included 2,000 away fans: a reduction of 14,000 and 6,000 respectively from last season's Sheffield fixture. The police had also closed the whole of the John Street Terrace closest to the away end. There were no 'plans', leaflets, or discussions about the day. The Blades met from 5.30 pm onwards in a city centre pub. All knew that no Leeds would be in the city centre because the police had it 'sussed'. The Blades walked to London Road pubs and then to the ground, entering variously the Terrace, Kop, and South Stand. The 3-2 victory for United enhanced a brief confrontation afterwards between twenty from each side near the railway station. Only two protagonists came to blows before police arrived - that was the extent of the violence.

The late bus: Leeds away - August 1986

For the next trip to Leeds the Blades reverted to 'coach' travel but deliberately altered their departure time and rendezvous. Fagin and South had booked a council double decker bus, departing at 1.00 pm. The aim of the day was to confront Leeds fans outside the ground; the city centre now held no opportunities because of police tactics. Two other operators had coaches going but there was no 'convoy' suggested; again, it was each to his own.

Departing with eighty Blades (plus two 'observers' - Nottingham Forest lads invited by a Blade mate) the journey was unusual for a number of episodes. About a dozen fans were the worse for drink; one had a pint glass and one a pool cue, taken from a local pub. Although potential weapons, neither were taken off the vehicle nor used for violence in the course of the day. Whilst upstairs was rowdy, downstairs was tranquil. Upstairs two urinated into the pint glass and poured the contents out the window, then one threw the glass at a passing car of Chelsea 'lads' who, on their way to Sheffield Wednesday, had driven by, gesticulating. Many downstairs considered the urine episode disgusting; whilst they could condemn it of mates, they had no power to demand uniformity of behaviour.

Approaching Leeds and seeing the floodlight pylons, everybody alighted, allowing the vehicle to drive to the car park empty. Along the one mile walk, the Blades quietly used both pavements and spread out to avoid being conspicuous. In their midst walked six unknowing Leeds lads. Ten Blades struck them as they made their escape, the rest watched. Minutes later the victims were standing with other Leeds lads pointing out Blades.

The Blades decided to go into the South Stand, reserved by the club for Leeds fans only, an idea mentioned on the bus. It was agreed that a 'quick scuffle' with 'Their Boys', ending with Blades getting removed by police to the visitors' terrace, "would look good." The primary aim was not to hurt rivals but annoy and humiliate them via a display of power. Hopefully, the media would report the disturbance and fellow hooligans would interpret such reporting, gaining Blades their peers' interest. However, Blades were 'sussed' by local lads whilst buying tickets from a cabin adjacent to the Stand; 'verbals' were exchanged as well as one punch. Three PCs radioed for assistance and within minutes police, on foot and mounted, escorted the Blades to the visitors' terrace. This meant passing the South Stand outside of which one hundred Leeds 'lads' had gathered. Exchanging threats and discreet punches, Blades with South Stand tickets showed them off, arguing were it not for police they would have entered the stand. The game ended in a 1-1 draw in front of a crowd of over 20,000.

A month later, six Blades appeared in a Leeds court to receive fines arising from minor public order offences related to this fixture. The magistrate voiced his concern that before him were some elements of an organized gang, provoked by his observation of the similar fashions worn by those convicted. This was nonsense. The man had been watching too much TV.

Taking it to them: Leeds at home - February 1987

Anticipating Leeds' arrival in Sheffield, and with the need to avoid police, the Blades moved their pre-match meeting for the first and only time to the nearby town of Rotherham. This innovation depended on Leeds lads thinking along similar lines to Blades and came about as a direct result of a local issue involving Rotherham Blades and Rotherham Whites (Leeds fans' generic name for themselves, taken from the team's all-white kit). Both groups used the same town centre pubs after their respective matches and some knew each other personally. One of the Whites had 'offered out' a Blade in front of their respective mates; however, the ratio was three to one in Leeds' favour. A fight did not take place; after much 'mouthing' no action followed and pub bouncers intervened. More importantly, though, a Blade had been bullied and this unworthy challenge had to be repaid. The Rotherham Blades informed their Sheffield colleagues of events at the next home match and invited them to Rotherham that day to 'get' Leeds in the pub they knew they met in on match days.

The Friday evening before the game, thirty Blades agreed to catch the 10.30 bus to Rotherham. In fact, only fifteen were on this bus; others came later by train and car. By midday there were eighty Sheffielders and thirty Rotherham Blades in various pubs; the only group missing were Leeds. Local police, suspicious of the large groups of lads, had requested reinforcements from Sheffield. Recognized Blades were given unequivocal advice: "Get back to Sheffield or you're nicked." By 1.00 pm, back in Sheffield, Blades bemoaned the futility of their plan. There was not a single incident with rivals all day. The game ended 0-0; the attendance was 12,500.

Hooligans in disguise: Leeds home and away - 1987/88

The hundred-strong Blades 'turn out' for the October 1987 home fixture knew that the chances of Leeds 'coming in' was remote. Meeting initially in a pub overlooking the railway station the group tired of police interest and moved to another pub, The Blue Bell. Already in were six Owls. Some Blades chatted with them, others urged Blades to 'do' them. One, whilst shaking hands with a Blade, received a punch in the face from another! Nursing his cheek, he and the others left; that was the extent of Blade-Owl violence today.

Other visitors of interest were two plain-clothes police aged around 30. One wore a waxed Barbour jacket, the other a 'floppy' cricket-style hat fashionable in the summer. Both wore trainers and jeans. The Blades spoke quietly and glanced at their rather obvious company who, realizing they had been 'sussed', drank up. While leaving, one stated loudly, for the benefit of a wider audience, "All the fuckin' idiots are out today ... we'll just have to crack some skulls later". The Blades made no reply.

The pre-match hours were eventless. In part, this was due to a small Leeds support (about 4,000) and to police monitoring closely the passage of Blades. Near the ground two men joined Blades' walk to the ground; they were immediately recognized as police (the pink ear piece was not totally covered by the upturned collar of the Barbour jacket); Blades fell silent and inscrutable. The Blades at the ground entered the uncovered area of the Kop (the fashion for about six months) to watch an entertaining 2-2 draw. Chanting came mainly from the John Street Blades and was monitored by forty PCs, supplemented by a mobile video camera carried by an officer, which supplemented the CCTV inside the ground. Although the match was officially all-ticket, shortly after kick-off around thirty Leeds fans were removed from the Shoreham End: a motley collection mainly of men, with a few women, within an age range of 16-50. They exited unhindered through the perimeter fencing gates, albeit abused as they walked under police escort, to the visitors' enclosure.

Because of a new police tactic, the Leeds coaches were under police orders to drive to the ground at the end of the match. Thus, thousands had only yards to walk to their transport, and police had only to protect against potential disorder in one particular street. Not seeing any 'mobs' who could be regarded as 'looking for it', Blades, by 5.30 pm, were quietly drinking in pubs. Ironically, intensive policing of the ground had no effect nine miles away, in a Rotherham suburb, where a pre-match battle outside a pub between a dozen Blades and thirty Leeds resulted in one broken window, no injuries and a front page story in Monday's *Sheffield Star*.

The away fixture in March was a miserable occasion for the 4,000 following Sheffield United, who lost 5-0. The Blades had no 'plan' whatsoever to face Leeds boys and none of the core hooligans even bothered to organize a coach. The demise of the team had seen attendances fall and hooliganism had been minimal over the previous few months. The low activity at either match may be partially explained by the intensified policing of Leeds supporters in this period, which came to a head during the season. Leeds United fans had been the subject of undercover policing and dawn raids ('Operation Wild Boar') in 1987 (see Armstrong & Hobbs, 1994). Eleven youths were arrested, and six were jailed in 1988: three for four years, two for two years, a sixth for eight months. The construction of the trial focused on cabalism and hierarchical organization within the group. The court was told how one accused was called 'The General', a title which was, in fact, a mock (and mutinous!) nickname regarding his former career as parachute paratrooper. The court was also told of the 'Leeds Service Crew' and 'The Yorkshire Army'. The former was a name which they used, but the accused informed me that it was adopted following its invention by British Transport Police in the early 1980s. The latter term was unknown to any of the accused. This contrasts with the Blades' experience of hooligan titles; 'Blades Business Crew' (BBC) was invented in 1985 to distract and parody police constructs of them, as well as to promote their reputation (Armstrong, 1992).

Christmas peace and Easter parades: Leeds home and away - 1989/90

An uninformed observer might think the hooligan issue was dying and that police had matters under control. They could take one fixture in this season to support their argument - the Boxing Day match at Bramall Lane. However, the Easter Monday fixture at Elland Road had all the ingredients of 'the bad old days'. One could then have argued the diametrically opposed view: that hooliganism was back. As per usual, the Boxing Day fixture was all ticket and furthermore arranged for midday on police 'advice'. A big crowd attended (28,000), reflecting traditional interest in Christmas football, but also the importance of the fixture - both teams were in the top three of Division Two. A good game ended in a 2-2 draw and the day passed without any fights. One reason concerns the Sheffield disassociation of Boxing Day with football disorder. There are drinks to be had and family to see. It is not a time to be in police custody.

This match saw three mobile police surveillance cameras and ten plain-clothes officers. For the first time ever at Bramall Lane the police introduced an 'Exclusion Zone'. They had, all around the ground to a distance of about fifty yards, erected metal fences manned by uniformed officers. Match goers had to produce their tickets to advance to the ground. Why this policy was implemented was a mystery. Was it to stop the potential thousands of ticketless fans storming the gates and gaining entry? (Not too far fetched a theory, given that only eight months previously the Hillsborough disaster had been precipitated by what local police believed, wrongly, to have been the organized storming of the gates). Or were these precautions simply symptomatic of the over-elaborate public order tactics deployed by the police around football? Either way if anyone wanted a ticket there were plenty being sold on the streets outside the exclusion zone; anybody who wished to could see the game.

The match passed without any crowd trouble, but once again shortly after kick-off various Leeds fans jumped out of the Shoreham End (a move now made easier by the removal of fencing, post-Hillsborough). The one hundred or so 'intruders', mainly men aged between 18-35, were not part of a 'mob'. The only rational explanation for their presence in the wrong end is that ground sections allocated to Leeds fans had sold out quickly, thus the visitors bought tickets for the home end. With the game underway, they made themselves known to police and requested a transfer to the visitors' end. They were abused by home fans en route and welcomed by colleagues on arrival.

Blades' intended taking Leeds by surprise four months later. The success of the team had generated huge away followings and a new *esprit de corps* amongst Blades. Many Blades were turning out regularly and fights with Owls became a regular event in the city centre. In part, it was anger at Leeds United FC which spurred many to action. Create an imposition and hooligans love to overcome it (cf. Giulianotti, this volume). It is part of the phenomenon. Attracting huge home crowds Leeds decided to allocate visiting fans only 1,200 tickets. This was a crucial match which would probably decide the Second Division Championship; thousands wanted to attend - including the Blades. Under some pressure, Leeds extended the ticket allocation to 1,800. The all-ticket match remained a 3.00 pm kick-off but the authorities did not take into account the convenience of credit cards and the short journey between the two cities. As a result, around three hundred Sheffield followers attended the match and sat in an area designated for Leeds fans, the East Stand; of these, about two hundred were Blades. Some Blades bought batches of ten and twenty tickets. One, Max, bought a total of 80 and then ran two coaches offering the package of transport and entry. The core Blades had their own arrangement; to avoid police capture, they decided on a convoy of cars. Police could control

318

coaches and trains, but could not stop all vehicles. Meeting at midday outside a pub, the eighteen vehicles and two vans took a combined total of one hundred fans on a 'convoy' along the M1 to an agreed rendezvous. After an hour's drinking, the convoy drove to within one mile of the ground, allowing a silent walk without incident.

The Blades entered undetected and took their seats at 2.30 pm. The Leeds lads entering looked in amazement and anger at over two hundred silent, smiling faces. When the teams took the pitch the Blades made themselves obvious and scuffling broke out and two Blades were arrested (one was Max). The fighting was small scale, just two scuffles and two more arrests. The Blades were amazed at how slow police were to intervene; this may have been due to the stand having no officers present, it being 'policed' instead by private stewards. Later, police arrived in number and sat on the stairways to separate the warring factions. The match was a disaster for the Sheffield team (they lost 4-0). Outside, Blades walked amongst the waiting Leeds 'lads'. However, with both sides aware of plain clothes police nearby, words were threatening, punches were sly, but that was it. The Blades travelled home and drank the night away, pleased with their performance and hoping the Owls would appear. They did not.

Leeds, home and away - 1990/91, 1991/92

These four fixtures did not produce any confrontation of significance between the rival hooligan mobs. This is due to a number of factors. Firstly, the all-ticket policy of Leeds United led to the allocation to visiting supporters of only 1,500 tickets, which went directly to official supporters' clubs. Thus, all unaffiliated supporters, including the Blades, do not travel; to do so would be futile.

Secondly, during 1991, the Blades had a more important issue to settle which coincided with the Leeds away fixture. Consequently, forty met on Saturday midday in a Sheffield pub and marched on a pub which they believed the Owls would be in before the latters' home match. The Owls had fled, however; the Blades' knowledge of their side's fixture at Leeds was gained through listening to radio reports while drinking. Thirdly, one simple, overlooked aspect of the control of the football ground is how, for over ten years, fights have been exceptional. Consequently, I will argue, the next generation of hooligan aspirants have not undergone the socialization into the proceedings which juveniles did during the 1960s and 1970s. In a sense, the next generation of supporters did not come through. Fourthly, Cohen (1972) and Clarke (1992) have pointed to structural and educational changes within the working class and the school curricula. Consequently, football is no longer the only taught sporting activity for boys, reflecting changes in working class and adolescent leisure. Put simply, not as many young boys attend football matches as before, nor are they as fanatical. Finally, we cannot disregard the impact of police tactics, surveillance and judicial sentencing. But in the absence of any study which can demonstrate a correlation between deterrence and offending, any connection here is necessarily speculative.

Conclusion

I would argue that the Blades' activities, over a lengthy historical period, are best understood through biography and anthropology rather than structure and sociology. 'Football hooliganism' lacks legal definition, structural coherence and precise demarcation of membership. It is ephemeral, renegotiated weekly, and constructs nomadic spaces for individuals and social groups to enter, perform and exit, through voluntary associations akin to Maffesoli's (1988) concept of the 'urban tribe'. It is also a contested site in which political structures and institutions endeavour to impose simplified, prejudicial readings of complex and evolving practices, through the agencies of the police and various expert opinions.

Evidently, the nature of Reputation is one that must be constantly contested within the hooligan formations. The Blades' collective perception is that by winning their competitions, Reputation is gained because Honour has been gambled and saved. Consistent victories produce a reputation for Hardness; thus, as Campbell (1964, p.268) defines it, "honour is whatever raises a man up in the eyes of others, and gives him a reason for pride." Internally, in attaining this reputation for Hardness, very low standards of personal behaviour were tacitly tolerated. The Blades exist as a loosely knit collection of individuals (young, male Sheffield United fans), segmentary to the utmost, without a leader and internal hierarchy. Blades are 'something happening' and someone to hang out with and enjoy time with. Because the range of needs it satisfies is fairly narrow, it is outgrown when other forms of satisfaction become more important. Even for core Blades, their Blade identity ends when those for whom they need support (i.e. fellow Blades, Owls and Their Boys) are not around.

The Blades are a voluntary association, consisting of individuals from extremely varied backgrounds, united by support for one club and a common antipathy towards another. They are no different from thousands of their peers in the city or for that matter, the country. No one theory can explain the Blades; all that could be said is that for a variety of reasons, some young men are drawn together around shared symbolism and common consumption patterns. Some stay only a few months, others remain for a decade. Time, here, is exchanged for the content of information and the form of identity.

There is no one Blade identity; there is great diversity within their group, as they realize, which takes on a contextual role and status. In the absence of leadership or stated norms, this heterogeneity produces a wide variety of behaviour. This is manifested through the 'disorganization' surrounding transport to away games; inconsistencies in the appropriate times for pursuing rivals, drinking, etc.; and, disagreements as to the correct treatment of Owls.

In relation to the police, and policing of football match occasions, it may appear that the Blades are constantly deterred, or dissuaded by the former's presence, from violent interaction with their peers. On a simple reading, this would suggest that police have effectively prevented hooliganism; however, there are more important processes to note. Bauman's (1991) thesis suggests to the student of public order that the police are no longer, in their strategies, legislating to neutralize phenomena. They are now interpreters, constantly using the most recent technology and surveillance strategies, to watch the hooligans, who are one step ahead. In this sense, the police are reliant upon the actions of the Blades to provide for arrests and therefore success against the hooligan. However, generally Blades enjoy confrontation rather than violence. Within this, the aim of humiliating rivals plays a larger part than injuring them. This provides a satisfaction which could obviate any need to inflict violence. What is being prosecuted is not simply violence against 'Their Boys' per se, but a semiotics of Reputation, Hardness, Smartness. When all is said and done, there are far more words spoken than punches thrown; this is the essence of hooliganism.

What it means to be a Blade is inherited, narrated, interpreted and enacted differently, through co-existent social groups at the everyday level by constantly changing participants. But the social dramas they enact renew the desired values and norms the participants hold or aspire to. Such dramas achieve 'communion' between disparate individuals pursuing achievement and selfhood. Blades provide emotional ties of shared ordeals, the pursuit of Reputation allowing a common theme of discussion. Blades offer the comradeship of fellow fans but, like similar groups, they are Janus headed; in group friendship is linked to hostility to others. But who gets drawn into this association, the circumstances under which they meet, and the precise role of 'enemy' can vary considerably.

Bibliography

Armstrong, G. (1992) 'Impartiality and the BBC', *Flashing Blade*, December.

Armstrong, G. (1994) *Blades, Pigs and Their Boys*, forthcoming.

Armstrong, G. & Harris, R. (1991) 'Football hooligans: theory and evidence', *Sociological Review*, 39(3).

Armstrong, G. & Hobbs, D. (1994) 'Tackled from behind', in R. Giulianotti *et al.* (eds.) *Football, Violence and Social Identity*, Routledge, London.

Bailey, F. (1969) *Stratagems and Spoils*, Blackwell, Oxford.

Bauman, Z. (1991) *Legislators and Interpreters*, Polity, Cambridge.

Bourdieu, P. (1970) *The Sense of Honour in Algeria 1960*, Cambridge University Press, Cambridge.

Bourdieu, P. (1977) *Outline of a Theory of Practice*, Cambridge University Press, Cambridge.

Brandes, S. (1987) 'Reflections on honour and shame in the Mediterranean', in D. Gilmore (ed.) *Honour and Shame and the Unity of the Mediterranean*, American Anthropological Association, Washington.

Campbell, J. (1964) *Honour, Family and Patronage*, Oxford University Press, Oxford.

Clarke, A. (1992) 'Figuring a Brighter Future', in E. Dunning & C. Rojek (eds.) *Sport and Leisure in the Civilizing Process*, Routledge, London.

Cohen, P. (1972) 'Subcultural conflict and working class community', *Working Papers in Cultural Studies No.2*, Birmingham, CCCS.

Dunning, E., Murphy, P. & Williams, J. (1988) *The Roots of Football Hooliganism*, Routledge, London.

Foucault, M. (1977) *Discipline and Punish: the birth of the prison*, Pantheon, New York.

Friedrichs, P. (1977) *Agrarian Revolts in a Mexican Village*, University of Chicago Press, Chicago.

Geertz, C. (1972) 'Deep play: notes from the Balinese cockfight', *Daedelus*, 101(1).

Giulianotti, R. (1994a) 'Social identity and public order', in R. Giulianotti *et al.* (eds.) *op. cit.*

Giulianotti, R. (1994b) 'Taking liberties: Hibs casuals and Scottish law', in R. Giulianotti *et al.* (eds.) *op. cit.*

Goffman, E. (1959) *The Presentation of Self in Everyday Life*, Penguin, Harmondsworth.

Haynes, R. (1993) 'Marching on together', in S. Redhead (ed.) *The Passion and the Fashion*, Avebury, Aldershot.

Leeds TUC & AFA (1987) 'Terror on the terraces', mimeo.

Maffesoli, M. (1988) 'Jeux de masques: postmodern tribalism', *Design Issues*, 4 (1 & 2).

Marsh, P., Harre, R. & Rosser, E. (1978) *The Rules of Disorder*, Routledge & Kegan Paul, London.

Marsh, P. (1978) 'Life and careers on the soccer terraces', in R. Ingham (ed.) *Football Hooliganism: the wider context*, Inter-Action, London.

Peristiany, J. (ed.) (1965) *Honour and Shame*, Weidenfeld & Nicolson London.

Pitt-Rivers, J. (1966) 'Honour and Social Status', in J. Peristiany (ed.) *Honour and Shame: the values of Mediterranean society*, Chicago University Press, Chicago.

Suttles, G. (1968) *The Social Order of the Slum*, Chicago University Press, Chicago.

Taylor, I. (1982a) 'On the sports-violence question: soccer hooliganism revisited', in J. Hargreaves (ed.) *Sport, Culture and Ideology*, Routledge, London.

Taylor, I. (1982b) 'Class, violence and sport: the case of soccer hooliganism in Britain', in H. Cantelon & R. Gruneau (eds.) *Sport, Culture and the State*, University of Toronto Press, Toronto.

Turner, V. (1974) *Dramas, Fields and Metaphors*, Ithica, Cornell University Press, New York.

Walker, M. (1982) 'Leeds, the Lads and the Meeja', *New Society*, 28 November.

Ward, C. (1989) *Steaming In*, Sportspages/Simon & Schuster, London.

Watson, D. (1993) 'Psycho Mike and the phantom ice-rink' in N. Hornby (ed.) *My Favourite Year*, Witherby/When Saturday Comes, London.

Wikan, U. (1984) 'Shame and honour: a contestable pair', *Man*, 19.

Williams, J. (1986) 'White riots', in A. Tomlinson & G. Whannel (eds.) *Off the Ball*, Pluto, London.

13 'Keep it in the Family': An outline of Hibs' football hooligans' social ontology

Richard Giulianotti

> (I)t is not a question of setting a collective identity against individual identities. *All identity is individual*, but there is no individual identity that is not historical or, in other words, constructed within a field of social values, norms of behaviour and collective symbols (Balibar, 1991, p.94).

Football hooligans: unredeemed 'folk devils'

Social knowledge and understanding of contemporary soccer hooliganism remains limited. Public knowledge of the phenomenon and its media representations tend to overlap more consistently than they diverge. Even *prima facie* empathetic studies of soccer's deviant dimensions succumb to reified sensationalism or effective hypocrisy. Stuart Cosgrove's (1991) recent work on Scottish soccer culture proclaims itself to be the book which 'brings the game into disrepute' and 'concentrates on the side of football that administrators and officialdom would prefer to suppress' (Cosgrove, 1991, p.7). In doing so, it reports rather than interrogates the hyperbole surrounding one soccer subculture, Edinburgh's Hibs casuals (the 'Capital City Service'). This gang has allegedly "turned parts of Edinburgh's city centre into a weekend war-zone and have been implicated in protection rackets, drug rings and criminal damage" (*Ibid*, p.136).

Sociological studies have done little to dispel the conjecture. Most youth subcultural 'folk devils' have attracted debunking treatises from interested researchers; not yet the soccer hooligan. Much of the research seems to be undertaken on the premise that the phenomenon's conventional meaning, as serious social malady, remains paramount. The most extensive research to date, carried out by Eric Dunning and his team at Leicester University during the 1980s had accepted as one of its analytical cornerstones the principle that the media

> contribute to the generation of a moral panic; that is, a reaction to a phenomenon that is perceived as constituting a social problem which distorts and exaggerates its dangers, leading to calls for draconian measures to deal with it - measures of a kind which, as we have suggested, appear to have had the unintended consequence of displacing and reinforcing the problem (Dunning *et al.*, 1988, p.10).

However, this position is rather vitiated by the sociological perspective upon which it is grounded, an approach introduced by Norbert Elias and termed as figurational or process-sociological. There have been numerous subsequent criticisms and restatements of the Leicester position on soccer hooliganism, which I do not propose to rehearse. I do seek to add the further observation that in their studies of soccer hooliganism, the figurationalists may have adopted wholeheartedly one feature of the Eliasian approach while ignoring some of the methodological and analytical strengths of another. In studying soccer hooligan subcultures, the Leicester team have relied almost entirely upon the theoretical searchlight of Elias' *The Civilizing Process* (1978a) (see especially Dunning *et al.*, 1988). The core hypothesis is a broadly historical, societal description of the processes underlying the gradual percolation through the social classes, of increasingly constrictive codes of behaviour and etiquette. The figurationalists argue that this process has failed to develop 'civilizing' norms within the lower or 'rough' working classes in particular, and therefore it is this group which is central to soccer hooligan violence. The picture of lower-working class communities provided by the Leicester thesis emphasizes their rather endogamous reproduction of self-evidently 'rough' values within 'rough' housing estates, apparently hermetically (and hermeneutically) sealed from the wider aims and values of more 'civilized' society (cf. Murphy, et al., 1990, pp.129-166).

Subsequently, the substantive part of the Leicester thesis relates to the *phylogenetic* study of English fan disorder: the historical development of the game, from folk football to soccer, and the continuities and changes in fan and player violence. The weaknesses are most acute in relation to explaining the *ontogeneses* of football fan disorder: the development of specific fan subcultures, within specific social *milieux*, at national, regional and local levels. In part, this oversight has been acknowledged by Eric Dunning (1994, p.153), when noting that Leicester's paradigmatic study *The Roots of Football Hooliganism* should have limited its explanatory purchase to England. However, the figurational, everyday question asked by Elias (1978b, p.134) - 'What makes people bonded to and dependent on each other?' - has wider reverberations upon social research. It requires the researcher to examine the social and normative 'interdependencies' between different groups at the microscopic level, to describe what commonalities (as well as differences) are prevalent between them.

In relation to the question of crowd violence, therefore, sociological analysis must move beyond the value-laden reading of its 'uncivility'. As historians such as E.P. Thompson and Natalie Davis have indicated, avoiding morally commonsensical readings of public disorder allows a critical insight into 'the ritualized and theatrical aspects of crowd action as cultural and communal expression' (Dean, 1989, p.48). In the field of soccer sociology it has taken the researches of an anthropologist (Armstrong, this volume, forthcoming) and a social psychologist (Finn, 1994), to provide a lead in situating the emergence and development of soccer hooligan subcultures *lococentrically*: that is within the value frameworks of specific social environments. In an earlier paper, I have also sought to show how the nascence of one such formation (the Aberdeen Soccer Casuals) in the early 1980s reflected a new sense of economic, cultural and soccer superiority throughout the city in relation to Scotland. The ASC's comparative decline was partially traced to deep-seated local mores, such as its cultural conservatism and isolation (Giulianotti, 1993).

These studies emphasize the extent to which identifiable British soccer subcultures draw upon club supporters' indigenous values to rationalize and legitimize their pursuit of, and partaking in, soccer-related violence and public disorder. My own ethnographic research recognises a similar process present amongst one soccer subculture, the Hibs casuals, who attach themselves to Hibernian F.C., a Scottish Premier League side from Edinburgh. This subculture has continued to counteract successfully two acute pressures operating against it. Firstly, there are the increasingly oppressive Scottish police and judiciary measures against the Hibs casuals, which have included the imprisonment of 'top boys', the arrest of scores of casuals, the proactive detention without charge of individuals prior to matches, and their routine panoptical surveillance on match-days and at other times (Giulianotti, 1994a). A second challenge to the CCS has been more symbolic than real: the somewhat exaggerated perception of a new youth cultural antipathy towards soccer violence through the rise of the 'rave'/club scene (Giulianotti, 1994b; Redhead, 1991).

Research with the CCS suggests that, in the process of counteracting these pressures, Hibs casuals have collectively germinated a unique moral and existential framework, a *social ontology*. This involves the establishment and transmission of a shared, locally-grounded perspective on other groups against which the Hibs casuals may define themselves, through a socio-normative *syntax*, to enable the construction of a collective identity and agency. The social ontology draws upon, re-codifies and re-orders established symbols within the vocabularies of both the Hibernian support and wider Edinburgh public, and the soccer subcultural argot of Scotland, or Britain as a whole. The accessibility of this social ontology to prospective CCS supporters - its demarcation of familiar and identifiable social groups within a coherent socio-normative framework - and its easy reproduction, are the principal bases for the longevity of the subculture as a whole. The maintenance of material and symbolic distances between the CCS and these social binaries is problematicized, through the experiences of eco-social, biographical and personal interdependencies. Before exploring the social syntax underlying the Hibs casuals' ontology, it is necessary to examine some semantic issues regarding the formation.

The Ideal Speech Situation and Number One status

The CCS is also sometimes known as The Brotherhood or The Mafia, though its nucleus and fellow travellers alike prefer The Family as an alternative *nom de guerre*. Two long-standing Hibs casuals explain The Family as a surrogate kinship network based on interdependent obligations:

> I'll tell you why we're called The Family. Because, see that boy there; if he got kicked out of his house tonight, he'd have about sixty places to stay. We look after one another. And if anybody has a go at a Hibs boy, we're after them....
>
> When something happens against any of us, there are Hibs boys there in no time. It's as though they're sensing a fight, with some kind of extra sense .... like a lot of little soldier ants, attacking a hostile invader. The best description of what Hibs casuals are like came from a Hearts boy I know. He said that when there's any hassle in the centre and there's a Hibs boy involved, the rest of us seem to come out of the cracks in the pavement.

The Family is Edinburgh's premier soccer casual movement. Technically, casuals are distinguished in appearance from other soccer fans by their disinclination to wear team colours in favour of expensive designer and sports leisurewear; and in cultural terms by their comparatively instrumental pursuit of violence, principally with opposition casuals.[1] The soccer casual style was Scotland's major youth subcultural identity throughout the 1980s, emerging chronologically in Aberdeen (Aberdeen Soccer Casuals), Motherwell (Saturday Service), Edinburgh (Capital City Service, Casual Soccer Firm), Dundee (Utility) and Glasgow (Inter-City Firm, Her Majesty's Service, Celtic Soccer Casuals) (Giulianotti, 1993a). In the latter half of the decade, Aberdeen and Hibernian casuals were at the forefront of Scotland's most serious casual violence. During this period, The Family progressively established ascendency over Hearts' casuals known as the Casual Soccer Firm (CSF), and the wilting casual scene throughout the country. The CSF's most prominent casuals do not appear in the city centre during principal leisure periods, such as weekends and midweek evenings. Additionally, a frequent grievance within the CCS is that most casual gangs in Scotland, with the exception of Aberdeen and possibly Rangers, no longer travel through for matches to Easter Road, the home of Hibernian and The Family.

The watershed in the formation's history is traced by leading figures to 23rd March, 1985, when over 500 Aberdeen casuals marauded through Edinburgh, leaving one Hibs counterpart close to death from a pre-match confrontation. For major occasions, the CCS has mustered in the range of 200 or more: at the 1991 Skol Cup Final, the gang produced upwards of 400 'boys'. Inevitably, there will be many within this total, or additional to it, who are not felt by its leading lights to merit inclusion. However, it should also be stated that if one were to take into account the number associated with the CCS, past and present, the total would spiral to well over 500. Some are on the interstices of involvement at soccer, others may no longer attend soccer regularly, but socialize freely with current CCS boys. These figures contrast with the regular Hibs home support, which for season 1991-92 averaged 9,841.

Within The Family there are also gradations of status, though cabalism is not evident (Giulianotti, 1994a). We have, for example, the 'top boys', the *noblesse oblige*, who consistently form the nucleus of the 'frontline' during confrontations with opponents. And, of course, there are also the relatively regular casuals for whom continuities within the gang, and the preponderant, routine reproduction of affiliations, will suggest limited importance of boundary maintenance with outsider formations. Analytically, however, the formation's syntactical definition remains central to its sociological possibility.

For each serious casual formation in Scotland, the pursuit of 'Number One' status remains a primary objective. Casual gangs are battling physically and semiotically for this precedence over each other: who have the best 'mob' in fighting and fashion leading terms, which mobs are 'game' or 'runners'. The very endeavour to achieve this competitive pre-eminence indicates that any casual formation is appealing to a common set of standards, a subcultural standard of 'truth', against which this claim to superiority may be judged. Habermas (1970, p.372) defines this underlying objective as the Ideal Speech Situation:

> No matter how the intersubjectivity of mutual understanding may be deformed, the *design* of an ideal speech situation is necessarily implied in the structure of potential speech, since all speech, even intentional deception, is oriented toward the idea of truth.

For Habermas, the difference between presaging and actually attaining the Ideal Speech Situation is the difference between *discourse* and *action* (Habermas, 1973, p.168). Action requires a background consensus, whereby modes and contents of linguistic communication are accepted, uncontested by all: it is apparently the mode of communication in which the Ideal Speech Situation has been attained. Discourses arise where this consensus collapses or has not been attained. Thus, for Habermas, once this Ideal Speech Situation has been attained, all inequalities and subsequent social conflict, contestation and debate are finished: discourse is over and harmonious action begins.

This reading of intersubjective harmony harbours two fundamental weaknesses. Firstly, Habermas's analysis is one which is classically modernist, in that it essentially seeks not only the end of politics but also the end of all social difference. It is a scenario in which the 'natural' status of a 'pure consensus' hides what Barthes (1972, p.155) terms a 'myth': in effect, 'a conjuring trick', whereby one group's power interests are hidden behind a 'natural' or 'commonsense' form of social order. In this sense, casual gangs may be termed postmodern. We not only have the celebration through contestation of 'difference' (different towns and cities, different local and regional cultures, different interpretations of the style itself). We also have the inherent acceptance that attaining the Ideal Speech Situation, and establishing a casual gang's 'Number One' status, necessarily entails the gang's demise - who can they define themselves against and compete with afterwards?

Secondly, the Habermasian distinction between discourse and action is too rigid. Disputes over each casual formation's relative strengths and weaknesses are both discursive and active. After fights, those involved with casual gangs develop distinctive interpretations of proceedings and competing interpretations between both sides emerge: what the numerical balance was between each side, which side had the advantage of surprise, which side was expected to take the initiative in a certain context, how many on each side were 'decked', which side 'backed off', etc. But, contrary to Habermas's consensual definition, action itself is the fundamental resource for pursuing a short-lived pre-eminence, a claim to 'Number One' status until the next time. To put this another way, one of the appeals of the actual violence itself is certainly existential, through 'the buzz' of being involved (cf. Finn, 1994); but, this should not ignore the microsociological factor, of seeking to 'settle old scores', of silencing rivals' perceivedly groundless claims to superiority on previous occasions. The Ideal Speech Situation is therefore recomposed as a preferred scenario where the 'good name' of a casual gang is re-established, through action, and with little room for subsequent debate.

The social ontology of a football hooligan formation

The Family's pentangular social ontology is depicted in Figure 1, consisting of a chain of negatively-grounded signifiers against whom the CCS is defined. Socially, at the everyday level, the rigidity of these boundaries is not absolute, but negotiated. The various meanings of these groupings are underpinned, and made communicable, by The Family's working of five existential categories. These are time, space, body, self and other. In a collective cognition and application of these categories, The Family utilize a major social grouping to embody each one. Highlighting the vagaries of cognitive classification, on the interstices of these existential categories are located other social groupings within The Family's lifeworld.

I should add that in piecing together The Family's ontology, I have sought to utilize terms of reference and social categories which the Hibs casuals regularly actuate, rather than those which sociologists would demand that they should. Accordingly, a gender categorization does not arise here, although there have been 'casualettes' associated with The Family, and a group of teenage girls known as the 'gobblers', the sexual exploitation of whom is graphically eponymous. Equally, there are the 'chavvies', whose lack of subcultural identity is their main distinguishing characteristic; and the 'big-wigs', the uniformed police who are on duty on match days.

The Other

This is the most important ontological category for The Family, as it also underpins the CCS cognition of the remaining four categories. It is not simply the case that the Other is syntactically aligned to other categories, against which each derives its Saussurian meaning. For the CCS, the Other's role in enabling their collective identity is profoundly ambiguous according to three ontological precepts: syntax, authority and politics. Firstly, the presence of others, and the

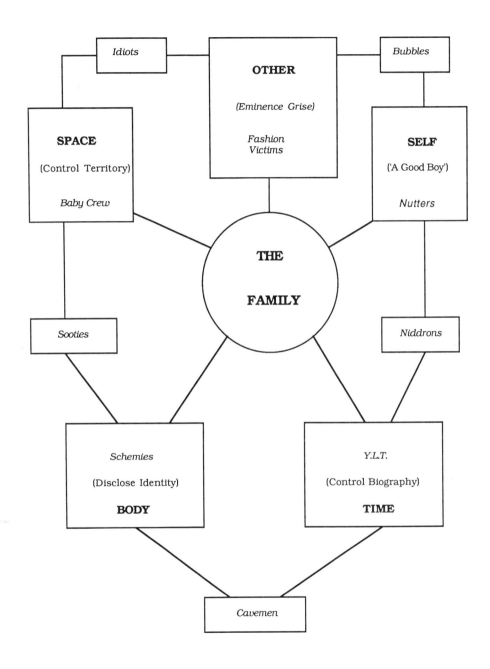

Figure 13.1: Hibs casuals' social ontology

fundamental Other, enables common identification and collective sociation:

> Being a friend, and being an enemy, are the two modalities in which which the *Other* may be recognized as another *subject*, construed as a 'subject like the self', admitted into the self's life world, be counted, become and stay relevant. If not for the opposition between friend and enemy, none of this would be possible (Bauman, 1991, p.54).

For the CCS, opposition casuals represent the essential 'other': enemies on match-days, but with shared and recognizable identities both on these occasions and outwith it. The ability of these others to perform positively, with honour, in pursuing Number One status, generates 'respect' amongst The Family. Here, the collective discrimination against these others becomes positive. Leading opposition casuals are discussed and praised internally; word filters through the hooligan grapevine of The Family's favourability towards these others' performances *via* common workmates, telephone calls, exchanges during court appearances, etc. Furthermore, individual and small group interaction between these seemingly 'rival' casuals tends to be consciously civilized, formal and entirely amicable on chance meetings outwith 'hooligan' contexts e.g. during holidays overseas, at worksites, at matches and nightclubs in neutral venues.

Underlying these consensual exchanges of violence, however, is the common authority which exists between The Family (*qua* aggregate of friends) and casual others (*qua* temporary collection of enemies): the desire to 'do the business', uphold the good reputation of the gang, and aim at asserting a discursive claim to Number One status through definite action. The Ideal Speech Situation, and the attainment of Number One status, therefore stands as what Derrida (1984) terms 'a transcendental signified', a legitimizing Other and ideal against which the actions of the casual formation are judged.

Thirdly, there is the final reiteration of the Other as necessarily an enemy, and which emphasizes an appropriation or consumption of the Other. To introduce Barthesian argot, the Other's desirable 'foreignness', by which we negatively and symbolically distinguish ourselves, is retained analytically; but at the additional expense of seeking to subjugate it politically. Baudrillard (1983) terms this process the *éminence grise*, the art of making the Other disappear. The neutralization is, in a transcendental sense, a simulation of the Ideal Speech Situation, which discursively renders the latter all the more viable to the CCS and its sympathizers. For The Family, invoking control of the Other physically and stylistically remains paramount; but its very attainment threatens entropy by eradicating the formal, parental boundaries facilitating collective identity. Consumption is negation is self-annihilation.

The Family combats this process by tenaciously refusing to allow former Others of the Scottish casual network the opportunity to depart from their stratification within its social ontology. As an act of cognitive brinkmanship, those former rivals seeking to disappear from The Family's hooligan ontology are reclassified to fit with the 'transvestite casuals', the would-be others who are 'all dress and all mouth', interested in the discourse but not the action (cf. Giulianotti, 1994a).

The embodiments of these pure Others, who are entirely negatively judged, are the 'Fashion Victims'. Of the five major social groupings, this is the one with whom The Family has empirically the least inter-relations. Fashion Victims are, as nomenclature conveys, at the mercy of sea-changes in the world of designer clothing, no longer within the casual league of style. The media are thought to exercise an unsavoury power in determining their quarries' attire. In utilizing this particular description of former 'trendies', The Family permits itself the space to continue to demonstrate its *physical* superiority: battle weary casuals seeking sanctuary in a different 'style', such as the anti-violence 'rave scene', have been assailed by offspring of The Family looking to reproduce old rivalries.

In identifying more specifically which social groupings are Fashion Victims, the Family's social ontology immediately indicates that it is not a hermetically sealed one. A Hibs casual from the city's West End references the long-running, Edinburghian antipathy towards the perceived socio-cultural vulgarity of Glasgow to characterize this category:

A Fashion Victim's somebody that dresses exactly the way magazines like *The Face* tell them to. They copy everything. Just about all the Wee-Gees (Glaswegians) are real Fashion Victims, you know; if they see pictures of modish suits in the media, they're all wearing them the next week ... I mean, you can see them on television, sitting there in their £300 suits, with their fake sun tans, looking at Oscar Marazoni photos of the Gorbals or wherever, saying, 'Yes that's the way it was'. All this City of Culture stuff ... its totally false.

Glaswegian ex-casuals are also considered to be particularly prone to involvement in the Fashion Victim's latest forum, the 'rave scene'. The latter is seen by some of the CCS as a platform upon which opposition casuals may act 'wide'.

'Wide' relates to actions designed to confuse subcultural categories for the benefit of their performer. In a conventional football sense, this may simply be an individual's open display of presence on territory recognized by both sides as not his own. Analytically more serious are instances where subcultural identities are played off against one another. Thus, 'Fashion Victims' align themselves with the presumed *avant garde* of raving, but still retain subcultural affiliations with casuals. Glaswegian casuals have been known to arrive in Edinburgh in an avowedly non-casual context for these activities, but still return to their native city with the casual 'news' that the CCS do not dominate in the way that they had in the past.

Flanking the Fashion Victims are 'Idiots/Wee Laddies' and 'Bubbles', which impinge upon the categories of space and self respectively. The former are Edinburgh based and, unlike the Fashion Victims, are definitively concerned with enjoining themselves to the CCS. In common with Fashion Victims however, their 'natural' understanding of youth subcultures, and The Family in particular, is derived principally from the latter's media representation. It is essentially the local, popularized notoriety of Hibs casuals which attracts this minor social grouping. Idiots/Wee Laddies are understood by the CCS to be utilizing the general public rather than the Scottish casual network, with The Family at its core, as a reference group for their meretricious behaviour. On match-day, the Idiots/Wee Laddies over-dress: an iconography of clothes rather than action. The wearing of bright colours and ostentatiously 'casual' attire attracts the police to them and, consequently, The Family, thereby stylistically and pragmatically undermining the formation. However, the artifice of the Idiots/Wee Laddies' casual presentation is most threatening to The Family in relation to opposition casuals - who may either attack or berate the former as 'Hibs casuals', act well against them, and thus undermine any of the genuine casuals' claims to Number One status.

In contradistinction, Bubbles are often former casuals (CCS or otherwise) who have vacated the terraces and train stations for the rave scene. This macro-style identification aligns them, in the view of the CCS, with Fashion Victims, though their historical and interactional links with the main corpus render boundary maintenance a good deal more problematic. The Family have been concerned that opposing casuals have metamorphosized into ravers, and are using Edinburgh Bubbles to ensure a peaceful reception when they travel through to Edinburgh. Although this issue has led to widely criticized internal fighting between representatives of the two polarities, shared biographies combine to de-amplify the animosity felt by some of The Family. One individual, prominent amongst Hibs casuals for eight years, reasons:

> You have to look it from both points of view. Some boys are not into soccer any more; a lot of them were never that into it in the first place, but some were good boys, and still are. They're more into having a good time at night; they want to go to raves and so on. Other boys are still into the violence...

Shared biographies (and therefore subcultural *savoir-faire*) accommodate the new, non-violent inter-subjective communication between Bubbles and their other, former soccer casual adversaries.

The Self

The individual self is an integral part of modernity, if not its *sine qua non*. Elias (1989, p.172) recognizes 'a distinctive social habitus which is characteristic of our age.':

> It induces in people the feeling that in some sense their individual self and, by proxy, every other individual, exists as a kind of monad independently of all others in a central position in the world and that one can explain all social events, including human communication, in terms of individual actions (*Ibid.*).

Sennett (1977) adds that the historical erosion of the public domain has facilitated the paradoxical advent of narcissistic self to new Protestant ethic.

Worldly asceticism and narcissism have much in common: In both, 'What am I feeling?' becomes an obsession. In both, showing to others the checks and impulses of oneself feeling is a way of showing that one does have a worthy self. In both, there is a projection of the self onto the world, rather than an engagement in worldly experience beyond one's control (Sennett, 1977, p.334).

From this, therefore, we have a vision of self which seeks perpetual validation through its controlled performance before others. Alternatively, through the prism of the 'looking-glass self', the self is also wary of excessive disclosure of its identity before others, who scrutinize its performances for clues to its real content.

The imputation of self through evaluation of limited action is a popular science also practiced by The Family. The type of self sanctioned by the collectivity is the 'good boy', an accolade accorded individuals 'clued up' on casual history, style and formations; and who are 'game' i.e. don't abandon fellow casuals, or blacken the CCS reputation by 'doing a runner', when confronted by opposition casuals. Outwith the context of formal Family activity, Hibs casuals are given a relatively wide berth for the pursuit of minor indulgences, idiosyncrasies and deviances. There is no recommended habitus for Hibs casuals *per se*.

Earlier studies of soccer hooligan subcultures have drawn attention to the proclivities of the Nutter (Marsh, 1978; Hobbs & Robins, 1991). Marsh attributes this individual's psycho-social infirmities from special types of non-rational behaviour. 'Nutters "go crazy" or "go mad" - they go beyond the fans' limits of acceptable and sane behaviour' (Marsh, 1978, p.70). Definitions such as these ignore the extent to which the actions of the 'Nutter' are goal-orientated within the framework of subcultural norms. It may even be argued that, categorically, the 'Nutter' is closest to the subculture's *conscience collectif*, given his perceivedly reckless and selfless upholding of the group's reputation. The 'Nutter' may simply extend the concept of 'gameness' into more enervating terrain yet uncharted by the current 'good boys'. These ambiguous evaluations of the 'nutter' are illustrated within The Family by its collective appreciation of the late 'Dodgy D', a Hibs casual said to be universally popular within the gang, but whose violent experiences against opposition casuals were considered to be excessive and beyond anyone's control. Dodgy D's exploits attained a maximum utility for The Family in the late 1980s, when fights with Aberdeen casuals acquired a particularly dangerous and unpredictable character. One casual reports:

> He did that Aberdeen boy ages ago, when we were still looking for our own back after the 1985 game at Easter Road. I was there and saw him that day, it was fucking excellent, excellent. Aberdeen came ahead and it went off. He was right in, out with the blade, in, gloves off, jacket, blade away. That was it; smooth as you like. Excellent, fucking excellent.

The Nutter is flanked by 'Bubbles' (straddling the other-self divide) and 'Niddrons' (on the self-time border). Links with both are secured by their disproportionate propensity to face the law in contexts which The Family consider unworthy of such personal sacrifice. Bubbles are by definition heavily involved in raving, which has been effectively criminalized at the macroscopic level, following police and popular press concern with its symbiosis to drug subcultures (Giulianotti, 1994b). The distinction between the two ascriptions is at the level of action: Bubbles tend to be non-fighters, whilst Nutters most certainly are.

Niddrons are understood to be even more liable to attract the attentions of the police. Authentic Niddrons hail from Niddrie, a heavily underprivileged council housing estate in south-east Edinburgh, a region traditionally given over to following Hibs. The Niddron habitus is classically lower working class: they are defined sardonically by one casual as, 'People from Niddrie. They're either a tramp or a thief, or both.' Niddrons are intrinsically criminogenic: legal biographies are typically littered with social work and borstal reports, and a lengthy criminal record with soccer-related violence a mere peccadillo. An engrained disinclination to apply the 'gaming approach' to involvement in soccer-related violence renders their presence to even front-line casuals 'pure jailbait' (cf. Berk, 1974). Another white collar Hibs casual states:

> You see the Niddrons being really game one week and not there the next, because they've been arrested for housebreaking or something. They're usually right good boys like, but they end up missing big games because they're getting lifted all the time. I've been to matches where they turn up when they've got a warrant out for them. You say to them, 'What are you doing here, the

police'll spot you a mile away?' 'Ah, I'm a Hibs boy.' 'Away home, you're no use to us here.'

Yet, this categorical distinction between Niddrons and Nutters, and The Family itself, is often transactionally curtailed. For the mainstream CCS, the exigencies of cementing the wider reputation may be so strenuous as to draw the entire collective into situations which are considered by others at the time to be 'jailbait' scenarios. At the everyday level, a common subcultural *langue* with Bubbles, social friendships with Nutters and Bubbles, and shared biographies with Nutters, Niddrons and Bubbles combine to deconstruct frequently the boundaries between these three categorical others and the mainstream CCS, thereby rendering the former groupings more proximate to symbiotic rather than outsider status.

Time

In articulating the underpinnings of The Family's categorization and working of time, I accept Giddens' (1984, pp.132-3) criticism of Hagerstrand, that

> 'clock-time' should not be accepted simply as an unquestioned dimension of the construction of topographical models, but must be regarded as itself a socially conditioned influence upon the nature of the time-space paths traced out by actors in modern societies.

Unfortunately, Giddens' failure to expand here leaves unresolved the issue of whether pure time, as linear, is an existential fact of life, or essentially a social construct. More sociologically certain is that a major ingredient of modernity is the rationalization and compartmentalization of time. All social structures valorize the control of time, or the mollification of its consequences in lieu of their mastery. Lives and careers are chronologized and planned; stages or 'phases' in the lifecourse may be terraced mentally, though their meanings are subject to personal reflection and historico-cultural change.

The Family, a subculture almost exclusively aged in teens and twenties, collectively establishes itself as more capable of rationalizing the linear social effects of time/history, than its subcultural ancestors. In this sense, The Family's social ontology does not attain *de facto* the hegemonic power capable of creating pure myth, in which history is denied in favour of a 'natural' Number One status. Alternatively, the continuous reproduction of Number One status, and the desire to cement hegemony over the Scottish casual scene which constitutes the Ideal Speech Situation, is an essential requisite of The Family's overall *raison d'être*.

One popular view is that soccer hooligan subcultures have attained their final incarnation as 'soccer casuals'; following this viewpoint, pretenders to the CCS's hegemony as Hibs fans' primary subculture can only espouse an 'Alla Non Violenza' ideology. The Family has itself displaced the 1970s Hibs soccer hooligan subculture, the Young Leith Team (hereon, YLT). Unlike the city-wide CCS, the YLT's centripetal pull only collated gangs from the Leith area of Edinburgh. Earlier confrontations with the YLT have now subsided, the YLT's heritage of affective and inebriated 'aggro' having been successfully purged by the designer style and relatively instrumental machinations of The Family.

The most pertinent characterization of the YLT by Hibs casuals concerns its failure to respond to social and cultural changes. The former's subcultural currency is now lowly valued, being still bedecked in attire that graphically explores the socio-economic and subcultural 'downward option' of 1970s Scottish football hooliganism (Giulianotti, 1993). Another Hibs casual ties the YLT's stylistic irrelevance to a generic biographical stagnation, a refusal to move into the next of the lifecycle's phases:

> You see them hanging about on Easter Road, outside the pubs and shop doorways when you go through for a match. They just hang around like they've always done, with dirty jeans on and their hair just a mess. They've got families and that now, but they're still like teenagers, no job or income except for the odd wee crimes. They're just a state. They look really pathetic, you know, bottom of the pile stuff.

Flanking the YLT are the Niddrons (on the time-self border), and the Cavemen (on the time-body border). The former represent the most tangible nexus between The Family and the YLT, but at a symbolic, cross-temporal level. Conceivably, Niddrons may take the place of the YLT in the future, as a displaced soccer subculture still trapped within a lower working class habitus. Both are considered to be obviously lower working class, with a criminogenic background only differentiated temporally. In contradistinction, predictable and irreversible biographies of violence and crime are not entertained by most Hibs casuals. Several keep scrapbooks of press cuttings on their own and other gangs' exploits, which will serve as compendia guaranteeing their offspring's respect in years to come. By this stage, another distinctive phase in the lifecycle will have been entered into by the first generation casual. One self-employed collector states:

> No one gets a shot of these. They're my pride and joy. I'm going to take them out when my son's about 15 years old or so and say, 'There you are, that's what I was doing when I was your age.'

It is only with the (largely symbolic) prospect of shared group biographies that The Family must countenance similitude with the YLT. For while the CCS do not encounter the YLT 'pagging' (fighting) for Hibs, they do enjoy the animated if irregular service of Niddrons. Conversely, on the other wing, the Cavemen are again generationally distinct from the main core. Cavemen represent another superseded lower-working class/supporter identity. They are classically depicted as obese through alcohol, intoxicated, wearing fat scarves, manically hypnotized by the game itself, and frequently tucking into a half-baked pie. In terms of time, therefore, Caveman are taken to epitomize a styleless masculinity and outmoded soccer identity synonymous with pre-1980s Scottish fandom (cf. Giulianotti, 1991, 1993). Within The Family's ontology, Cavemen are distinguished from the YLT, in that they actuate a fan rather than gang identity. But, the CCS nexus with this minor grouping is far more tenuous than their singularly symbolic linkages with the Niddrons. Though Cavemen are thought to have an element of inverted pride in the nationally recognized activities of their casuals (with Cavemen songs such as 'Hi-bees and Casuals don't go' now unheard), there is no foreseeable prospect of the majority of The Family allowing support for Hibs to outweigh their casual identification. The Cavemen, for their part, are known, in extraordinary circumstances such as super-charged derbies with Hearts, to have removed their scarves to augment the CCS numbers, and gone in pursuit of the opposition. Yet Hibs casuals remain sceptical about the sincerity of the Cavemen's empathy towards them in tackling tough opposing fans. A white-collar casual who has been at most major Hibs fixtures since the mid-1980s reports:

> They (Cavemen) do like us, but it depends on the circumstances. When we went down to Millwall, or when we go through to Glasgow, they find us useful: they know they're not going to get battered outside the ground. Some of them, I think, are quite proud of us, that we're number one. They think, 'At least Hibs are good at something'. But when it comes to European games, they don't want us fighting, damaging Scotland's reputation and that.

The Body

> Within consumer culture the body is proclaimed as a vehicle of pleasure: it is desirable and desiring and the closer the actual body approximates to the idealized images of youth, health, fitness and beauty the higher its exchange-value. Consumer culture permits the unashamed display of the human body. Clothing is designed to celebrate the natural human form ... (Featherstone, 1982, p.23).

With the body functioning as such a central vehicle for the disclosure of personal self and inclusion in a collectively consumerist culture, it is surprising that the corporeal tends to be ignored in sociological studies, 'as if this dimension were of a purely biological nature' (Berthelot, 1990, p.399).

Maffesoli (1988, p.150) takes Featherstone's contemporary reasoning a stage further. He argues that in the role-orientated 'tribes' of our complex, postmodern times, the body is the major resource in promoting a tribal icon through which individuals may specify their collective empathies.

> In the solitude inherent in all urban areas, the icon is a familiar image - a sort of group 'uniform' - that acts as a point of reference and becomes a part of daily life.... It also allows for the recognition of oneself by oneself and by others, and finally, of others by oneself.

The body thus becomes a signifier itself for the reading of both the self contained and the social identity of the individual. The Family both reflect and deploy this popular philosophy. The body is an instrument for the active pursuit of the focal objective, in relation to being Number One. It is utilized materially in violent confrontations with others; and symbolically, as the personal space upon which group identity and styles are consciously etched.

For The Family, casual identity *qua* bodily display is structured within a wider social and historical economy, which conceives of fashion as a flotation of all-embracing signs. Evidently, The Family signify a continuity with the long historiography of violent youth subcultures in Scotland (Murray, 1984), or Britain generally (Pearson, 1983; Hebdige 1988). However, the immediate context in which Hibs casuals operate is relatively different, due to intensified policing measures at fixtures, but more importantly through changes within the subcultural soccer hierarchies of Edinburgh and Scotland (Giulianotti, 1993, p.170). Where violent interaction with rival fans and casuals has been significantly undermined through public order measures, the body accentuates the value of symbolry in promoting subcultural claims to pre-eminence. Across segregationary fences inside football grounds and through the police escorts outside, epithets fly between rival casuals on the relative failures of opposing numbers to maintain reasonable levels of designer 'style'. Redhead (1991; with McLaughlin, 1985) has indicated that 'soccer's style wars' offer a symbolic parody of Thatcherism's consumerist individualism. In this context, we may observe that the competing casual gangs are also attempting to produce a shared ontology in which their own Ideal Speech Situations *qua* Number One is central, and judged by bodily demeanour. A prerequisite for this attempted discourse is the maintenance of a strong categorical distinction between other, Edinburgh subcultures at the everyday level.

The fundamental bodily outsiders to The Family are the Schemies, a social category identified negatively by wider social groups within Edinburgh. The Schemies' characteristics are not solely incarnate, but it is the body upon which these are all accessibly codified. Their attire is considered far removed from that of the casual. Instead of wearing designer labels and styles, Schemies wear garments that are the lower working class equivalent of the macro-culturally attuned Fashion Victim: flared jeans, pseudo-designer tops, the proletarian 'raver' look. The Schemie title is itself spatially grounded, within the vast postwar housing schemes on the geo-social periphery of Edinburgh. Their negative typology relates to the socio-cultural characteristics discursively appended to these locales: lower working class, riddled with unemployment, drug misuse, AIDS (cf. Giulianotti, 1994b). The cultural connotations of these estates are not the exclusive property of The Family; they are themselves in debt to publicly sanctioned discourses for such knowledge. A local housing report on one 'Schemie' area states:

> Crime and vandalism continue to figure highly as areas of concern, and this is reflected in complaints to advice agencies. Pilton *is known as* one of the main concentrations of drug abuse in Edinburgh, and the combination of heroin abuse, the incidence of the AIDS virus and drug related criminal activity has a serious impact on the area (L.R.C., 1988, p.6, my emphasis).

The Schemies are flanked by the Cavemen (on the time-body border) and the 'Sooties' (on the body-space border). All three are distinguished from The Family by their intrinsically disenfranchised reading of fashion. The Caveman-Schemie axis bridges the hiatus between old working class and new underclass identity. Depicting the semiotics of manual labour, Cavemen are also sometimes referred to as 'Sweaties'. The debauched depiction of Cavemen noted above, and their corporeal display of copious alcohol consumption, can be contrasted with their latter day incarnation, the Schemies, signifying materially a new stylistic disability, in conjunction with the postmodern hedonism of hard drugs, as inscribed upon the body through emaciation.

Alternatively, Sooties (dressed in suits, of an evening 'on the town') epitomize the proletarian divide of formal-informal attire. Sooties are subculturally criticized according to stylistic and interactional criteria. They are caught in the old binary of scruffy leisure attire (perhaps even that of their younger siblings, the Schemies) against the 'respectable' evening wear which is little more than a variation upon their parental groups' fashion. Conversely, The Family's *a priori* 'smart but casual' attire elides the modern dichotomy of the informal and formal (Giulianotti, 1993). It is as functional in nightclubs as it is on the terraces. But casual attire also provides a semiotic critique of the old, 'respectable' working class equivalence in which the sign of proper, formal dress sought to be a masculine referent for good character and financial security. The actual attire of Sooties tends to be less expensive than 'legitimate' casual wear; additionally, their 'respectable' facade is expected to collapse with ridiculous ease when they've enjoyed a few drinks and are challenged.

Space

The modern understanding of space, according to both Sennett (1977) and Foucault (1977), is instrumental. Sennett (1977, p.14) argues that "public space has become a derivative of movement", whereby "we take unrestricted motion of the individual to be an absolute right". Foucault locates modern society within the *episteme* of Panopticism. This rationalizes, anatomizes and economizes space: it is mapped, zoned, and partitioned. Therapeutic and carcereal institutions represent the fullest manifestation of this *mentalité*.

Space therefore exists as an essential resource; claims of territorial rights are made, expectations of mobility are mapped out. The 'space' of individuals and collectives is acknowledged and respected, ignored and trespassed upon. Goffman (1959) indicates through a dramaturgical model how this division of private and public space is negotiated. 'Back regions' are where individuals and self-identifying 'teams' expect to be unobserved and undisturbed, where they prepare privately for public performances given in 'front regions'. One of the symbolically challenging features of youth subcultures such as The Family is that they oppose this private-public binary. Public spaces exist as both front and back regions for its team interaction. Hibs casuals' use of public space thus provides it with a volatile potential in confronting opposing groups seeking to claim access:

> Buildings have functions, forms and structures, but they do not integrate the formal, functional and structural 'moments' of social practice. And, inasmuch as sites, forms and functions are no longer focused and appropriated by monuments, the city's contexture or fabric - its streets, its underground levels, its frontiers - unravel, and generate not concord but violence. Indeed space as a whole becomes prone to sudden eruptions of violence (Lefebvre, 1991, p.223).

It is the fear of these eruptions that leads the Panoptical *mentalite* into surveillance of public spaces.

There is an established, militaristic lexicon for describing the subcultural 'gang wars' that arise between the changeable rulers of any 'no-man's land'. Space does not exist alone as the categorical referent for these rekindled gang animosities. Time is also a co-arbiter for when a material space has its subcultural symbolry activated or deferred. Throughout most of the day, a public space's utility remains uncontested, weekends and evenings being the principal hours for asserting subcultural claims to its control (Armstrong, forthcoming).

Mobility is a key resource in the quest to control space. Interaction and confrontations between soccer subcultures are secured by effective movement to and from the major territories of the 'home' subculture. Public transport points at which rival subcultures are expected to either pass through or alight are often reactively staked out by both the opposition and the police, in their diverging endeavours to ensure that something or nothing 'goes off' between the two 'mobs'. Pro-actively, the authorities can employ the tactic of policing subcultures in transit, or even denying them access to transport. In July 1990, Hibs casuals set to travel south for a 'friendly' at Millwall had their buses turned back at Edinburgh; they responded by travelling by rail, and some flew down. A proactive strategy may also be adopted by the subcultures themselves. During the 1989-90 season, the CCS headed off the widely touted arrival of Motherwell casuals in Edinburgh, by travelling through to Motherwell before their rivals' departure. In general, the success of the police in zoning and physically partitioning the spaces within which the CCS and other soccer subcultures can operate has had two major effects:

(i)   An increase in the confrontations between splinter groups from rival soccer subcultures, in contexts peripheral to soccer, and in spaces less assiduously controlled by police. One example of this has been the violence between Hibs casuals from north Leith and Hearts casuals from the Broughton and Muirhouse districts.

(ii) A reduction in the animation of the space-violence nexus, in relative proportion to the increase in the use of space for the display of stylized control. 'Swaggering' through an opponent's territory on match-day communicates a claim of subcultural superiority.

Amongst the CCS, territorial pre-eminence in the city centre is a prized authority. This really only impinges fully upon other casuals, particularly any Hearts casuals and those from outside Edinburgh who would otherwise entertain a night out in the city. The presence of the YLT and the Schemies may also gain a hostile response, though both, like opposition casuals, tend to curtail their forays into the centre in favour of remaining within their substantial home loci. The general age of the CCS ensures that its presence in the city centre tends not to be externally visible; affiliates will look to congregate inside central pubs, clubs, and wine bars to the maximum extent.

To the outsider, the most obvious, territorially concerned grouping of the Hibs casuals is their Baby Crew. Unlike The Family *per se*, this entity is either too young or unwilling to inhabit the back regions of CCS pubs. The Baby Crew is, by definition, the next generation of The Family; its affiliates are most active and numerous during school summer holidays. Though the age distinction translates itself into culture, and the CCS does not consider the current Baby Crew to harbour casuals *de jure*, the boundary between the two can be diachronically weak. As one ex-Baby Crew associate remarks:

> One Hibs boy used to see the Baby Crew when they were out in the town during the summer. He'd point at one of them and say, 'Right, you... over, here!' And the boy from the Baby Crew would be with him for the next few weeks, like his apprentice kind of thing. Everybody would know him as a Hibs boy after that....

Conflicts between The Family's main body and the Baby Crew, over control of key subcultural resources within the city centre, have emerged to redraw the loose demarcation of the two. In the most notable instance, a gang of seasonally inflated Baby Crew raided a shop regularly utilized by the CCS. The same shop was later informally assured by The Family that this piece of larceny would not re-occur.

Flanking the Baby Crew are the Sooties (on the body-space border), and the Idiots/Wee Laddies (on the space-other border). All three consistently inhabit the centre of Edinburgh during premier leisure periods. The Sooties are distinguished from the younger Baby Crew by the codified spaces of lounge bars and night clubs in which they present their formally manicured selves. Alternatively, there is no generational distinction between Baby Crew and Idiots/Wee Laddies. Both dominate the symbolic spaces of the city centre, but are

350

distinguished by The Family according to their degrees of casual *savoir-faire*. Those involved with the Baby Crew are prospective Hibs casuals, in temporal abeyance: they are cognizant of what is casual style, who the opposition are, and what is expected of them should they be encountered. In Wittgensteinian terms, they are already socialized: they understand The Family language game, follow the rules and conventions within it, and are learning how to enforce, adapt, and add to them.

In contradistinction, as noted above, Idiots/Wee Laddies do not possess this engrained knowledge; their posturing as Hibs casuals is essentially an exercise in embraced notoriety. The final prospective generation of the Baby Crew, during the early 1990s, provoked a marked ambivalence amongst Hibs casuals. Some felt that the 'taxing' of non-associates in the city centre, through the theft of money and/or clothes, had become uppermost in the new Baby Crew's set of priorities. Thus, the expectation arose that the new Baby Crew were simply Wee Laddies presaging careers in prison rather than on the terraces.

Acknowledgements

My thanks to Mike Hepworth, Norman Bonney and Barrie O'Loan and thanks to Janet Tiernan.

The research for this chapter has been assisted by the University of Aberdeen and the ESRC.

Notes

1. The term 'Leicester School' came to be applied to this group of researchers in the late 1980s (Giulianotti, 1989; Clarke, 1992). However, the methodological and everyday unity implied by this term is no longer applicable, since John Williams' split with the 'process-sociological' approach to explaining fan behaviour (see Redhead, 1991a, p.480; Williams, 1991; Dunning, 1994).

2. The strongest methodological criticisms come from Armstrong & Harris (1991), Giulianotti (1989) and Hobbs & Robins (1991), all of which lead into further critiques of Leicester's empirical findings. Alternatively, Taylor (1987, 1989) and Clarke (1992) provide criticisms regarding the Leicester sociologists' weak position on football's relationship to traditional working class culture and changes in British political economy. The strongest defences of the Leicester findings appear in Dunning (1989, 1992, 1994) and Dunning *et al.* (1991).

3. The term 'casual' has now entered mainstream English and political discourse. It has been defined, somewhat whimsically, as a noun and adjective, originating in 1986.

    > A youth cult that emerged in Britain in the mid-1980s, its members were distinguished by their taste for expensive designer clothing, which was combined with an equally enthusiastic taste for hooligan violence, often exhibited on the terraces of football stadia (Green, 1991, p.45).

    Meanwhile, Hebdige (1989, p.89) locates 'casuals' within a wider cultural-demographic community of 'style-setters', 'innovators', 'empty nesters', 'dinkies', 'woofies', and other analogues of the post-modern New Times.

Bibliography

Allan, J. (1989) *Bloody Casuals: diary of a football hooligan*, Famedram, Glasgow.

Armstrong, G. (forthcoming) *Fists and Style*, Ph.D. thesis, University College, London,Department of Anthropology.

Armstrong, G. & Harris, R. (1991) 'Football hooligans: theory and evidence', *Sociological Review*, 39 (3).

Balibar, E. (1991) 'The Nation Form: history and ideology', in E. Balibar & I. Wallerstein, *Race, Nation, Class: ambiguous identities*, Verso, London.

Barthes, R. (1972) *Mythologies*, Jonathan Cape, London.

Baudrillard, J. (1983) *Les Strategies Fatales*, Grasset, Paris.

Baudrillard, J. (1993) *Symbolic Exchange and Death*, Sage, London.

Bauman, Z. (1991) *Modernity and Ambivalence*, Polity, Cambridge.

Bellah, R. *et al.* (1985) *Habits of the Heart*, Hutchinson, London.

Berk, R. (1974) 'A Gaming Approach to Collective Behaviour', *American Sociological Review*, 39.

Berthelot, J.M. (1990) 'Sociological Discourse and the Body', in M. Featherstone, M. Hepworth & B. S. Turner (eds), *The Body: Social Process and Cultural Theory*, Sage, London.

Clarke, A. (1992) 'Figuring a brighter future', in E. Dunning & C. Rojek (eds) *Sport and Leisure in the Civilizing Process*, University of Toronto Press, Toronto.

Clarke, J. (1978) 'Football and working class fans: tradition and change', in R. Ingham (ed.) *Football Hooliganism: the wider context*, Interaction Imprint, London.

Cohen, P. (1972) 'Sub-cultural conflict and working class community', *Working Papers in Cultural Studies 2*, CCCS, Birmingham.

Cosgrove, S. (1991) *Hampden Babylon: Sex and Scandal in Scottish Football*, Canongate, Edinburgh.

Dean, S. (1989) 'Crowds, Community, and Ritual in the Work of E. P. Thompson and Natalie Davis', in L. Hunt (ed.), *The New Cultural History*, University of California Press, London.

Derrida, J. (1984) *Octographies*, Galilee, Paris.

Dunning, E. (1989) 'The figurational approach to leisure and sport', in C. Rojek (ed.) *Leisure for Leisure*, Macmillan, London.

Dunning, E. (1992) 'Figurational sociology and the sociology of sport: some concluding remarks', in E. Dunning & C. Rojek (eds.) *op. cit.*.

Dunning, E. (1994) 'The social roots of football hooliganism: a reply to the critics of "The Leicester School"', in R. Giulianotti *et al.* (eds) *Football, Violence and Social Identity*, London: Routledge.

Dunning, E., P. Murphy & J. Williams (1988) *The Roots of Football Hooliganism*, Routledge, London.

Dunning, E., P. Murphy & I. Waddington (1991) 'Anthropological versus sociological approaches to the study of soccer hooliganism: some critical notes', *Sociological Review*, 39 (3).

Elias, N. (1978a) *The Civilizing Process*, Blackwell, Oxford.

Elias, N. (1978b) *What is Sociology?* Hutchinson, London.

Elias, N. (1989) 'The Symbol Theory: An Introduction, Part One', *Theory, Culture & Society*, 6, 2.

Featherstone, M. (1982) 'The Body in Consumer Culture', *Theory, Culture & Society*, 1.

Finn, G.P.T. (1994) 'Football Violence: a societal psychological perspective', in R. Giulianotti et al., op. cit..

Foucault, M. (1977) *Discipline and Punish*, Penguin, London.

Giddens, A. (1984) *The Constitution of Society*, University of California Press, Berkeley.

Giulianotti, R. (1989) 'A critical overview of British sociological investigations into soccer hooliganism in Scotland and Britain', *Working Papers on Football Violence*, 1, Department of Sociology, University of Aberdeen.

Giulianotti, R. (1991) 'Scotland's Tartan Army: the case for the carnivalesque', *Sociological Review*, 39 (3).

Giulianotti, R. (1993a) 'Soccer Casuals as Cultural Intermediaries: the politics of Scottish style', in S. Redhead (ed.) *The Passion and the Fashion*, Avebury, Aldershot.

Giulianotti, R. (1993b) 'A Model of the Carnivalesque? Scottish football fans at the 1992 European Championships in Sweden and beyond', *Working Papers in Popular Cultural Studies No.6*, Institute for Popular Culture, Manchester Metropolitan University.

Giulianotti, R. (1994a) 'Taking liberties: Hibs casuals and Scottish Law', in R. Giulianotti et al. (eds.) op. cit..

Giulianotti, R. (1994b) 'Scotland, Drink and Drugs: Another Generation of Casualties', in P. Lanfranchi & F. Accame (eds) *Gli Aspetti Sociali del Fenomeno della Droga nello Sport*, Soc. Stampa Sportiva, Roma.

Goffman, E. (1959) *The Presentation of Self in Everyday Life*, Penguin, Harmondsworth.

Green, J. (1991) *New Words: a dictionary of neologisms since 1960*, Bloomsbury, London.

Habermas, J. (1970) 'Toward a Theory of Communicative Competence', *Inquiry*, 13.

Habermas, J. (1973) 'A Postscript to *Knowledge and Human Interests'*, *Philosophy of the Social Sciences*, 3.

Hebdige, D. (1988) *Hiding in the Light*, Routledge, London.

Hebdige, D. (1989) 'After the Masses', in S. Hall & M. Jacques (eds.) (1989) *New Times*, Lawrence & Wishart, London.

Hepworth, M. (1987) 'The Mid Life Phase', in G. Cohen (ed.) *Social Change and the Life Course*, Tavistock, London.

Hobbs, D. & Robins, D. (1990) 'The Boy Done Good: Football Violence, Changes and Continuities', *Sociological Review*, 39(3).

Lefebvre, H. (1991) *The Production of Space*, trans. D. Nicholson-Smith, Blackwell, Oxford.

Lothian Regional Council (1988) 'Pilton/Muirhouse: Local Profile and Context Statement', Department of Planning, November 1988.

Maffesoli, M. (1988) 'Jeux de Masques: postmodern tribalism', *Design Issues*, 4(1-2).

Marsh, P. (1978) 'Life and Careers on the Soccer Terraces', in R. Ingham (ed.) *Football Hooliganism: the wider context*, Inter-Action, London.

Murphy, P., J. Williams & E. Dunning (1990) *Football on Trial*, Routledge, London.

Murray, B. (1984) *The Old Firm: Sectarianism, Sport and Society in Scotland*, John Donald, Edinburgh.

Pearson, G. (1983) *Hooligan: A History of Respectable Fears*, London: Macmillan.

Redhead, S. (1991a) 'Some reflections on discourses on football hooliganism', *Sociological Review*, 39(3).

Redhead, S. (1991b) *Football With Attitude,* Wordsmith, Manchester.

Redhead, S. & E. McLaughlin (1985) 'Soccer's Style Wars', *New Society*, 16 August.

Sennett, R. (1977) *The Fall of Public Man*, London: Faber & Faber.

Taylor, I. (1987) 'Putting the Boot into a Working Class Sport: British Soccer after Bradford and Brussels', *Sociology of Sport Journal*, 4.

Taylor, I. (1989) 'The Hillsborough Disaster', *New Left Review*, 177.

Williams, J. (1986) 'White Riots', in A. Tomlinson & G. Whannel (eds.), *Off the Ball*, London: Pluto Press, London.

Williams, J. (1991) 'Having an away day', in J. Williams and S. Wagg (eds) *British Football and Social Change: Getting into Europe*, Leicester University Press, Leicester.

14   The birth of the 'ultras': The rise of football hooliganism in Italy

Antonio Roversi

Introduction

In this chapter, using the results of research carried out by the Istituto Cattaneo of Bologna between September 1989 and May 1990, we would like to try to provide an initial quantitative estimate of the incidence of hooliganism in Italy for the Football League seasons during the period 1970/71 - 1988/89 for divisions A and B (the two professional divisions of the Italian Football Association). Basically, we will address ourselves to three types of problem:

1. How many incidents of football violence have been caused in Italy in the top two divisions since the appearance of the first organized groups of young fans? Which groups of supporters have been the most dangerous? Is there a category of high-risk matches, and if so which are they?

2. Has football violence in Italy always taken the same forms or has it changed overtime? Can we draw up a picture of the development of football violence from its first appearance to the present day? What are its latest features?

3. Can we draw up an identikit picture of the phantom called the 'ultra' who has been haunting Italian stadiums for so long?

Quantitative aspects of football hooliganism in Italy

Incidents related to League matches

First of all, we should specify exactly what we mean by the expression 'football hooliganism'. It refers to the forms of violence between spectators in England, where it appeared for the first time on a larger scale. Football hooliganism may be defined as the combination of acts of vandalism and systematic, often bloody aggression, carried out by specific groups of young fans against others like themselves inside and outside the grounds. In Italy this form of violence first appeared at the beginning of the 1970s and was closely linked to the birth of the groups of young fans who are known as 'ultras'. It should be added - and we will discuss this later - that these groups have a history which extends beyond the use of physical violence alone. In the absence of official data, the main statistical sources on the phenomenon for the period 1970/1989 are newspaper reports as featured in Table 14.1.

However, we must emphasize that these figures, like any official figures are always underestimated. They only record episodes which have been fairly serious - and have therefore attracted the attention of the press - or have occurred in the presence of the police. In any case, statistical monitoring will never be able to record the countless incidents which have occurred and continue to occur every Sunday involving 'ultras', but which have not made it into the official files because they do not fulfil these two conditions. For example, during the research we carried out in Bologna, the young 'ultras' interviewed several times, mentioned incidents which do not appear in the newspapers, in the ANSA dispatches or in the Ministry of the Interior lists. It is impossible to attempt a numerical estimate of these incidents. Given this situation, there is only one possible conclusion: the data does not reflect the real scale of the phenomenon, but only gives a general idea of football violence over time and space. To complete the picture we should combine the data with figures from the 'grim chronicle' of deaths, injuries, arrests, etc.

Table 14.1: Incidents related to league matches in Serie A and B seasons 1970/71 - 1988/89

Year	no of incidents	no of games	% incidents	Year	no of incidents	no of games	% incidents
70/71	2	620	0.3	80/81	17	620	2.7
71/72	5	620	0.8	81/82	25	620	4.0
72/73	9	620	1.4	82/83	41	620	6.6
73/74	9	620	1.4	83/84	37	620	5.9
74/75	12	620	1.9	84/85	45	620	7.2
75/76	16	620	2.5	85/86	55	620	8.8
76/77	8	620	1.2	86/87	59	620	9.5
77/78	18	620	2.9	87/88	61	620	9.8
78/79	6	620	0.9	88/89	65	686	9.4
					(72*)		(10.5)
79/80	13	620	2.1				

Source: from 1970/71 to 1979/80 newspapers (*Corriere della Sera, Resto del Carlino* and *Stadio/Corriere dello Sport*) from 1980/81 to 1988/89 newspapers (*Corriere della Sera, Resto del Carlino* and *Stadio/Corriere dello Sport*) + ANSA Archive.
* Ministry of the Interior figure

Overall, the figures inform us that football violence, as the expression of organized groups of young fans, has been constantly on the increase since the early '70s, apart from seasons 1967/77, 1978/79 and 1983/84. Even though the data here covers only three seasons, the number of injured also shows an upward trend, while the number of people arrested and reported to the police increased during the second year and dropped off during the third, with a larger fall in arrests. It is very difficult to interpret this last fact since it would seem to indicate a reduction in the police effort to control football hooligans, although this is very clearly not the case.

Table 14.2 : Official arrests, injuries and deaths of Italian fans

	86/87	87/88	88/89
Arrests	183	283	123
Been questioned	360	440	407

Injuries	432	510	513
Deaths	-	-	2

Source: Ministry of the Interior

Involvement of 'ultras' groups in incidents of football hooliganism

But now let us turn to problems of another kind. Is it possible to draw up a 'league table' of the most violent supporters, showing the clubs whose fans have been responsible for the largest number of incidents? If we take the estimated data for incidents during the period 1970/89 as a basis, the 16 highest ranking groups of supporters are as in Figure 14.3. There is no proof that fans with the highest scores have necessarily always been those most involved in episodes of football violence: some may have been more violent in the past and have become less so today, and vice versa.

If we divide these figures into four periods, the first three of five years each and the last of four, we can note that, during the first five year period 1970/71 - 1974/75 the clubs whose fans were involved in the largest number of incidents were Roma, Napoli, Milan and Lazio, in that order.

During the second period 1975/76 - 1979/80 Milan were still in the top four, but they were now joined by Juventus, Bologna and Torino. During the third period 1980/81 - 1984/85 Roma fans again achieved the highest score, followed by those of Fiorentina, and these two groups remained at the top of the table during the subsequent period 1985/86 - 1988/90, together with the new groups from Atalanta and Verona.

Table 14.3: **Involvement of 'ultras' in incidents of football violence: seasons 1970/71 - 1988/89**

Serie A and B

Team	no of incidents	no of incidents	% no of incidents
Roma	90	574	15.6
Fiorentina	66	574	11.4
Juventus	61	574	10.6

Milan	61	590	10.3
Lazio	54	630	8.5
Verona	51	606	8.4
Atalanta	50	624	8.0
Inter	50	574	8.7
Bologna	49	584	8.3
Torino	34	574	5.9
Napoli	33	574	5.7
Genoa	32	636	5.0
Ascoli	31	554	5.5
Cesena	26	662	3.9
Sampdoria	25	584	4.2
Pisa	22	382	5.7

Source:Corriere della Sera, Resto del Carlino, Stadio/Corriere dello Sport + the ANSA Archive

However, apart from the variations in the violence of their behaviour over time, which can only be explained by specific reference to the histories of the particular groups of supporters, the overall impression from this table is that incidents of football violence, in addition to growing in number more or less constantly over the two decades considered, have been distributed more or less evenly over the whole country, even if to varying degrees. Moreover, the incidents covered in Table 14.3 show only the tip of the iceberg of a phenomenon which now affects virtually all football teams in Italy.

Spectator disorderliness

At this point we shall provide a few comments on a different form of violence: 'spectator disorderliness'. This refers to all forms of spectator violence which occur in the stadium and are directed against those taking part in the match itself: players, referee, linesmen, managers, trainers etc. These acts are normally much less serious than football hooliganism per se, since they are unplanned and those involved are rarely seriously hurt; their origins generally lie in the excitement generated by the match itself. Those responsible are not usually hooligans. While in hooliganism as such those responsible can easily be identified as young 'ultras', here we are dealing with violence which generally involves ordinary supporters.

In the main, these are acts of 'adult deviancy', which is quite clearly different from the 'youthful deviancy' of the 'ultras'. Moreover, unlike hooligan violence, spectator disorderliness is rarely reported in Monday's newspaper reports and television news.

The data shown here refers to episodes of spectator disorderliness at division A and B matches, starting from the 1970/71 season. The data are taken from rulings by the Football League Disciplinary Committee against clubs, which are based on reports by referees. The data does not include measures taken after the throwing of fire-crackers or peaceful pitch invasions - which normally occur at the last matches of the season - since these acts are not intentionally violent, being simply spectator expressions of joy and celebration. The incidents include pitch invasions (and attempted invasions), with or without attacks on the referee' incidents (and this is the most common category) where items such as bottles, cushions, fruit, stones and coins are thrown onto the field, sometimes hitting the referee, linesmen or players; attacks on the referee (including those outside the stadium); and attacks on the players' buses (usually those of the visiting team).

Table 14.4: Spectator disorderliness: League matches in Serie A and B 1970/71 - 1988/89

Year	No. acts of disorderliness	No. matches	% acts of disorderliness
70/71	69	620	11.1
71/72	39	620	6.2
72/73	57	620	9.1
73/74	92	620	14.8
74/75	83	620	13.3
75/76	75	620	12.1
76/77	47	620	7.5
77/78	46	620	7.4
78/79	64	620	10.3
79/80	48	620	7.7
80/81	62	620	10.0
81/82	83	620	13.3
82/83	44	620	7.1
83/84	49	620	7.9

84/85	52	620	8.3
85/86	68	620	10.9
86/87	70	620	11.2
88/89	103	686	16.6

Source: *Processing of Football League Data*

If we compare Table 14.5 with Table 14.3, which lists the number of incidents of football hooliganism, we notice several differences. First of all, the leading teams in Table 14.5 include some which play or have played only in division B, while Table 14.3 features only division A teams and those which have gone constantly back and forth between the two top divisions. Secondly, Table 14.5 includes a considerable number of teams from Southern Italy which, apart from Napoli, do not appear in Table 14.3 at all.

Table 14.5: Football disorderliness, seasons 1970/71 - 1988/89: Serie A and B

Team	No of acts of disorderliness	No of matches	% of acts of disorderliness
Inter	76	574	13.2
Milan	71	590	12.0
Catanzaro	68	590	11.5
Catania	64	478	13.3
Roma	57	574	9.9
Taranto	54	772	6.9
Sambenedettese	54	532	10.1
Atalanta	52	6 24	8.3
Sampdoria	49	584	8.3
Genoa	46	636	7.2
Palermo	46	562	8.1
Napoli	44	574	7.6
Lazio	42	630	6.6
Perugia	40	560	7.1
Foggia	39	424	9.1
Fiorentina	3 7	574	6.4

Source: *Processing of Football League Data*

This indicates that even if football hooliganism has now become widespread at a national level, at least in the two top divisions it is more noticeable in the Northern cities. In contrast, in the South of the country football violence related to more traditional forms of spectator disorder seems to dominate.

Can we draw up a provisional balance sheet of the mass of data we have presented so far? Overall, the image of the Italian football scene which it provides does not seem very encouraging, and would appear to confirm the statement made a few years ago by a member of the Federation's top management that "stadiums are not churches". Spectator violence, whether in the form of football hooliganism by 'ultras' or misbehaviour by the general public, seems to have solid roots reaching well back in time. However, we must remember that these two phenomena are clearly different, and not only in the level of the threat they pose to society. Spectator disorders have more or less always been part of the atmosphere of the football stadium. (Without looking back to the pre-war period, our search through the newspapers confirms that they were constantly present in the 50s and 60s).

This type of behaviour really goes hand in hand with the game of football itself. It can be found in virtually all countries where the sport is practised, and in all periods when modern football has been played on the continent of Europe (see Dunning, Murphy and Williams 1988). It is an immediate, spontaneous expression not only if individual excitement, but also of the collective participation which is the most typical, most popular characteristic of this sport. However, from our point of view the important factor is that this behaviour is stable in the sense that there has been little change in the phenomena involved over the years, except for pitch invasions which have probably become less common. When we turn to football hooliganism, the picture is very different. Here we are facing a more complex phenomenon, with wider social roots - which are only partly related to the world of football - and which above all has taken different forms over time. Unknown before the '70s, it swept through the Italian stadiums, driven by absolutely new forms, causes and protagonists, and has grown constantly since. Our next section will consider its development during the last twenty years.

Evolution of the features of hooligan groups in Italy

The rise of the 'ultras'

As we have already stated, the birth of the 'ultras' movement in Italy can be dated to around the early 70s. Those years saw the appearance on the Italian terraces of small groups of young fans who gathered behind banners with intentionally threatening messages, and who stood out from the rest of the spectators because of the more colourful, lively way in which they expressed their passion for the game. For example, there was the birth of the yellow-blue 'Brigades' at Verona, the 'Granata Ultras' at Turin, the 'Fossa dei Leoni' at Milan and the red-blue 'Commandos' at Bologna.

This phenomenon was completely new for Italy, but it was not exactly original. In England a very similar movement had been in existence for almost a decade (see Dunning, Murphy & Williams, 1988). So should we consider Italian hooliganism as a purely imitative phenomenon? Or better, that it is the result of the direct importation from abroad of the first germs of this new type of football 'madness'? We must first of all remember that what is happening in Italian stadiums, is also happening, or will soon be happening, in other European countries. Germany, Holland, Belgium and Austria are amongst the countries where similar hooliganism appeared at about the same time as in Italy, but in each of these countries it occurs in specific forms and by specific channels of transmission (see Roversi, 1990; Broussard, 1990), confirming that we are not dealing with pure imitation.

This is a more complex process of cultural diffusion which has spread from its original centre to surrounding areas, adapting to local situations. But we must also add that the ways in which the 'ultras' movement put down roots and took its first steps in Italy have always featured at least one characteristic not found elsewhere which identifies, as we might say, the 'Italian way' in football hooliganism. First of all, let us try to reconstruct the main events in the small revolution which our home-grown hooligans have brought about.

Before we start, we must note that most young people who gathered behind those banners were definitely not new fans, but had already been there for some time. Many of them had been introduced to the Sunday rites in the usual familial way, picking up the passion for football at home. Others were drawn into the world of the stadium by so-called clubs of organized fans - groups of older supporters, officially recognized by the football clubs, which were founded above all to guarantee their members tickets for matches, and to organize trips to support the team. In short, these young people had already been part of the 'football culture' for some time. However, they suddenly decided to form independent groups and to go to the ground without adult supervision.

What was behind the formation of these new groups? We can provide a short list. Doubtless an initial element of cohesion within the early 'ultras' was provided by the existing friendships between the young founders. Friendships between neighbours, schoolmates and users of the same bars seem to have formed the first informal network of relationships on which the groups at the stadiums were founded. They were not necessarily groups of peers, but the distance between them in terms of age was definitely fairly limited. Secondly, and this was the special feature which marked the birth of hooliganism in Italy and was to accompany it for some time, this friendship was refined in many cases by common membership of an extreme right or left-wing group, even if discontinuous and never especially intensive, or at least some kind of shared political experience (see Segre, 1979). It is worth remembering here that in those years the term 'ultras' was mainly used in Italy to describe left-wing political extremists. These elements were bonded together by the ingredient which probably served to ignite the whole process: knowledge of English football hooliganism which some of these young people acquired in a number of ways - by watching Cup matches where Italian teams played English clubs, by reading the sporting press; and for the fortunate few, during trips to England.

The 'ultras' appearance represented an important new beginning in the history of football supporters in Italy. Since then violence by young fans has become an increasingly common feature of Sunday life in our country, even if its form and intensity have differed significantly over the intervening years. It is worth analysing its development, trying to identify its main stages.

The learning years

The first phase in 'ultras' football support covers more or less the whole of the 70s. The phenomenon had various features during those years. The first was definitely the new ways in which these groups supported their teams, since it is undeniable that their appearance coincided with a change in the appearance of the stadium. The terraces, especially behind the goals, filled up with large banners and flags, and were often covered with a coloured fog from smoke-bombs. The sound of the crowd changed, too. Drums of all types and sizes appeared and were pounded incessantly for long periods; shouts and chants were no longer the opportunity for expressing spontaneous, immediate participation in the events of the game, becoming an independent, prolonged din with an obsessive rhythm of their own. As was the case for similar groups in other European countries, a special uniform was adopted for going to matches, although in Italy this was an adoption of the student style of dress. Parkas and camouflage jackets, decorated with trimmings and symbols referring to football, were the outfit of the first young hooligans, showing the extent to which the political climate of those years was reflected in the atmosphere on the terraces.

Another factor which must be emphasized, again in line with the behaviour of young supporters abroad, was that these groups considered the areas behind the goals as their own exclusive territory, and strangers were not welcomed. As is well known, in those years this need to defend the 'home end' was the reason for many incidents between hooligans, since one strong element in the aggression between groups of 'ultras' was the attempt to invade the adversaries' territory and if possible capture their flags and banners. This was considered as out and out profanation by all hooligan groups and could trigger a chain of revenge attacks over time, ready to explode whenever the two teams met.

But why did this 'game' of violence start? What are the real reasons for the fights and the incidents, with their inevitable corollary of injuries, arrests and sometimes deaths? If we ask today's young 'ultras' about this - or at least, this was what we found in our research among younger Bologna hooligans - the replies are usually very vague and evasive. "It's always been that way" or "It's because we hate each other". One almost gets the impression that all this has happened, and continues to happen, by a kind of inescapable destiny, under a rule which is vaguely seen as something greater than the individual, which must be obeyed. In reality, these events had more concrete origins. First of all, it must be noted that in many ways hooligan violence is related to and a continuation of the consolidated tradition of fighting between older supporters. If we continue to look at Bologna, this is true of their fans' battles against the supporters of Fiorentina and, to a lesser degree, of Pisa and Arezzo, or with fans of other teams in the Tuscany region. As we were told by an old Bologna fan in an interview in the course of our research: "The Tuscans are terrible. It's in their blood. We used to turn up in a friendly mood, not wanting to start anything. But we always had to fight". And another: "At Pisa we always got knocked about. It was normal".

Many of those hooligan groups spontaneously took as their adversaries the supporters of those teams with whom their father had already done battle. These 'natural enemies' were then joined by groups of fans with different political ideologies, since, as we have already mentioned, contrasting political views overlapped with and fuelled the behaviour of young hooligans. This does not mean that groups of political extremists played a direct role in the life of the terraces, but there is no doubt that many of the young people who joined the 'ultras' groups had marginal experiences of this kind. And it is equally certain that political extremism was definitely a glamorous example for the young hooligans, not only because its symbolism coincided with the hard line image they wanted to create for themselves, but also because the organizational and behavioural model it offered fitted their aims like a glove.

This difference in political and ideological positions, which often only existed in the imaginations of those involved, gave birth to rivalries between the groups of various cities. For example, supporters of Milan and Bologna were considered left-wing, while those of Lazio, Ascoli and Verona were believed to be on the right. And to finish our list of the reasons which lie behind incidents of hooligan violence, we must also remember what has been called, not without irony, 'the Bedouin syndrome' (Dunning, Murphy and Williams, 1988). This is the principle by which the friend of a friend is a friend, the enemy of an enemy is an enemy, the enemy of a friend is an enemy and the friend of an enemy is an enemy. Although it may seem paradoxical, this principle often lies at the basis of clashes between groups of supporters who would otherwise have no reason for enmity, and also fosters good relations between others. Another comment from the Bologna 'ultras':

We never met up with the 'purples' (Fiorentina supporters) while our team was in division B. But we had plenty of contact when our team was playing away against Modena and coaches used to arrive from Florence ... We were playing Brescia and we found ourselves up against the Cesena banners.

So, Modena and Brescia officially became enemies. And the same mechanism led to the formation of 'triangles': Milan, Bologna and Genoa against Inter, Sampdoria and Fiorentina. Although there were fewer incidents in this period than during the next decade, they almost immediately became very violent. This is confirmed by many episodes. We can list a few as examples. Milan-Juventus in February '75: rockets and fire-crackers were repeatedly thrown onto the field from behind the goal, where large numbers of young hooligans had gathered behind the banners of the 'Commandos Tigre' and the 'Fossa dei Leoni', hitting a number of players. Masked youths from the two factions armed with sticks fought on the terraces. When the fans had left the ground the incidents started up again and a young Juventus supported was stabbed. Juventus-Sampdoria supporters were joined by Torino 'ultras', who urged on Juventus's adversaries noisily during the match and unfurled their huge standard, a wine-red skull at the 'away' team end. Inter-Milan in March '77: the red-blue Brigades and the Inter Boys met up inside the stadium, armed with knives: there were a number of injuries. Vicenza-Verona in January '78: incidents inside the ground between the two groups of fans involved firing rockets and throwing iron balls at one another. In short, even if they have only been around for a few years, the Italian hooligan groups seem to have wasted no time in reaching European standards in football hooliganism. On the other hand, we must also emphasize that during this same period they were lagging behind on a number of important factors in their development. In general, they were few in number compared to the dimensions they were to achieve in the 80s: they were not yet present in all towns with teams playing in Serie A and B; not all of them followed their teams to away fixtures, since away games involved a level of organization and expenditure which many were unable to provide; and finally - and this is another Italian characteristic still present today - they did not consider that matches played by the national side provided an opportunity for 'ultras' from all over the country to launch a combined offensive.

In the years which followed, between the late 70s and the mid 80s, some of these features seemed to disappear, making way for a new phase. Violence now tended to move outside the stadiums and almost always occurred before or after the matches themselves. From 1977 onwards, virtually all the games at which clashes between 'ultras' groups occurred showed this constant feature (cf. Borghini, 1987). In most cases, disorder took place in the immediate vicinity of the stadiums, but the reports also sometimes refer to clashes in town centres or at railway stations. This may be partly considered as resulting from restraining security measures adopted by the sports authorities, football hooliganism now being viewed with apprehension by public opinion and the mass media as a serious law-and-order problem. In this period, strict segregation of opposing fans inside football grounds was introduced, and the number of police drafted onto the terraces and around the pitch was also greatly increased. Moreover, October '77 saw the inauguration, at the Rome Olympic stadium, of the first closed-circuit television system for surveillance of supporters, and during the following years similar systems were to be installed at Milan, Torino and Verona. In addition, after the death of the Lazio fan Paparelli in October 1979, the use of metal- detectors was introduced in Italian stadiums for a certain period of time.

This second period also seems to see the emergence of a new generation of hooligans who differ in a number of fundamental ways from the previous, 'founder' generation. First of all, these groups generally place less emphasis on support for the team as an element of internal cohesion. Support for the team remains, but very often it becomes a general background element, easily removed. In this period, the behaviour of these supporters often became completely independent of the original foundation of the groups - the wish to support the favoured team, even if in an unreasonably violent manner - and chose the way of violent aggression and clashes with the supposed enemy, the opposing 'ultras', at all costs. Secondly, probably as a direct consequence of this change of tone, the hooligan groups became more generally and more noticeably militarized. Clashes were often now prepared well ahead and with great care. As the newspaper reports show, the 'ultras' outfit for matches now included iron bars, sticks, knives, catapults, chains, rocket-firing pistols, bolts and knuckle-dusters.

The consequences of all this were only too obvious. Let us look for example at what happened in a number of cities on the day when the Lazio fan Paparelli died in Rome, 28 October 1979. At Ascoli, at the end of the Ascoli-Bologna match the hooligan element amongst the Bologna supporters vandalized cars parked near the stadium. Pursued by the Ascoli 'ultras', the fans clashed in incidents which left seven injured. The Bologna coaches were searched by police and turned out to be arsenals on wheels. In Milan, at the conclusion of the Inter-Milan derby, violent disorders broke out between the rival 'ultras', leaving eighteen injured. In Brescia, where the division B match between Brescia and Como took place, there were more violent clashes after the match. Many rockets were fired into the crowd and several were again injured.

The picture provided by this second phase of Italian hooliganism therefore shows more organization, planning and co-ordination than the previous stage. The 'ultras' now showed that their organization was less spontaneous, more stable and with a clearer hierarchy: within each group there was often a clear allocation of roles and tasks, with well defined career structures; strategies were carefully worked out, aiming at violent physical clashes, especially on the dates of certain matches; a network of lasting alliances by twinning relations with similar groups from other cities was constructed, while consolidating positions of implacable hatred against other groups. Referring again to our research, the Bologna 'ultras' entered into stable alliances with the red and black brigades of Milan, the Pescara Rangers, the Udinese Teddy boys, the Padova Ghetto and the Sambenedettese 'Onda d'Urto' ('shock-wave'), while the Cesena WSB, the Fiorentina 'Collettivo Viola', the Ascoli Settembre 'Bianconero', the Inter Boys and the Juventus Fighters became their historic enemies. Basically, a phenomenon which the ordinary supporter or outside observer saw as an increasingly incomprehensible grey area, made up of abstruse symbols, often proved, in this period, to be a formation of young people not lacking in organization and structured around a core of fairly strict and coherent rules.

Recent developments

If we now consider what happened starting more or less from the

1983/84-1984/85 seasons, the impression is of a further rapid transformation. In a situation which shows a constant increase in the level of violence in the clashes and the number of incidents caused by hooligans, as indicated by the figures in the previous paragraph, some apparently contrasting elements were suddenly attracting attention. On the one hand, new groups were proliferating more or less everywhere, both in cities which had hitherto been unaffected by the phenomenon, such as southern Italy, or in towns where the local team played in lower divisions, or in cities where the 'ultras' element had already been around for a while, but had gathered around one or two slogans. Especially in the latter case, an important factor was the appearance of new groups which arose independently, identified by their own banners and with widely varying origins: groups of skinheads and punks, groups of friends, neighbourhood groups etc. Some of these groups were short-lived, disappearing almost immediately, often reappearing under another name, in line with the latest fashion. Others consolidated their positions and, even if their numbers varied over the years, were a constant factor in life behind the goal.

Together with some of the largest groups with the longest tradition, these small groups seemed to signal a peaceful return to the terraces by the 'ultras', since their main contribution was to provide an original input to the overall choreography of the stadiums. Secondly, there was a significant lowering of the age-group in certain elements of the latest recruits to the 'ultras' bands. This change can easily be noticed with the naked eye in Italian grounds, and the older hooligans view it with a mixture of disdain and worry. For example, one of the 'ultras' we interviewed in the course of our research told us:

When I started to go to matches I had more respect for those who had been inside the organization for a number of years. Now if you ask a kid to help put a drum together he tells you he's not your porter.

The fact is that these latest recruits, described by their comrades as 'newly-fledged ultras', have normally not supported football teams before. They have no background in football behind them and do not seem interested in acquiring one; above all they give little importance to group bonding and identity. The 'us' feeling - so strong amongst the traditional 'ultras' (cf. Salvini, 1988) - now rarely goes beyond flaunting the group's emblem, and participation in the group event of the match itself often becomes just individual exhibitionism.

In other words, these 'newly-fledged ultras' seem to introduce a kind of behaviour which the hooligans who have been on the terraces for the longest had difficulty in accepting and over which they had little or no control. Thirdly, in some cities large cores of 'ultras' are splitting up and no longer identify with a single system of rivalries and twinning alliances. Returning to our example of Bologna, the 'Forever Ultras' enjoy excellent relations with the Genoa and Milan fans, while the Mods and Supporters consider the 'Fossa dei Grifoni' (Genoa) and the red and black Brigades (Milan) as their greatest foes. A fourth and last reflection: the newspaper reports for the last few years show a large number of acts of minor vandalism by fans against trains, buses, railway stations, cars parked along the roads leading to the grounds and so on.

To this list we have to add attacks on normal fans or 'ultras' of the same team, theft from ordinary citizens, the sacking of bars near football grounds or motorway service stations and finally episodes of racism, which for the moment are few and far between. Overall, these are acts of petty crime, very different from incidents normally considered as football hooliganism, but often carried out when away matches are played. It is virtually impossible to prevent them, and it is equally difficult for the police to identify those responsible.

Who are the 'ultras'?

Young men ... young women

At this point, it only remains to try to form an identikit picture of the 'ultras'. To this end, we will use 264 young Bologna 'ultras' who were handed a questionnaire of 46 questions during the trip to the away game at Verona on 18 March 1990. Naturally, the analysis of these data will not provide an ideal image of the Italian hooligan - who has already been quite rightly described (see Moscati, 1988) as having a 'variable geometry', both because his social face changes over time, and because his identity is, of course largely dependent on the urban social context from which he originates. In this case we are dealing with Bologna and its province, an area with a fairly stable socioeconomic environment. The sample which we are about to analyse can never be more than relatively representative, although it offers significant features which deserve consideration. As Table 14.6 shows, and as was to be expected in our sample, the vast majority were males. However, the female component was greater than many would think. More than half the 45 girls present in the sample stated that they did not belong to any traditional, historic group and had therefore circumvented the problem of acceptance in this strongly masculine culture.

Table 14.6: Composition of 'ultras' sample by sex and age

	%	Age	%
Males	82.9	15 and under	1.1
		from 16 to 18	25.8
		from 19 to 21	31.4
Females	17.1	from 22 to 24	22.3
		from 25 to 27	13.4
		from 28 to 30	3.0
		over 30	3.0
Total	100.0	Total	100.0
(n)	(264)	(n)	(264)

What is more, 65.9% of the females stated that they had only been with the 'ultras' for less than three years (i.e. since Bologna F.C. returned to division A). They can be described as the 'weak segment' of the female 'ultras'. On the other hand, there is also a 'strong segment' amongst the girls at the ground, consisting of a small group of females who have been full members of the 'ultras' scene for some time, without being pushed into the background or subordinated to male fan roles. In Bologna - and this also happens at the ends of other Italian stadiums - there is an all-girl 'ultras' group (the URB Girls) and girls occupy positions as recognized leaders in two historic groups.

This aspect of the phenomenon is certainly worthy of further investigation, but provisionally it can be linked to a well-grounded tradition in Bologna of 'female' fans which clearly emerged during our research, and which is symbolized by a number of now elderly women fans firmly implanted in the memories of several girl 'ultras'.

On the question of age, Table 14.6 shows that the modal category is the group between 19 and 21 years (31.4%), followed in second place by the 16 - 18 band (25.8%). Taking the sample as a whole, 58.3% of the young 'ultras' are less than 21 years old, but it must also be considered that in this case the number of youngsters under 15 is very probably underestimated.

When asked whether they belonged to an 'ultras' group, 66.2% said 'yes' and 33.8% said 'no', confirming the reduced influence held by official 'ultras' over young fans. But when asked "How long have you been with 'ultras'?", even those who answered no to the previous question gave a reply showing that they still considered themselves part of the 'ultras' scene. All in all, although there is a 'hard core' of 28.8% of young fans who have more than six years as 'ultras' behind, 41.6% of fans only started their 'careers' when the local team returned to the top division, even if in some cases they had already been attending matches for some time.

We can further differentiate these 'ultras' according to their membership or otherwise of groups, separating those organized into the most numerous groups with the longest traditions (49.8%) from those belonging to small, unstable, usually recently formed groups (16.3%) and those not organized in any groups (33.9%). Finally, 91.2% were born in Bologna or surrounding communes.

The social background

But now we come to an important problem, on which common sense and public opinion generally hold very stereotyped views: the social background of the young 'ultras'. Are they really, as some people believe, a sort of aristocracy of the sub-proletariat? If we consider the activities of the Bologna 'ultras', this does not seem to be the case. Out of 259 who answered the question about their job or studies, 20.5% said they were students while 79.5% said they worked. One of the first features of the sample starts to emerge: the majority of the young 'ultras' are from the working class. But let us analyse the composition of the two groups, the students and the workers, separately.

The first group, the students, consists of 46 males and 7 females. Most of the group (60.4%) are between 16 and 18 years of age and within this age-range the vast majority (78.1%) attend technical or vocational high schools. Around this central core there is a group of university students (24.5%), a small group of grammar school students (7.5%) and the remaining 7.6% containing university students who have fallen behind with their studies and students of 18 years of age attending technical schools.

The group in employment contains 169 males and 46 females. In this group the skilled and unskilled blue-collar workers visibly predominate, both compared to workers of other kinds and within the sample as a whole; they represent 80.3% and 51.9% respectively. They are warehousemen, porters, shop-assistants, bricklayers, carpenters but above all shop-floor workers, and it is significant that almost all of them, like those working in other sectors, have steady jobs and not temporary or casual employment (out of 187 workers interviewed only 17, equivalent to 9% said they had a part-time job) and moreover 77.3% said they liked their work a lot or that it was not bad. It must be emphasized that only 3.9% of the entire sample admitted to being unemployed. Therefore these initial data seem to provide an image of the social composition of this group of 'ultras' as a pyramid where the base is much larger than the tip.

122 subjects specified their father's profession, and these data would seem to confirm the picture, even if there is a certain tendency to downward mobility compared to the father's professional status. 66 subjects, equivalent to 54.1%, had retained their father's professional standing, while 9.8% were upwardly mobile and 36.1% were downwardly mobile. This last last figure is definitely anomalous compared to Bologna as a whole. In general, these young people live with their parents (87.7% compared to 12.3% who say that they have left home). And life at home does not seem to cause inconvenience or conflict, since 85.3% say that they get on very well or quite well with their parents.

Lifestyle: a universe with few ways out

And now we come to another aspect of fundamental importance in the life of the 'ultras': relationships outside the home. The questionnaire included a short set of questions to check the young fans' integration in the young scene outside football. When asked: "Do you have a group of friends outside the 'ultras' environment?" 247 subjects out of 257 (96.1%) replied "yes" and only 10 (3.9%) replied "no". However, to the next question, "Do you see the other 'ultras' during the week?" 67.9% said that they did, and when asked, "Of

378

your three closest friends, how many are 'ultras'?", no less than 54.5% replied 3 and 27.2% answered 2. So it would seem that, although the initial statement gives the impression that many fans are capable of abandoning their Sunday life as 'ultras' during the week, moving on to other leisure activities, in reality things are rather different. The last two replies indicate that the 'ultras' scene provides a protective shell which is never left even during the days which pass between matches.

Basically, this would seem to be a universe with few ways out, and which it is difficult for stimuli and experiences from the young lifestyle in general to penetrate. However, the contradiction here is only apparent. As we saw in the previous section, the 'ultras' group is often the sum of a number of preexisting groups of friends, on which it imposes itself, moulding them to the culture of the stadium's end, but leaving their basic personal relationships largely unchanged. So it is no surprise that a large number of young people claim that they have other activities but still say that they have close friendships with other 'ultras'. In fact, for these the worlds inside and outside the ground are often mirror images of one another, each acquiring importance depending on the circumstances: where everyday experience is the dominant factor, the private aspect of friendship comes to the surface, while when the group experience of the terrace prevails - inside the ground, during trips to away matches, during preparations and when looking back at events over the following days - the public dimension of the role as an 'ultra' takes precedence.

And this role has led many young 'ultras' to take an active part in episodes of football hooliganism. Here again, we used a short set of questions to assess their attitudes and their real involvement in acts of violence. To the question: "Do you cause trouble at the ground?" out of 258 subjects 26.0% replied "I keep out of it", but 49.2% replied "only if I'm provoked" and 24.8% answered "whenever I get the chance". To the question: "Have you ever been involved in a fight at the ground?" out of 260 subjects 49.2% replied "yes". Finally, when asked "Have you ever been in a fight for reasons apart from football?" 65.5% said "yes". Even if very probably they replied in the affirmative partly because they wanted to emphasize their own 'tough' image, this does not seem to alter the basic fact that the experience of fights and clashes with opposing fans forms the common heritage of many young 'ultras' and is a more general part of an experience of violence which has also been expressed in contexts outside football.

Those who have taken part in episodes of football hooliganism are above all the youngest. 64.7% of those who claim to have been involved in incidents relating to football matches are less than 21 years old. In this case the girls are a tiny minority: only 8.4% of the female 'ultras' seem to have taken part in this type of incident. Again, students account for only 16% of those who replied "yes", compared to 83.0% of those in employment. The most active of this faction who participate in acts of violence seem, by far and away, the blue-collar workers, with a proportion of 85.2%.

One last note before we conclude. Out of 261 subjects in the sample, 49.4% take part in sporting activities themselves, and of these more than half play football in amateur teams, some even play in a variety of amateur league, as emerged from the interviews carried out during our survey. This gives the impression that the concept of sport as 'healthy', as a kind of social healer capable of bringing these fans back to real sporting values, is probably a 'de Coubertinian' idea which is now out of date and without any real effectiveness.

Note

This chapter is based on a paper published in the *International Review of the Sociology of Sport*. It is published here in this form with the kind permission of the author.

Bibliography

Borgini, F. (1987) *La violenza negli stadi*, Manzuoli, Florence.

Bromberger, C. (1987) 'L'Olimpique de Marseille, la Juve et le Torino', *Espirit*, 4.

Broussard, P. (1990) *Generation supporter. Enquete sur le ultras de football*, Laffont, Paris.

Dunning, E. (1986) 'Sport as a Male Preserve: notes on the social source of masculine identity and its transformations', in N. Elias & E. Dunning, *Quest for Excitement*, Basil Blackwell, Oxford.

Dunning, E., P. Murphy & J. Williams (1988) *The Roots of Football Hooliganism*, Routledge, London.

Moscati, R. (1988) 'La violenza negli stadi e i giovani', in Labos, *Giovani e violenza*, T.E.R., Rome.

Murphy, P., J. Williams & E. Dunning (1990) *Football on Trial*, Routledge, London.

Onofri, M. & A. Ricci (1984) 'I ragazzi della curva', *Il Mulino*, 5.

Roversi, A. (ed.) (1990) *Calcio e violenza in Europa*, Il Mulino, Bologna.

Salvini, A. (1988) *Il rito aggressivo. Dall'aggressivita simbolica al compartamento violento: il casa dei tifosi ultras*, Giunti, Florence.

Segre, S. (1979) *Ragazzi di stadio*, Mazzotta, Milan.

Triani, G. (1990) *Mal di stadio*, Edizioni Associate, Rome.